SECRETS OF
LIFE AND DEATH

V

Renate Siebert studied at the Frankfurt School in the 1960s as a doctoral student of T.W. Adorno. She is currently an associate professor of sociology at the University of Calabria.

Liz Heron has translated many Italian and French authors, including Nanni Balestrini, Giorgio Agamben, Anna Maria Ortese and Hervé Guibert. The most recent of her own books is a short-story collection *A Red River*.

SECRETS OF
LIFE AND DEATH

Women and the Mafia

RENATE SIEBERT

Translated by Liz Heron

VERSO

London • New York

First published by Verso 1996
This edition © Verso 1996

Translation © Liz Heron 1996
First published as *Le Donne, La Mafia*
© il Saggiatore 1994

The right of Liz Heron to be identified as the translator of this work has been
asserted by her in accordance with the Copyright, Designs and Patents Act 1988

Verso
UK: 6 Meard Street, London W1V 3HR
USA: 180 Varick Street, New York NY 10014–4606

Verso is the imprint of New Left Books

ISBN 1–85984–903–2
ISBN 1–85984–023–X (pbk)

British Library Cataloguing in Publication Data
A catalogue record for this book is available from the British Library

Library of Congress Cataloging-in-Publication Data
A catalog record for this book is available from the Library of Congress

Typeset by M Rules

Printed and bound in Great Britain by
Marston Book Services Ltd, Oxfordshire

Contents

CONTENTS

CONTENTS

Translator's Notes

Books quoting from many different works originally published in other languages require tricky decisions from translators about consistency and accessibility. Here, all quotations from the Italian have been newly translated, with the exception of those from Pino Arlacchi's *Mafia Business*. Likewise, quotations from the French are translated from the original. In the case of German-language authors I have quoted and referenced English editions and where none is available I have had to translate from the Italian and give page references for the Italian editions while also noting original editions in the bibliography. My thanks are due to Chiara Levrini for her help with bibliographical research.

The following acronyms are used in the text:

CSM – Consiglio Superiore della Magistratura (superior council of the judiciary)

USL – Unità Socio-sanitaria Locale (public health centre)

Sisde – Servizio informazioni e sicurezza democratica (non-military secret service)

L.H.

I'd like everybody back there to remember me as I was, generous and full of life. Decent and honest. And not the way I'm being made to look at the trial. They are running me down so as to destroy my character and weaken my testimony. And they are intimidating the other witnesses. But I am decent. I'm asking the friends I used to have to remember me that way. What has hurt me most is that there are people who were at school with me who are now saying: 'I never knew what she was like.'

Rosetta Cerminara

This work is dedicated to Rosetta.

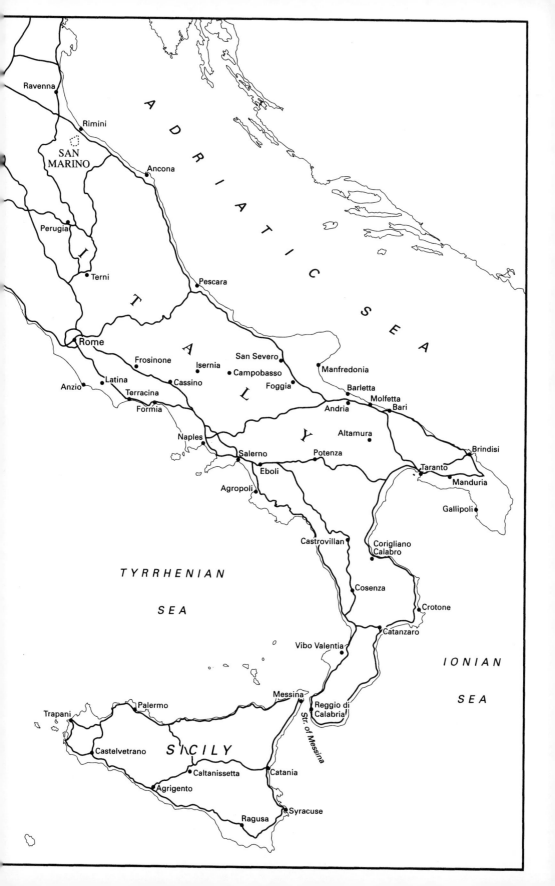

Introduction

What truth may objectively be is difficult enough to determine, but we should not, in our dealings with people, let this fact terrorize us. To this end criteria are used that at first sight seem convincing. One of the most dependable is the reproach that a statement is 'too subjective'. If this is brought to bear, with an indignation in which rings the furious harmony of all reasonable people, one has grounds, for a few seconds, to feel self-satisfied. The notions of subjective and objective have been completely reversed. Objective means the non-controversial aspect of things, their unquestioned impression, the facade made up of classified data, that is, the subjective; and they call subjective anything which breaches that facade, engages the specific experience of a matter, casts off all ready-made judgments and substitutes relatedness to the object for the majority consensus of those who do not even look at it, let alone think about it – that is, the objective.

Theodor W. Adorno

This study stems from a very intimate, private and personal need, the need to understand the nature of the world I live in from day to day and the furthest edges and limits of what my consciousness can take upon itself. Beyond these limits I feel myself to blame. Beyond these limits, for the sake of peace of mind, my consciousness succumbs to false consciousness.

I was first impelled to undertake this 'journey into Hades' by the powerful jolt of a discussion with Gianfranco Manfredi, a journalist and a southerner who made me aware that none of the women of the South who tell their stories in my book *È femmina, però è bella* had mentioned the problem of the mafia or the *'ndrangheta*.

Exactly. Because I, quite unconsciously, had no wish to talk about it then. Neither at the time of meeting these women, nor, even less, in my subsequent interpretation of their accounts. What little had been confided to me by the women I interviewed – for all my obvious resistance to discussing it – stayed on my tapes and was not introduced into the work I did on interpretation.

After that my friend's words gnawed away inside me. Why so much resistance, why so much dread?

As a *child*, growing up in Germany during the Second World War and the immediate postwar period, I was surrounded by adults devastated by events 'on a scale beyond their reach', as they were fond of saying; I grew up in anxious expectation of imminent and unavoidable atrocities to come. A new war, another catastrophe. A savage, inscrutable destiny.

As a *girl* I rebelled against the adults' world, a world which then seemed, quite simply, one stamped with racist crimes or, just as much, with silent complicity. Gripped by some manner of magical belief, I was convinced that crimes and brutality of this kind could in the future be prevented by force of will and reason. We only had to be watchful, alert and intelligent. To remember, not to forget: most of all, not to forget. 'We are all guilty,' Sartre said. We called it revolution, then.

As a *woman*, with whatever contradictions, I still believe in utopia. Yet my focus, I could say my hope, has been shifted from society and collectivity to the individual, to woman or man in the singular. I set out to ask myself the troubling question: what is going on 'inside' the subjects? What is their relationship with life and death, with their own existence and that of others, with the likelihood of their own death and with the occasion of causing the death of someone else? And more than that, what are the thoughts and everyday feelings, about everything they do, of individuals who are accustomed to killing for money, in cold blood, as if it were an ordinary job? And how do people live in close proximity with individuals like themselves, 'monsters' of a spine-chilling normality? According to crime statistics, the category of those who kill is made up almost exclusively of men. As a result, we find a high proportion of women in the second category: women who connive and are complicit, women who are subordinate and women who rebel.

The problem of the 'mafia' – perhaps in this respect like the problematic of racism – has now become a thorny and crucial issue for our civil consciousness, both individual and collective. The cultural and political elaboration of phenomena such as these marks a watershed, a point of no return between civilization and barbarism. Our everyday connivance with these shadows hanging over our lives, unwilling as it is – though often with a tacit assent bred of tiredness, fear and indifference – tends to become routine. We have accustomed ourselves to the 'banality of evil'.

It is my belief that this concept, developed by Hannah Arendt in her analysis of totalitarianism, can be used to highlight certain significant and specific features of the mafia, especially with regard to its ruinous impact on the democratic fabric of society. Dictatorship, be it Fascist or Stalinist, and the mafia are clearly historical phenomena, distinct sociocultural entities. Yet it seems to me that common elements can be identified. I believe that it was precisely the resonance between those vague 'memories' of the National

2

Socialist terror and mafia terror which unconsciously prevented me from thinking about these phenomena for so long.

The element they share is the totalizing nature of the all-embracing system of surveillance, terror and blackmail which strikes at the individual's emotional attachments and hangs over every one of his or her daily activities. Such is the collusion between illegality and legality, between crime and politics, that the very foundations of our democratic arrangements appear to be in doubt. 'Inside this Italy . . . there are factions in struggle. This is in other words an Italy where . . . battle rages – in terms of civilization and freedom – between what, for simplicity's sake, I shall call good and evil.'[1]

From this perspective the mafia functions as a 'total institution' (though an informal one) which stands in the way of the affirmation of privacy, suspending all guarantees of the individual's mental and physical safety, terroristically denying all rights to individuality. These aspects of mafioso activity impact all the more sharply on the cultural and social fabric where interpersonal networks tend towards traditional values of belonging and community, in other words where the individual as a social unit and as lived experience is still weak. In these conditions, perhaps, the appalling harm done by the mafia to individual rights is often not perceived as such. 'So many people still defer to the "family", to the "clan", to the "capo", to the "mafia organization". There are still so few who imagine that there can be individual choice.'[2]

Like totalitarian dictatorships, the mafia endows itself with the right over life and death; where mafia 'law' is in force there is capital punishment. We live in a democratic country, under a rule of law which shelters within itself enclaves where, in broad daylight, all these laws are suspended. The mafia exerts what Umberto Santini* calls 'territorial sovereignty' over entire areas of the country, with the connivance of complicitous factions in the state, and with capital punishment in force and civil rights abolished. This is so disturbing that it is worth repeating it and reflecting upon it. Yet by now it seems obvious, as if we had gradually got used to this state of things.

It is a mystification to split off the 'old' mafia from the 'new', precisely because such a distinction usually serves to blur the clarity of this basic characteristic. Sciascia relayed a passage from the interrogation of Tommaso Buscetta during the maxi-trial:†

---

* Umberto Santini is one of the founder members of the Giuseppe Impastato Centre in Palermo. See pp. 278–82. [Trs.]

† The maxi-trial took place between 10 February 1986 and 16 December 1987. It made legal history in Italy by bringing together an unprecedented number of accused, 475 in all, on charges related to mafia activities. They were tried by a pool of judges and the sentences included nineteen life sentences which were later confirmed by the Court of Cassation. It was this trial and its outcome that provoked the subsequent mafia killings of a number of the judges involved, among them Giovanni Falcone and Paolo Borsellino. [Trs.]

The lawyer Maffei: 'Do you remember through what channels the meeting between Sindona and your friends Bontade and Inzerillo took place?'

Buscetta: 'We never talked about it . . . Bontade told me that Sindona was just a madman . . . there was nothing to talk about.'

Maffei: 'But Sindona talked about a revolution. Was Bontade not concerned about being privy to this kind of secret?'

Buscetta (laughing): 'Sindona's secrets! They were like a feather in comparison with the secrets Bontade had.'

If Sindona's secrets were like a feather, we can imagine how much lead was in the secrets of the old, good and noble mafia that Bontade was looking after.[3]

In the course of this work I observed something which greatly disturbed me, and I became gradually filled with rage and hatred. Almost more than towards the mafiosi and their complicit women, these feelings were directed towards those representatives of the institutions without which the mafia could not exercise its dominion of death. Rita Borsellino, the sister of the murdered judge, said in one interview: 'Hatred is a feeling that is alien to me, that I try to keep at arm's length. . . . However, I have to say that I find it difficult to rid myself of hatred for the "pen-pushers" who could have been a party to the vile planning of the carnage.'[4]

The negation of individual rights by the mafia takes on a particular relevance for women who, even within the Western democracies which are founded upon the declaration of such rights, have had to struggle bitterly to enjoy them. Women's perception of themselves as individuals has always fuelled in men the fear that freedom could lead women to abandon responsibility for relationships. In 1848 the American feminist Elizabeth Cady Stanton wrote to a journalist: 'Put it down in capital letters: SELF-DEVELOPMENT IS A HIGHER DUTY THAN SELF-SACRIFICE. The thing which most retards and militates against women's self-development is self-sacrifice.'[5]

In order for there to be any substantial, not to say formal, recognition of one's own and others' right to individuality there has to be a margin of freedom, both cultural and material, that few women can claim for themselves even today, when the average level of education is high. And this is even less the case in the Mezzogiorno.

I should like to try to take up the 'challenge' that evil makes to thought, as Hannah Arendt said, and try to imagine how it can be possible for brutality, complicity and normality to have become fused in such a pervasive way.

I should like to attempt a double reading of the 'mafia' phenomenon; on the one hand I should like to bring in my own perceptions, my sensibility and my curiosity: a woman's observations and questions about a phenomenon which appears almost exclusively male. On the other hand, and precisely because I am a woman, I should like to research the specific involvement of women who, one way or another, are connected or have been connected with the mafia.

A strong sense of mortality informs our daily life and the way we live together socially and politically in this phase of our history. It has become hard to avoid asking what is going on, what in the course of some people's lives has gone on in their relationships, attachments and socialization to make them apparently so indifferent to life and life's potential, whether their own or that of others. This question comes up every time the newspapers give us the latest news about the mafia. Nowadays the level of mafia delinquency is not connected with poverty, but is an index of the wealth of our society. 'And, I repeat, we need to rid ourselves once and for all of the mistaken theories that make the mafia the child of underdevelopment, when in reality it represents a synthesis of all forms of illicit exploitation of wealth.'[6] The spread of violent death and the spread of industrial consumption go hand in hand.

There is no doubt, however, that these questions should be put to men and women separately, that there should be gender specificity in how the self is related to life, death and perhaps even consumerism.

The sense of mortality which pervades our daily life has many faces, lurking not only at deep levels in our psyche, but in our thoughts, in our fantasies and in the forms and objects of consumerism. Often work and leisure alike impinge on death. Without the aspect of death, power and politics can scarcely be defined. Saying mafia and thinking of death are one and the same.

Mafia activity seems obsessed by death. Beneath the surface of a society in overall balance, beneath the surface of a peace lived out with difficulty (under conditions of nuclear threat), it comes to mind that the disturbing 'success' of all the forms of violence connected with the mafia phenomenon can be linked to the fact that mafia violence also functions as an equivalent of war in times of peace. On the spread of violent types of behaviour which perform a vicarious function in relation to the major explosion of death and destruction caused by a war, Winnicott wrote: 'We have to carry on now on the basis that there *is not going to be another war*. . . . When we think of the notorious atrocities of modern youth, we must weigh against them all the deaths that belong to the war that is not, and that is not going to be.'[7] The specific contamination of every aspect of daily life with death, fear, blackmail and persecution, the virtual elimination of every individual will for the sake of one imposed collectively, by the group, suggests that mafia violence is particularly appropriate in fulfilling the social function of 'total war'.

Blackmail, threats, mistrust: the components of the mafia style, originally directed outwards, are ultimately twisted back against the group's own members. The sense of death, manipulated and rationalized as a means of achieving certain ends, is revealed for what it is: quite simply the annihilation of life and therefore, in the final analysis, of one's own life.

Threats which are not explicit, but only hinted at, create an atmosphere which increases the effect of intimidation and the need for protection. If you do not know when and from where the hit will come, anxiety and mistrust are intensified; fear becomes hazy and generalized. The acute, almost paranoid, sensitivity to signals which develops transforms the raising of an eyebrow into the most horrific threat.[8]

My thinking aims to look at the mafia from a hitherto little explored perspective. On the basis of my research work and my everyday life as a woman living in Calabria, I want to put questions to myself about the subjective implications and the ethical dimension of our everyday coexistence with a phenomenon which, like it or not, concerns us all.

In the context of this work, by the word *mafia* I mean both the Sicilian mafia and the Calabrian *'ndrangheta*.

I have excluded the phenomenon of the *Camorra,* whose specific aspects are least familiar to me, and included the *'ndrangheta* for the opposite reason. This decision would seem to be supported by the judgement of experts who identify the Sicilian mafia, known as *Cosa Nostra*, as the dominant criminal organization, able to transmit and impose its own codes even on the other organizations. Those collaborating with the law have also mentioned that many *capi* of both the Camorra and the *'ndrangheta* are 'men of honour'. The Parliamentary Anti-mafia Commission* writes:

> The mafia association Cosa Nostra, moreover, has an overriding importance compared to the others through longstanding tradition, an organized force both within and beyond national frontiers, and criminal and financial capacities. . . . In fact, in relation to other forms of organized crime, it succeeds in fulfilling a general strategic function, imposing its own behavioural models, taking on the role of middleman in large-scale trafficking, and constituting a definitive organizational model.[9]

I want to understand from a woman's perspective and I want to give a voice to the women who for one reason or another have found themselves entangled in the business of the mafia. It is my aim to combine attention to

---

* The Parliamentary Anti-mafia Commission was set up in 1962. There were few results in its first decade of existence. By the early 1980s it had formulated a number of anti-mafia laws, whose proposed enactment was given increasing urgency by an outbreak of mafia killings in Sicily, Calabria and elsewhere. One of these was the La Torre law, put forward by the Communist parliamentary group, with Pio La Torre as its first signatory. He was murdered in Palermo on 30 April 1982 and in September of that year the legislation, known as the La Torre-Rognoni law, was passed by the Italian Parliament. Under its powers, mafia association was for the first time defined as a crime. See also note p. 115. [Trs.]

subjective experience of the mafia with a theoretical analysis. This is therefore an interpretation interwoven with my subjectivity, as well as that of the women and men who have been involved in this book. In one sense I do not feel alone in this undertaking: the mode of observation and many of the categories of analysis which I have used are the legacy of the women's movement, to which I owe a great part of my theoretical formation.

Obviously not all the women who have had dealings with the mafia will be found in these pages. I have preferred to give space to those who have contributed first-hand testimony: interviews, stories, comments. Moreover, there may be distortions; my sources are largely made up of previously published material: newspapers, books, periodicals. I therefore feel that I am only partially responsible for the sources, while naturally I take full responsibility as far as the interpretation is concerned.

If it is true that the exclusion and estrangement of women have marked our history, this applies all the more to everything concerning the organization and culture of the mafia. The mafia has always rigidly excluded women. Yet women and the feminine are strongly present – by their absence, one might say – in the rituals, myths and, willy-nilly, in the everyday life of mafiosi. We know very little from the literature.

> The study of the complex and dramatic relationships which women conduct with the mafia remains still to be done. There would be much to say, not just about the figure of the mother, the pivot of the Sicilian family, but also about the fact that it is precisely widows of mafiosi or of victims of mafia killers who have been the first to dare open rebellion against the power of the *Honoured Society*.[10]

Historical memory delivers up more silences than words about the 'complex and dramatic' relationships which women conduct with the mafia. Therefore this work becomes like an archaeological excavation, re-examining existing materials so as to 'read between the lines', and grasp the nexus between the mafiosi's 'social representation' of the feminine and of women on the one hand, and what the women involved at first hand have to say about themselves.

In the process I asked myself what might be my 'real', personal interest as a woman, in a world like that of the mafia, which excludes me by definition? Besides my ethical indignation and political indictment, what do I have to do with the mafia? The answer is neither simple nor unequivocal.

It is true that the mafia comprises an ensemble of exclusive groups. 'The esoteric structure of the mafia cell, the *cosca*, has reference to some kind of group narcissism, a kind of lethal romance.'[11] The exclusion of women seems a fundamental element in the cohesion of the group. Yet, on the other hand, by this exclusion the mafia imaginary produces a feminine and sanctions feminine roles on which to found an instrumental use of family relationships, which in turn becomes a functional part of mafia criminal activity itself.

This is where we find a first point of contact. As a woman, I am affected by this use and abuse of the feminine. I believe it is important to build solidarity with women who are victims of the mafia. We must, together, break the silence and give them ever more space to speak, not leave them alone but reconstruct their stories and build a historical memory of their actions, bringing their subjectivity into focus.

In the second place my curiosity is aroused and I am affected by the 'fates' of the women who are complicit with the mafia. What do they feel, what do they think? How do they coexist day by day in the shadow of the death of their own fathers, husbands, brothers and sons? What do they feel about their men's collective 'lethal romance'? Envy? Admiration? Contempt? Estrangement? It will not be easy to deliver answers to these questions, but I believe it is still worthwhile asking them.

I believe that precisely as women we must denounce the complicity of women with the mafia and, most of all, the impunity which has protected them until now. That the judiciary should assume them to be not responsible, and therefore inferior — yet another negation of individuality and equality — offends us as women.

Yet I am aware of the difficulty of defining probable complicity, partly because from the 'outside' it is not easy to imagine in what ways and to what extent the women have knowledge of the bloody and criminal activities of their husbands, brothers and sons. Moreover, and here we touch on a far-reaching problem, it is surely arbitrary to draw a clear line between mafiosi and corrupt politicians/administrators. Presumably, however, the private life of the 'collusive' public politician's and/or administrator's wife is more remote and less involved in the husband's activity. Since they are not related, the 'pen-pushers' of mafia crimes remain more remote (albeit no less responsible) from the rituals and locations of death. Their own lives and those of their families therefore appear less immediately in thrall to the honoured secret society.

Finally, reading and rereading, I am convinced that the question 'and the women?' can substantially enrich general understanding of the mafia phenomenon and its implications for the fate of our civil society. Adopting the perspective of the women necessarily focuses a series of aspects centred on subjectivity, on structures of consciousness, on forms of socialization and upbringing. The problem of the mafia is undoubtedly a problem of markets, economics and politics, but it is not the aim of this project of mine to explore these aspects primarily. Instead, I am interested in the issue of education and civil consciousness which underlies and goes with the mafia phenomenon. The mafia represents a radical negation of what is widely considered one of the highest achievements of our civilization, which is to say the rights of man.

INTRODUCTION

Giovanni Falcone* often used to say: 'Cosa Nostra is not invincible. It is a structure built by men and like all things made by men it has had a beginning and will have an end.' If this is true, and I believe that it is, I hope that in the future the women will be able to contribute increasingly towards bringing about its end.

The mafia denies the individual's right to his or her freedom. This denial strikes at women as much as at men. What we are concerned with here is reconstructing the experience of the women, on the basis of a woman's sensibility.

This work gradually developed and grew in close contact with Anna Puglisi and Umberto Santino. With generosity and implacable critical judgement they advised me and discussed things with me on many occasions, offering me hospitality at the Giuseppe Impastato Sicilian Centre for Documentation in Palermo. As well as the Centre's resources, Anna and Umberto also made available to me their interviews and unpublished articles. Despite disagreement on some awkward interpretative points, a relationship of intellectual trust and affection developed between us which has a firm place in this book. I would also like to mention Gianfranco Manfredi, someone with a deep knowledge of the mafia/'ndrangheta phenomenon, especially as regards Calabria. Without his critical annotations to an earlier project of mine, this book might never have come about.

Anna Puglisi, Umberto Santino, Gianfranco Manfredi and Donatella Barazzetti read the whole manuscript, giving me useful advice and also expressing some reservations.

In addition I want to thank the women from the editorial group of *Mezzocielo*† – some of whom are also active in the Association of Sicilian Women against the Mafia, others in the Comitato dei lenzuoli [Sheets Committee] and others in Digiuno [Fasting] for the generosity with which they welcomed me in Palermo and offered me important materials to reconstruct the road they had taken.

The first part of this book was read by Laura Balbo and Marina Piazza who gave me useful advice and formulated further questions. I am grateful also to Pantaleone Sergi who provided information and material relating to Calabria. My thanks to Roberto Cipparrone of the Department of Sociology at the University of Calabria for his careful technical contribution. I also want to express my gratitude to the group of colleagues and friends in the department which, because of intellectual affinities, we call the 'Little School of

---

* Giovanni Falcone, anti-mafia judge who died in 1992, the victim of a mafia bombing which also killed his wife and bodyguards. [Trs.]
† *Mezzocielo*: a Palermo-based feminist magazine.

9

Arcavacata': Antonello Costabile, Piero Fantozzi, Paolo Jedlowski, Carmen Leccardi, Anna Rossi-Doria and Anna Salvo.

Finally, a particular thank you to Paolo Jedlowski who agreed, irritably but reliably, to give the text a final reading, without which I would have felt bereft.

This book is dedicated to the many women who have suffered unspeakable violence at the hands of the mafia, to the many women who have rebelled against the outrage of violent death. Thanks cannot be enough; my gratitude goes to them and to the memory of their actions.

This study was carried out with support from the CNR (Consiglio nazionale delle ricerche) research project 'Belief in legality and social stratification in the contemporary Mezzogiorno', coordinated for the University of Calabria by Professor Paolo Jedlowski.

Arcavacata di Rende, November 1993

PART I

The Mafia through the Prism of Gender

A Men-only Society

Initiation rites

When I read about the mafia, when I listen to the news and try to understand, I feel like someone spying through a keyhole. Admittedly, there are many other phenomena linked to power of the so-called legal variety, the logic of certain kinds of speech and action for example, which inspire the same feeling in me. It is a profound sense of estrangement. I do not want to be misunderstood; I do not mean (hypercritically) that I am 'better', remote from any criminal temptation, let us say. What I am talking about is an inner remoteness, an absence of empathy, of desire, of pleasure, of complicity. I feel this both about negative, manifestly criminal events, and about stories and descriptions to do with obviously pleasant and exciting experiences, like the sociability of the group, initiation rites, entertainments and privileges deriving from mafia power.

The historical estrangement and exclusion of women from the public sphere and from power are undoubtedly the frame in which to set this perception. And it has been precisely women's entry into the public sphere, formally legitimated and to some extent a *de facto* occurrence, which has highlighted the unease and estrangement felt by those women who, while gaining access to hitherto male occasions and bastions, do not give up their own femininity. Estrangement is bred from that gap between a world of social relations built on the fundament of a masculine model on the one hand and an interior landscape invisible to the eye on the other, modelled on the basis of a woman's body.

Furthermore, everything to do with the mafia provokes this sense of being alien in women like me and many others, as we try to understand and lay our claim to the ways in which we are equal with men and the ways in which we are different, either necessarily or from choice.

The mafia is a secret society which by definition excludes women. Secrecy appears to be a potent cohesive element for the men who are in the ambit of the mafia or are members of it. It is this secrecy which symbolically marks out

13

an insurmountable boundary for those outside the organization, at the same time as having the effect of disproportionately inflating its presumed merits. 'Since the exclusion of others from a possession will apply particularly when this is something of great value, the converse, whereby what is denied to many must be something especially endowed with value is psychologically apparent.'[1] Simmel emphasizes that secret societies, based on unconditional trust in the keeping of the secret, constitute 'an extremely effective education in the moral bond between men'.[2] Secrecy, silence, betrayal, exclusion: so many elements which characterize what he calls 'the group egotism' of secret societies.

What strikes me spontaneously as a feeling of estrangement from the mafia is undoubtedly fuelled by this boundary traced between me and them both through the exclusively male membership and through the secrecy. Yet I wonder what are the spontaneous feelings of other women, particularly those who live in close daily contact with mafia men. What is the fascination that, even nowadays, can bring about that reversal of values which Simmel talks about? Is it conceivable that the very fact of being excluded, a fact sealed by secrecy, could constitute an attraction for the women, those excluded by definition? There is of course no doubt whatsoever that this very configuration has a potent hold on male fantasies.

In fact, on the basis of a look at the mafia phenomenon through female eyes, everything suggests that material factors, such as income and status, are not enough to justify the extraordinary fascination which the mafia obviously exerts over young and not so young men who are prepared to do anything just to join this exclusive organization. I have an impression that, deeper than the attraction to what is dark and secret, these men have some kind of special relationship with both the male and the female.

Mafia values (or would it be more correct to speak of non-values?) seem in many respects to be an exacerbation of the values upon which male identity is founded in our civilization. Masculinity, which is erroneously taken to be a 'natural' given, appears in reality a somewhat difficult goal to achieve. ' "Be a man" implies something which cannot be taken for granted and that virility is perhaps not so natural as some would like to suggest. . . . *Duty, test, proof:* these words signify that becoming a man entails the fulfilment of a real task.'[3]

Many of the rituals, habits and customs which mark membership of the mafia seem like so many signals which communicate:

> We alone are real men, we are superior, joining us is extremely difficult, hazardous and irreversible. The pact is sealed with blood, the stake is high. Ritual is not a mere external ceremony, it commits the new initiate to a trial of courage, it marks the passage to his *manhood*.[4]

But looked at more closely, the pathetic *mise-en-scène* has but a single goal: power. Pierre Bourdieu observes that 'the "virile" *illusio* is the basis of *libido dominandi'* but we could reverse the formulation and say, with Elisabeth Badinter, that 'the *libido dominandi* is the foundation of virility, however illusory it may be'.[5] The widespread advance of female emancipation and women's mass entry into the public sphere may also have accentuated certain men's wish to show off their virility to themselves and to others at whatever cost.

The initiation rites seem to be very important, both in order to erect boundaries and barriers and to create bonds. Bonds exclusive to men, boundaries in the way of other men, an insurmountable barrier in relation to the world of women. The initiation rites thrust open the door on a narrow world of 'real men', aspirants to absolute power.

For the mafia does not just explicitly exclude women (whereas the public sphere is now accessible to both sexes) but also exerts a pervasive iron grip on the private sphere, the antonomastic female zone. It is forbidden for women to join the 'mafia' secret society; women are excluded from this power, excluded from the public – political – role which, albeit secretly, attaches to the mafia.

> Not everybody can belong to Cosa Nostra. This university of crime lays down the obligation to be courageous, capable of carrying out violent actions and, therefore, of knowing how to kill. But this is not the fundamental quality. Knowing how to kill is a necessary condition, but not a sufficient one. Many others must be satisfied. In the initial phase, belonging to a mafia environment and having family ties with men of honour are a great advantage. Among the indispensable qualities required, the *pentito*★ Salvatore Contorno brings up the fact of being male.[6]

It seems precisely the fact of being male that is the fundamental element in the initiation rites. The initiation ceremony represents the culmination of a period and a process of observation and selection. It is the older men, already united by the blood bond, who keep an eye on the new generation. The *pentito* Antonino Calderone said:

> The best of the young ones are carefully watched and studied by the older men. The oldest of the mafiosi, friends of the father, relatives of the mother, keep an eye on the kids, and some of them stand out from the others. . . . These fine male children are studied by the whole group, and when one of them makes an impression because he is smart and sure of himself and bossy he is immediately taken in hand and encouraged by the adult men of honour who teach him and show him the ropes, take him along with them, start giving him things to do.[7]

★ A *pentito* is someone who gives up criminal allegiances and turns state's evidence. The word's literal, original meaning – a penitent – carries religious and moral connotations of remorse that suggest a status beyond that of mere witness. [Trs.]

You don't choose to join the Honoured Society, you have to go about being chosen. 'It is the *'ndrangheta* which chooses its soldiers, nobody can put himself forward.'[8] These formalities hugely reinforce the latent bonds between men of different generations, marking out specific forms of authority and having the effect of surrounding the mafia with heightened fascination, secrecy and fear.

The *pentito* Leonardo Messina said:

> It's not as if you get up and join Cosa Nostra. It's a kind of outlook, they keep an eye on you as a child, they bring you up, they teach you to shoot, to kill, to plant bombs. You're a robot, you're marked out. The way you come into Cosa Nostra is as 'avvicinati', hangers-on, for a period that can last twenty years, or five years, or one year, and depending on individuals, then somebody tells you the time has come. But by the time they call you you already know that it's Cosa Nostra because you have already served these men for ten years. There's always one person who guides you, each man of honour has something like five, ten or fifteen people hanging around. . . . In Cosa Nostra the first murders are done by 'avvicinati'. When there's a meeting in a village to bring men in as new members, you'd think it was a party.[9]

In this sense the mafia seems the bearer of a charismatic power, a charisma with which certain men of honour in particular are endowed, but which resonates through the whole organization. The likely candidates for initiation are predominantly the sons, cousins, nephews and grandsons of the mafiosi themselves, but they can also be boys from anywhere else, offspring of the criminal community, noticed and carefully picked out. As Calderone says, 'this outer circle of young men willing to do anything' surrounds the mafiosi, depends on them, but also constitutes an essential part of the mafiosi's 'public' recognition: 'The mafioso seeks power and takes it, and is proud of it. But a great deal of his power is given to him by others.'[10]

Initiation therefore begins much earlier than the actual rite. The single-sex configuration of the mafia, its halo of mystery and the charisma that is thoroughly anchored in values of virility mean that the father/son relationship and the 'strong correlation between self-image and image of the parent of the same sex'[11] assume an overriding role for the constant regeneration of the mafia. Ianni, too, in his study of an Italian-American 'crime family', underlines this constellation: 'The Lupollo family is a man's world. The strength of this male bonding is such that sons spend considerable time with their fathers not only in business but in social activities.'[12]

The initiation ritual represents both a promise and a threat. Joining this elite entails a high price: the devil demands a soul in exchange for his services.

> But an oath is not a promise, as the kids being sworn in believed. I realized this because I was older than them and I knew the environment. It is a threat. The

16

guys around the table do not say: swear to be faithful for ever. They say: if you are not faithful you will die.[13]

The moment itself and the initiation rites have a powerful significance, committing the individual for his whole life and determining an unequivocal change of status. But above all they seal the new membership, with everything it involves.

All the signs indicate that the mafia ritual is practised for purely internal reasons. . . . The ritual has the property of a *concentrated calling up of strength* typical of the rituals present in oral cultures. . . . The ritual undermines rational expectations. . . . The ritual by itself grants an ephemeral certainty.[14]

You can enter the mafia, but you can never leave it, except as a dead man. 'Joining the mafia corresponds to conversion to a religion. Priests never stop being priests. Nor do mafiosi stop being mafiosi.'[15] The initiation ceremony seals a bond between men of different generations, emphasizing an 'endogamous' aspect: 'that of not desiring the woman of any other men of honour'.

Likewise, the importance contained in the blood symbolism of these rites suggests bonds that go far beyond those between mere business partners. Besides the warning never to betray, 'because you enter Cosa Nostra with blood and you only leave it with blood',[16] the ritual touches on a new bond, a closeness between males that is impregnated with a pervasive, albeit latent, homoerotic overtone. Bonds of libido between the members of the group, and between them and the various *capi*, are inaugurated, sealed and made visible through the initiation rites. 'Heart and "love" within the group, guts and *omertà* outside it.'[17]

The spilling of a drop of one's own blood signifies that one's own life has been given as a pledge, the drinking of the blood of others refers to archaic and mythic relations of acquired consanguinity. In many initiation rites adolescents suck the blood of a man's wound, so that they may become men. 'By sucking mother's milk boys are feminized and by drinking male liquids they become virile.'[18] Serafino Castagna, a historic *pentito* of the Calabrian *'ndrangheta*, describes his initiation: 'I had to duel with my friend until I wounded him. . . . "You must hit three times," the master explained, "when you have struck him and he begins to bleed, you must suck his wound." '[19]

With initiation the mafioso becomes part of a new universe, and is introduced to languages and forms of communication that are codified and structured by the shared secret of 'being the same thing', of belonging body and soul to a violent elite. 'From that moment on the one who has been baptized will no longer be like others, like the mass of his acquaintances and his fellow citizens. He will be a Christian with two baptisms.'[20]

Hunting and banquets

Membership of the mafia is something absolute. The bond is severed only with death, and after the initiation oath both the private and the public life of the mafioso is within the compass of the organization. It is well and truly a pact with the devil. But so long as everything is going well, according to the accounts of various protagonists, this exclusively male social existence seems to sparkle with frequent pleasures and entertainments. The sense of belonging to an elite, which Calderone emphasizes, on the one hand reinforces the bond between the mafiosi and, on the other, constantly enlarges the gap between them and those outside. 'You must excuse this distinction I'm making . . . but it is important to me. It is important to all mafiosi. It's important: we are mafiosi, the rest are ordinary men. We are men of honour.'[21]

Hunting features as one particular mafia pastime. This is an activity which in exemplary fashion combines links with the past and present and future aspirations. Materially and also symbolically, hunting ratifies the bond with the earth and with a personal history as peasant and farmer, but equally with the seemingly ever-present dream of attaining feudal power. 'Much of the language and the imagery which comes out of the trial documents is permeated with the countryside.'[22] Hunting, with beaters in the grand style, also symbolizes the achievement of social mobility, setting the scene, even if only momentarily, for a feudal style of life. 'But, as serfs turned masters, their vices were those of their ancient masters,' Sciascia wrote.[23] And indeed, the *pentito* Antonino Calderone offered an extremely vivid picture of these vices:

> The Costanzos knew that we enjoyed the company of important people, powerful figures. . . . They knew about our passion for hunting, for example. A lot of men of honour are hunters. . . . I remember a shoot at the start of the season on a wonderful hunting reserve the Costanzos owned on the slopes of Etna. . . . Michele Greco, Totò Minore and Totò Riina had come especially from Palermo and Trapani. . . . Then there was Nitto and other prominent mafiosi from Catania who had brought several crates of fish to roast.[24]

The bond with the earth, the bond with life and death and with weapons, the ancient bond between men: hunting offers an ideal framework for reinforcing relationships that are nurtured by violence, as well as by a fear of death, day in day out.

> At midnight we would sit down around the table and enjoy the food prepared by some of the guests. The men cooked, as was traditional at banquets among men of honour. . . . We would feast away to our hearts' content, laughing and joking until the next morning. Nobody thought about danger and death.[25]

Dinners and banquets with exquisite food and copious wine, toasts that combine jokes, obscenities and coarseness, high spirits shadowed by death and looking it in the face, become significant in all the autobiographical accounts and writings. In the Anonimo (Anonymous) account: 'There were parties once a month and in some cases more often. Don Peppe was playing host to important friends from other villages; from the car numberplates you could see there were some who had even come from Palermo. We men were preparing all the food and the youngest had the job of getting the animals.'[26]

The anthropologist Peter Schneider, in the course of his research in Sicily, also witnessed a great banquet at which friendships were forged on various levels:

> Consistent with tradition, no women attended these affairs. . . . Great emphasis was placed on eating and drinking and on the fraternal bonds created when men break bread together. Some of the participants then parodied women, dancing erotically alone and together, applauded and encouraged by the others. . . . What better way to reinforce solidarity among men who belong to the town, church and family but who have also an important and exclusive life beyond?[27]

The absence of women on these occasions seems a precondition of a particular emotional component marking these moments. 'Meals such as these, prepared and presided over by us men only, were fraternal occasions that ranked among the finest pleasures of life. We'd drink, eat, sing, recite poems, tell jokes and swap stories. Every five minutes it seemed someone or other would be raising his glass to propose a toast.'[28] Joe Bonanno talks about parties, for instance at the end of some bloody war between rival clans, which would last for as long as a week.

Ideally these banquets would be held, and still are held, in country places, at farmhouses or lodges. The resonance with a feudal style of life again comes to mind. Michele Greco, for example, kept an entire property for his friends' use: 'The villa on the Favarella estate was used by the men of honour just to get together for carousing, as you could see from the sixty-odd chairs, the huge ovens and the enormous grills lying all over the house.'[29]

Here we have entertainment, the exclusive bond between men, manly pleasures and the temporary repression of imminent death. But these banquets also have the function of forming and reinforcing friendships with a purpose, making and unmaking alliances. Friendship, even when it has an instrumental character, still contains an emotional component to be cultivated and nurtured. 'Equally important, we think, the banquets provide a context for elevating friendship to an ideology, thus lending additional stability to alliances formed in its name.'[30]

Backwoods violence

The mafia disputes the state's legitimate monopoly of violence; the mafia makes use of violence either for the purpose of internal cohesion within its own organization, or externally. 'I stress that the mafia fulfils its function with violence, with internalized violence, inflicted violence, threatened violence.'[31] The very definition of the mafia, in the final analysis, is anchored in the usurpation of a 'right' over the life and death of individuals. 'I am often asked if a man of honour can choose not to kill. My answer is no.'[32]

A careful reading of the means, times and sites of mafia violence indicates a fairly complex interconnection between archaic and industrial forms of threats, reprisals and killings. Yet there is no doubt that mafia violence has a purpose, that strong-arm tactics, murders, attacks and threats are functional to the accumulation of power and money. 'There is a widespread belief that the mafia privileges certain murder methods over others. This is a mistake. The mafia always chooses the quickest and least risky way. And this is its only rule. It has no fetishistic preference for one or other method.'[33]

From this point of view, as Judge Falcone rightly emphasizes, the mafia is an extremely modern criminal organization, with national and international ramifications. Yet, from a subjective point of view, in terms of the men actually involved and rooted in their own local culture and territory, it is pertinent to ask which, for them psychologically, is the 'quickest way'.

It is a delicate and difficult matter to analyse the outlines and overlays of what anthropologists call 'folk culture' and the distortions and manipulations which this culture undergoes at mafia hands. There is no precise line of demarcation, no crystal-clear truth. There is no doubt that much of the mafioso language, its signs and gestures, have roots in popular culture, just as there is no doubt that all of this is placed in the service of a criminal plan of extremely rational ends and means. I believe that the mafiosi themselves are unaware of this, just as I believe that many people become drawn into this 'mafia culture' at some subterranean level for the very reason of its multiple resonances with their own folk patrimony. As it modernizes itself along the way, the mafia undoubtedly feeds off the traditional patrimony, and manipulates and fuels a widespread nostalgia for what is irreparably past. 'Any particular secret society is probably an attempt to cling to a threatened social, economic or political order.'[34]

A large part of the violence practised by the mafia is marked with the ways and customs of the rural world. As one *pentito* put it: 'The boss's men are *dead meat*. They are used up and thrown away.'[35] Anonymous puts things similarly: 'And he was not under Don Nino's protection: my friend Saro Menzapinna was pigmeat. Nobody minded if they took his life.'[36]

The mafioso murderer often exhibits a relationship with the body and blood of his own victim akin to that of a peasant with sheep or with the killing of a pig.

Before the man fell down I was on top of him and I fired into him a few more times. When he was on the ground I saw that his head was shaking convulsively and there was a faint rattle coming from his throat. His body was quivering all over; I rested the pistol butt on the back of his neck and shot him one last time . . . then he stopped moving.[37]

Giorgio Bocca quotes the words of the 'ndrangheta pentito, Scriva: 'To find out where the Tripodis were hiding, they took one of their relatives, a guy called Seminara, made him sing and then killed him. The actual business was taken care of by Antonio, the butcher, who pulled him between his legs and cut his throat like a goat kid.'[38]

This corporeal and visceral relationship with blood and death harks back to a peasant culture, where blood was of 'decisive importance', as observed by Luigi Lombardi Satriani with reference to Calabria. Blood is central in numerous religious rites, in apparitions, in rituals of a magical nature and, finally, in the rituals which accompany violent death. 'There is a belief that the assassin who does not taste his victim's blood by licking the murder knife will remain at the scene of the crime unable to flee, and therefore the first thought of the knife murderer is to lick the knife.'[39]

I am far from wishing to 'ennoble' mafia murders with folkloric explanations. Yet I believe it is important to grasp and recognize the twisted elements of traditional culture, because I imagine that they represent a powerful element of 'deception', both for those who are threatened by the mafia and for those who become members of Cosa Nostra itself. Homicidal practices make a similar combination of the archaic elements of peasant society and the pragmatic elements of industrialized consumer society, for example the trussing, goat-style, which is ordinarily practised so as to fit a corpse into the boot of a car for convenient transportation. A similar confusion between barbarity and professionalism prevails at the level of conscience. The *pentito* Francesco Marino Mannoia expressed it in these terms to Falcone:

> Do you realize how much strength is necessary to strangle a man? Do you realize that you can take as long as ten minutes and that the victim breaks free, and bites and kicks? Some even manage to get out of the noose. But at least these are professional-style murders.[40]

A cynicism that has its roots in modern genocidal society is mingled with (badly assimilated) traditional cultural models in which violence in the face of nature is part of everyday experience. Antonio Zagari, a member of the Calabrian 'ndrangheta, serves as an example of the coarse arrogance that this mixture can produce at an individual level.

Killing a man, even though it was the first time, left me completely indifferent, maybe I even liked it because what I felt was like a sense of wellbeing, a really strange pulsating sensation . . . between my stomach and my brain. But the blood I found on myself made me feel sick.[41]

An esoteric group?

The reading of the mafia phenomenon thus far developed represents an attempt on the basis of a woman's subjective sensibility to identify the over-riding cohesive element of the mafioso group as the fact of being exclusively male. Yet, I should not like to be misunderstood: I most certainly do not want to construct an equation between mafia identity and male identity *tout court*. The sense of being a mafioso, the behaviour and the particular staging of mafioso identity, appear rather like an intensification of masculinity and the values traditionally linked to the male. A hypothesis could be made that the mafia offers a route that can be taken, an answer to the difficulty and fragility of the male condition. A 'wrong' answer to the perennial fear of men, faced with the dilemma of whether or not to accept their own female aspects, the fear, above all, of appearing female.

'A man's first duty is not to be a woman.'[42] Male-gendered sexual identity is founded on the painful act of separation from the mother, on the refusal of the feminine. Hermann Burger writes that each man is confronted with the following problem: 'On the one hand actively to proceed against the mother; on the other to suffer passively through her. . . . We must kill her and be killed by her. In making himself, man must take care not to wound his female soul.'[43] The initiation rites of so-called primitive societies have the decisive meaning of wrenching boys away from the world of women, often through very painful and cruel rituals. The pain functions to erect boundaries, to cut off every way back to the realm of the mother. Amputations, symbolic wounds, circumcision itself all function to take the boy away from the mother and introduce him to the community of men.

> This builds enormous tension into contemporary conceptions of masculinity. Fear is defined as an unacceptable emotion, but in disowning our fear and learning to put a brave face to the world, we learn to despise all forms of weakness. Strength is identified with a stiff upper lip, as we learn systematically to discount any feelings of fear. We learn not to show our feelings to others, since this is an immediate sign of weakness. This is a deep cultural inheritance.[44]

The equilibrium of masculine identity seems a fragile one, for the very reason that it swings constantly between a social ban on recognition of one's own feminine components and the intimate nostalgia for a regression back to that femininity which is held and buried within every man.

By cutting short his identification with the mother and his dependence on her, the male risks total loss of his capacity for reciprocal recognition. The boy develops his gender and identity by means of establishing discontinuity and difference from the person to whom he is most attached. This process of disidentification explains the repudiation of the mother that underlies conventional masculine identity formation, and results in a kind of 'fault line' running through the male achievement of individuality.[45]

The man is compelled to show proof of his masculinity over and over again; it can never be regarded as secure. 'In breaking the identification with and dependency on mother, the boy is in danger of losing his capacity for mutual recognition altogether. The emotional attunement and bodily harmony that characterized his infantile exchange with mother now threatens his identity.'[46]

The mafia group represents a strengthened defence against all intrusion of the feminine. Externally, the group defends itself by admitting only men as members. Internally, at the subjective level, all are obliged to reject and excise the feminine sides of their own character, if necessary under threat of death. This alienation from the needs of affection, dependence and vulnerability is something fundamentally imposed upon the psyche of every single mafioso. 'A mafioso who allows any signs of psychological unease to leak out and therefore shows evidence of insecurity risks being silenced for ever.'[47]

Giuseppe Marchese, a ruthless killer apparently without any scruples, was watching the funeral of Falcone and his wife and their bodyguard on television. He was in prison, along with other *picciotti* (young southerners) when Rosaria, the very young widow of the police officer Schifani, turned weeping to address the 'men of the mafia', and screamed: 'Too much blood, there is no love here, there is no love here, there is no love at all.' For Marchese, the feeling of being moved by this and the immediate sense of mortal danger, the threat of being killed by his own cellmates, were one and the same. 'They were all impassive, but there came a point when I couldn't stand it any more. I had to leave so as not to let them see that I was moved.'[48] Marchese knew that this 'surrender' corresponded to a sentence of death. His decision to testify, shortly after, was also a consequence of this awareness.

Self-control, the denial of feelings and the rejection of others' feelings are invariably the foundation on which membership of the mafia is developed. The mafioso is compelled to suppress all those feelings which do not fit the pattern of ends and means imposed by the secret organization he has joined. In short, the mafia man, to an even greater degree than other men in our society, becomes 'invisible to himself': 'This instrumental relationship to language and to feeling is ultimately expressive of an instrumental relationship to self which grows from the denial of particular realms of human experience. . . . So it is that men become strangely invisible to themselves.'[49] This, however, does not mean that the bonds between members of the mafia are bereft of feeling, quite the contrary.

Homophobia – by which I mean a hatred of feminine qualities in men – seems to be a constituent element of the bonding between mafiosi. This is where the argument becomes complicated. In this sense, being a man corresponds to not being a homosexual. 'Homophobia is such an integral part of heterosexual masculinity that it performs an essential psychological role: it indicates who is not homosexual and points out who is heterosexual.'[50] Homophobia acts as a psychic defence mechanism. It is a strategy for avoiding recognition of an unacceptable part of the self: passivity, identified in the feminine. In fact, *passive* pederasty is considered a disgrace, an impossibility for anyone who wants to apply for membership of the 'family'.[51]

Simultaneously, however, the bonds between mafiosi often take on a marked emotionality, seemingly drenched in latent homosexuality. We can trace these features in all the autobiographical accounts. Let us quote one example from the text of Joe Bonanno:

> If Anastasia had told Costello, Willie wondered, why hadn't Costello told his right-hand man? Moretti felt betrayed and diminished by Costello's new 'love'. . . . Costello wanted a strong man next to him – first Moretti and then Anastasia – in order to thwart Genovese. To counter this, Vito made an alliance of his own with Tommy Lucchese, who at that time was the second in Gagliano's family. It was common knowledge that Tommy and Vito were close. The expression I like to use is 'They were making love'.[52]

Freud identifies a strong component of sublimated homosexual desire in friendship between men. Nevertheless, in patriarchal society a certain manly overtone in relationships between men intimately expresses violence and contempt for what is different.

> There is a certain gesture of virility, be it one's own or someone else's, that calls for suspicion. It expresses independence, sureness of the power to command, the tacit complicity of all males. . . . The pleasures of such men, or rather of their models, which are seldom equalled in reality, for people are even now better than their culture, all have about them a latent violence. . . . In the end the tough guys are the truly effeminate ones, who need the weaklings as their victims in order not to admit that they are like them. Totalitarianism and homosexuality belong together. In its downfall the subject negates everything which is not of its own kind.[53]

Sticking with the same analogy, Joe Bonanno speaks in these terms about Stefano Maggadino, his friend/mortal enemy and cousin:

Our silent stares expressed what we could not in words. We knew we would never be friends again, but we were past the stage of reproach and denial. We were beyond that. We were in the occult stage of final affirmation. With our eyes only, we said to each other: 'You know what you know. I know what I know. And no one else will really know as we know.'[54]

An understanding of the strong bond connecting mafia members can be helped by going back to Freud's analysis in *Group Psychology and Analysis of the Ego*, as does Filippo Di Forti. Like the group of brothers which is formed on the basis of a negative response to a severe and oppressive father and which is united by the group members' shared love and hatred, according to Di Forti, the mafia group can be understood as a brotherhood:

The mafia shows itself to be like a fraternal community born from the negation of a father's authority, an authority which is, however, internalized by the group as a phantom presence of which the mafioso's sense of honour is one manifestation. . . . One feature of the mafia is its esoteric structure which originates from a split between official society, the society of the fathers, and a mafioso society, a 'fraternal community'. . . . The mafioso brotherhood is born out of the negation of the father's authority and that of his representatives and therefore sets itself in opposition to the authority on which the laws of official society are founded.[55]

Intensifying a particular bellicose and fascistic masculine ideology, mafia ideology exalts brotherhood between 'real men', soldiers and combatants.

It must also be like this between soldiers in wartime: they know themselves to be men who may die from one moment to the next. And even if they live through it, in the end they go back to civil life and never meet again. But through those days they were brothers. Because among soldiers needs and thoughts are the same. And so there are some words that even if spoken softly, very softly, ring out like the bells on Easter Day.[56]

And again:

If you've ever been in battle you know that in the face of danger most people take cover and wait to see what everybody else is doing. But a man, the pure warrior, knows what to do. He just does it. Everyone else on the battlefield looks at him and says, 'That man looks like he knows what he's doing.' Soon everyone on the battlefield follows the natural leader. . . . Everybody grouses, everybody wants to go to sleep. Only one man, the pure warrior, is off in the corner oiling his rifle, arranging his gear, darning his socks. Everybody feels like going over to him and saying, 'Hey what is it with you? Let up.' But in his heart everybody knows the pure warrior is right. The pure warrior is alert only to the present. And everybody starts cleaning his rifle.[57]

Like it or not, mafia ideology exalts and sometimes deforms characteristics which as a rule belong to the male gender, and which subtly bind men together, be they mafiosi or not. Sciascia testifies to this in the relationship he draws between Don Mariano and the *carabinieri* captain, Bellodi: ' "You, even if you nail me on these papers like Christ on the cross, you are a man." . . . "You too," said the captain with some emotion. And in the unease he immediately experienced from this armed salute exchanged with a mafia *capo*, in mitigation he thought . . .'[58]

The sociocultural context which fosters mafia ideology is historically situated on an intermediate terrain. Even from a historical-anthropological point of view being a mafioso has meant and still means existing on a hybrid cultural territory. Discussing mafia culture, Luigi Lombardi Satriani asserts:

> Its immediate surroundings are bourgeois culture and lower-class culture, but it is towards the first that it inclines, attempting to connect with it after a predatory journey into plebeian culture. But this attempt by mafia culture to connect with bourgeois culture should not be surprising, because the mafia is historically the creature of this culture and the relationship between the two can be patterned in the image of an incest, prolonged throughout time, between mother and daughter.[59]

Therefore at the historical level, but also at the level of psychology, the mafia is the bearer of a strong ambivalence. 'The mafioso internalizes the power and arrogance of the barons of the period of Bourbon domination in Sicily and, at the same time, his society is born out of a reaction to the barons.'[60] Put differently, in psychoanalytic terms, the mafiosi, in uniting against the law of the father, combat it with its own means. 'The "law of the *lupara*" [the shotgun] is the law of the father which is taken on by the mafia brotherhood as its own law.'[61]

Moreover, the object of love and of hatred for whose defence and for whose possession the brotherhood was born, in conflict with the law of the father, is the mother, who symbolically represents possession of the earth. The secret which unites the fraternal members of the association, the *omertà* in effect, is the weapon turned against the father, the law, the state, the outside world, in defence of the world inside, in defence of a mother, fantasized as uniquely good, a 'holyholymother'.

> The esoteric structure of the mafia can be traced back to the desire to keep secret a relation with an object of love and of hate; the mafiosi mean to preserve this object from attacks coming from outside. The secret, therefore, can be

traced back to this attachment to the mother whose bad parts and relative hostile feelings are negated and who, thereby, comes to be named holyholy-mother.[62]

So this is a group made up of men only and marked with a radical ambivalence in relation to the feminine: a union between brothers on the one hand in the name of attachment to the mother, and, on the other, in the name of fear and contempt for the feminine. An exclusive group. An esoteric group.

The Family

Exploiting family networks

Any attempt to read the mafia phenomenon from a woman's perspective can only underline the ambivalence of mafia codes in relation to the family. The importance which this institution assumes in mafia strategies appears to be motivated principally by opportunism. Applauded as a value and rigidly defended on the basis of formal and functional criteria, the family takes on a dual aspect: it is on the one hand a pivotal means of exercising territorial sovereignty, on the other an organizational model for criminal activities. This second aspect, moreover, promotes the reproduction of an ideology which matches up criminal organization with family, conferring on the former a halo of protectiveness and benevolence that is altogether familial. 'The *cosca* takes the family as a model, expanding it, and the reason for its strength lies precisely in the enormous potential of the family model of organization to penetrate the social system.'[1]

The manipulation of family relationships and the exploitation of family attachments even to the point of sacrificing the lives of close relatives are commitments that the aspirant mafioso undertakes to respect at the moment of initiation. 'Cosa Nostra comes before everything – our blood relatives, our religion, our country.' Thus runs the testimony of Joe Valachi.[2] Tommaso Buscetta uses similar words: 'Cosa Nostra comes before blood, family, relationships and country.'[3] And again: ' "In honour of the Family, the Family embraces you." The counsellor ... asked one of the new recruits if he would leave his mother on her deathbed were he to be called by "The Cosa Nostra". "Would you do it now?" he was asked, and he answered: "Yes." '[4]

Outwardly, as an explicit ideology, the mafia presents itself as the defender of the family and its values, while within it individual men of honour are well aware of the cynical use to which these values must be put. Calderone explains:

> Family relationship and friendship are worth nothing compared with fidelity to
> Cosa Nostra. If the interest of the family is involved, all these feelings disappear,

moving into the background. They are actually made use of to strike all the better, to achieve the desired end more easily. No one feels particularly embarrassed by this, and no one talks about 'betrayal' in these circumstances.[5]

Family ties, even matrimonial strategies, serve to augment the power of the *cosca*. The patriarchal form of the family predominates in the mafia world, and it could not be otherwise. Marriages cement alliances between the families and open up prospects of fresh profits and greater power. In the maxi-trial indictment, for example, we read:

> To this let it be added that Giacomo Giuseppe Gambino was present at the wedding of Giovanni Grizzaffi, nephew of the Corleone man Salvatore Riina, and that one of Gambino's sisters is married to Giovanni Pilo, who has been identified as a 'man of honour' of Buscetta and Contorno's San Lorenzo family, while another sister is married to Calogero Spina, the son of the well-known mafia *capo* of the della Noce district mafia.[6]

Such is the strategic significance of marriages for the structure of the criminal organization and the arrangement of alliances between the different cells, that by following a trail of weddings, christenings and confirmations, the judges managed to gather information about internal changes within organized crime.

> In the '162 report' written up by the Palermo police in 1982, we read, and with a sense of revelation: 'Pietro Marchese, brother-in-law of his namesake Filippo Marchese (both of the Corso dei Mille family) who had married one of his sisters, was also a brother-in-law of Giovanello Greco (Ciaculli family), whose sister Rosaria he had married.' This prompted the Palermo police to guess at an earlier alliance between the families of Corso dei Mille and Ciaculli, which remapped the organization![7]

In these marriage contracts, the woman's role is obviously central. On the one hand, through them, the men of honour increase their own power, plotting alliances with other cells, while at the same time matrimonial strategies can also be focused on smoothing out otherwise irreparable conflicts between rival families.

> The woman emerges distinctly as a central figure and as an exchange commodity when ending a feud was at issue; the offering up of the virgin blood of the woman brought as a bride to the male of the enemy family compensated for the blood spilled hitherto and sealed the pact that no new mourning be provoked between the families that are henceforth related and joined by a bond of blood.[8]

In his autobiography, Joe Bonanno draws significant distinctions between 'family' and 'Family'. Despite repeated declarations of love and affection for his close relatives, his account demonstrates the unquestionable subordination of the interests of his family – with a small 'f' – to those of the Family – with a capital 'F'. It could be objected that this hierarchy, in which concern for family attachments is subordinated to concern for one's work, is not entirely peculiar to mafia men, but is a general male characteristic, at least in our culture.

> It was the Enlightenment which universalized a particular morality, premised on a radical division between reason and emotion. It still casts its shadow over the visions we inherit of ourselves.... If men carried power in the structures of capitalist society, it was becoming clear that this was at a considerable price in terms of their own capacities and desires.[9]

The industrial work ethic and the splitting off between affective functions and instrumental functions have accustomed us to a male socialization which privileges a commitment to the sphere outside the family. This is undoubtedly true. But what appears to be specific to the mafia ethic is both the ambiguous mixture of respect, honour and exploitation in relation to the family, and the contamination of family attachments with a ferocious obedience to the mafia codes, with blood and with death.

> In other words: the family tie which tends to be the basis of mafia partnerships, known – not by accident – as 'family', is used to facilitate the elimination of mafiosi who are aligned on the side of the enemy by the dynamic of mafia war, but who imagine that they can save their own lives by relying on the family relationship, especially if it is a very close one, thereby delivering themselves into the hands of the killers. A deadly mechanism which restructures mafia organizations on the basis of interests that use family relations as a trap.[10]

A conception of family ties and attachments that is very exploitative: it brings home the totalizing claim on the lives of others in general and of close relatives in particular. A visceral idea of possession, perverse in some respects, which cancels out the actual individual, only affirming possession as such.

> The boss Pietro Marchese had his throat cut like an animal in prison on the orders of his brother-in-law, Filippo Marchese, but at the hands of five prisoners outside the family. I remember the *pentito* Salvatore Contorno, while deploring the fact that Filippo Marchese had not personally carried out the sentence, uttered these words: 'On my blood I alone can lay hands . . .'[11]

In some cases it has been this very conflict between obedience to the secret society and an almost ritual sacrifice of the life of some family member that has caused an internal rupture, even the decision to give testimony. In his statement, Giuseppe Marchese recalls an event that happened years earlier but which seems with hindsight significant in his trajectory as a *pentito*. When he was sixteen he was in love and wanted to marry a girl from what the rules of Cosa Nostra held to be an 'irregular' family: her parents were separated. Giuseppe's brother, who was also a man of honour, made the suggestion that he 'clean up the family mess' and marry an orphan instead of the daughter of separated parents.

> Do you understand what I had to do: kill Rosaria's father . . . I hung around playing for time, then there wasn't any time left. My brother confronted me and said: 'Well, Pino, do we all have to keep banging our heads against the wall? You're wearing yourself out with this wedding and you're wearing out your family. If you don't kill him, we'll kill him.' I immediately broke it off with Rosaria.[12]

This example is a good illustration of the implacable ferocity of mafia blackmail, its radical intent to condition and model in its own image the affective sphere of its own members. What characterizes the mafia as an all-embracing institution seems precisely to be this aim of annihilating individual personality. The reporter describes the *pentito* with a 'motionless profile, like stone . . . Marchese seems to have no emotion when he speaks. He is cold, almost mechanical, pedantic about memories and details. He narrates his life as it were someone else's. He narrates this with an icy sense of (apparent) estrangement.' The reporter's doubt about whether Marchese's emotional coldness is apparent or real remains open, a crucial question: to what extent does the mafia succeed in freezing, annihilating and ravaging the inner, affective life of its own members? And what do women in intimate relations with such men think about it?

There is reason to wonder what kind of family we are talking about. Does the mafia's interference with decision-making in specific families meet with resistance? What is the role of women in these contexts? Are they able to grasp where decisions are fully worked out, in the bosom of the Honoured Society, or in the bosom of their own family? Or are they in fact the same thing? Clearly there is no simple answer to these questions.

Hitherto, most analyses of the mafia have overlooked any investigation of the gaps between 'family' and 'Family', taking for granted an equivalence between two things that are not identical. Salvatore Lupo is right when he writes: 'Hess and the others do not try to understand how cultural codes, networks of patronage, or even blood-related families are the backbone of mafia organization, precisely because the one is never regarded as distinguishable from the other.'[13]

At first glance it seems that as regards the role of women in mafia-dominated society, the mafia family does not correspond either to the typical family of traditional peasant society or to that of bourgeois society. While in the peasant family, as a rule, women's role was *de facto* powerful, although with the outward appearance of patriarchy which formally denied them any power,[14] in the bourgeois family the asymmetrical division of functions between the instrumental (equalling male and public) and affective (equalling female and private) conceals a deeply unequal condition beneath the appearance of formal equality. This second contradiction – between formal, judicial equality between men and women and differential treatment in terms of economic and social realities on the basis of the disparity in family roles – has none the less engendered and fuelled the process of female emancipation in modern societies.

In the mafia family, a hybrid of peasant culture and petty-bourgeois culture, the woman seems trapped within the worst aspects of both: she is denied both the *de facto* power which prevailed in the peasant family, and the access to formal equality and emancipation typical of the lower-middle- and middle-class family.

In relation to the categories of *private* and *public*, the mafia in fact assumes very particular features. Its connotation as a secret society by definition suggests that, in some oblique way, it infiltrates both the private and the public spheres whenever the opportunity arises. In pursuit of its own ends – 'the mafia is . . . an association of mutual assistance which acts at the expense of civil society and to the advantage only of its members'[15] – the mafia follows an extremely pragmatic logic and has no specific interest in either one of the two spheres to the detriment of the other. Its relationship with both seems to be essentially manipulative.

Nevertheless, the mafia's greatest strength, its ability to exert widespread control over its territory, naturally means that its interest in using individuals through control over families, and therefore over the private sphere, appears to be pre-eminent. A sense of belonging, territorial rootedness, social control and a deep knowledge of traditional codes of communication allow mafia leaders to rule their own 'Family' in the image and likeness of the blood family.

From this point of view the man's patriarchal hold over the family and its members, which in traditional peasant society appears to be counterbalanced by women's considerable silent power in family management, acquires an incomparably greater dimension in mafia families. Having total say over his family members, even to the extent of life and death decisions, is a function of an individual's power within the mafia organization. The 'public' role of the mafioso above all presupposes a total hold over the 'private' sphere. The mafioso's undisputed control over his own family and his power to manipulate family relationships in an authoritarian manner appears to be a prerequisite for being acknowledged and esteemed as a 'man of honour'.

Being and seeming

The manipulative pragmatism which permeates mafia behaviour is particularly focused on appearances. The mafioso is defined by formality, rigid rules
and total obedience to the internal statutes of the Honoured Society. Here I
am thinking most of all of the rules of conduct imposed on different aspects
of the family. Pino Marchese's story shows us how in order not to break the
rule that forbids a mafioso to marry the daughter of a separated couple, there
has to be resort to murder. In order to appear to be upholding mafia-decreed
standards, you either are or you become a murderer.

In *The Day of the Owl*, Sciascia indicated the dangers of such formalism,
with reference to Sicilian culture:

> In Sicily, thought Captain Bellodi, the crime of passion is not triggered by gen-
> uine passion, passion of the heart, but by a kind of intellectual passion, a passion
> or preoccupation for – how to put it? – judicial formalism: in the sense of that
> abstraction whereby laws are pared down by the degrees with which we make
> judgements according to regulations, to the point when we reach that formal
> transparency where *merit*, that is the human weight of facts, no longer counts;
> and, with the image of man removed, the law's mirror of itself is the law.[16]

A connection should probably be made between the rigidity of this formal
adherence to the patriarchal family model and the fact that the mafia family
is in reality substantially different from the traditional patriarchal family which
it claims to typify. The need to *appear* is in inverse proportion to the absence
of *being*.

> The distribution of prestige and power within the family (typical of mafia
> zones) is not predetermined, as in the case of the patriarchal-style family, but is
> formed through a series of very intense conflicts. The entire domestic universe
> is dominated by relationships that are *vertical* in nature (parents–children; hus-
> band–wife; older brother–younger brother, etc). Customary family solidarity
> only applies in the case of conflicts with an outside group.[17]

Family ties, once binding because part of collective solidarity and reciprocity
behind an unchanging façade, have become the object of individual
manipulation.

The ban on divorce furnishes an eloquent example. This ban is so strictly
enforced that 'Buscetta himself was expelled from the mafia for having had
too disordered a family life and, particularly, for having divorced his wife'.[18]
But what really lies behind so much 'uprightness'? 'When the Anti-mafia
Commission asked a *pentito* why it is that a man of honour cannot have a wife
and a regular lover, he answered that if a man has a wife she will never give

him away to the police, but if he has two women, sooner or later one of them will give him away.'[19] The criterion preventing the man of honour from having regular extramarital relations does not derive from any moral principles. It derives, instead, from the need to avoid either of two women feeling betrayed and resorting to giving the man away to the police. 'It is utilitarianism which inspires rules and behaviour that are otherwise inexplicable.'[20]

It is important to bear in mind that family and Family, in Joe Bonanno's terms, are being overlaid and it is this superimposition which creates confusion, deception and error, even perhaps among the protagonists themselves. As a mafia organization, the Family represents 'a second world alongside the visible world' (Simmel), that is the family, which it resembles and seems to be like. But inevitably, whenever conflict arises, it is the family which loses.

> Among all the ties of the individual the one arising from a secret association always assumes a privileged position, by comparison with which those open to view – family and state, religious and economic affiliations and those of class and friendship – however complex their content, carry quite a different weight and impinge more superficially.[21]

Regarding my specific interest, that is the position of women within this 'confusion', there is a further distinction to be made: apart from secrecy or otherwise, the family is a heterosexual organization, while the Family is strictly monosexual. The strength of the male/male bond constitutes the foundation of the secret mafia organization. And it is the mafiosi themselves who excel in playing off the appearance of sameness in what is not identical.

Current analyses of the mafia, however, do not seem to attach much weight to this difference. Indeed, Ianni denies it any relevance: 'If the real function of kinship is to affiliate individuals into a system of reciprocity and exchange, there seems to be no reason why kinship relationship cannot be artificially produced among males and why a non-biological, extra-genealogical family unit and spirit cannot be engendered.'[22] I fear that arguing in this way obfuscates precisely the gap which is produced when what seems is passed off as what is.

This gap represents the space and area of displacement upon which critical discourse and insight can be based. And this is the mafia's weak point as a social construction. Why the fanaticism over formal strictures? Why the inflated death toll and the omnipresent fear of death? If this fabric, this solid base to which the equation between Family and family refers, really existed, perhaps the mafia enterprise would be less deadly. But the fabric is not there. 'Rules constitute the mafioso's only safeguard.'[23]

The mafia, therefore, does not merely effect a ruthless manipulation of kinship networks, but it imposes an intensified regime of rationality which is instrumental, dictatorial and absolutist, even in some respects obsessive, completely obscuring the relation between the formal strictures and what these very strictures really mean. Let us take for example the cardinal rule, often emphasized by Giovanni Falcone, of speaking the truth as a man of honour and in relation to other men of honour, always the truth, 'because for him the truth constitutes a rule of survival'.[24]

We might legitimately wonder which truth we are talking about: a circumstantial truth, bent to circumscribed requirements, a truth in the service of mafia power and abuse. And yet the strictness and severity with which the mafia demands the application of this rule, blindly we could say, blurs the perception of what may be untruth. The moralistic appearance of the abstract rule always to tell the truth has been substituted for the substantial essence of a moral judgement of the truth or non-truth of an action, a fact or an event. Truth, yet again, assumes a purely instrumental character: 'Thus by the rules of silence and the obligation to speak the truth, there is a certainty that the circulation of news will be limited to the essential and, at the same time, that the news reported will be true.'[25]

I should like to quote in full one example of this kind of instrumental rationalism, described by Giovanni Falcone:

> It is the rule that the son of a man killed by Cosa Nostra cannot be received into the organization to which his father belonged. Why? Because of the famous obligation to tell the truth. From the moment when he joins Cosa Nostra, the son would have the right to know why his father was killed, the right to demand explanations which would be the source of huge problems. So the decision was made to forbid him access precisely to avoid being placed in a situation where it would be necessary to lie to him.[26]

Being a murderer can therefore *seem* like having a passion for the truth.

Honour, shame, vendetta

In the traditional organization of Southern society, honour, shame and vendetta are fundamental social institutions, each in its different way relating very closely to women. These institutions simultaneously involve values which assumed a central function in the overall balance of the community, during a historical period in which the presence of the state was minimal.

To examine these institutions from a woman's point of view is all the more urgent given that both women's complicity and their manipulation in mafia activities appear intimately connected with these values. The mafia's exploitation of honour, shame and vendetta corresponds precisely to its skill in making what is largely obsolete in structural terms appear to be still valid and socially desirable. The mafia has succeeded in using central elements in the culture for its own ends, thereby 'exploiting the ideas of honour and shame as political ideologies which governed relations of power among men'.[27]

The concept of *honour*, as John Davis has clearly argued, designates a system of stratification, marking off dominant positions and subordinate positions. It presents itself as an absolute system, so that 'each competitor occupies a unique position in the hierarchy. One of the weapons in such discrimination is the distinction between honour-virtue and honour-status. The weapon is used by rivals ...'[28] The terrain on which rivalries are played out is a man's good name, or reputation, which is supremely anchored in the conduct of his women. The outcome of these rivalries assails the man in his entire being, that is to say his honour.

The ghost of honour reverberates through the life of every day and every night, through minute daily activities. This all-pervasiveness endows it with a terrible power and guarantees social control. This is why it seems important to investigate the workings of these mechanisms in a perspective of understanding through the subjectivity of those implicated. This observation by Davis therefore appears sacrosanct, above all as far as women in the home are concerned: 'So while an anthropologist may write resonantly of honour and of the sense of shame which preserves it and the reader's heart may swell as big as a Grandee's in response, nevertheless most concern with punctilio, for the greater part of the Mediterranean population, is pettifogging, concerned with the minutiae of day-to-day domesticity.'[29]

What in the traditional society was an element of social regulation between families, and based on a complementarity of masculine and feminine roles, becomes coopted and distorted by the mafia. 'In fact, women assume no specific, direct function within the cells, whose activity and development seem to be based exclusively on male membership. Despite this absence of female involvement, mafia ideology makes frequent reference to feminine purity.'[30] Honour, based on an exaggerated concept of individual strength, becomes the pivot of mafia ideology, 'a way of *singularizing* the different cells one from the other and singularizing the mafioso within his own society'.[31]

The stereotype of the mafioso as a man of honour, with all this implies for women, as we discussed above, still represents a central pillar in the social construction of the image of the mafia. In a situation of widespread mistrust, the idea of being able to turn to courageous men in order to secure agreements and contracts, in accordance with the example of gentlemen of rank in bygone days, represents a potent lure to draw in the faint-hearted. 'This amounts to the structuring in "elevated" terms of a code used in plebeian milieux for different ends from those for which it had originally been developed.'[32]

Shame has a direct relation to honour. 'As with honor, the idea of shame serves both to defend or enhance the patrimonies of families and to define the family as a corporate group.'[33] But even more than honour, shame is part of people's inner world, and is not subordinate to conscious control. Shame in some way sanctions the working of codes of honour, being released like a conditioned reflex. From earliest infancy, shame is the fruit of the process of socialization.

'Shame eats the soul. It pushes you to become other than what you are, and it creates its own reign of constant fear. It is a powerful form of social control, though we barely acknowledge it because it works away in individual psyches.'[34]

Shame is the expression of an inner fear, linked to fear of humiliation (*Schamangst*), and is therefore a product of intra-psychical dynamics, of a struggle between drives and internalized social impulses. This kind of dread is generated in the ego to forestall even the most remote threat of danger. As such it is infinitely more potent than real fear (*Realangst*), which represents a reaction to actual situations of danger. 'True anxiety is produced through the threat of an external object; neurotic anxiety, which may also have a real basis, on the other hand is produced from within, through the ego.'[35]

A form of social control exerted through violence can at least be escaped from, while there is no way out from one imposed through shame; it is a form of control that individuals exert upon themselves.

If honour demands women's involvement, bestowing on them the task of maintaining the reputation of the family and therefore of the man of honour, shame, by underhand means, fetters women and makes them intimately complicit in the perpetuation of abusive and dominating relationships. The inner turmoil which we are accustomed to call shame is both the expression of an unconscious assumption of guilt and a defence. Defence from any real likelihood of being attacked, guilt at having a woman's body and therefore in any way provoking acts of aggression. Thus the circle closes up, imprisoning women, because honour, what men strut and swagger over, when taken on as women's duty and moral challenge, becomes the tombstone of all female freedom.

If in the past the socialization of women and children into shame had the purpose of making them 'bear part of the defensive burden themselves',[36] nowadays, with the mafia distortion of these values, women are put in the position of having to bring respectability and prestige to arrogant male competitiveness. 'This reference to feminine purity serves a man's good reputation when it is a matter of the purity of his mother, sister, wife or daughter, initially assisting his introduction into the cell, and subsequently serving to uphold his prestige, both inside and outside it.'[37] As codes of assigning resources and status and as deeply felt values, honour and shame have lost much of their meaning and power.

Mediterranean families are no longer so totally preoccupied as they once were with the virginity of their daughters and the shame of their wives, and they are becoming less so all the time. Many of the customs associated with such pre-occupations cannot possibly survive the diffusion of an international youth culture, let alone the impact of women's liberation when it eventually reaches this area. Moreover, the expansion of state institutions undermines the need for them.[38]

However, their persistence in mafia ideology and control seems all the more dangerous. Bereft of their cultural authority and material roots, these codes tend to become the expression of a violent authoritarianism directed above all against women, whether they be complicit or not, whether they be mothers, daughters or wives.

And finally the *vendetta*. Since vendetta too, in common with codes like honour and shame, has been ideologically swallowed up by the criminality of the mafia, it makes sense to recollect the meaning it bears in folk culture, if only in order to measure the level of manipulation and exploitation which the mafia brings to it; also in order to throw more light on how and where the female role has been unduly endowed with traditional tasks and expectations which happen not to be traditional at all.

'The vendetta is a cultural response, set up in defence against the danger of being killed. . . . For the survivor the danger and the threat of being killed contain the risk of loss of presence, just as the avoidance of the right/duty of vendetta contains the risk of the loss of social presence.'[39] The period of the vendetta is as long as the period of mourning; until the execution of the vendetta, reconstructing the social crisis provoked by the offence, mourning cannot end. 'We should remember that the traditional community does not regard itself as merely a community of the living, but includes the dead as part of itself, in a link between mythic time and historical time, articulating the relation between history and meta-history.'[40]

It is not surprising that the mafia, so close to death in all its forms of expression, whether practical or rhetorical, should have drawn in full measure on the symbolic values and burdens of the ceremonial procedures of vendetta. 'The fear of death which seems to fuel peasant feuds and constitute them as a part of mourning also supports the development of mafia power.'[41] The street and the square, which constitute a scenic space for ordinary people, are cunningly exploited; just as a vendetta was often announced publicly, giving notice of guilt and condemnation, the mafia too threatens by way of signs and gives prior notice of its sentences of death.

I will illustrate the mechanism of appropriation, perversion and manipulation operated by the mafia in relation to popular cultural codes by citing one crystal-clear example. The vendetta was a commemoration of death; for instance, feuds in Calabria are tied to dates and anniversaries, a strategy of memory which reconnects the vendetta with the trauma suffered. 'By killing at this specific time, it is as if the dead man, through his historical substitute, were acting directly, renewing that principle of reciprocity which regulates and inflects relationships.'[42]

The mafia too is attentive to dates and anniversaries, with such arrogance and cynicism as to plan to kill a son on the anniversary of the father's murder:

> A new *pentito* from the Catania *cosche* told the magistrates that he had been given the job of killing the Rete Member of Parliament Claudio Fava....The hitmen had planned everything for the evening of 5 January last, the anniversary of the murder of the MP's father, the journalist Pippo Fava: a blood-chilling detail meant to serve as a warning to the men who symbolized the struggle against the mafia.[43]

I believe that this example is very illuminating: by formally imitating an ancient ritual, emptied of its meaning of reciprocity and reparation, the mafia implies a claim on popular roots and affiliations, while at the same time pursuing its own aim of intimidation and domination which has nothing to do with the balance of traditional community. A moment of truth – the common denominator of death – becomes the basis for a false ideological construction – the assumption of complicity between folk culture and mafia culture. 'The mafia obsession with power takes shape on this culture of killing, this fear of death.'[44]

It may be that the mafiosi themselves have a clear perception of the gulf between an action weighted with collective significance and score-settling. Anonymous, for example, writes: 'But by then I was an old hand. It was no vendetta. . . . I held the pistol to his heart and goodbye Paolino.'[45]

From this perspective, there is considerable mafia ambiguity. By drawing ideologically on the past and legitimating its own operations by recourse to traditional codes, the mafia manages to draw a veil over its own most significant features, and those most deeply at odds with popular culture.

> It seems to me that mafia culture exists as an intermediate territory, a double-sided phenomenon; on the side facing towards the subaltern classes its values are formally identical with folk values and this side could be termed populist; on the side facing the classes in power, its real interlocutors, it transforms the values it has taken 'from below', the values of the people, inserting them into a project of individual and group hegemony, which is not in this respect dissimilar from the ethics implicitly promoted by capitalist mores and is deeply a function of these.'[46]

The institution of the vendetta specifically puts women at issue. 'The blood memory is passed through the women.'[47] It is their funeral lament that urges the men on to vendetta. As custodians of family memory, custodians of rituals linked to life and death, and custodians of objects held as 'disturbing tokens of the pedagogy of the vendetta', women have traditionally been central figures within family life, transmitting culture, carrying out the pedagogy of the vendetta.

> At Drapia, in the province of Catanzaro, one woman kept for years the jacket that her husband was wearing when he was killed; her son, who at the time of his father's death was two years old, wore the jacket to kill his father's killer on his release from prison. The woman inculcates the waiting and, in the end, it is as if the father himself, through the son's adopted dress, were living again to kill his killer.[48]

The vendetta as the task ideally befitting women as guardians of family memory seems none the less also to be a social construction fuelled by male fantasy. The ideology-freighted image of the vengeful mafia woman is offered to us by the old mafia leader Nick Gentile:

> Here I must mention something which, although incidental, is typical enough to convey the sense of honour in force in the mafia. During the period of the vendetta, one day when Leonardo's widow was with her nineteen-year-old son, she met her husband's killer. Quick as lightning, she gripped his chest and told her son: 'Here is your father's murderer, kill him!' The boy took out his pistol and let the unlucky guy have it without thinking twice.[49]

Joe Bonanno's memory seems closer to reality:

> My grandmother Bonanno . . . lived on to the age of ninety-seven. She could often be heard reciting the rosary, or talking to herself out loud. Sometimes in the midst of her monologues I would hear the name of a Buccellato who had just passed away. It was as if she were keeping count of the enemy dead on her rosary.[50]

Here we touch on an area where, as we shall see further on, the interests of women and mafia interests easily concur; but this also is dangerous territory for mafia interests, and radically so. Through contact with schooling and with different cultural models, even as regards childhood in general,[51] the furious attachment of mothers to their own children, mother love, can take on new shades of meaning which are wholly antagonistic to the mafia's bloodthirsty interests. There have been recent reports of women who have had their sons snatched away from them at a young age by men of the Honoured Society, because they could no longer be counted on, they could no longer be guaranteed, to inculcate death.

> Domenico and two other sons were taken away from Carmela. She was told

that they were being rescued from death. The boys lived with trustworthy substitute parents and for a long time they didn't set foot outside the house.
Domenico was afraid of everything, he would eat then vomit, he had cold
sweats and at night he would have nightmares, shouting that they wanted to kill
him, that there was someone waiting to shoot him; he stayed shut up inside, he
wouldn't even step out onto the balcony. . . . There are other children living like
Domenico. . . . When 'the family' puts them in a safe house, it is nearly always
in order to ensure the possibility of future vendetta.[52]

In February 1993 the newspapers reported that a child of twelve, the son of
a murdered boss, had been identified in Tuscany. He had been taken there from
Sicily, and hidden and brought up by his uncle in order to become a killer and
a boss in his turn. 'He is twelve and he goes around armed. . . . There are already
two sentences weighing upon his twelve years: the deadly one decreed by his
family's rivals and the cruel one willed by his own clan.'[53] And what of this
child's mother? We have no means of imagining her relationship with this son.

Yet, imagining how a young woman today might experience a relationship
of this kind, it occurs to me that traditional codes like honour, shame and
vendetta, exploited and uprooted from their original cultural context, can
no longer continue to have such a hold on women. While these codes have
become powerful elements in mafia ideology, the fact is that they have become
internalized values rather than material aspects of social regulation. The feelings of love, hate and fear of humiliation are no longer the cornerstones of
social relations, are no longer elements of public life, but have been made
private and become the property of the individual. But it is this very right to
individuality which is denied by the mafia when it invokes honour, shame and
vendetta in order to give a semblance of popular legitimacy to its crimes. I
believe that this is a dawning source of conflict which cannot but involve
women deeply.

Transmission

'Listen, sweetheart, I have just one thing to tell you. . . . If we had stayed there
and somebody like me, a mafioso, had come and asked to marry you, I couldn't
have said no. You would have married a man like me. And you've seen what
kind of life we led in Sicily. I was never at home, always sleeping in different
places, coming back or disappearing suddenly in the middle of the night. Do
you think that was nice? . . . You can be free and independent. . . . You don't have
to become the wife of a mafioso and lead a life of hardship. I don't mean
hardship from lack of money. I mean the hardships of suffering because of
fear.'[54]

These are the words of Antonino Calderone, addressed to his daughter to explain his turning state's evidence. These words made a strong impression on me, because they speak an important truth. They are very simple words, but they are born of a reality where what appears simple is instead extremely complicated and disturbing. They are born from within a world where individual rights, particularly women's rights, are totally subordinated to clan imperatives. We are talking about the relationships between generations in mafia families, relationships of sons and daughters with a father who is a member of Cosa Nostra.

Clearly, there are many ways of being sons and daughters in such a situation, and the stronger the influence of secondary socialization, like schools, universities and diverse affiliations, compared with the primary influence, the influence of the family as most narrowly understood, the less predictable are the outcomes of a mafia upbringing. Leonardo Messina explained before the Parliamentary Anti-mafia Commission: '. . . these days even a roadsweeper or a cobbler can have a son with a degree who might become a Member of Parliament or a doctor. There isn't the same submission to the mafia. This is a positive thing.'[55]

Yet, if we go by autobiographical accounts, biographies of famous mafiosi and newspaper reports, it would seem that even now the will of the father lies heavy as a stone on the boys and girls of this world. *Honour Thy Father* is the significant title of the biography of the son of Joseph Bonanno, the Italian-American boss, also known as 'Joe Bananas'.[56]

I think it is appropriate to trace the fates assigned to sons and daughters separately. The shadow of the father hangs equally heavily over both, however, and in both cases it is the mother through whom a Law of the Father is ultimately transmitted.

> Inside the family and within the mafia domestic universe, the fundamental relation is one of subordination, dominated by the vertical nature of relations and by a complex of obligations, and is not one of intimacy or solidarity. . . . Even in her role as housewife the mother has a primary function in giving strong support, albeit often not explicitly, to the model transmitted by the father. . . . The mother is authority. But it is the father who, for the child, *has* authority.[57]

In the mafia milieu, the bonds that are most charged within the family dynamic seem those between the males, between father and sons most of all, but also between brothers.

> Each boy tries to copy his older brother, his father, his uncle. He mirrors himself in them and there comes a point when he begins to feel and see like them. When a boy lives and grows in a mafia family, kinship network and neighbourhood he realizes it, guessing at it even if he doesn't know it.[58]

References to transmission through the male line take on a mythic character in the memories:

> Even when I was a seven-year-old, my father addressed me in a dignified manner. He said, 'You are a Bonanno. Be proud . . .' [and, dying] his last words were: – Your name is Bonanno. Always be proud of your name. – He died while clutching me to his bosom.[59]

The bond between the men of the family, particularly that between father and son, seems the most fertile ground for the unbroken reproduction of the myth of the mafia, of the myth of its *omineità* – its manliness – its invincibility, a myth just as important in itself as weapons and other material features. Diego Gambetta has amply demonstrated how, as an illegal protection industry, the mafia itself is compelled to make constant reference to its reputation, its appearance, its image, to a mythic invincibility, esteem and strength in order to set out its wares in the market, the selling of violent protection, after having violently sowed the seeds of fear.

> The problem of trusting someone in a world where trust is scarce highlights all the more the split nature of reputation. Those who live in a world without trust have all the more extreme a need to be able to trust someone. But if the rule is 'trust no one', why on earth should you trust mafiosi? There is a cognitive leap that has to be made between those in whom you trust and all the rest; perhaps, of all human constructions, myth is the most suitable for building such a bridge.[60]

This work of imagination is meticulous and essential for the reproduction of the mafia family enterprise, allowing no room for mistakes and investing every member of the family with its authoritarian properties – rigidly and hierarchically, of course.

There is also a very banal, quantitative aspect that is part and parcel of having male offspring in mafia families, and that can be summed up in the toast (baleful to female ears): 'Here's to male children!' The evidence suggests that families from mafia groupings have a much higher rate of demographic growth than non-mafia families in the same environment, which can be related to a 'strategy of *maximizing the number of descendants*': 'This strategy consists, basically, in the production of as many male children as possible and the practice of an increasingly rigid endogamy within the ranks of mafia groups.'[61] Recalling a discussion with his brother Pippo, Calderone himself emphasized this tendency. 'Can't you see how those Cavaduzzi know-nothings are running a race for male children, like the barbarians in the Middle Ages? Look how an idiot like Salvatore Ferrara – a guy we all laughed at to his face – has become strong and respected because he has had three sons? . . . Who was

Salvatore Ferrara before he had all these sons? He was nothing.'[62]

So what are girls for? The daughters seem less directly drawn into things, because they elude immediate investiture in the law of the father. Yet, their lives are doubly valuable in mafia strategies. The rhetoric of honour is founded on keeping them in check and their good behaviour increases the father's prestige. At the same time, and most importantly, daughters are invaluable in building up status through advantageous matches. Marriages are made in order to set up alliances with important or territorially close mafia groupings. Another aim, though less widespread, is access to the legal market by way of family connections. 'Much has been written about the tendency of mafia families to make their way back into the legitimate world by marrying their descendants to the heirs of *respectable* citizens, which does seem to have played a very important role in the history of the American mafia; but no such tendency seems to have operated among Calabrian and Sicilian *mafiosi*.'[63]

If there is any space within such a constellation for the articulation of inter-generational conflicts, the question of a symbolic 'killing of the father', which is usually so fruitful for the growth of the individual, is a very delicate one. Might not opposing the father, perhaps even just from the necessities of adolescent maturation, be misunderstood as dangerous opposition to the mafia, and not trustworthy? Might it not even be fatal?

Vera Pegna tells the story of Alberto, a young man from Caccamo, a village where this young Communist militant had been elected local councillor. This was in 1948. Alberto was a student from a middle-class family and had recently joined the Italian Socialist Party. The family kept giving him a hard time about his political activities and one day Alberto showed Vera a letter that had been sent to his father by an uncle who had emigrated:

> I really have to come out with it and tell you I was surprised, I mean surprised and humiliated to hear from friends of mine that Berto isn't only involved in politics against certain local people, but he is going in for a propaganda campaign against the mafia. This is humiliating for all the relatives without exception and it's dangerous, blackening everyone's name so publicly. I'm telling you that when they told me this I couldn't believe it. I hope it's a slander, because if it was true you would all have to get out of Caccamo or else cover yourselves in mud. There have never been people like this in our families. I would like to be reassured about this matter, I repeat be reassured by you and by Berto himself.[64]

How heartrending and extreme it can be to rebel against your own mafia father is exemplified by the story of Peppino Impastato, the young left-wing militant in the seventies at Cinisi, a village under the mafia rule of the Badalamenti. His younger brother Giovanni relates:

It was no accident, as we can read in his writings as far back as 1965, that he came to politics on an emotional basis, from the starting point of his need to react against a family set-up that had become intolerable. From then on he categorically rejected the figure of his father as head of the family and as a mafioso.[65]

[Peppino] waged a struggle in Cinisi which combined denunciation with mockery through 'Radio Aut' ... [organizing] unemployed building workers in the area and farmers whose land and livelihood had been taken away from them for the construction of that suicidal airport put up in one of the windiest areas of the Mediterranean.[66]

In the life – and death – of Peppino Impastato conflict between generations and political conflict are profoundly intertwined. What gave him strength in this situation were the ideals of '68, the solidarity of his comrades. Thrown out of his home by his father, and secretly supported by his mother, in 1978 Peppino was killed by the mafia, after his father had died in an accident.

Giovanni Impastato continues:

For my brother the struggle against the mafia represented the human and civil affirmation not just of a political idea of social justice, but above all of a new way of being and living; he made it very clear that it is possible to struggle against the mafia even if you come from a mafia environment and a mafia family, but then the price you pay, starting with your day-to-day life, is terribly high.[67]

'Revolution at home, before anywhere outside it; revolution in thoughts and emotional attachments, in everyday life, before political revolution', Anna Puglisi and Umberto Santino write in their introduction to the life story of the mother of Peppino and Giovanni.[68]

Undoubtedly, the social position of the mafioso, whether lower class or upper, as well as his education and training, upbringing and sensitivity, play a decisive part in the form assumed by any inter-generational conflict. In this respect the Bonanno case is extremely relevant, since we have access to two (auto-)biographical reconstructions, that of the father, Joseph, and that of the son, Salvatore. There are signs of an extremely strong bond, of Salvatore's difficulty in adapting to his own destiny as the boss's oldest son, but also an awareness of the conflicts between the individual's life and the father's clan strategies. With hindsight, the father still feels obliged to justify his heavy interference in his son's life:

I was very pleased with the romance. Their marriage would bring together two eminent families. But it would be unfair to infer that I had forced the marriage on Salvatore, regardless of his personal feelings. No doubt, especially when they were young, my own children saw me as an authoritarian and, at times, even a forbidding father.[69]

His 'independent-minded' daughter Catherine regarded this marriage as 'a marriage of fathers' and, when her father asked for her opinion, she answered frankly.

> She was about to say something else when, suddenly, she felt a hand slap across her face, and fell back, stunned, confused, then burst into tears as she ran, never before having seen her father that enraged, his eyes fiery and fierce.[70]

The Sicilian-American Joseph Bonanno has a very lucid grasp of the conflicts and contradictions encountered by his own criminal organization, to the extent that the new generations, the sons, and the nephews who are cousins of the sons, are socialized simultaneously in the family by the weight of 'Tradition' and in life outside the family by the values of American society overall.

> American values, therefore, conflicted with our traditional values. And pretty soon, people in our own world began to think of themselves as 'individuals'. . . . This individualistic orientation . . . sapped the authority of the Father. It destroyed the Father as the symbol of moral order.[71]

It is difficult to foresee how much the cultural gap between one generation and the other will influence mafia destinies. There is no doubt, however, that the transmission of mafia values, whether explicitly through the will of the father, or implicitly through relationships, attachments and hierarchies, cannot but be placed in a constant dialectic with the wider society. The rising social mobility of many mafia families puts at risk the tight control of the father and mother over the sons and daughters. In Sciascia's novel *The Day of the Owl* the *carabinieri* captain puts his finger on this wound, when he tells Don Mariano:

> '. . . And you have guaranteed a wealthy future for your daughter. . . . But I don't know if your daughter could ever justify what you have done to guarantee this wealth for her. . . . I imagine that you will find her very changed: kinder, compassionate towards everything that you scorn, respectful towards everything that you do not respect. . . . And when your daughter is so different that you no longer recognize her, she will in some way have paid the penalty for wealth built on violence and deception.'[72]

And is it here perhaps, in the impossibility of the desire to bequeath both everything and its opposite – to impose the status quo by violence and to dream of change – that the murderous fury of the mafiosi could come to its limit?

It is surely in relation to their children, as they look – metaphorically – into a magnifying mirror, that the doubts, uncertainties and contradictions of the mafia identity assume substance. In his farewell letter to his wife, before attempting suicide, Tommaso Buscetta wrote: 'And you must explain to our children that this has been the only gift I could leave to you. Teach the boys that their father is not to be avenged in any way. What a paradoxical fate: I am abandoning you because I love you, I am killing myself so that you can all live.'[73]

Even though it is doubtful whether Antonino Calderone's reason for turning evidence was his relationship with his children, it is my belief that his experience prefigures possible scenarios for the future.

> Even in my earlier life I took care of my children, but the fear of being killed from one moment to the next made me think about them in pretty limited terms. The only question I would ask myself was: 'Who can I leave them to? What will their lives be like without me?' There's no room in your head to think about anything else. And you're not in a state of mind to understand what a great treasure they represent.[74]

3

Women

Myth and reality

Although, or perhaps precisely because, the mafia is deeply structured as a 'society only of men', the feminine is ubiquitous on the mafia horizon. Attraction and repulsion, idealization and coarse abuse, at one and the same time appear to be characteristic of the mafia outlook towards women and the feminine in general. In explicit mafia ideology the relation to women appears unequivocal: they are to be dominated, used and, paternalistically, kept in the dark about the secrets of the Honoured Society. The world of women is thought of as 'naturally' subversive of mafia order, and in the initiation rites the aspirant mafioso undertakes to keep these two worlds separate.

Rather than being grounded in a peasant world, mafia ideology in relation to women seems deeply bourgeois, naturally with the nuances of the milieu in which the mafioso moves. In some respects women appear to have a terrible responsibility conferred upon them: responsibility for reputation, a fundamental prerequisite for the success of a mafia career. In the sphere of the mafia protection industry 'a protector must in the first place be able to protect the morality of his own wife, in order not to fall into the dishonourable state of the "cuckold"'.[1] The double standard of bourgeois morality, which has been perfectly assimilated, then allows him to have lovers, occasional affairs and women who are paid for sex. On one condition, however: the marriage is indissoluble. As far as appearances are concerned, his own wife must be respected, not so much because she is a woman to be respected, but because she is the mother of his children.

As his own wife is to be respected, so are the wives and daughters of the other men of honour; none of the women of one's own clan is to be touched. Calderone relates: 'Heaven help the man who looks at anyone's wife or daughter. If he does he's a dead man. As soon as it's known that a man of honour has bothered another man's wife, he has to die.'[2]

The initiation oaths are binding. A mafioso must not attempt to seduce the

48

women of other men of honour, and in general he is compelled to lead a spotless family life in the eyes of everyone.

Even the mafia attitude to prostitution seems an expression of the bourgeois double standard of morality. 'I would have endured being accused of anything, however serious, except living off women. Such a vilifying accusation made me go out of my mind, because besides ruining me it would have stained the honour of my whole family,' writes Nick Gentile.[3] The (partial) renunciation of this source of profits is recompensed by the appearance of conservative decency. The image of the man of honour and the ideology of the mafia as a benevolent society of mutual aid are founded on the myth of the upright head of the family who honours and protects women, first and foremost the mother of his own children.

The autobiography of Joe Bonanno, dedicated 'to the memory of my humble, faithful and devoted wife Fay', well illustrates the space–time constellation reserved for the woman married to a mafioso.

> She had waited and loved me throughout all the disruptions [the so-called Castellammarese war between different mafia factions], loving a man part of whose life would always remain secret, loving a man of whom she could not ask certain questions. . . . Fay always put up with my defects, and, moreover, she knew how to bring out the best in me. Fay's favourite room was the kitchen. . . . Although respectful towards men . . .'[4]

Mrs Bonanno's role seems a strategic part of the constructed image of the family as 'decent' and of the conquest of bourgeois respectability among the notables of Tucson, Arizona, far from the turbulent 'volcano' of New York.

It is in keeping with this reassuring image of normality that when the police burst in to search the house it is presented by Joe Bonanno as an act of barbarism on the part of the American government towards his wife. 'Fay took it badly: the devastation of her domestic haven dazed her. And she cried. Never, in all my years as a top man of my world in New York, had any man invaded her house and defiled it. . . . Haven't these people any heart? . . . haven't they any children?'[5] From her husband's description Mrs Bonanno does not appear to be a naive person, but no direct testimony of her experience is available. We know, however, from her son that towards the end of her life Fay suffered from repeated crises because of a nervous illness.

A woman is basically considered to be a man's property, and the bond that ties the man to the woman is that of possession. This ancestral, almost meta-historical bond is the background that men share, be they farmers, bourgeois or mafiosi.

But what distinguishes a mafia environment from some middle-class domestic novel? It is Bonanno who in fact gives us an answer to this, when he talks about the rules of his 'Tradition': 'If a family member discovered that his wife had gone to bed with another Family member, he was justified in killing him. No one had to tell the cuckolded Family member what to do and he didn't have to tell anyone else. He simply did what was necessary.'[6] The curiosity and questions aroused by trying to imagine how life is lived inside the mafia world always meet with the same obsessive and unvarying answer: death.

When translated and assimilated by the mafia, the sexual double standard of bourgeois myth is infected with death. Regardless of any love and affection there might be, violence and death nail family members to their destiny. Feelings are a danger to order, and especially to mafia order. And women represent the quintessence of this danger. It is perhaps not by chance that a killer like Zagari should fantasize about death with a woman in mind: 'Death is like a nymphomaniac woman, never sated by embraces, and when you lead a certain kind of life, so as to avoid being gripped in her arms, or at least to delay this as long as possible, you must send someone to her to distract her, to satisfy her just enough to postpone her embrace of you until the next time . . . until it's OK.'[7]

The coarseness of the killer compared with the educated boss should deceive no one. The distance between them is cultural, a 'class' difference within the mafia world itself; but in substance their framework is identical. In fact, Zagari relates: 'My father reproached me for being a cuckold because Angela had got a legal separation from me. . . . In my father's opinion I should have killed her, as he said: "A real man of honour with balls in the right place can only allow his wife separation and divorce to the sound of a sawn-off shotgun." '[8] The myth is honour, the reality 'divorce Italian style'.

A woman is useful, she has a function as the mother of male children. 'Indeed, it is the birth of male children which makes it possible to have human material for the substitution and replacement of the inevitable losses.'[9] This accountant's reckoning brutally highlights the reality of being a girl, the unwished-for female child, and a woman. Women are useful, in Zagari's words, so as to 'multiply the family of the *Honoured Society, Mother Stepmother* who is pregnant year in year out'.[10]

There is a demarcation line between one's own women, who are chained by myth, kept a watch on, protected and forbidden things, and all the others, who are really just scorned. 'What emerges is an intensified and extreme notion of domination over women, who are considered by natural right to be the exclusive and private property of men.'[11] The myth of manliness, on which mafia self-representation rests, requires and allows violent attitudes towards women. Enzo Ciconte cites various episodes of assault, rape and mistreatment of women by *'ndranghetisti*: 'Isolated cases? Perhaps. . . . Yet they are significant of a tendency and an attitude of violent and total lack of respect for women which is distinctly at odds with the image of itself that the *'ndrangheta* has wanted to present. The reality is different from the image. But it is the image that has prevailed over time.'[12]

From the point of view of subjectivity, given the intimacy of the relationships, it seems difficult to imagine that the contradictions of this double life, bourgeois and mafia, are not felt. Antonino Calderone confides: 'I got married in Catania, to the girl who worked at the Agrarian Consortium and who has followed me through all the ups and downs of this strange life of mine. I have always tried not to tell her anything about my commitment to the mafia, keep her away from the problems, the fear and the hatred. I have kept up a pretence as much as it has been possible.'[13]

It is in this guise, the guise of subordination which inevitably becomes weighed down with complicity, that the role of women in relation to the mafia becomes meaningful. It is in this guise that dependency is transmuted into participation, responsibility and – it must surely be said – guilt.

Love and sexuality

Discussing sexuality is not easy, be it one's own or that of others; that minefield, that impetuous 'subsoil' that stirs up such fear and hope in us. For a woman like me, foreign by background and personal history to the world of the mafia, it seems all the harder and more hazardous to speak about the private life of these men with their vow of silence and *omertà*. Yet I believe that I should attempt some reflection on these factors, precisely because it is the realm of subjectivity which seems basically the most deeply shaken by contradictions which could lead to change.

'A very current saying in the Cosa Nostra world goes: "Better to command than to fuck." '[14] Power and command, although longed for, exercised and enjoyed in a deeply felt way, as seems to be the case with mafiosi, require alertness, coldness and self-control, characteristics acquired to the detriment of other aspects of intra-psychic life, to the detriment of eros. The man of honour does not speak, he does not let emotions and feelings leak out. This strongly imposed and self-imposed attitude cannot but have lasting consequences for the way in which these men express their own sexuality. One is prompted to think that the culture of death must infect ways of relating to living bodies, erecting boundaries and limits beyond which danger lies, the danger of losing oneself, of letting go, of becoming weak – the danger of loving. A 'professional ethic' which is a systematic training for murder, as we also know from the history of totalitarian regimes and acculturations, demands psychic sacrifices which have repercussions most of all for sexual life and erotic fantasies.[15]

'The mafioso is unable to love, only to fuck ... his sexuality is exclusively genital and consumerist, the mafia imagination being phobic about sex. . . .

The ideology of his emotions is possessive, but his attitude is masculinist and genital-centred; a man must be a "man", no messy feelings, no room for erotic communication.'[16] We do not know whether these evaluations are the product of clinical work or some kind of generalization, albeit a legitimate one. Whichever, it seems to me that here Filippo Di Forti has touched on a deep issue which is corroborated, sometimes directly, more often indirectly, by what the mafiosi say about themselves. Relating the macabre details of a murder only just committed, Zagari says: 'I couldn't wait to have it all over with and be back at home, get under the shower, wash all this mess off myself with plenty of soapy lather from my favourite apricot-scented foam bath, and then to relax making love. At times of tension and difficulty having sex always restores my psychic equilibrium.'[17] The poverty and the brutality of these words, the fantasizing about the foam bath, reveal a deep incapacity for human relations which seems in proportion to the proven capacity for strangling, shooting and mutilation which Zagari demonstrated in his career as a 'ndrangheta hitman.

These intra-psychic dynamics – self-control and the cult of death at the expense of eros – are backed up by cultural and social conditioning. On the one hand, as Leonardo Sciascia maintains, male sexual behaviour is conditioned, through Sicilian peasant culture, by a form of

> idealized version of the 'cock', which in the peasant world is the animal that represents a perfect sexuality, being readily aroused, quick, insatiable, and able to give a worthy response to all approaches. It is clear then how the sexual act often becomes reduced to a tawdry affair dispatched without great pleasure, fleetingly, even painfully in its spasm-like briskness, and it is clear how sexuality, through never being 'enjoyed' as such, belongs to the world of the unreal.[18]

Moreover, the man of honour is strongly conditioned by the conservatism which dominates the mafia organization from top to bottom. Family life and sexual life are strictly regulated, appearances are what matter. The bourgeois double standard is an internalized value: 'It is important that the lawful wife is not humiliated in her social milieu.' In many respects sexuality appears to be subordinated to outward show. On the one hand in the service of the family and the production of honour, and on the other, ambiguously, in the service of a man's manly image. 'Indeed: sexual exploits can increase the mafioso's "professional" authority, so long as they maintain a relative degree of secrecy and are not flagrant.'[19]

Emotional anxiety is a sign of untrustworthiness. It appears that with strict (formal) adherence to the paramount rule that marriage is not to be touched, from one instance to the next mafia morality applies varying judgements to the matrimonial infidelities of its members. These would of course reflect shifts in power relationships. Yet one could also hazard that they depend on some subjective evaluation: there are different ways of expressing 'libertinage'. For some, these transgressions are a way of further displaying potent and virile manhood, and there are others who, by contrast, conduct an intimate rebellion against mafia totalitarianism, giving precedence to a personal love affair. Despite his high status, Tommaso Buscetta 'was *posato* [suspended from the organization] because he had a turbulent emotional life'.[20]

What seems dangerous is less the infraction of a rule, in terms of its content, than the fact of emotional surrender which might seriously endanger the organization. In very ordinary terms, moreover, the security of the Honoured Society, which is anchored in secrecy, is put at risk. Even the most commodified and alienated sexuality involves some regression, some shortlived turn inwards, some yielding to the pleasure principle, weakening the reality principle. For a man of honour, to lower his guard is dangerous in any circumstance, whether at a private or a material level. If these rules have a purpose other than that of mere conformity to conventional values . . . a less obvious purpose could be that of preventing illicit sex from becoming an unconscious way of transmitting confidential information.'[21]

In such a context, sexuality and death appear closely interwoven. Just as the resonance of death becomes particularly intense in moments of surrender to pleasure, sexuality tends to be lived out, or rather consumed, in the frenzy of the flight from death. Lying low between one murder and the next, Zagari has his wife taken to a friend's house. 'I asked him to go and get Angela and bring her to me . . . so that evening and the one after I wasn't on my own any more. After two days when we only stopped fucking just long enough to eat something and satisfy bodily functions, Angela had to go back home.'[22]

A woman's body incarnates a temptation that is deeply threatening to the discipline and cohesion of the organization. The reduction of erotic communication to genital sexuality demands from the individual a huge sacrifice whose recompense, albeit partial, is the mafia ideology of manliness. 'There is a sado-masochistic component which is recycled into a macho and consumerist mode of behaviour. . . . The positive value which obsesses the mafioso is death.'[23] When Anonymous writes: 'This pistol was my wife,'[24] he is saying something extremely pertinent. He is referring both to the dangerous character of his love for his wife (she is dangerous like a pistol), and to his instrumental relationship with her (I hold her in my fist like a pistol), and, finally, to his control over his passion for her (I must hold my dangerous feelings in my fist as if they were a pistol).

For example, the contempt implicit in the expression 'fucking' yet again bears witness to fear of women, the fear of one's own feminine side, the fear of the anarchic power of eros. Lombardi Satriani underlines this ambivalence:

Being men means, in any event, being males . . . ; being ready – theoretically

53

available, that is – to demonstrate one's own sexual potency. Not to be all these things involves being regarded as not amounting to much, as being not a whole man, effeminate, the ultimate negative value . . . ; playing the next guy for a sucker, or pulling a fast one are more often expressed as 'fucking', 'screwing' and the like, to the point where some kind of 'symbolic sodomizing' becomes an all-encompassing process.[25]

Recent newspaper reports offer us a particularly significant episode, one which has come to light with the stories of a 'ndrangheta grass. At Gioia Tauro, in 1990, a young man who ran a fashion shop, Ferdinando Caristena, was killed – 'he was well liked, pleasant and good-looking, but his lack of manliness was a longstanding piece of gossip'. What did he do wrong? 'Caristena – the grass tells the Public Investigators – was chasing after Gaetano and Domenico Mazzitelli's sister; Domenico is the brother-in-law of Mommo Molé. He was really unhappy about Caristena hanging out with the Mazzitelli girl because the guy was known all over the district as a homosexual, which was the truth, and it would have meant dishonour for the entire family.' Besides his interest in the girl there was talk of what people thought was a relationship with one of her brothers: 'The rumour going around was that Caristena had actually had unnatural relations with Gaetano Mazzitelli, so Domenico Mazzitelli's wish to punish him was even stronger.'

After the murder a woman made a number of anonymous telephone calls to the investigators to identify the Mazzitelli brothers as responsible for the crime. 'The Mazzitellis' sister – the grass went on – left Gioia Tauro after that crime, I think she went somewhere near Modena or to France, out of the bad feeling she bore her brothers, since she "liked" Caristena and was even thinking of shopping them.' But before she left the unfortunate girl spent three weeks in hospital 'because of the beating she took – according to a police report at the time – from the brothers, because they were against her relationship with Caristena'.[26]

Fear of women, fear of one's own feminine side, fear of the anarchic potency of eros; the ferocity and gratuitousness of the killing of this nice young guy who is 'different' contains within it all these elements in a paradigmatic way.

This extreme revulsion for any form of 'perverse' sexuality – let us recall the explicit ban on membership for homosexuals, especially passive homosexuals – sounds the alarm about a more general tendency in the mafia world to keep sexuality at bay through a subordination of the pleasure principle to the reality principle. The disruptive force of eros, its promise of happiness, of amorous regression, of tenderness and life, binds sexuality to the pleasure principle; a diffuse, not merely genital sexuality, which stimulates communication and connectedness. The baleful compulsion to 'fuck', however, channels sexuality into a one-dimensional trajectory, harnessing it to the reality principle of reproduction and that principle to the service of a phantom virile potency.

Suspicion

It is not lack of emancipation that keeps women out of the mafia. The mafia organization, as Judge Falcone told Giovanna Fiume in an interview, is 'totally a male one. Either there are no women or they have a subaltern support role.'[27]

Both women and men are involved in plots, mutual projections and fantasies about the mafia. But as far as mafia practice is concerned, the resoluteness with which mafia men exclude women from active participation expresses a truth: the truth of women's untrustworthiness for the trade of killing.

This difference is usually made manifest in distinct roles, occupations and behaviour. But in a more radical way this difference is located at a deep level. And deep structures alter at an imperceptibly slow rate. Concealed here, I believe, is a deep barrier to any 'emancipation' of women in the mafia world.

Mafia men mistrust women, maintaining that women, in the final analysis, can never truly become mafiosi. Here, contempt for women's presumed inferiority is peculiarly mixed with a degree of admiration for their intransigence and a strong recognition of their otherness. According to Antonino Calderone:

> The men of Cosa Nostra are very careful about what they tell their wives. This is based on the notion that women's minds work in a certain way. All women, including those who have married mafiosi or who come from mafia families. When something touches the attachments that matter most to her a woman no longer thinks clearly. Omertà no longer counts, and neither Cosa Nostra nor any rules or arguments can then hold her back.[28]

This awareness entails not a few problems for the mafioso himself, since it places him between two loyalties, between two contradictory orders, that of his oath to the mafia and that of his oath before the altar. Calderone continues: 'The Sicilian man of honour knows this, and tries to keep wives, sisters and mothers well away from mafia affairs. He does it to protect them, to safeguard them, to save them, because if a woman knows something in the end either he has to kill her or he has to have someone else kill her.'

The rule of silence, the omertà which is regarded as a quality proper to brave men, is applied most of all to women. And it is rigorously pertinent when it comes to those women who are closest. 'At the top of the list is the rule of silence; a man of honour must not reveal his membership to any-one. . . . It is especially necessary to take care not to speak of it with women ("women are not to be spoken to about problems concerning Cosa Nostra", says Contorno).'[29]

Mafiosi spy on one another, in the mutual suspicion that the other might show weakness in relation to his woman. 'Nitto gave everything away to women, and then he insinuated that I was the one who talked too much to my wife!' Calderone exclaims.[30] When it comes to silence, female otherness provokes dread, fear and a sense that everything might escape that iron control which is imposed with the threat of death.

When it is a matter of other men's women, it seems judgement is sure, condemnation easy: 'Cosentino was pissed off. He couldn't get over it that someone like Tano had thought fit to confide in some *whore* or other.'[31] Whereas things change whenever one's own life falls foul of this dilemma. Silence does not come easily, unless you completely give up intimate relations. 'Cortimiglia told me that in Corleone's day:"A man of action should be free. Either a wife or a pistol." He knew he was right to talk like that. But, God in heaven, without a wife and without any children what kind of man is a man?'[32]

Confiding in a woman automatically assumes the meaning of betraying one or more men. Here too there emerges that very strong bond between males which has already been discussed. 'What kind of man are you to go and tell your mother about things that happen between us?' With these words a mafioso reproaches a young man who had worked in his fief. The young man, coming to grief shortly after this while negotiating a cattle theft, was killed. This was in the twenties, an episode narrated by Anton Blok.[33] Confiding in women, aside from the 'cause', means above all the betrayal of the pact between men. 'If I go and tell a woman:"That person committed such and such a murder," the subject in question will come and confront me:"You have put me in the hands of that woman. . . . How could you trust her, even if she is your wife or your sister, when women are known to talk?" '[34]

But what does feminine otherness consist of, for it to be perceived by mafiosi in such a radical way as to set up a rigid incompatibility between the mafia and women?

There appear to be two interwoven factors in 'mafia psychology', if we can call it that. On the one hand the strong homophobia, which marks out many men of honour and which is an integral part of mafia ideology, gives a solid basis for mistrusting women. 'It [homophobia] is linked to other fears, primarily the fear of equality between the sexes. Homophobes are conservative, rigid people, favouring the preservation of traditional sexual roles.'[35] Mistrust of women and mistrust of giving way to one's own feminine aspects are one and the same. 'Homophobia strengthens the fragile hetero-sexuality of many men. It is therefore a psychic defence mechanism; a strategy for avoiding the acknowledgement of an unacceptable part of the self.'[36]

On the other hand it may be that the historical and anthropological experience of a strong maternalism, like that handed down in the peasant cultures of the Mediterranean, has played a part in establishing the mixture of resentment, mistrust and awe that defines femininity for the men of these regions. The perception of a difference and a strong dose of misogyny are closely compounded. I believe that the very harsh judgement on Sicilian women given by Leonardo Sciascia can serve as an example for this masculine ethos:

> Many misfortunes, many tragedies of the South have come to us from women, especially when they become mothers. The women of the Mezzogiorno have this fearsome aspect. How many crimes of honour have been provoked, instigated or encouraged by women! By women who are mothers, by women who are mothers-in-law. Suddenly we find them capable of the worst infamies in recompense for the oppressions undergone by them in their youth, and resorting to the most appalling social convention. . . . In southern society these women constitute an element of violence, dishonesty and abuse of power.[37]

Here we enter a kind of vicious circle. The female ambivalence between *appearing* weak and *being* strong, which is characteristic of many peasant societies,[38] is the product of complicated power relations between men and women in these societies. The exercise of patriarchal power on the female body has engendered unhappiness and resentments. Being weak in 'sexual dealings', women have taken revenge on men in 'family dealings'. This dialectic of oppression is none the less recognized by Sciascia, who, not by accident, links these delicate entanglements with the 'sense of being mafioso'.

> When I denounce the mafia, at the same time I suffer, since in me, as in any Sicilian, there are still present and vibrant the residues of feeling mafioso. So by struggling against the mafia I also struggle against myself, and it is like a split, a laceration. The same thing happens where Sicilian women are concerned; in my manner of describing and condemning them there is also a condemnation of myself. . . . In the very same moment as I judge them, I feel myself responsible for their condition, atavistically responsible.[39]

In my view, the ambiguous fantasy of *matriarchy* which marks Southern society takes on the character of a masculine projection on the feminine, one which can offer some rationalization, some pseudo-rational explanation, of the mistrust which men foster in relation to women and their difference.

Women or mothers?

'The only woman who is really important to a mafioso is and must be the mother of his children. The rest "are all whores".'[40] The doubling of the female figure as saint and mother on the one hand, woman and whore on the other, is not only the province of the mafioso, but is a very deep-rooted cultural legacy. It should moreover be emphasized that the ambiguous interplay of feminine strength and weakness is primarily set in motion by women themselves. It is expressed in the very forms of female complicity with their own subordination. 'The complement to the male refusal to recognize the other is woman's own acceptance of her lack of subjectivity, her willingness to offer recognition without expecting it in return.'[41] Usually, it is only by desexualizing herself that the woman manages to acquire power.

A particular 'shrewdness about female powerlessness'[42] prompts women in patriarchal peasant contexts to conform outwardly to the subordinate role prescribed by the social order, so that they can in practice act with all the power over people and things that is available to them as mothers in the family sphere. These are everyday strategies of resistance, secret female strategies, among them the shrewdness of strongly confirming their own powerlessness, in order to avoid any challenge to their own position, which in reality expresses a *de facto* power.

None the less, the coercive character of this configuration tends to distort maternal capacities. Angela Lanza writes: 'In these areas the centrality of motherhood in thought and action, constrained as it is to assume the values of patriarchal society in conflict with those of industrial society, becomes crushed and twisted, effectively losing its authority, which resides in a different "maternal knowledge".'[43]

The ambiguity of this situation, the flagrant discrepancy between *being* and *appearing*, bears risks and costs for the individual woman, regardless of any gains. The costs of these entangled forms of complicity – with the other women in exercising family power, with the men in complying with their presumed supremacy – seem high, extremely high in terms of intimate relations. The negation of self as a woman, for the sake of assuming power as a mother, creates imbalances within relationships, above all in relationships with the children.

The shrewd complicity between women, as already discussed, has a correlation in complicity of another kind, with the male: that complicity which, contradictorily, attributes splendour, potency and wondrous things to virility, while seeking to hold it imprisoned in one's own bonds. I am talking about the mother's relationship to the male child. The birth of the male allows the woman, if only at second hand, to participate in the splendour of the male principle – the dominant principle of the public sphere – and, simultaneously, it gives her the opportunity to form it and bind it, to make it dependent and make it hers by proxy – in private. The possession of a son, inevitably influenced by mother-love, thus reveals its doublesidedness: it is an exclusive possession, enjoyed in private, which gratifies and gives value to the woman as mother and, simultaneously, it is a licence for the son to act as a male within the social, with all the attendant consequences that this licence has for the mother herself, as a woman.

To bring up her own son in the illusion of his supremacy, involves the woman's tying him to her, being his witness, his guarantor of this superiority, in which she has an illusory participation by virtue of being the mother; yet it also involves instilling in him and confirming for him the negative value, whether latent or manifest, of the female, perhaps even contempt for women. By this way of giving value to the maternal, mothers contribute to devaluing the female, to devaluing women.

I have digressed in this way in order to stress that women are deeply complicit in this process, whose outcome is the adulation of mothers at the expense of women. Clearly, this does not dispense with the huge male responsibility. Men often shackle women to the simultaneously threatening and reassuring stereotype of the 'mother of my sons': 'nor could I have killed the mother of my children for any reason in the world!' exclaims Zagari,[44] when his father, also a member of the 'ndrangheta, suggests murder as a way of solving the problem of a separation. The words imply that perhaps it could be an option were she to be thought of merely as a woman.

It is likely that this harshness regarding women, operating through ambiguous respect for mothers, might denote a deep fear of the psychic implications of the sexual connection. Again, Sciascia confirms this hypothesis.

Racked by profound insecurity, existential dread and a deep-seated instability, the Sicilian cannot but answer the pull of sex. However, circling around sexuality there is the religious or rather bigoted notion of the family, whose organizing core is that of woman. Thus woman is desired as woman only in so far as she is *other* (either belonging to another man or to no one, but in any event not to him), but once she has become his wife she at once becomes transmuted into an institution, she is transformed into the family and disappears as woman and individual.[45]

For mafiosi the mother patently embodies a strong symbolic value. It was Erich Fromm who stressed the defensive properties of the projection of the maternal imago on to collective bodies.

The transference of the motherly function from the real mother to the family, the clan, the nation, the race has the same advantage which we have already noted with regard to the transformation from personal to group narcissism. . . .

Empirically the fact can easily be established that there is a close correlation between persons with a strong fixation to their mothers and those with exceptionally strong ties to nation and race, soil and blood. . . . It is interesting to note in this context that the Sicilian mafia, a closely bound secret society of men, from which women are excluded . . . is called 'Mama' by its members.[46]

The psychoanalyst Di Forti makes reference to Fromm to highlight the centrality of the maternal imago for the cohesion of the esoteric group (a union between brothers, in the name of the mother and against the law of the Father) which in his view, as we have already seen, constitutes the mafia. His hypothesis is an interesting one, even if for the time being we lack any deeper clinical insights. 'The mafioso is a rebel on the outside, since he denies the authority on which the laws of official society are based, but a conservative on the inside of his group, since he must protect the secret on which the group's life is based; he must preserve the imaginary mother from attacks coming from the outside.'[47]

The widespread cultural tendency to double the figure of the female as a woman on the one hand and, on the other, as a mother who can in some way suitably placate men's fear of women, becomes particularly acute within mafia ideology. The obsession with death which pervades it infects every area of the emotions. By denying women autonomy and individuality, men defend themselves from the 'danger' of loving, from the danger of betraying 'Holyholymother' and her ravenous hunger for death. I quote Filippo Di Forti again:

> Behind the appearance of the 'Holyholymother' there is death, which re-emerges beyond arrogance and outrage. The maternal imaginary, the imago of the mother softens the world of the mafia. . . . The negation of women's subjectivity hides fear and dependence on the maternal imago; behind the masculinist language there is symmetry and powerlessness, and so manliness (*omertà*) hides the fear of the dialectic, the interruption of speech, the displacement on to silence. The mafioso is not able to love, he does not know equality in power and he displaces the conduct of things towards death. No less is the spirit of the mafia deceptive, which makes it also seductive, a seduction deferred to the negative, a displacement towards death.[48]

4

Death

Power

Not those who die, but those who die before they must and want to die, those who die in agony and pain, are the great indictment against civilisation. They also testify to the unredeemable guilt of mankind. Their death arouses the painful awareness that it was unnecessary, that it could be otherwise.[1]

The mafia, without doubt in accord with the repressive tendencies of the overall society which gave rise to it and which continues to give it sustenance, is a maximum expression of the 'unredeemable guilt of mankind' to which Marcuse refers, the unforgivable guilt of our society and its rulers, we might say. Violent death and the ever-present threat of violent actions are what characterize the mafia more than any other aspect of its being and operation. 'The most direct form of power is the pure power of action: the power to bring harm to others with a direct act against them, the power to "do something" to others.'[2]

The awesome strength of the mafia organization derives from the determination of its members. When all is said and done, beyond the craving for wealth which is undoubtedly an important motive in criminal activities, the mafia's paramount aim is power.

The mafia's raison d'être is to create a hierarchy that is autonomous from the *general* hierarchies of economics and politics, with the prominent notables and big landowners at their apices. At the point when society *in general* ceases to be strictly ordered by a legitimated absolute authority, the mafia no longer recognizes anything above it.[3]

In the final analysis it is this primary objective which inspires all its actions at the deepest level, and, in my view, it helps our understanding both of the mafia's internal structure and its relationship to the local area. The passion for

61

power pervades the entire network of relations, inspiring and conditioning the relationship to women and functioning as a basis for the reproduction of a mode of being, thinking and feeling that is mafioso.

Roberto Scarpinato, assistant prosecutor in the Palermo anti-mafia team, relates:

> Marino Mannoia once told me: 'A lot of people believe that you join Cosa Nostra for the money. This is only part of the truth. Do you know why I became a man of honour? Because before in Palermo I was Mr Nobody. Afterwards, wherever I went, people showed me respect. And this was something I couldn't buy.'[4]

What the mafia sets out to claim, its challenge to the state and, in some respects, also to the Church, is synthesized in its abrogation of absolute power to itself, the power over life and death. Territorial sovereignty, the *signoria del territorio*, is founded on this claim.

> We are in places where the 'death penalty' is in force, and has always applied. Accepted. This is why young children are taught to deprive themselves of speech, of sight, of hearing – you must not talk, you must not see, you must not listen. Because everyone knows that they can kill you and that they'll get off scot free.[5]

Calderone explains:

> Any mafioso knows perfectly well where his power comes from, when all is said and done. People are afraid of being physically hurt, and nobody wants to take even the slightest risk of being killed. Whereas the mafioso is unafraid and takes risks, and as a result puts others' lives at risk.[6]

This spiral of terror, primed by fear, is exactly what most acutely characterizes mafia power. The mafia manipulates anxiety, invading by stealth private and intimate spaces, stifling at birth every individual freedom, every sense of civic duty. Mafia power, by definition, is totalitarian. 'On January 6, 1941 President Franklin D. Roosevelt proclaimed the Four Freedoms: Freedom of Speech, Freedom of Religion, Freedom from Want, and *Freedom from Fear*. . . . Anxiety impairs the freedom of decision, indeed it may make such freedom impossible – only a fearless man can decide freely.'[7]

The mafia does not only stir up fears that can be traced back to real dangers. A good part of its power is based on the collusion of people who, at a personal level, feel themselves to be terrorized, intimidated by threats and blackmail. 'The extreme nature of the mafia phenomenon lies in this power to evoke primordial fears.'[8] Fear is synonymous with unfreedom. There can be no freedom where fear reigns.

> To live without anxiety is indeed the only uncompromising definition of freedom because it includes the full content of hope: material as well as spiritual happiness. But there can be (or rather there should be) no life without anxiety as long as death has not been conquered – not in the sense of a conscious anticipation and acceptance when it comes anyway, but in the sense of depriving it of its horror and incalculable power as well as of its transcendental sanctity. . . . Man is not free as long as death has not become really 'his own', that is, as long as it has not been brought under his autonomy.[9]

The power of the mafia owes its cutting edge to its offensive capacity. 'In the directness of the offensive action there is a more flagrant demonstration than in any other way of how crushing can be the superiority of men over other men.'[10] Power as exercised by the mafia is absolute, total, not open to appeal.

> The mafia does not leave things unfinished, half done. . . . There is no way out, there is no appeal. . . . They will not forget. The mafia does not forget. And if you leave it, you leave it with blood because they kill you. You cannot get away, you cannot betray Cosa Nostra, because it comes above everything. It comes before your father and your mother. And your wife and children.[11]

Calderone's anguished words, expressing an experience lived through, clearly illuminate the mechanism whereby, through the all-encompassing mark of death, butcher and victim become as one. The destructiveness upon which power held through death is based tends to overflow. 'On the other hand, destructiveness cannot but produce death, not only that of the other, but also one's own; a shorter way is therefore revealed which leads to self-destruction.'[12]

Elias Canetti's analysis of the link between power and death – 'The passion is for power. This is so much linked to the fact of death that it seems natural to us' – is very pertinent to an understanding of what deeply motivates mafia members. There is a fundamental horror of death that is common to all mortals; a void, an unsayable, an enormity. 'To confront a dead man is to confront one's own death, a lesser death because one does not really die, a greater death because there is still another to come. Even the professional killer, who takes his lack of feeling for boldness and courage, does not escape this confrontation: in some hidden recess of his soul he too is terrified.'[13] Before the body of the dead man, beyond horror, overwhelmingly, a sensation of euphoria builds up, the euphoria of having survived.

Talking about a murder he had committed, Buscetta says: 'Really young. It's so easy to pull the trigger and see the other guy drop. And you immediately get a sense of release; I did what I had to do, and the best way.'[14]

The man watching is not the dead man, but he could have been. Dread is transformed into satisfaction, into euphoria.

> The fact of this is so horrible that it is masked in every possible way. Whether shame is felt at this or not is a key to the worth of the man. But this changes nothing in relation to the fact itself. The circumstance of survival is the central circumstance of power. . . . The real content of this power is the burning desire to survive great numbers of men. It is more useful to the powerful man that the victims be enemies; but friends too could serve his purpose. In the name of manly virtues, he will demand of his subordinates the most difficult, impossible things. That these should be their downfall matters not in the least to him. He can make it known to them that this would be an honour.[15]

The skilful manipulation of such deep and fundamental feelings as the horror of death and the compensation of surviving typifies the exercise of the power which circulates within the mafia, between the men of honour. In relation to the outside these feelings are given potency, made explicit and translated into physical threats. The euphoria of survival is rationalized and given strategic value. 'A mafia killing, far from being uniquely or cardinally the product of a bloodthirsty uncontrollable instinct or a marginal subculture, is primarily a premeditated killing, in other words inspired by a strategic logic.'[16] Judge Falcone also stresses this aspect of mafia killing: 'The nature of the killing and the weapon are determined only by strategic and technical conditions.'[17]

For the victims, but also for the mafiosi themselves, the effectiveness of the threat lies in the irrevocable nature of the sentence. 'The fact remains that in 99 per cent of cases when a man of honour gets the order to kill, he has no other choice but to obey – this is Falcone again – without questioning himself or others. Anyone wavering before the necessity to kill is a dead man.'[18]

For the victim, the potency of the threat is amplified by imagination, tending to erase limits and boundaries. Strong emotions connected with bodily injury ensure that it is not only bodily integrity which is stricken, but inevitably also that of the person as a whole. And this is where the mafia blackmail lurks. 'Imagined violence glitters like a jack-o'lantern in daydreams and nightmares of all kinds.'[19]

The mafia's claim on total power also covers the past, memory. In this respect also akin to a totalitarian regime, the mafia tends to rewrite history, any and every time that the axis of power within it shifts. Before the Parliamentary Anti-mafia Commission, Leonardo Messina explained the killing of Ignazio Salvo in these terms:

Salvo belongs to the Salemi Family, very important men of honour. There's a long, historic line of Salvos there; all those who have had contact with politicians must, in some sense, die out. There should be no traces or historical memories of the past. This is because they're turning their coats.[20]

The power targeted by mafia strategy is power over a geographical area, a 'territorial sovereignty' which in many respects seems 'like absolute dictatorship'.[21] In this guise, that of the total privilege of power, the mafia differentiates itself from other forms of common criminality. 'The mafia attempts to control all economic activities, whether legal or otherwise, that are practised on a given territory; this fact of territorialism is the matrix of how mafia power is delineated.'[22] Evidence corroborated in the territory of Ciaculli, the 'fief' of the Grecos, seems relevant to these dictatorial targets. Whole families have been condemned to eviction and exile because they are regarded as insufficiently 'trustworthy'. Under the threat of arms these people have had to give up their land and their homes to go and live elsewhere.

> The most famous case was that of a widow who had refused to move out and saw her own house being walled up by Pino Greco's men; she had to get out very quickly to avoid being permanently imprisoned by bricks and mortar. Her house is still today an oddity in Ciaculli, with no doors or windows.[23]

The aim of mafia strategy is to render others powerless. Assuming power over life and death, playing clever games of blackmail, intensifying fear and terror through the imagination, the mafia also sets itself up as lord and master over the corpse of the defeated. 'The killer's triumph can also be prolonged beyond the act of killing if, by mutilating the corpse and refusing its burial, he destroys the hope of an afterlife for the soul of the victim.'[24] The many cases of *lupara bianca*★ [disappearance] emphasize the shadowy and disturbing atmosphere which characterizes the social experience of living under mafia domination.

The cult of death, iron discipline and the macho idea of taking justice into your own hands – 'a man of honour asks no one for justice, least of all the state'[25] – are the ingredients of a thoroughgoing mafia ideology. The figure of the hitman, sketched out here in a political satire, is one of the potent images of this ideology:

> I could see the Invisible. I named the Unnameable. I possessed the Elusive. I was a fellow citizen of the Citizen through antonomasia: the Hitman. . . . How casual, undeliberate, illogical, uncoordinated were the gestures of the crowd; how geometric, elastic, tight and precise to the last millimetre were the

★ Literally: white, i.e., phantom, shotgun. [Trs.]

gestures of the Hitman. . . . The Hitman would turn up out of the blue and dis-
appear in the blast of his custom-made weapon. He would produce the most
deadly effects and, were there not a corpse to bear witness to his passing, one
would have said: he isn't there, he has never been. No one sees him, for fleshly
eyes cannot hold the sight of him. Fortunate this city that has Citizens the like
of him, envied the world over! Which appear and vanish like phantoms. Which
come from afar and from very near but as if they came from anywhere and
nowhere. They are everyone and no one. And yet being so omnipresent and
all-powerful they are sons of this people. Attached to duty and the family.
Kindly, open-handed. And their metal hand can be made of all these hands
which seem so thick-set and plain. Pushers and swindlers and bag-snatchers.[26]

In fact, ideology marks itself out and becomes powerful precisely by virtue
of the fact that it contains within itself intricately combined elements of
truth and falsehood in relation to what it claims to express. 'This is no straightforward criminal organization, but an ideology which, however distorted,
has elements in common with the rest of society,' Falcone explained in one
interview.[27] Arlacchi, for his part, talks about a 'vision of the world which can
be defined as "heroic" and "anti-Christian"': 'the mafioso seems able to accept
death by making a qualitative distinction between human beings. His frame of
mind appears in many ways elitist and anti-egalitarian. Since not all men are
seen as being on the same plane, not all lives have the same worth in mafia
eyes.'[28] This is confirmed by Zagari's words: 'I have my own ideas, according
to my standards, about who it was OK or not OK to kill and those ideas, right
or wrong, were what I acted on.'[29]

One milestone in this vision of the world is *omertà*, the quality of silence
which is identified with real manliness. A quality and at the same time a frailty,
a further pull towards death: the negation of communication.

> *Omertà*, silence, heralds this message of deathly narcissism: it is not mere chance
> that we talk of being silent as the grave. He who does not speak estranges him-
> self from shared subjectivity, from dialogue; as a concrete flesh and blood subject
> he is already dead.[30]

How far are women strangers to this ideology? We do not know. Yet we
have, once more, some indications that support their *effective* outsider status
from the 'profession of killing'. Relevant researches show that murder, mafia
murder in particular, 'is first and foremost a crime of males, not only as
authors but also as victims'.[31]

But there is a worrying suspicion that women do know a lot more than is
supposed. What follows is the account of a murder, through an intercepted
phonecall between the wife and the sister of one of the accused in the maxi-
trial:

Pia: Scumbags, if you wanted to kill him, kill him and get it over with. What's all this cutting up for?

Maria Cristina: Cutting . . . cutting . . . because, what I think I'll do is ask where he is. So as to . . .

Pia: Yes, yes . . .

Maria Cristina: And they stuck the knives into him, pulled out his teeth and other stuff . . .

Pia: Into his head, his shoulders . . .

Maria Cristina: And they shot him in the end.[32]

These ladies seem to be condemning the gratuitous cruelty of the murder. Yet their way of commenting on it gives us an inkling that violent death is accepted and endorsed by them as a daily routine. 'Their being in the know and their apparent indifference leads us to suppose that this was not an exceptional occurrence for these women and that they are in the know about the commercial practices of their relatives, down to the last detail.'[33]

It is hard to weigh up the difference between doing, being active protagonists, on the one hand, and being present, knowing and continuing to observe, on the other. Yet I am convinced that close involvement and active participation in the mafia organization demands that the individuals concerned cultivate a psychological predisposition for violence, power and unnatural death. In an essay on love for death and love for life, Fromm writes:

Characteristic for the necrophile is his attitude towards force. Force is, to quote Simone Weil's definition, the capacity to transform a man into a corpse. Just as sexuality can create life, force can destroy it. All force is, in the last analysis, based on the power to kill. . . . The lover of death necessarily loves force. For him the greatest achievement of man is not to give life, but to destroy it; the use of force is not a transitory action forced upon him by circumstances – it is a way of life.[34]

What is the 'way of life', in psychological and social terms, of those women who are closely bound up with a world imbued with death, but do not themselves actively cause death? Do they live in conflict and in contradiction? Is their complicity dictated by terrible fear? By inner involvement? By considerations of convenience? Or perhaps by indifference?

For mafiosi, death undoubtedly holds a powerful fascination. Sometimes it even occurs to me that this attraction is an even stronger motive than the 'banal' desire to get rich. Giovanni Falcone has some fine and deeply felt thoughts about these 'fates':

'Brother, remember that you must die' the Catholic Church teaches us. The unwritten catechism of the mafiosi suggests something analogous: the ever-present risk of death, the paltry value given to others' lives, but also to one's own, compel them to live in a state of perpetual alert. . . . In melancholy moments I let my thoughts wander to the fate of men of honour: how can it be that men like others, some of them gifted with real intellectual qualities, are compelled to forge a life of crime in order to survive with dignity?[35]

Compulsion to kill

From the heroic to the commonplace, from the mythic to the bureaucratic, is but a short step, one that precisely marks out the tension between ideology and reality in mafia business.

'The mafioso kills to avoid being killed, the hitman is moved by a compulsion to kill, an attempt to displace death outside himself, on to an enemy, to defer his own death.'[36] The death of the other and one's own death are much more interwoven and connected than perhaps might at first appear to the mafioso himself. After having betrayed and killed another man of honour who trusted him, on orders from above, Anonymous glimpsed for the first time that ineradicable bond that now truly pinned him to a fate that had seemed at first to be a choice:

> As far as Tano was concerned it had never crossed his mind: that was the only certain thing. And it was the thing that kept me awake. Tano was smart, but he hadn't realized that he was getting ready for his own party. And, in his shoes, I would have come to the same end. Now I knew that it could happen to me too, Christmas night, Easter morning or any other day.[37]

Antonino Calderone's testimony allows us to travel along the road leading to this awareness that Anonymous expresses of the verdict's certainty. The mafioso with his back to the wall, imprisoned in that very net which he has helped to weave, knows there is no way out. 'The Santapaolas would have interpreted my absence as a sign of withdrawal or betrayal in relation to them. But I was in danger even if I turned up, because it's by keeping appointments that you get killed.'[38]

Paolo Pezzino comments:

> Look at the rituals, which show that it must always be the best friend who kills the one they've decided to eliminate: both to avoid arousing his suspicions and to compel respect for the basic rule of obedience. A world of cruelties in which violence appears detached from any purpose.[39]

As if in a whirlwind, deceiving themselves that they know no fear, that they feel no human feelings and sensations, these men are compelled by a perverse mechanism of their own creation to raise the stakes ever higher. We return to Calderone:

> Some of them think they can protect themselves from this curse by having power, and they try to stay up there on top because they think that as soon as they come down, even a little, they'll be killed. And so they keep on killing. They kill so that they can keep on being in command, and by then there is nowhere to turn. They can't give up being in command because so long as they command they live and when they stop being in command they die.[40]

Here we can touch and feel the very dialectic of power, its extreme limits, its infection with death.

> What the real man of power has in mind is in fact unbelievably grotesque: he wants to be the *only* one. He wants to survive everyone, so that nobody will survive *him*. He wants at all cost to escape death, which means that there must be no one anywhere who can put him to death. So long as there are men, any man at all, he will not feel safe.[41]

The world of Cosa Nostra is a paranoid and demented one that often reveals its true nature to its own members only at the very last. Obviously, at the start of a career in the mafia this perception is less sharp, if it is there at all. On the contrary, according to Di Forti, there is the prevalent illusion of a release from the fear of death, which comes about by deflecting the death drive outwards. Moreover, for the individual there is a psychic gain in the gratification of merging with the esoteric group:

> The neophyte must give up his own Ego-ideal and accept the ideal of the group as his own. This total devotion to the mafia conceals a 'symbiotic fixation' on the mother; the new initiate must exact a high degree of masochism from himself. He must be prepared to die for the mafia, to give his blood to the mafia.[42]

Lu sangue fa lu murmuru (blood is not quiet). This popular saying comes to us by way of the Sicilian folklorist Giuseppe Pitrè. Who knows better than the mafiosi that the culture on which they depend, albeit by distorting it, makes children and relatives take on the burden of any injury suffered by their kin? This close awareness imposes vigilance, foresight, preventive action. The documents of the Anti-mafia Commission tell of the hitmen of the La Barbera group: 'who, having to eliminate Pietro Prester, did not hesitate to sacrifice the brother too in order to avoid any eventual reprisals'.[43] The hellish and inexorable compulsion to kill is protracted potentially to infinity.

> And you will die, and your children will die too. . . . Death calls to death as blood calls to blood. It is a thing without end. Nitto Santapaola was scared stiff about this, but the only way he could deal with it was to say: 'We must also kill the sons of those we have killed.' He said this because he was afraid that the sons of the dead men would grow up and then kill him, or else kill his sons. This is where all your terrible fear comes from, you mafiosi.[44]

Sometimes nerves give way. Nick Gentile talks about an accomplice racked by suspicions of imminent death:

> He saw a hired killer in every single person walking along the pavement outside the bar and it got to the point where he would often tell his crony Don Piduzzu about it. He was so jumpy that he took everything the wrong way round. I don't know if I should put this terror of his down to some kind of bad nervous collapse, but the upshot was that he killed himself in his own house one morning.[45]

For an outside observer like me, it really seems very hard to grasp the sense of such compulsion. Mafiosi behaviour even undermines any reasonable perception of the relationship between 'guilt' and 'vendetta'. Giovanna Fiume talks about the carnage in Piazza Scaffa, where 'eight men were killed for seven horses', and comments:

> The bloodletting was out of all proportion . . . it brings home the difficulty those studying the mafia have in understanding a cultural universe where death is not a punishment for repeated infractions of the mafia code, but often for the first and only time this happens. In cases like this it seems vendetta is not a matter of degrees and it takes no more than a small wad of banknotes to pay off a young hitman.[46]

It is not surprising, then, that in circumstances like these mafia murder should become a factor independent, as it were, of conditioning and social change. Arlacchi talks about 'a phenomenon of exacerbated sociocultural disintegration': 'Once they exceed a certain level, in fact, mafia murders begin to develop a powerful *multiplier effect* which has devastating consequences for the structure of society.'[47] Death comes ever faster, with reproduction and the relationship to wife and children betokened by the increase in the birth of sons – and death comes at an ever younger age. 'There are very few who reach old age. The turnover has escalated . . . the old men have to keep their wits about them, they can't bow out. . . . And a boss without power ruins the image of the society, so he is killed.' This is what a young mafia lawyer in Palermo told Giorgio Bocca.[48]

The imminence of death and the prospect of a short life lead mafiosi to live intensely and to

> value men on the basis of sharp anti-egalitarian distinctions, and to let nothing stand in the way of strengthening the power and size of their families, whose most marked features are large numbers of children, male pre-eminence, the subordination of the women, children and old people, and endogamy within the social group.[49]

It is very important to consider the consequences these tendencies have overall for the quality of interpersonal relationships and the quality of life in collective terms. How do women adapt in this climate of permanent bereavement? What is the outcome for daughters and sons? The compulsion to kill involves a compulsion to mourning in extraordinary forms, it leads to brutalizing and submission. Marcuse wrote:

> Whether death is feared as a constant threat, or glorified as supreme sacrifice, or accepted as fate, the education for consent to death introduces an element of surrender into life from the beginning – surrender and submission. It stifles 'utopian' efforts.[50]

And being brought up to accept violent death seriously accentuates this mournful stifling of hope.

The celebration of death as such, of death as a value in itself, is a basic feature of Fascism. The illusory release from the fear of death through the displacement of death outwards, killing as a form of self-defence from death, and finally, the compulsion to kill, all represent the gravest of dangers for our culture, its ever-present shadow. Umberto Eco writes: 'Whenever death is not regarded as a means towards some other end but a value in itself, then we have the seed of Fascism and we should name as Fascism whatever brings this about.'[51] Historically Fascism and the mafia have taken up apparently antithetical positions. Yet it is my belief that their mutual animosity is based on a jealous rivalry for power which emanates from their very closeness to one another, a closeness so profound as to make them almost identical when it comes to such central features as the relationship to death, to authority and to women.

The 'banality of evil'

Mafia violence exhibits specific characteristics, some of which are mutually contradictory. The blood relationship, which in some respects implies powerful emotions, is none the less instrumental, rational and cold in nature. Where feelings and sensibilities are concerned, mafia ferocity seems to oscillate constantly between an inside and an outside. Murder is a run-of-the-mill administrative measure whose purpose is to impose total control. The Palermo judges write:

> In this session it is of great importance to stress unequivocally that murder is not an exceptional event or at any rate one cut off from Cosa Nostra's ends, but a routine means whereby the organization achieves its purposes and affirms power; everything else is deceit and mystification.[52]

Mafioso language and idioms disclose a way of thinking about the job of killing which is designed to shore up the enormity of their crimes in a guise of routine, normality and bureaucratic ritual. 'In February it became necessary to have further recourse to murder,' writes Zagari.[53] Calderone brings up sinister jokes made by his accomplices Stefano Bontade and Michele Greco:

> Bontade arrived an hour later in his Porsche Carrera. He was very fed up and he made this excuse: 'Sorry for being late, but I got a puncture and I had to throttle Stefano Giaconia.' This was fine with Michele Greco: 'No problem, Stefano. We've waited for you. Anyway you've done a great job taking Giaconia off our hands.'[54]

Sinagra's revelations, the detailed and spine-chilling stories of the 'suppressions' and tortures in the Sant' Erasmo 'death chamber' at Palermo, offer a picture which is appalling precisely in that it alternates between cold-blooded extermination, only comparable with the logic of the concentration camp, and bloodthirsty 'backwoods' violence.

> Even the use of acids to dissolve the bodies of those killed can be inscribed in this logic, which couples the efficacy of the technical means used, with its capacity to pile horror upon routine administrative horror, so as to discourage any response from their adversaries, and inflicting brutal humiliation upon them by putting the bodies inside rubbish bags or melting them down and flushing away the remains.[55]

In this lucid strategy of terror, contempt for life, most of all for that of others, is the supreme weapon. Terror, notoriously, is 'blind'; it is carried out with a target in mind, but is always accompanied by the arbitrary, by the unpredictable, and can strike at anyone. The boundary between 'the guilty' and 'the innocent' is abolished. Terrorist violence fires into the indiscriminate mass.

We have excluded the definition of 'accidental' death for those who, although not the predetermined victims of the mafia, have been struck down in the course of attacks which, by virtue of the methods used and the time and place of their execution, could not but produce other victims besides those 'designated'.[56]

As far as the rules of *omertà*, obedience and expediency will allow, hitmen are free to give way to their own sadistic or merely aggressive tendencies. Caponnetto relates:

Sinagra also told us about young Inzerillo who wanted to avenge his father's murder and went around spreading the word on the mafia scene that he would kill Totò Riina. So Pino Greco, who was a notorious big-time hitman who was later wiped out by the Corleones themselves, cut off his arm, and told him: 'You won't be able to shoot Totò Riina now.'[57]

Calderone recalls: 'Luciano Liggio was a bloodthirsty one. He took pleasure in killing. . . . When you were with him you had to watch out. . . . Everyone uneasy, mouths shut, and you could feel death in the air. . . . He would kill as a game, out of sheer malice.'[58]

From the informers' stories in particular there emerges a baleful picture, a gallery of portraits of men who, to say the least, are hardly attractive – looked at from a woman's point of view. 'A ghastly tangle of terror, vice, brutality and death. A blend of coarseness and subtlety, of the feudal-archaic and techno-crime modernity.'[59] Thus delineated, the mafia seems an organization likely to attract, with its promise of heroic conquests, many mediocre men, with a mechanism analogous to what comes into play in wartime: 'War thus gives the ordinary man, who in peace time had no means of advancing himself as someone of importance, an opportunity to experience power; and at the very point where this experience has its roots: in surviving piles of dead. . . . A certain splendour of invulnerability irradiates the man who returns unharmed.'[60]

After months and months of interrogation, Caponnetto commented:

With the exception of Bono and a very few others, it is my impression that the human raw materials involved were depressingly squalid: coarse characters who left you wondering how they were able to run a criminal organization on that scale. And the fact is they left no impression on me, nothing to remember. . . . I have to admit that I was disappointed [by the boss Michele Greco]; what I found was a very lightweight personality, lacklustre, with no charisma, in whom you could sense the complete absence of cultural baggage.[61]

This brings to mind Calderone's words, already quoted: 'The mafioso seeks power and takes it. . . . *But a lot of his power is given to him by others.*'[62]

These features of the mafia phenomenon should give us pause for thought. The realistic image of men who are unpleasant, mediocre, insensitive and brutal (with due recognition that there are a few exceptional charismatic figures) is at odds with a widespread preconception that gives emphasis to a social depiction of a heroic nature. As far back as 1886, Alongi wrote: 'The mafioso dresses shabbily, adopts a demeanour and speech of monk-like, naive, foolishly attentive geniality, patiently suffering insults and injuries, but at night . . . he shoots you.'[63] If we combine this image with the squalid features that mark out the new generations that have taken over with drug trafficking, we contemplate the picture of a social evil worrying by virtue of its very 'quality'.

A crude, gratuitous, passionless evil. As if life, the joy of life and its vividness, had been benumbed and impoverished. Brutality and normality mingle and merge. Without wishing to construct misplaced historical comparisons, I feel a strong affinity between what we are discussing and what Hannah Arendt has called the 'banality of evil':

> It is indeed my opinion now that evil is never 'radical', that it is only extreme, and that it possesses neither depth nor any demonic dimension. It can overgrow and lay waste the whole world precisely because it spreads like a fungus on the surface. It is 'thought-defying', as I said, because thought tries to reach some depth, to go to the roots, and the moment it concerns itself with evil, it is frustrated because there is nothing. That is its 'banality'. Only the good has depth and can be radical.[64]

Max Weber's words also come to mind, when he describes the outlook of mere 'power politics': 'It is a product of a shoddy and superficially blasé attitude towards the meaning of human conduct; and it has no relation whatsoever to the knowledge of tragedy with which all action, but especially political action, is truly interwoven.'[65]

An absent 'knowledge of the tragedy' and the 'banality of evil' are, I believe, terms that meaningfully refer to the alliance between politics and the mafia which has laid waste civil society in Italy in the postwar period.

Hannah Arendt talks about the 'banality of evil' with reference to Nazi crimes and with particular reference to Eichmann, an emblematic figure in any engagement with the genocide of European Jews.

Eichmann was not Iago and not Macbeth, and nothing would have been farther

74

from his mind than to determine with Richard III 'to prove a villain'. Except for an extraordinary diligence in looking out for his personal advancement, he had no motives at all. . . . He *merely*, to put the matter colloquially, *never realised what he was doing.*[66]

Even though Hannah Arendt's analysis is focused on the phenomenon of Nazism, I believe none the less that the specific component of evil which philosophy identifies as 'thoughtlessness' is a habitual feature and a defensively directed one, marking many criminals and many crimes in advanced industrial societies, whether governed by dictatorships or more or less democratic orders.

I was struck by a manifest shallowness in the doer that made it impossible to trace the uncontestable evil of his deeds to any deeper level of roots or motives. The deeds were monstrous, but the doer . . . was quite ordinary, commonplace, and neither demonic nor monstrous. There was no sign in him of firm ideological convictions or of specific evil motives, and the only notable characteristic one could detect in his past behaviour as well as his behaviour during the trial . . . was something entirely negative: it was not stupidity but *thoughtlessness.* . . . Clichés, stock phrases, adherence to conventional, standardised codes of expression and conduct have the socially recognised function of protecting us against reality, that is, against the claim on our thinking attention that all events and facts make by virtue of their existence. If we were responsive to this claim all the time, we would soon be exhausted; Eichmann differed from the rest of us only in that he clearly knew of no such claim at all.[67]

What seems most disturbing of all is the fact that this kind of criminal, or hitman, as he is called when referring to the mafia, is like so many others, and like so many others is neither a pervert nor a sadist, but just dreadfully normal.

This way of looking at the mafia, I realize, clashes with that of someone with a deep knowledge of the phenomenon, like Judge Giovanni Falcone. Falcone emphatically stresses the human and moral aspects of many of his mafia interlocutors, whether they be informers or otherwise.

I have learned to recognize humanity even in its apparently worsened state; to have not just a formal, but a genuine respect for the opinions of others. . . . The categorical imperative of the mafiosi, to 'speak the truth', has become a cardinal principle of my personal ethics, at least where the truly important relationships in my life are concerned. However strange it might seem, the mafia has taught me a lesson in morality.[68]

The contradiction is perhaps more apparent than real. Both ways of seeing – the *overriding* perception of the 'banality of evil' on the one hand, and on the other the *overriding* perception of the continuity of moral codes, albeit frustrated ones, with their ethnic and cultural attachments – select elements which most deeply touch whoever is looking.

What overridingly disturbs and touches Falcone, the Sicilian, implicated professionally but most of all existentially, is probably closeness and similarity, what he shares with the mafiosi in terms of his own attachments. Indeed, it is precisely the relevance of ethnic attachment, in its explosive mixture with the processes of internationalization at a highly technologized and mediatized level, which makes organized crime so dangerous for the future of social coexistence in global planetary terms.

> In order to survive and develop, organized crime needs to draw support from local particularities and archaic cultures which will ensure that it is adequately impermeable in relation to the outside world, and at the same time it needs to build models which are universally workable as a basis for future international agreements.... Meanwhile this unitary model is taking shape, founded on the strong tradition of ethnic groupings, on an extraordinary capacity for territorial control and for acting on decisions taken; on the development of primitive forms of trading, like the barter of old.[69]

However, what most of all disturbs someone like me, a woman who was born and grew up in Nazi, then post-Fascist Germany, without any roots, bereft of a sense of belonging, is precisely the formal and manipulative nature of that categorical imperative which Falcone talks about. What meaning can there be in 'always speaking the truth', at a formal level, if everything is still brutally subordinated to the maintenance of power, at all costs? The elision of substantive rationality and instrumental rationality, which is so important in fully understanding the apparent paradox of the meticulously planned atrocities of Fascist terror, is what strikes me here too: the rigid and formal morality of the mafia code is a function of what could not be more ethically repugnant: total contempt for the freedom of others.

The price of life

The changes manifested in mafia organization over recent decades come under the heading of market logic: these are inflationary times. The amount of money in circulation, which has been hugely increased by drug trafficking, has meant a dizzying drop in the price of life. The inflation of easy money means the inflation of deaths by killing. Yet what has remained unaltered is the usurpation of the right over life and death as such.

In *The Day of the Owl*, Sciascia had Don Mariano say: 'But if you're asking me, just making conversation on my views about life, if it is right to take a man's life away, I'll tell you, first you have to see if he is a man.'[70] In terms of this code, nowadays even the decisions that lie behind the death sentences seem more hasty, although this makes little real difference. Zagari writes of 'my Calabrian friends . . . who gave me the job of eliminating some people whom the organization wanted dead'. This is all it takes to activate the hitman, because in the end, as Zagari maintains further on:

> dying is as natural as being born. There are those who are born after the normal nine months of gestation in a perfectly normal birth and there are those who are born premature perhaps by a Caesarian section, which has nothing normal about it at all. More or less by the same token, with ways and means that replace and anticipate the natural event, there are those who are made to die, 'simply' by rearranging the date of a fated moment that is yet to be confirmed.[71]

'There are those who are made to die': just as if the murderer disappears. The hitman's ideology has adapted to the spirit of the time: death is no longer administered even in the name of manliness, but in terms of the technical perfection of a quasi-'surgical' intervention.

Antonino Calderone also confirms this tendency. 'These days it's money that has taken over everything. . . . The way people think nowadays, in this kind of case things would be done differently. An investigator like Cipolla would just be wiped out, with no time or money wasted on recommendations and getting people transferred.'[72]

The drug millions have had effects on both the functioning and mode of organization of the mafia and on the everyday life of its members. Overnight luxury and extravagant consumerism must have produced changes and generated new elements in relations both between the sexes and between the generations. This is posed as a question.

> And 'the cousins' [the Italian-Americans] started paying for everything at a different price. Up until then the word 'millions' was something I had read in the newspaper. It was when they talked about state finance. Then there came a time when I heard it on the lips of people who five years before were counting the change from a thousand lire note. It was a bit like being in a *putia di vinu* [a drinking haunt] like the ones there used to be in my village. When you went there late in the evening it was full. Everybody was talking loudly and nobody was listening. One way or another there wasn't one of them fit to make any sense. With the wine in their bellies and their heads they were always quick to come to blows or start singing, depending on the turn things took. Palermo was like that for a decade or so, until I left. All drunk on millions.[73]

What was the outcome of so much wealth? More and more 'stuff', more and more death. Once more it is Sciascia who gives us a key to decipher this frenzy:

> Stuff, which could be land, a house, crockery, linen, animals, food stores, seems just to be a casual source of income; it is not *used*, it is *left* after they've died. . . . The more wealth grows . . . the more our own death grows and is amplified. The rhythm of accumulation as a rhythm of death . . .[74]

5

Eros against Thanatos

The quality of life

Palermo is fetid and infected. In this burning July, it gives out the sickly-sweet smell of blood and jasmine, the pungent odour of creolin and cooking oil. Like a huge dense cloud settled over the city, the miasma of the rubbish burning at Bellolampo. . . . The corpses of the murdered, hands and feet tied like goats, throttled, decapitated, castrated, left inside car boots or black plastic bags, already number more than seventy this year. . . . Behind these cool tufa walls rubbish piles up – from the market, from those who live here, bones from butchers' shops; and children scratch around there, along with dogs and cats, and darting rats. This part of Palermo is another Beirut destroyed by a war that has now lasted forty years, the war of mafia power against the poor, the city's disinherited, the war against culture, civilization and decency.[1]

By following a thread of argument which seeks to locate a woman's point of view we have reached a crucial point: the contradiction between the growing material wealth of the mafiosi and their families and what we might call the congenital obstacle to the enjoyment of this wellbeing. 'Of course they're rich. But the villas they are shut up in are like fortresses. They were locked inside them. . . . Owning a villa is a symbol of belonging to the bourgeoisie, but culturally those arrested are lumpen.'[2]

The conditions of illegality, criminality and violence necessary for the accumulation of this wealth are exactly what later prevents the enjoyment of all this accumulated 'stuff'. The story of the Palermo gang boss, Salvatore Anselmo, appears an emblematic one. Locked away inside his bunker apartment, he had 'connected live wires to his doorbell and the iron grille. Anyone who touched either of them would be electrocuted . . . Salvatore Anselmo lived in a state of fear.'[3] His murderers got him to open the door all the same, probably being relatives or close friends.

In particular, those who belong to the 'losing' clans lead a wretched life. Felicia Bartolotta Impastato relates:

Before, the balconies would be open and everyone would be out on their balconies, and people going around by car. Now these people are nowhere to be
seen. As for the four who were arrested, they were totally buried. . . . One of
Gaetano Badalamenti's sons was arrested and the other escaped from prison, I'm
not sure where. Then there was Nino Badalamenti's son, they murdered him.
There are other mafiosi's sons who've shut themselves away, collapsed . . . it's
nervous collapse they get, because they can't go out. They can't go out and
they're going crazy . . . so it means they see nobody, men or women. The lot of
them are scared stiff. Whereas before you were always running into them,
because the village is small.[4]

The promise of happiness which is the mirage of consumer society turns out,
in the case of the mafia world, to be all the more a mirage. 'Even when he's
wealthy, the mafioso isn't likely to enjoy his wealth. Take the case of De
Stefano. He was supposed to have property in Switzerland, but he died in the
Aspromonte with his Dupont lighter in his hand. Once he's been involved in
mafia business, the mafioso can never get away, not even if he makes millions.
He always has to live a mafioso's life,' says one interviewee.[5]

This estimation is all the more credible when it is expressed by someone
who, like Calderone, can judge from the experience of being inside a mafia
perspective.

These days Totò Riina is on top . . . he's above everybody. But at the same time
he's reduced to a pathetic state because he can't go out and about, he can't leave
the house, he can't sleep, he can't sit out in an orange grove in the evening and
enjoy the cool air and the scent of the orange blossom; he can't do anything
without worry. He's absorbed in his dread of being killed . . . what can a man
like Totò Riina say he's seen of the world, in hiding for twenty-five years and –
even if he is super-rich and owns villas and apartment blocks – has never left the
pastures and the caves and the company of the animals right there where he was
born?[6]

We know now that Riina lived in Palermo, and in well-to-do circumstances. Yet this doesn't alter the fact that his days must have been marked with
dread.

Judge Falcone too was of the opinion that the temptations of consumerism
represent a new element which may alter rules and principles.

The mafia is made up of human beings whose needs, desires and behaviour alter
through time. Sometimes I have observed signs of irritation with regard to the
harshness of certain rules. I have remarked that, after turning evidence, men like
Buscetta, Mannoia and Calderone would in some wise lay claim to a certain
quality of life that is incompatible with mafioso principles.[7]

These seem like explosive contradictions, because it is often this dream of a life of luxury which has pushed young men towards the mafia organization. 'Francesco Marino Mannoia sighed as he spoke to me recalling the time when he joined: "What a tragedy! And to think I was so fond of beautiful women and Ferraris!" ' And Falcone again: 'I have often tried to picture his life as a "mafia chemist", spending his days refining dozens of kilograms of base morphine, locked up in some makeshift lab that's uncomfortable, smelly and insalubrious.'[8]

This impatience with wretched living conditions, more a case of survival than living, could in years to come be aggravated by the everyday experience of the poor quality of life in high-density mafia zones. Because in addition to the hardships of clandestinity and fear there can be living conditions brought about by the degradation of all public resources because of mafia power. In Palermo, Reggio Calabria or Agrigento private wealth is powerless in the face of water shortages, uncollected rubbish, filthy hospitals, etc. . . . .

> The mystery is the contempt which the gentlemen of the mafia display towards their own homeland and their own people, underneath all the claptrap about codes of honour. Even in the Medellín of the cocaine barons, the Escobar clan and the Gavirias wanted an ultra-modern airport, a futuristic elevated metro system, and first-class hospitals. But in Cosa Nostra's Sicily, in the 'ndrangheta's Calabria, in the Camorra's Naples, yesterday's ragamuffins turned into today's gang bosses exploit without putting anything back in except the frills and fancies of fly-by-night consumerism.[9]

But this is not the end of the story. Loyalty to Cosa Nostra also involves concessions and sacrifices in terms of the quality of emotional life and relationships. Matrimonial gambits and power alliances impose obedience on both young mafia members and the daughters of mafiosi. Mannoia, for example, had had to marry Rosa, the daughter of the gang boss Pietro Vernengo, even though he loved another woman, Rita, who was also expecting his child. 'He's never forgiven himself, he's still eaten up with remorse over that business. In the end Rita was his partner when he decided to turn himself in, masterfully carrying out the negotiations with Gianni De Gennaro for his surrender. . . . So Mannoia chose life. . . . There came a point for him when he opted for love over the traditional family values that conformed with the mafioso code.'[10]

Naturally, wealth and quality of life are not totally separate. Yet, as the testimonies of the mafiosi themselves make quite clear, the unsettling wealth that came in the wake of drug trafficking has drastically highlighted the limited possibilities for enjoying this wealth, in the context of the mafia way of life. Clandestinity, paranoia, enforced personal relationships, constricted emotional life with others: 'Cosentino gave him a dirty look. . . . He did not realize you should never ask questions, because if something has already been decided questions are superfluous, and if it hasn't been decided questions are futile'[11] – as time goes by all these limitations are liable to produce ill-humour and dis-affection in the most demanding and sensitive.

The discrepancy between the consumer society's promise of happiness and everyday impoverishment is much more acute in the case of the mafiosi, because there is not even an appearance of this promise being kept. With a greater urgency than 'normally' rich men, men of honour can experience the limits of wealth, but obviously on condition that they reach an age that allows them such experience. 'In one of his most advanced formulations, Freud once defined happiness as the subsequent fulfilment of a prehistoric wish. That is why wealth brings so little happiness: money was not a wish in child-hood.'[12]

In response to this reality, whose combination of extreme precariousness and ever-growing material possibilities makes it in some respects schizo-phrenic, these men have developed their own ideology, a cinematographic image of life as brief but intense. This heroic – and, we should say, deeply false – image is locked into a reality – one that is indeed true – in which the men of honour are seen to be active at multiple levels. Calderone gives many examples illustrating their varied activities. By day they run companies and businesses and do deals, by night they rob, kill and conspire. Sumptuous parties, vast orgies of food, weddings, christenings and confirmations with hundreds of guests. Gold bathtubs, glaringly expensive cars and other objects at sky-high prices. The ideology behind this divides men into heroes, the few whose life is short, and sheep, the many whose life is long and tedious. 'Better a day as a lion than a hundred years as a sheep,' thundered Fascism's lethal slogan.

This picture is well illustrated in an informal talk between an investigating magistrate and a prominent Palermo mafioso which is recorded by Arlacchi:

> *Magistrate:* Totò Inzerillo was killed. He was only thirty-seven. Isn't it a shame to die so young? At that age so many important experiences still lie before one. . . . So many goals to reach, so many things to do and see . . .
>
> *Mafioso:* Inzerillo died at thirty-seven, it's true. But his thirty years amount to eighty years for an ordinary person. Inzerillo *lived well.* He got a great many things out of life. Other people will never get even a hundredth of those things. It's not a shame to die at that age if you have done, had and seen everything Inzerillo did, saw and managed to get. He didn't die weary of life or dissatisfied with it. He died *full up* with life. That's the difference.[13]

The new styles of living consonant with an industrialized society divide public from private life, introducing new needs, like the need for privacy, raising the issue of the quality of life as a public value and encouraging the idea of the individual and individual freedoms. School and education in general are potent vehicles for these new realities. These, quite evidently, are values that are diametrically opposed to mafia domination. 'It is interesting to observe how the mafia's long rejection of the values of formal education has, until now, produced barely literate mafiosi.'[14] The illiterate lived 'embedded in the totality of social relations', very much inside his own culture and, in consequence, was extremely useful. Yet today, not least as a result of their relative material wellbeing, the new generations in general are getting educated and the children of the bosses go to university.

We have few facts with which to speculate on the long-term consequences of schooling and the encounter between these young people and 'high' culture. Yet it seems clear that material wellbeing and higher status will prompt many children to move away from their fathers' 'profession as killers'. When it comes to Cosa Nostra in America, Caponnetto talks of 'a wholesale crisis of vocations': 'the sons of the bosses who are now bourgeois and absorbed in professional life as lawyers or bankers don't want to know anything about their fathers' career'.[15] Yet it is also common knowledge that Michele Greco's brother is a doctor and Giovanni Bontade's was a lawyer.

Let us take, for example, Giorgio Bocca's conversation with the Costanzo brothers, Catania businessmen and sons of *Cavalier* Carmelo Costanzo. Even though they are not mafiosi, 'merely' businessmen firmly linked to the mafia, problems emerge which are engendered by education and produce what I would call fruitful contradictions between the generations. Vincenzo Costanzo, an architect, says: 'The other day Orlando and Fava from the Rete went to my daughter's secondary school (in Rome) to give a talk on the mafia; they talked for two hours about the Costanzos and my daughter came home in tears.' And again: 'I'm at home with the children and their cousins, I turn on the television and there's somebody talking about the Costanzos and the kids ask me if it's true.'[16]

Anonymous talks about a meeting with Di Cristina at Riesi, when the boss confesses to him that having 'studied too much' has made him less fit, less smart and less fierce as a mafioso. 'My father and Stefano's [Bontade] made us study because they wanted us to become better than them. They were wrong, Giovannino, they couldn't have done us a worse disservice. I saw this. . . . If you make a lion study, he's worthless and the jackals are all over him. Do you know what I mean?'[17]

But when ignorance (in educational terms) is combined with poverty – as in the case of groups marginalized by society – the path is extremely hard and full of pitfalls, demanding the investment of exceptional energies. Rita Borsellino talks about this. After her brother's death she led discussions in a lot of urban and village schools, at great risk from the mafia:

One girl said in class: 'When we heard that Borsellino* had been killed, we drank a toast at home!' Not even this sort of comment put a stop to the dialogue. By talking to this girl in an unheated way a point was reached where she more or less conceded that it is not right to celebrate the death of six people. It is work that has to be done in depth and with patience; our society (including many so-called 'respectable' parts of it) is mafia through and through. The roots have to be pulled out by digging up the earth all around them. If all you do is cut them with a hatchet, the cut-off roots will grow again.[18]

Personally, I believe that the change will come very much through education and cultural factors. Subjectivity deeply affects how things will change, but in some respects subjectivity also puts up strong resistance to these processes. Eros against thanatos: a fierce and hazardous conflict for those who have embarked upon a mafia career. Thanatos gets the upper hand by stifling imagination, fantasy, utopia. Hannah Arendt affirmed that Eichmann '*never realized what he was doing*'; the 'banality of evil' resides essentially in a subjectivity which is flat and bereft of dimensions, thought, imagination. Involvement, be it through thought or feeling, takes the individual towards a pluridimensional relationship both with the self and with others. To the all-engulfing dimension of *what is* there can be brought and integrated the supplementary dimension of *what could be*. 'In its refusal to accept as final the limitations imposed upon freedom and happiness by the reality principle, in its refusal to accept what *can be*, lies the critical function of phantasy.'[19]

This pluridimensionality impacts upon individuals' perception of themselves, impacts upon the depth of their thought and brings oxygen to their relationship with others. The eros then released into these relationships is supremely antagonistic to the culture of death that is inherent in the mafia.

The hope for the growth of a greater imagination and capacity of thought about what one is really doing can be applied to everyone. The new generations, however, seem privileged in this respect.

Making a new start

It seems to me that the phenomenon of turning state's evidence — *pentitismo* — produces certain compulsions. Even when their motivations are to do with vendetta or merely with anxiety about survival, the *pentiti* open themselves up to new ways of thinking and allow themselves feelings which mafioso terror had formerly stifled from the start. Moreover, it is the *pentiti* who allow us, on

---

* Judge Paolo Borsellino, who was murdered by the mafia in the Via D'Amelio bombing of July 1992. [Trs.]

the outside, to establish some contact with the inside and approach some grasp of what remains incomprehensible to outsiders. 'By breaking the law of *omertà*, they open the way to the most recondite secrets of the top mafioso ranks and bring about a psychological shift in the mafia world.'[20]

Crossing the frontier, the internal frontier between the world of mafia values and that of societal and humanistic values that are the basis of our culture, Calderone perceives Cosa Nostra like a world beneath a glass bell: 'I watched Riina getting carried away with his speech and then I realized that I was now a stranger to that world, for I observed it with detached eyes and impassive heart, as if behind a window of frozen grief.'[21]

In the progress of *pentimento*, this phase of dawning awareness and distancing appears extremely delicate and hazardous – necessarily, if we consider the mafia interests liable to be harmed. Nothing must leak out. It is certainly in this phase, when mafia values are being undermined, that anxiety about the fate of close family members grows stronger. Leaving behind the iron law which privileged the Family, the *cosca*, the esoteric group, the man on the brink of leaving Cosa Nostra trembles for the fate of those close to him, who in this phase take on a growing importance. He sees his ex-comrades in all their ferocity. 'It had also crossed my mind that Nitto, my close friend whose wife and mine were friends too, knew me so well he would realize that to do the job properly would also mean eliminating my wife, since it would occur to him that I must have told her things,' relates Calderone.[22]

Judge Falcone was one of those who most closely witnessed the inner torment of these men. His empathy enabled him to attempt to reconstruct their psychological itineraries. 'Those who have rejected Cosa Nostra have become aware of the culture of death it spreads and exalts and they have chosen life.'[23] Commenting on Mannoia's experience, Falcone remarks: 'He chose what offered the prospect of protecting his partner and his children in terms of what was most vital and joyful. I think that his experience is revelatory.'[24] I think it is not wrong to say that, by opting for the family instead of the Family, the *pentito* has finally listened to himself, to his own feelings and attachments. This is precisely what seems to mark his new beginning: a meeting with himself.

His relationship with his children and the future they represent assumes a central role in this development. By turning his back on Cosa Nostra he can at last allow himself a different, new relationship with his children. It is now possible for him to listen to his children, instead of, as before, merely giving them orders. In a telephone call from his hiding place abroad, made during a television broadcast commemorating the Capaci massacre,* Antonino Calderone said:

---

* The bombing at Capaci, on the motorway between Punta Raisi airport and Palermo, which killed Judge Falcone, his wife and bodyguards, in May 1992. [Trs.]

Just think that the other day my daughter told me: 'Daddy, if you hadn't given yourself up, if you'd just stayed in Sicily, I would hate you; you did the right thing.' Now, if these gentlemen want to be hated by their children for the sake of their greed, to stay the rotten way they are, what does it mean? It means that they are not with their children, that they do not love their children.[25]

This is of course a valid consideration for the 'big shot' *pentiti*. However, for the 'small fry', things are more complicated. Their families cannot be – or do not wish to be – completely protected and therefore remain at the mercy of what is known as the transversal vendetta. Just how devastating mafia domination can be at the level of personal relationships is amply shown by the recent case of the *pentito* Marco Favaloro, who accused Salvatore Madonia of killing the entrepreneur Libero Grassi by shooting him in the back.

As soon as she heard that her husband had informed, the wife Giuseppa Mandarano swiftly distanced herself from what he had done. Dressed in black, with great histrionics, making use of newspapers and television, while refusing any protection – 'I don't want to live my whole life armourplated like those judges' – the woman stated: 'He is not a *pentito*, he's a filthy wretch. The very evening I found out I opened the wardrobe and took out all his clothes and burned them. There's nothing of his left in the house, not even a shirt or a handkerchief.'[26] And again: 'I'm in mourning. My husband is dead even if he's alive physically. I'm asking for a divorce. That wasn't the man I married, I married a decent person. Whether it was freely or against his will, he now is what he is; they're welcome to him.' Favaloro was rejected not only by her but by his four brothers and his children, Giuseppe, Raffaele and Lucia. His wife also said: 'What was I to do? Countersign the death sentence on my family? It's my belief that they forced him to say those things, by putting pressure on him, manipulating him. But I don't care if what he says is lies or the truth. He and I are finished now.'[27] Another young woman, Daniela Scalzo from San Cataldo, responded to her husband's *pentimento* by setting fire to the room where she lived with him and then to her parents-in-law's room. She too had refused the 'protection' that had been offered to her by the state.[28]

Two fiercely divided worlds, the world of legality and civil society and the world of mafia illegality, two worlds openly at war: the conflict has devastating effects both materially and in terms of personal life. A war that will be won only with the conquest of minds.

The separation between one world and the other seems marked not so much by *pentimento*,* in the judicial meaning and the narrow sense of

---

* The Italian word contains a range of meanings, from the ordinary 'second thoughts', 'grassing', or 'informing', to the religious connotations of 'repentance' or 'conversion' which encompasses regret, remorse and recognition of guilt. [Trs.]

informing, but by that inner turning point, that change of register which Calderone talks about when he perceives Riina as being shut behind a glass. It is this altered perception which frees the energy drive from the domination of thanatos and makes it available to eros. The pleasure of living also illuminates everyday life in modest circumstances.

> We set to work and we were happy, happy, happy. . . . In Nice I rediscovered life, I was reborn, I developed morally. It was there that I discovered my children, I understood what it means to bring them up, follow their progress, see them grow in a certain way. . . . Throughout my whole life as a rich man in Catania, as a powerful and respected mafioso, I had never been at peace, or as happy as in those three years we spent in Nice.[29]

Rita Atria: do not forget

To achieve this turnaround, to restore one's own life by reversing values, convictions and habits is not easy, either from the perspective of inner worlds or from any 'external' perspective. Mafia terror tends heavily to discourage any second thoughts. Nevertheless, the stories of the *pentiti* display a range of possible motivations for decisions of this kind, which in their diversity have a common basis: the choice of life over death.

Pentimento, the decision to make a new start, for good or ill, means becoming a protagonist, acting in the first person, being active again. And, again, I believe that in these situations the outcome for women is more difficult, because it is mediatized. In a situation marked by dependency, becoming a protagonist demands a special effort, an even greater effort. Acting for oneself in the first person has, in these cases, to be invented from scratch; there are no traditions or cultural models, there are no examples to emulate, no known paths to follow.

Often, there is not even *pentimento*, remorse, because the only 'guilt' is for having been born and grown up in mafia families. The tragic story of Rita Atria seems exemplary here. For me, her suicide carries the following message: 'I did my very best, to the last; individual and lonely as it was, my choice was the right one. But now, with nowhere to turn any more now that I have lost my only certainty of protection and affection – Judge Paolo Borsellino – I can see no future.' Rita's strength failed her because she was truly alone; she had no examples or models to inspire her. She herself was the example.

A year after her death, her sister-in-law and friend Piera Aiello tried to make sense of her suicide:

> I have thought about it a lot. And I'm convinced that Rita had made the decision to take her own life some time before. With her revelations to the

magistrates she had fulfilled her duty as a citizen and felt at peace with her conscience, but there was still a great source of unresolved pain: her relationship
with her mother. As a little girl Rita Atria was very fond of her mum, but her
mum never accepted her decision to collaborate with the law. I remember that
there were stormy telephone calls, furious quarrels that left her in a pitiful
state.... The judge's death was the final blow for her; she felt she was abandoned
and the only adults she loved had become unreachable.[30]

Rita's is not a case of *pentimento*. She had committed no crime. Simply, like
so many other women, she happened to live in a mafia family. Her decision
to collaborate with the law, without any contingent motives (such as the
wish to 'avenge' the death of family members), was the choice of emancipation. In the difficult post-adolescent phase of her life, Rita made a turning
point in her own trajectory. Taking flight towards some dream of freedom is
a common move for many young women of her age; but it is a forbidden
dream for those who grow up in the shadow of mafia (negative) values.

Rita's sacrifice moved people and disturbed them. The women of
Castelvetrano and Partanna write: 'Now we are the ones who must isolate the
mafiosi, not the other way round. Rita we ask your forgiveness for having
ignored you.'[31]

Rita Atria was a pioneer, one of a slender vanguard of women from her
background who are all paying a very high price as they affirm their right to
their own individuality. In the families they come from, their battle for freedom – that freedom of the individual, whether male or female, which is
guaranteed by the Constitution – has no traditions, has no examples to call
upon. It is a freedom that has to be invented from scratch, a precious possession of which there is still scant experience. 'She could have defended herself
from everything, but not from the grief of being left alone.'[32]

I would like to suggest we think about Rita's story using the reconstruction of her life that is presented by Sandra Rizza, a reconstruction which
stresses the tragic character of this short life through the opening quotation:

> if I die
> Before my time, why then, I count it gain;
> To one who lives as I do, ringed about
> With countless miseries, why, death is welcome.
> For me to meet this doom is little grief; . . .
> And if you think it folly, then perhaps
> I am accused of folly by the fool.[33]

It is important to remember that Rita was very young. In the transition
between adolescence and a young adulthood, Rita lived through many hard
experiences that weighed heavy upon her: the murder of her father when she

was eleven years old, the murder of her brother a few years later, her mother's hostility and incomprehension, the decision of her sister-in-law, Piera Aiello, to collaborate with the law and Rita's subsequent isolation in the district as the relative of a notorious *pentita*, then her boyfriend's desertion of her for the same reason. Rage, desperation and loneliness.

Rita's short life unfolded in the shadow of two powerful and overbearing male figures who absorbed her love, her tenderness and her devotion: her father and her older brother. Mafia men, albeit of small standing, violent men who died in a violent way. With them Rita had a strong bond, both while they lived and after they died, a bond fuelled by pride in being an Atria and the wish to avenge their death, to carry out the intentions of the brother, who had died in his turn to avenge the father.

None the less, her relations with the living were above all relations with women. She has a place in a tragic, deeply conflictual triangle of three women: Rita herself, the daughter of Giovanna Cannova and the sister-in-law of Piera Aiello; Giovanna, Rita's mother and Piera's mother-in-law; and finally Piera, the young widow, Rita's sister-in-law and the daughter-in-law of Giovanna Cannova. This irreparable conflict which set one against the other, separating the two young sisters-in-law from the older woman, can be summed up by their differing conceptions of love and feelings of vendetta for Nicola, Rita's brother, Giovanna's son and Piera's husband. An age-old struggle, full of ancestral echoes; a new struggle, brand-new, opposing recourse to the law with the idea of *omertà* and vendetta waged alone.

This implacable and dreadful struggle borders the territories of both the living and the dead, both reason and madness. Traces of it may still be found in the way the graves are laid out in the small cemetery at Partanna. Nicola, the son, is buried at a distance from the father, and next to him his sister Rita now lies. This was what Rita had written; she wanted to be buried in the same grave as her brother, not her father's. The photograph of Rita on the stone and the words carved into the marble, 'Truth lives', were chosen by Piera Aiello. But on All Souls' Day, the mother, Giovanna Cannova, reasserted her authority over her daughter, destroying the photograph and the inscription with a hammer. 'Nobody had the right to put that photo there. Rita must be kept away from here.'[34] She did not attend the funeral. 'On that July day when the funeral cortege was carrying her Rita's coffin through the streets of Partanna, she shut herself up at home with a cushion over her face.' However, Rita had decreed in her diary: 'My mother is on no account to attend my funeral or see me after my death.'[35]

These words in Rita's diary contain a dreadful, desperate message. 'She wasn't yet seventeen, but she knew she was going to die and that she would die before her mother.'[36] For a long time, the primordial dread of abandonment and the fear of death – the sharpest weapons of the mafia's hold on people – had overshadowed this young girl's life.

The life of Rita's mother, Giovanna Cannova, was scarcely a happy one. Subordinate to her mafioso husband, a brutal womanizer, she took things out on her children. 'This ill feeling in the Atria household, screaming, beatings, nerves ready to explode with tension . . .' With her husband and son both murdered, her daughter-in-law's decision to report everything she knew and had seen threw her into panic. She perceived the risk of her daughter Rita following her sister-in-law's example. Distressingly torn between the old and the new, she made a furious defence of *omertà*, engaging upon a struggle with the magistrature. She made a charge against the Marsala Prosecutor's Office and the *carabinieri* for the abduction of a minor, after Rita's decision to collaborate with the law as well. In her powerless desperation she did not even stop short of threatening her daughter with the same fate as her brother; in other words, she threatened to have her killed. The only language she knew was mafia language. Harsh with herself and with others, filled with dread, she lived out a drama where she was deaf in her loneliness and rancour. She was incapable of seeing, beyond all this, that Rita had taken a step towards freedom.

After Rita's death she collapsed and spent months in a rest home, where the nuns had to spoon-feed her like someone paralysed. 'She had a husband and a son killed, her daughter died of despair, and all she can do is go around alone and in mourning, carrying a hammer through the deserted pathways of a cemetery.'[37]

The other woman to make a powerful mark on Rita's experience was Piera, the wife of the adored brother Nicola. 'My name is Piera Aiello and my life can be easily summed up: at fourteen I became engaged, at eighteen married, at twenty-one a mother, at twenty-three a widow.'[38] Piera came from a non-mafia family, but she was well aware of the milieu in which she was born and grew up. She knew Rita from a very young age: 'I first knew poor Rita when she was six. I was sixteen and I was already engaged to Nicola. He would lift her up in his arms and cuddle her. And, after Don Vito's death, when the mother decreed that the two of them were not to see one another any more, they started meeting in secret, at Sciacca.'[39]

After she had been engaged for a few years Piera wanted to leave Nicola, 'but I hadn't reckoned with the honour of the Atrias', she explains. 'They forced me to marry him.'[40] She concealed this bullying from her own father so as to spare him problems, and tried to influence her husband to give up the mafia and the vendetta. But by now Nicola was 'part of the gang' and, in any case, was stubborn in pursuing the vendetta over his father. His enemies beat him to it, however, killing him in front of his wife's eyes.

Now, years later, Piera says: 'The women of mafiosi always know everything. If they talk, it's all over for Cosa Nostra. . . . I myself was on the point of persuading my husband Nicola to collaborate with the law. I'm sure that if the mafia hadn't killed him first he would have managed it. A woman can lead her own man where she wants. Even if the man is a super boss.'[41] Widowed at twenty-three, Piera decided to take her own revenge. 'I loved Nicola, he was the father of my daughter . . . my daughter should never be ashamed, neither of being an Atria, nor of being Sicilian.' But she decided to avenge herself differently from the traditional concept of vendetta, by going to the police with everything she knew and everything she had seen. The fact that Piera came from a non-mafia family doubtless influenced this decision, helping her to see that this could be a real way out. The price, as we now know, was very high. But Piera also gained something from it: 'It is good to be clean, to feel clean and untroubled. There is a wonderful difference between having to appear untroubled and really being so.'[42]

The sense of vendetta that accompanies Piera's decision, as it did Rita's, in no way detracts from the explosive force and liberating significance of their actions. I believe that it was a deep feeling, one perhaps necessary to give them the courage, even the reason, demanded by such a rupture. I am convinced that no outsider has the right to judge these feelings. The words of the vendetta are part of a well-known lexicon, one familiar even when, in such cases as these, they express undertakings that are in essence new and different. Taking hold of a weapon and taking the law upon oneself (or else inciting someone to do so), on the one hand; going to a judge and asking that justice be done, on the other, are, from a social and civil point of view, radically different actions, yet they are triggered by feelings of rage, hurt and vendetta which can be the same.

Piera's words are eloquent. The dialectic between old and new, pride and an armed bodyguard, family attachment and the rationality of universal rights seems inscribed in her very actions: 'From time to time I go back to Partanna, and there I am. I go to visit the cemetery, to pray at Rita's grave. I go with an armed bodyguard, people see me, everyone sees me but no one can come near me. All they can do is look at me and I walk with my head held high, like a grand lady.'[43]

How is Piera perceived by the people who see her there? Doubtless not with indifference. Some, for obvious reasons, will hate her; others, however, will be curious, astonished, shaken. Margherita Cacioppo writes:

Piera Aiello sat in the back seat of one of cars, 'alone', although protected by a lot of bodyguards, resigned, but smiling shyly, sad at certain moments, in no way perturbed, hidden behind her mirror sunglasses. I read an infinite loneliness there, certainly more tragic than the person I saw so many years ago, when we often used to have an ice-cold beer on a hot summer evening in her bar at Montevago, the only one that stayed open late. She would be behind the counter, silent but uneasy, sweet-natured but suspicious, her husband's liveliness a strain: Nicola Atria. Now, the only people around her are those with whom she shares the pain of running risks. . . . Remember that you aren't alone.[44]

Piera seems very clear-minded, aware of the risks, but also aware of her rights. 'I myself have never caused anyone any trouble: and this is something known to the gentlemen I have put behind bars. Some of them don't even know me; I'm the one who has been given the trouble.'[45]

But she also seems very much alone, really missing the infinitely remote normal life she once had. Now there are two of them confronting the Partanna mafia in a trial currently in progress: she and Rosalba Triolo, the ex-girlfriend of one of the incriminated hitmen. During a television interview Piera Aiello was asked what she had to say to the women of her town:

> The only thing I want to say to these women is to walk with their heads held high in their town. Let them help me if they can, but I do not want help in any other way, I only want their support; if there are things they want to denounce, they must do so, they shouldn't be ashamed to be from Partanna. Because I think Partanna is a wonderful place. I've lost any hope of going back now, yet, perhaps in the bottom of my heart there is a still a hope that some day I'll be able to take a walk in my own Piazza Garibaldi.

A year after Rita's suicide Piera sent a message from her secret refuge to the women who in spirit had been close to her throughout this period:

> Some day when this is all over, when I am free, I would like to meet each one of the women of the 'Sheets Committee', the ones from the 'Fasting' group, all of the women who edit Mezzocielo, and thank them, for it's all I can say to them. But I'd like to thank them one by one. Because there are so many of them, aren't there? All I need is a little sign to tell me that I am not alone, little things that give me the strength to go on, because there are times when courage can fail, when you're alone and there's nothing for it but loneliness; this happened when they killed Paolo Borsellino and when my sister-in-law Rita Atria killed herself, but I've kept going just because those women are alive.[46]

At seventeen, in her rage and grief for the death of her father and her brother, in her rebellion against her mother, Rita Atria must surely have been drawn by Piera's example, having been her friend already.

Reading Rita's story, trying to put myself in her shoes at seventeen or eighteen, I was struck most of all by how *tough* her experiences were. I can't find any other word.

The pages in her diary bear witness to fear and terror:

> It is four in the afternoon. A little while ago while I was outside hanging out the washing I saw Claudio Cantalicio go past my house in his car. It isn't the first time I've seen him. . . . Claudio lowered his head, and the other person turned to look at me. . . . Better to be in a cage full of starving lions than be facing the

hatred of the Accardos; I could leave and find the smallest hole in the world and stay in it for ever, but if they wanted to they would find me and kill me.... One a.m. and I can't sleep ... I am very scared ... tonight around eleven thirty-five I heard someone knocking at the door ... they kept on knocking, insistently.... It was Andrea D'Anna ... I know too well that he always carries a pistol.... Andrea wasn't drunk tonight, he would have been able to do what they ordered him to, which is to kill me and my mother. He was being nice but too insistent. I told my mother that everything was fine, I made up excuses to set her mind at rest, but I'm really scared that they'll kill me tomorrow.[47]

Where was I while Rita was spending nights like these? I was in the same country, in the same South of that same country, unknowing, like so many people, nearly everyone, engaged in a quiet normal life. It is a thought that troubles me a lot.

Rita, however, was fearful and alone in a very deep and far-reaching way – bereft of her mother, her home, her family. Her experience can perhaps be understood by means of the Freudian category of the uncanny, the *unheimlich*:

The term *Das Unheimliche*, 'what belongs to the sphere of the frightening, what generates dread and horror', is set by Freud alongside *heimlich* (from *heim*, home), what is familiar and habitual, through its opposite. Indeed nothing disturbs us more than an alteration in our normal field of experience, a variation suddenly arising in the very place where we feel at home. Freud observes that the dream of home is always accompanied by a feeling of nostalgia and when someone dreaming of a place or a landscape thinks: 'This place is familiar to me, I have already been there,' an interpretation replacing the landscape with the mother's body would be valid. Indeed there is no other place where we can assert with such certainty that we have 'already been there before'.[48]

After choosing the path of the new, after opting for freedom, Rita found herself completely homeless, with no home and no mother. Being without a home, metaphorically, circumscribes the human condition of modernity; we are all more or less drawn into this process. Yet – and this is where I perceive the intolerable burden of Rita Atria's experience – this process is usually lived in solitude, but alongside many other solitudes. We are alone, alongside many others who are alone. Rita, however, did not have time to experience all those other solitudes around her.

Even before it becomes a material reality, homelessness is a mental condition. Alone, in front of her diary, in her own town and in the midst of neighbours who have always been there, in the room next to her mother's, Rita conquered freedom and lost her sense of 'being at home', even before her flagrant break with her world. To the solitude produced by the death of her father and brother, by her boyfriend's desertion and her mother's hostility, Rita added her decision to break away. She was the one who took the road of no return.

In the short term this decision was made easier by Piera's presence. Piera too had taken this road. Yet, Piera's decision was made in conditions that were more emotionally protected. At least it seems so. Piera had a small daughter, on whose behalf she felt impelled to make her move, Piera had a non-mafia family which was on her side. On the first anniversary of Rita's death the women who came from Palermo met Piera's grandmother at the cemetery. She wept as she told them:

> My granddaughter Piera was my favourite, and now I don't know where she and her little girl are . . . when they telephone me I can't even speak, because I get upset and I start crying. . . . Here nearly everybody has cut us off. There's one family near where I live of people who ended up in prison after Judge Borsellino's investigations. Whenever they see me go by they scream 'Curses on your granddaughter and your whole family . . . may you end up like Rita Atria.'[49]

But Rita was alone, with only one friend who mattered: her brother's widow.

Away from Sicily, by virtue of being state witnesses, in the early days the two young women enjoyed a new life in the guise of freedom. In Rome they were 'tourists', having a good time, getting to know other young people, going dancing. They almost led a normal life. But they had to move from house to house all the time. For security reasons, lasting relationships could not be formed. After suitable investigations, the security services made an exception for Gabriele, a young sailor, Rita's new boyfriend. But, deep down, Rita was suspicious. Not so much of him, but of his family. She lived in fear of the moment when his mother would get to know her true identity.

Rita did not have time to discover that there could be love and trust for her too. She did not have time to experience new forms of solidarity between people who were homeless, all existentially exiled and alone. The murder of Borsellino cut into the bond between the world of before and the world of after, between belonging to family and place and new forms of freedom, the bond represented by this judge who was so human, so fatherly, so Sicilian and so opposed to the mafia. He represented a guarantee that the transition from one world to the other would be possible. And the fine thread that bound the judge to the young girl in some way endures even after both of them are dead.

The judge's sister, Rita Borsellino, said:

> I know that Paolo talked to his daughters about Rita both because he actually

thought of her as being like them so as better to understand the psychology of such a young girl. He called her *a picciridda*, and it was as if she was his daughter. I can still see how Paolo was with this girl to whom he was deeply bound. . . . All of us who could went to the public demonstration [in Partanna, commemorating Rita's death]: my sister, my brother, some of my sister's children and two of mine, and myself. And it was the first time we went on a demonstration. We did it to underline what Rita Atria stood for.[50]

At seventeen, Rita was too fragile to withstand the further blow of the judge's death. Thanatos won in the end.

In the theatrical performance of *Il sogno spezzato di Rita Atria* ('The broken dreams of Rita Atria'), Gabriello Montemagno has Rita say: 'Everything is over now. We got away from the mafia which has everything it wants, to take refuge in the law which lacks weapons for the struggle. We ended up alone. The old world doesn't want us any more, as a matter of fact it hates us, and we don't know if we'll ever see the new one.'[51]

Rita was really a girl, on the threshold of becoming a woman.

If I was really a woman I would be a woman; what is it precisely that makes the difference between me and a woman? Maybe it's that I haven't yet tasted the pleasures of the flesh? I didn't realize how important this is. Maybe I'm not old enough to be a woman. Maybe I haven't got a woman's ideas and ambitions. If this is all that differentiates me from her, then take me before an audience, stretch me out on a bed and only then will you understand how old I am. I am younger than you can know, but I will give you such great pleasure that your soul will delight more than you can dream of. If there is an adjective greater than womanly, well that adjective will be mine.

These are Rita's words, written in her diary in the final months of her life, when she was in Rome.[52]

Rita Atria's funeral brought to the fore the enormous rifts provoked by her decision. 'They are burying her in her home town, at a funeral with no relatives, with no males. Those who are there have come from far away. They are women. Still, above all.'[53] Those absent are the mother, the Partanna community, the state; those present are a few relatives, one or two girls who were schoolfriends, some teachers. The coffin was carried by women from the Fasting group, and the Association of Sicilian Women against the Mafia who had come from Palermo; the magistrates of Trapani, Marsala and Sciacca sent a message of condolence. But, even with tears in his eyes, the priest insisted that suicide is a sin.

Rosaria Schifani writes:

There was even someone who wanted to bury her as a sinner. And Don Russo, the old curate in Partanna, sweating in front of the little altar and the light wood coffin, chose psalms from the holy scriptures that only referred to sin rather than innocence. When this priest spoke about 'the violent hurricane which has uprooted a flower and an action that was objectively rash', he fell short of blaming the mafiosi who ruin life and the peace of a community, because for him the devil is nothing more than 'human wickedness'. Rita a sinner? What sin? The sin of speaking out? It was a good thing that there were women who shouted: 'Rita did not sin. Rita spoke out. Never again will we leave a woman all alone.'[54]

On the first anniversary of Rita's death (and after the full Requiem Mass in Ravenna cathedral for the captain of industry Raul Gardini who committed suicide), the Borsellino family issued a hard-hitting press release, which includes the following:

> The priest in her town denied her a funeral: only a benediction outside the church.... Now the doors of the Church open to give solemn funeral rites to a man who took his own life when facing serious charges. We are sure that God's mercy exists and is equal for all, making no distinction between persons: rich or poor, powerful or lowly; accused or accusers. While trusting that the Church will use the same yardstick for everyone, our thoughts go out in gratitude to Rita Atria, who died, like Paolo Borsellino, for the love of truth and justice.[55]

Not long before she fell into the void, Rita wrote in her diary: 'Before taking on the mafia you have to examine your own conscience, and then, after defeating the mafia inside yourself, you can take on the mafia around you and among your friends; the mafia is us and our mistaken way of acting.'[56]

Many other women are beginning to see themselves in the loneliness of Rita and Piera: 'If Partanna is Sicily, Rita and Piera are us, and a part of us dies every day like Rita, and a piece of us goes into exile each day, like Piera.'[57]

Rosetta Cerminara: an exemplary tale

> I would like some day to be able to go back to my family, to have friends again, to talk to my father and mother and feel them close to me, hugging me and touching me. And for my brothers and I to tell one another things, as we once did. A life without fear. But I am afraid that it will never be like that; they tell me that the mafia has a long memory. And so I know that I have to disappear, that we will never have a life as it was. That I cannot have relationships and must always be careful about who I see and talk to.... I cannot give a definition of the mafia, I can't manage that. But I know it is something that has ruined my life and the life of my family.[58]

These are the words of another young woman, a 21-year-old Calabrian, an office worker and militant Catholic – from a family of shopkeepers – who bravely spoke out about what she saw at Lamezia Terme, on the evening of 4 January 1992. Inadvertently, along with several other people, Rosetta witnessed the killing of Police Superintendent Salvatore Aversa and his wife Lucia Precenzano.

> I know that an awful lot of people saw what I saw, in the town centre at seven in the evening, and yet they are keeping their mouths tight shut. They're afraid. I'm afraid too, yet I've found the courage to speak out. I'm now even more afraid than before, because they haven't spoken out. Not even now, when the trial is taking place and people are being charged, will anyone come forward.[59]

Who is Rosetta Cerminara? An ordinary girl, from an ordinary family, a casual passer-by on that stretch of road where the mafia set an ambush for the police superintendent. As usual in a provincial place, where everyone knows almost everyone else, Rosetta knew the Aversas and had acknowledged the superintendent as he went by in his car. And likewise, Rosetta knew the hitmen. One of them, Renato Molinaro, had been her boyfriend two years before. She knew him well, she was still fond of him. In those days she knew the other one, Pino Rizzardi, because he went about with Renato.

As is their way, the mafiosi made their move with brazen arrogance. Even though they lived in the same town, they acted quite openly, carrying out the shooting at seven in the evening in a busy town centre street. Usually, as if by some enchantment, *omertà* and impunity are on their side. But this time the spell was broken. A crack opened in the enchanted sleep of the fairytale village. Could Rosetta have been impelled to testify by the shock of a memory of love and tenderness stridently evoked in the present through a bloodily violent event? 'I remembered him when we were together as nice, gentle, attentive. Then he got involved with a drug crowd . . .'[60]

Her decision was undoubtedly strengthened by her direct acquaintance with the protagonists, with the murderers, but also with the victims. In her interview with Sandra Bonsanti, Rosetta explains: 'And then the *maresciallo's* murder at that very moment when he had only just waved to me, and he was smiling and serene, maybe not even realizing what was happening to him. How could I go on keeping this vileness to myself? I felt the need to unburden myself, I started asking for advice and telephoning the Aversas' son.'

But the hitmen had also recognized Rosetta (as, probably, they had been recognized by and likewise remarked other passers-by). Usually straightforward administrative matters in a world under the mafia thumb. In fact, her ex-boyfriend turned up to see Rosetta. In the girl's statement to the District Prosecutor's office she spoke of 'successive meetings with Renato, who stopped in front of the Automobile Club office where she worked, in an insistent manner, slowing down his car and looking inside; and the later meeting in a sandwich bar with the aforesaid Renato who came up to her and told her "not to talk too much if she wanted to go on breathing" '.[61]

In the stage monologue 'Woman of Honour', Rosa Masciopinto has Rosetta say:

> I could be wrong, I said to myself. When you're frightened everything is bigger, everything is ghastly. Then they threatened me. It was like flinging a fear of responsibility into that fear, into my fear. A fear of choice. Of separating the better part of something from the worst part. Separating my courage from my fear. They're both in the same place. Courage is a feeling of the heart.[62]

Renato's was a counterproductive move, a further shock perhaps for Rosetta to see the Prince Charming of memory as none other than the ice-cold bully of the present.

> Now he was there with the gunmen. I had told myself: he just happened to be there, passing by, he's not a bad person. Then, in the days that followed, he came and threatened me: say nothing, otherwise . . . keep your mouth shut, or else . . . And that was when I decided to talk, because I thought of the harm they could do to my brothers . . . I wanted to protect my brothers.[63]

To begin with Rosetta deliberately put the investigations off the track, and she is honest about this. 'When she opened up on the telephone a few days after the crime, first of all to Paolo, the Aversas' younger son, then to the investigators, she only partially spoke the truth and even lied to deflect the investigations from Molinaro.'[64]

In the days following the crime Rosetta's decision to rebel came to a head. When I think of the terrible days she must have gone through, I can picture a confused sense of rebellion, a *no* to her injured memory, to the *omertà* of this environment, to the killers' threats, to her family upbringing.

> I spoke out because it was horrible, it is horrible that they murder so many people in Calabria. In '85 they killed an uncle of mine, Pino Cerminara, who got caught in crossfire. Ever since, I've thought it was a pointless way to die. For all Calabrians. . . . When I decided to speak out, at the end of January, I told my dad Michele and my mother Teresa. We'd always been more like friends than parents and daughter. I would tell them everything. I said: I got a good look at Aversa's murderers. What should I do? Their first answer was: what you feel you should do. Then caution and fear entered into it. My family, Calabrian families, often teach their children: mind your own business. I transgressed. I disobeyed. I've been the ruin of my family, they're now compelled to live like outlaws, far away from Calabria, under surveillance. My mother, my father, my two brothers.

Everything's over, they've lost their home, their two shops, their work, people close to them, their friends, everything. We live under permanent surveillance.[65]

Rosetta's story is totally exceptional. In that moment which for ever marked her life and that of her close relatives, Rosetta was an ordinary witness, a 'free' citizen, with no family ties either to the victims or the executioners. She was like me, like everyone. Each and every one of us could find ourselves in a similar situation. It is a hard thought to bear. 'In spite of all our history of struggle against the mafia, thinking about what Rosetta did, thinking it over, I'm not sure I would have been as brave as her. What she did is really something very big.'[66]

As far as I know, before her there was only one other case of voluntary testimony by an ordinary citizen in a mafia killing: the travelling salesman who was an eyewitness in the murder of Judge Livatino, who had radically to change his life, his work, habits, relationships and place of residence after his testimony.

'Those who have lived in mafia lands', Graziella Priulla wrote in *L'Unità*, 'know the weight of everyday life; they know that when the spotlights are turned off, the effects remain and last. That when the initial burst of interest dies down, the sense of things loses its original sharpness, alignments dissolve and people are left alone with their questions and their splits from others. A void is created around the protagonists.'

Hannah Arendt's words come to mind: 'Only good is deep and can be radical.' Good and evil, life and death: Rosetta's action forces us to look at ourselves in the mirror, to ask ourselves uncomfortable questions. 'Each one of us women could have been in your place that evening,' wrote some women in an open letter to Rosetta. Rosetta speaks for herself. And this is what is exceptional about her, on reflection this is precisely what is shocking. Rosetta is not moved by any vendetta, nor does she enact any mourning through her actions.

> Rosetta is . . . unprecedented because she is not moved by something maternal . . . Rosetta speaks for herself, she does not have to demand justice and satisfaction for the grief and mourning of others. She speaks out because she saw something and does a reckoning with herself, she speaks out and alters her life for ever, from this moment on. . . . Thinking about Rosetta also means giving thought to the meaning of the mafia for those inside, for those who withdraw from it, for those who are outside it.[67]

I believe that the break with the obvious, the break with habitual patterns that was produced by Rosetta's resounding action, was a source of scandal, scandal at two distinct but interactive levels.

On the one hand there was the reaction of the community, of the people who knew Rosetta, or perhaps didn't personally know her. Silence, maybe even embarrassment. 'Not even the parish priest [showed his face] with whom we spent so much time, in the apostolic groups and in the parish work with drug addicts.'[68]

This silence from 'her' Lamezia, from 'her' Calabria, is a bitter wound for the young woman, representing a point of contradiction in her experience. Rosetta confided to the journalist Sandra Bonsanti:

> There hasn't been a single friendly voice to reach me from Lamezia in these months. Never, nobody. And I believe that nobody will want to be involved in what I am living through. . . . I believe that everybody in my town is on my side, but they won't admit it. . . . So many people know and won't talk, I believe that an awful lot of them saw what I saw. But nobody has talked. And I am very frightened.

Very frightened, indeed, probably everybody who has anything to do with this murder, or with other similar murders, is very frightened. Speaking out against *omertà* seems easy and obvious. Yet I share what Donatella Mauro expressed in a solidarity meeting for Rosetta Cerminara: 'This subject needs a lot of attention, because I don't know how far *omertà* goes when you realize that speaking means dying.'[69]

Embarrassment and silence are, I believe, so many spies of a deep dread, and can also be read in terms of a defence mechanism whose aim is to distance from us the challenge which Rosetta, even in spite of herself, throws down. As in a checkmate, Rosetta's move has cut off our avenues of retreat; it becomes impossible to count ourselves out, to maintain that we are not involved, that this was yet again, for the nth time, a settling of scores 'between them'. 'And if we stop and think for a moment, the realism of it is appalling, and so it is, and I think that our long silence is also because of our incapacity to speak about this action, because it is so stunning we've been left without words.'[70]

But it should also be said that this appalling initial silence has gradually lessened. There have been gestures of solidarity, letters and postcards to the President of the Republic, activities in schools and so on. Perhaps Rosetta has not been left altogether alone.

I talked about two distinct but interactive levels of reaction. The other is the level of reaction of those who have no interest in things changing. I'm thinking of the defence's explicit insinuations during the trial, but I'm thinking also of common sense. Common sense, whatever is most comfortable and simple to think when we are confronted by somewhat upsetting and difficult problems, is deeply imbued with the male symbolic order which marks our history and our society.

The male perspective on the social and on us has moulded what common sense 'has always' known, which is to say that women are emotional, unreliable, irrational, passionate and vengeful.

A woman in a courtroom is, first and foremost, a female body, an obstruction on the straight road of the search for 'their' truth. The defence tried to insinuate that Rosetta invented everything as revenge for a betrayal in love.

> Her testimony is deeply felt, tortured, with the anguish of her feelings coming through very clearly: 'I didn't love him any more,' she says, 'but I was still fond of him.' . . . Questions came at her thick and fast, some of them out-and-out trick questions, a tough confrontation, no holds barred. The state's lawyer, representing the Ministry of the Interior, complains: 'This is an attempt to destroy the witness psychologically!' And from the defence benches they reply: 'And what if it is?'[71]

A comparison has been made between the trial for the murder of the Aversas and a rape trial, because the prosecution witness, Rosetta, was transformed from accuser into accused. This is exactly what happens in rape trials: the violence suffered is transformed into guilt, the original guilt of the female body. There is a common denominator in the disavowal of the head and the heart which, along with that obstructive body, makes this witness a woman.

A systematic disavowal of the 'civil', ethical aspects of a woman who assumes the freedom (and perhaps it is this that is most scandalous) to denounce the violence suffered, whether as a body or as a moral being, as an individual among other individuals.

A disavowal of the emotions. And where is it written that the emotions are less true than the cold, rational calculation which seems to be the principal motive of the pitiless executions carried out by mafia hitmen?

Rosetta has given us a lesson about this too. With the intelligence of her emotions, all alone she held up throughout the long cross-examinations intent on discrediting her.

The gentlemen of the mafia did not expect this. They gave vent to their fury over the corpse of their victim, desecrating the Superintendent's grave and burning his coffin. The first trial was annulled on the grounds of technicalities, the Public Prosecutor resigned after receiving death threats.

Rosetta did not give way, but at what a cost!

> These days . . . I am left with no one. From time to time I go home, by 'home' I mean the house where my parents now live, the last time I was taken there was three months ago. . . . Yes, perhaps this is a possible wish, I would like to be remembered for who I was and not for who they say I am at the trial, so that not even those who were my friends know me and take their words back. I often weep. I hope I have the strength to go on.[72]

Rosetta Cerminara's life and that of her whole family was turned upside-down:

> My life has changed enormously, I had a fairly normal life. In the mornings I
> would drive to work and in the afternoons I would be at my mother's or my
> father's shop, then on Sundays I would go to football matches and spend my
> time at the stadium. Now I'm not living, because I'm in a hotel. All I do is think
> about what can happen to me, about what my family will have to face, about
> all the problems we will have to deal with. I'm in a state of armed siege.[73]

Meanwhile, the trial began for the second time before the Court of Assizes
at Catanzaro. Despite everything, Rosetta testified and stuck to her version of
things. But she was tired and disheartened. Even in this case the institutions
did not seem equal to what was demanded of them, they seemed weak in
their protection of the witness, just when the all-pervasiveness of the mafia
threat and the exemplary nature of this trial demanded a commitment of a
different order. Answering a question about why she had failed to appear
when called on an earlier occasion, Rosetta said:

> Because I am stressed, because I can't cope any more with coming here, because
> I am repeating the same things for the fourth time. The first time at the pre-
> liminary hearing which was annulled, then at the cross-examinations, which
> were also disqualified, both times because of technicalities. And now I am here
> again to repeat what I have already said which is what I saw, always the same.
> And I am not even believed. What's the point in me coming here? . . . It doesn't
> seem to me that I am treated as a witness.[74]

Treated as a witness . . . in this unequal struggle Rosetta has taken on the
most uncomfortable and simultaneously the most important role. Materially
and symbolically she has taken up the highest challenge to mafia domination:
by testifying publicly she is cracking open the mafiosi's customary impunity
and embodying the possibility of breaking the vicious circle of the violent
hold over people which makes the mafia invisible, cancelling out the possibility of bearing witness to its existence.

> The systematic and implacable suppression of the witness is the most obvious
> (though not the only) aspect of this organizational characteristic of the *cosca*; it
> seems to have incorporated within itself a conscious and extremely stubborn
> line of defence against the 'repressive interference' of public forces. And more:
> in pursuit of this it has instigated a mechanism and a reliability of application
> which are eminently akin to the state's. In fact in striking with thorough and
> implacable severity at every 'informer', the organization established the univer-
> sality of a norm: the *certainty of the sanction*, it could be said. Therefore exactly the

same certainty that the state was unable to guarantee in the work of crushing criminals or in the action of defending and protecting citizens who took on the burden of testimony.[75]

But it is not only the institutions which seem culpably weak, it is the whole of Calabria's civil society in this case which appears forgetful, absent-minded, incapable of giving the attention and the solidarity which Rosetta deserves. At this point the political forces were pursuing the mayoral elections in the various local councils, the women were nowhere to be seen, the associations likewise. There prevails a tragic incomprehension of the fact that Rosetta is there, suffering, giving testimony, standing her ground for all of us, at any rate for that part of society which identifies itself with the ideals of freedom.

Rosetta represents hope, the force of the emotions and the intellect against the forces of evil, the potential of eros against thanatos – yet it would seem that we have still not realized this.

But will *her* life have a future? 'I think about the future all the time, and I'm frightened because I don't know what I'm heading for. I'm so frightened,' Rosetta said in the interview with Sandra Bonsanti.

Paul Celan wrote in one of his poems: 'Nobody / bears witness / for the witness.' The scene of the crime that evening was crowded, yet nobody observed Rosetta, just as nobody saw the murderers. Only the presence of the dead could not be denied.

Rosetta Cerminara has given us hope; we would like to be able to give it back to her, we would like to send her strength for living and, most of all, for enjoying life. We would like to become all of us witnesses to her testimony.

Postscript

In mid-January 1994 the trial concluded, in the first instance, with a life sentence for Rizzardi and a twenty-five-year prison sentence for Molinaro. The day after the sentencing, the state awarded Rosetta Cerminara a silver medal for civilian valour.

More than a year later, on appeal, the accused were acquitted and Rosetta's testimony was deemed false. Subsequently, in January 1996, the Court of Cassation overruled all of these judgments, compelling a retrial.

PART II

Women with the Mafia

6

Emancipation?

Estrangement and complicity

We know very little about the women who live in mafia families or are, at various levels, involved in mafia criminality. Moreover, the sources are distorted: those inside do not speak, those who come out focus above all on certain subjects: making the break, bereavement and feelings of revenge.

There must be very many ways of being and feeling, there must be very many different levels of involvement, in the mafia universe. Nella Condorelli remarks: 'Of all the women I've met who are variously connected with mafia business, on my travels all over Sicily as a reporter on women's issues, I've yet to meet any two who were the same. In terms of education or literacy, emancipation or subordination to their own social condition. In the feudal mafia of old this complexity did not exist.'[1]

It is as if, paradoxically, we were living in the same society at the same time, but were caught up in radically different systems and discursive and legitimating orders. Our official language, the language of broadcasting, newspapers, cinema and education (for those actually attending schools), is the same, giving us all the same cultural models. What differs is the way in which these models are assimilated, absorbed and made personal. What is different, in my view, is the way in which we perceive ourselves in relation to others, the ways in which we perceive prohibitions and freedom, our ways of locating ourselves in time and space.

If the formal, official language is the same for all of us women, the language of intimacy, the 'mother tongue' – the one in which we talk about our victories and defeats, our fears, joys and desires – seems profoundly different. As we have already seen, the mafia universe is a closed, hermetic world. 'The mafia is an organization "of otherness" ... in relation to society; its legitimacy resides solely in violence, and *omertà* is correlated only with violence in so far as this is imposed upon the rest of the society through terror. Codes of honour and *omertà* are values that are internal to the sectarian group.'[2]

In other words, *civil society*, awareness of rights and restraints and a person's various subjective aspirations, on the one hand, and the *mafia ethos*, with its loyalties, hierarchies, ambitions and prohibitions on the other, represent essentially different contexts, even though they overlap in space and time. If we think about society as a whole this observation appears self-evident in some respects. If we think about single individuals and their subjective perceptions, their everyday life, the decisions they have or don't have to take, this doubling is perhaps something as yet little explored. 'Within an organized-crime family, authority – that is, legitimated power – does exist. There is a sense of legitimacy that permits the family to organize power into a hierarchical pattern, so that some members hold authority roles and others do not.'[3]

The intimate context for the actions, feelings and modes of perception of the women who inhabit the mafia ethos seems to me a central question if we are to investigate the relevance of the concept of emancipation against this background.

The belief in legality which, according to Max Weber, is the basis for legitimate power in modern societies, 'derives from the relation arising between modes of legitimation internal to the person and those assured externally. . . . In other words faith in legality comes from the coexistence of traditions, interests, ideals, religious experiences and the law.'[4] We need to reflect on the weight exercised by informal mafia control on personal perceptions of the individual's democratic rights and duties and at the same time on how much historical circumstances and cultural traditions have the effect of modifying the boundaries between legality and illegality.

The mafia has always proved adept at responding to the cultural universe of broad strata of the population, making itself a surrogate for the presence of the state and acting in parallel. 'Just as the presence of the state in Sicily is weakening, the level of conflict is raised. . . . The state/mafia dialogue both at high and low levels between the two orders plainly shows that Cosa Nostra is not anti-state, but rather an organization which aims to exploit the distortions of economic development.'[5] In these conditions, faith in legality develops diverse forms of skewed vision. The displacement between formal legality and merit is such that it is taken for granted that nowadays the lowest social groupings are liable actually to acquire 'a faith in illegality'.[6]

Economic achievement, an important yardstick for the attainment of status, becomes increasingly fetishized as opportunities for professional achievement are increasingly lacking. Faith in legality is not and cannot be divisible from the material conditions of the subjects' self-affirmation within the social. 'The only, and the most attractive, way of finding a shortcut to self-recognition is the excursion into illegality. If this works it enables both a rapid integration into the world of the comfortably off, and – most importantly – the expression of one's own potential and one's own personality, which are otherwise "ignobly" repressed by the dominant society.'[7]

In this context, the meaning I want to give to the concepts of legality and illegality refer not merely to the social actions of the self and of others (stealing, killing, etc.), but also, and most particularly, to individual rights, civil rights and the subjective perception of these rights. What are the boundaries between legality and illegality with reference to a woman's body, a woman's head, a woman's heart? And what of the women themselves? What perceptions do they have of the freedom and/or unfreedom which characterizes their lives, day and night?

Reverberating around faith in legality is a sense of belonging, a cultural identity and, not least, the gender identity of each man or woman. Analysing the proceedings of a trial at Palermo in the eighteenth century, Giovanna Fiume highlights the conflict between reforming, enlightened magistrates and the deep-rooted culture of the people. This 'estrangement from judicial institutions' discovered in those proceedings does not seem so far from the alienation still felt today by many citizens when facing the authority of the state and its institutions. 'Our characters are unable to defend themselves nor do they understand exactly what it is they must defend themselves against. Justice places in a different order of discourse and in a different system of meaning an action which finds its own context in a cultural universe that is altogether different, and where the concepts of legality and illegality have no place.'[8]

How far the idea of 'estrangement' is relevant and contemporary is shown by an episode that took place during Angela Casella's pilgrimage to Aspromonte in search of her abducted son. During a meeting with local women in the village of San Luca, a young girl handed out a letter she had written to Cesare's kidnappers.

> I join this mother in her grief and her fear . . . my humble appeal echoes the voice of that healthy part of civil society which is the majority . . . release him! Give the son back to the mother. I am the daughter of Arcangelo Messineo and I, my mother and brothers are suffering the same fear as this mother, Signora Casella, because as I think everyone now knows, my father too is the victim of a kidnap, but a more painful and humiliating kidnap because he has been kidnapped by the law.[9]

Her father, needless to say, was at that time in prison, suspected of involvement in a kidnapping.

My understanding of the role of women in the mafia is that it takes place within an oscillation between estrangement and complicity. Subordination and submission are closely compounded by a more or less conscious perception of women's own vital importance to the functioning of the mafia as such. Subordinated and deprived of individual freedoms, deprived of civil rights, but at the same time abstractly venerated as custodians of honour and respectability, and materially recompensed by the indirect reflection of their men's mafioso power – only thus can and must women exist inside the mafia universe. The mafia cannot do without them and yet can only make use of them by denying them the right to individuality.

Well before it is felt or perceived by the women themselves, *estrangement* from the mafia is what the Honoured Society has decreed for them, translating a profound distrust into a formal prohibition of membership. Estrangement is simultaneously potential and *de facto*.

Complicity, the age-old feminine vice, has the ambiguous seductiveness implied in Zerlina's *Vorrei, ma non vorrei* ('I'd like to but I dare not') to Don Giovanni; being there, making the most of opportunities, but without taking any responsibility. A shortfall in individuation, an accommodation with subordination. The illusion of the easy way out, the line of least psychic resistance – an illusion, precisely that.

Complicity can also be born of the attraction to a violent man, it lurks in the myth of the anti-hero. Antonino Calderone relates:

> Women are drawn to the mafia. Until they are stung by grief and the appalling things that happen in Cosa Nostra they have a very good life inside it. Mafiosi are sexually attractive. I can't forget that time we went somewhere around Enna to meet a big shot who'd been on the run and hiding out for thirty years. . . . We went to a restaurant for dinner . . . and there was a woman coming in and out of the building bringing us the dishes. She was the owner's wife. When she saw us she exclaimed: 'Aaaah! What a lot of handsome mafiosi I've got here today! What a delight to see all these handsome young men in the mafia! Come here so that I can give you all a kiss!'[10]

There are many situations in our society where women are torn between estrangement and complicity. In the abstract this conflict as such and the individual responsibilities which follow from it do not appear to be specific only to women in the mafia sphere. As wives, but also as daughters, sisters and mothers, women often give credibility to the shady activities of their men, particularly when these take place behind a façade of respectability.

But there is something specific to the mafia condition, a dilemma of sorts, which makes existential choices more radical, which makes inner anguish more acute, and which in the end has the effect of stimulating the faculty of putting up with things. This is the infection of death, it is the totalitarian hold over people, the categorical imperative, the cowardly subterfuge, the humdrum resolution of every conflict; it is the threat of violent death that hangs over women's lives too in the mafia setting.

I would suggest that within the mafia environment itself there are different frames of reference for men and women as regards action, thought and feeling. Once again the dividing line is violence, the violence of death. When he was interviewed for the Marisa Bellisario Foundation research on *Women and the Mafia*, Franco Cazzola maintained:

> The fact is that mafia power is male power, precisely because it is extremely violent. But this force of male destruction comes up against and – it seems to me – clashes with that 'purposeful' sense of solidarity which is very strong in women. Which means that the conflict is between the sense of wider (more feminine) solidarity and the sense of clan solidarity which reproduces the violent mafioso power of the male.[11]

The story of Giacoma Filipello, one of the first *pentite*, seems very pertinent here. Giacoma was the partner of Natale L'Ala, the Trapanese killed in 1990. Her complicity and 'collusion' with mafioso power seem indisputable and she admitted this herself. But her story also conveys an experience which ranks her with the many women who, in Cazzola's words, 'are the hidden everyday victims of mafia power by the mere fact of living in those nuclei of "violated" solidarity'.

So let us listen to Giacoma:

> I loved Natale, but I know today that I spent twenty-five years of hell. For me that life was irresistible . . . [but then] it was hell. We became wary, I spent long periods shut up at home. . . . I couldn't cope with seeing all those corpses any more. The cruelty. Wives without husbands, mothers waiting for their children to grow up so they could have their revenge. . . . They were years of fear and terror. . . . I was scared stiff, I was afraid for him and for myself. I would have liked to break that circle of violence, but if I had done it when Natale was still alive, he wouldn't have understood. He would have thrown me out, or I would have had to leave. And I loved him.[12]

Businesswomen, front women, intermediaries

At this point we must ask ourselves whether the very concept of female *emancipation*, and the aspirations and utopia connected with it, can be reconciled with the underworld, with the 'world apart' of the mafia.

The idea of emancipation has a history; it is constantly being redefined, swinging and twisting and settling between two shores. On one of these emancipation implies the process of individuation, denoting female individuality as something acquired and not as a mere family role defined solely in relation to others. On the other, female emancipation is thought of as a specific valuing of the quality of motherhood which functions as a base for a new self-valuation for women, socially and collectively. Equality, which is based on each individual's full individuality, is conjugated with difference, whose value derives from the psycho-physical potential for mothering.

Historically, it is the conquest of *individuality* which is at the centre of women's struggles for their emancipation. 'Not even in its most purely liberal suffragist strand does the demand for equality ever rule out the recognition of difference between the sexes. . . . The British suffragists never regard equality as synonymous with sameness: indeed their difficulty is that they affirm difference while fighting against inequality.'[13]

From praxis is born thought which, in its turn, influences praxis. Women's way of situating themselves and perceiving themselves – what we could call mothering thought – is precisely the fruit of that ambivalence which marks female experience in our society. The sense of omnipotence which accompanies the experience of motherhood is closely interwoven with the everyday experience of female powerlessness in the social and in the public sphere. The two strands – equality and difference – still do not easily intersect.

Sara Ruddick has made a substantial theoretical commitment to developing what can be defined as *maternal thinking*.

> I speak about a mother's *thought* – the intellectual capacities she develops, the judgments she makes, the metaphysical attitudes she assumes, the values she affirms. A mother engages in a discipline. That is, she asks certain questions rather than others; establishes criteria for the truth, adequacy, and relevance of proposed answers; and cares about the findings she makes and can act upon. . . .
> To describe the capacities, judgments, metaphysical attitudes, and values of maternal thought does not presume maternal achievement. It is to describe a *conception* of achievement, the end to which maternal efforts are directed, conceptions and ends quite different from dominant public ones. . . . I am not saying that mothers, individually or collectively, are (or are not) especially wonderful people. My point is that out of maternal practices distinctive ways of conceptualizing, ordering and valuing arise. We *think* differently about what it *means* and what it takes to be 'wonderful', to be a person, to be real.[14]

Sara Ruddick's thinking can help us to understand the extent to which the enforced and rigid stereotyping of the figure of the mother in mafia iconography remains remote from the prospect of maternity as an expression of female freedom.

Women in public life as mothers – women in private life as individuals: this dialectic is hard to reconcile, a conjoining of constellations which, half accomplished, opens the way to constrictive ideologizing and constricted freedom. Only the simultaneous recognition and realization of individual freedom and maternal specificity contain the promise of happiness, linked to the utopia of emancipation. However it may be, emancipation is indivisible from self-determination and female freedom.

Here, very summarily, lies the historical/conceptual horizon of the idea of female emancipation.

It is female ambivalence in relation to both of these thorny issues which, together with the male tendency to counterpose mothers and women, has contributed to the formation of 'the woman question'. Rather than being mothers in the social sphere and individuals in the family, at the best of times women are mothers in the family and individuals in the sphere outside the family; at the worst of times they are mothers in the family and nothing more. A reductive version of the concept of emancipation allows women an incursion into professional and political life outside the family, while solidly maintaining their fundamental function within it.

As I have tried to demonstrate in the first part of this study, mafia organization and the everyday practice of mafioso conduct as a rule confine female space to the domestic sphere. Yet, while sticking to the absolute principle of the subordination of the women of the family to the men of the family and at the same time of all members of the family to the authority of the Family, meaning Cosa Nostra, in its evolution from feudal to market economy and high-level financial transactions, the mafia also uses women in the non-domestic sphere.

'The mafia organization continues to be masculinist, power continues to be in the hands of the men, but for some years now women have begun to have an active role not only as drug pushers, but also as traffickers,' Anna Puglisi explained in an interview.[15]

News coverage and evidence that comes up in trials throw light on how mafia women's role 'outside the family' is taking shape.

Of the 474 accused in the maxi-trial, four were women. This is not many, but their presence as accused is frequently interpreted as a significant sign of a change taking place. Let us look at them.

Anna Colizzi, who lived in Turin but originally came from Puglia, and was engaged to a cocaine and heroin trafficker, was accused of having made her villa in Sicily available to be used as a heroin refinery; she is connected to Buscetta and through him to Gerlando Alberti.

Antonietta Giustolisi, a Sicilian and the wife of a 'respected member' of the Catania clan, was accused of having given refuge in her Rome apartment to notable fugitives from justice, like Nitto Santapaola; as intercepted telephone conversations show, she ordered *camicie*, that is kilos of drugs, and took care of payments and deliveries.

Anna Ianni, an Abruzzese and the wife of another trafficker, was accused of having made her living room in Rome available as a clearing house for international drug trafficking; she was a member of a Rome gang that imported huge quantities of drugs from Thailand in 1980.

Carmela Migliara, a Sicilian, was accused of hiding in her Caltanissetta house her cousin Giuseppe Madonia, a boss and fugitive from the law, hitman in the Captain Basile murder.[16]

At different levels all four have shown a degree of involvement in illegal trafficking, which is proved by intercepted telephone calls, although subsequently they were all either discharged, found not guilty or amnestied. In each case the 'domestic sphere' has a bearing on the nature of the crime: the woman's home, place of residence or 'living room' turned to use as a strategic site of wrongdoing. A vision of home that is a long way from the mafia stereotype of the respectable house, with the wife who is only a housewife and 'knows nothing'.

Undeniably, their presumed illegal activity has partial connotations of work outside the family, even if the physical and interpersonal context is still the family and the home.

Besides the four accused in the maxi-trial, crime reporting in the daily newspapers tells of many other women who are either accused or suspects in mafia activities: most are front women and intermediaries of various kinds, a few are businesswomen involved in shady dealing.

Gianfranco Manfredi writes:

> We still have no way of knowing whether these are hangers-on, weak links in the mafia chain, or second strings to the bosses. What is certain is that in Calabria we are witnessing the disturbing phenomenon of women's entry into mafia activities. . . . Caterina Corse, an office worker, is suspected of being the 'telephone caller' for the gang that kidnapped the pharmacist at Montebello Ionico. . . . At San Luca, Maria Strangio was arrested along with her husband and other accomplices, while laundering a hundred million in dirty money, with the purchase of building plots in tourist areas.[17]

Also in Calabria recent newspaper coverage presents two other women active in the criminal businesses of the 'ndrangheta: Giuseppa and Caterina Condello, respectively wife and sister of the boss Nino Imerti, also known as 'Nanu Feroce'. From intercepted telephone calls it emerges that Giuseppa was in constant contact with her husband when he was on the run (Imerti was arrested in 1993). One name that keeps coming up in these conversations is that of the young, go-getting Caterina, known also as 'Junior'. In the provisional custody order of the Reggio Calabria Tribunal, in November 1990, the judges wrote:

> Giuseppa Condello does not limit her own role to that of enforced and unwilling participant in Imerti's illegal activities; she is actively involved, and her function is by no means a superficial one; in all the criminal operations of the organization, and specifically: A) in her contacts and connections with her own

114

family . . . B) in preparing and carrying out acts of extortion. . . . . Caterina Condello, otherwise 'Junior'. Her role is fundamental within the organization. There is practically no sphere of the group's activity which does not involve the energetic operational skills of 'Junior' . . . 1. Basic logistic support . . . 2. Co-extortionist . . . 3. Front woman for Imerti . . .[18]

The same phenomenon can be observed in Sicily:

The screen of a woman manager with her down-to-earth, energetic dealings on the telephone over the sale and dispatch of large quantities of varnishes to Italian and foreign customers, functioned as a perfect cover for the true activities of 'Sicilpierre' . . . the firm's owner . . . set up a convincing and high-profile operation in order to hide the illegal activities . . . of her brother Salvatore and her cousin Francesco . . . but was first and foremost a cover for her partner.[19]

And there is more. In the charges of the Palermo judges, incidentally, we can find details of the contract of sale for the estate of Prince Francesco Lanza di Scalea, which was heavily in debt:

Well now, Salvatore Graziano is accused, in these proceedings, of mafia associations, and the buyers represented by him are 1) . . . , 2) . . . , 3) . . . , 4) . . . , 5) Gaetana Riccobono, wife of Antonino Porcelli, an influential member of the Patanna Mondello family and cousin of Rosario Riccobono, representative of the same family; 6) Maria Spatola, sister of Bartolomeo Spatola, long-since identified as a mafia member . . . ; 7) Rosalia Di Trapani, wife of Salvatore Lo Piccolo, who is charged with mafia association in these proceedings.[20]

Or this: Nicolò Maugeri turns out to be the owner of numerous vehicles, some of them armoured, among them 'a Jaguar 4200, registration MI 99837M, in the name of his wife, Anna Finocchiaro'.[21]

The function of front woman, which is now widespread among the wives, sisters, sisters-in-law and daughters of mafiosi, is both to connect with the substantial wealth which is produced by drug trafficking and with the way that assets are made more public in the wake of the La Torre law.*

If there is a possibility of any of these front women having done what she did lightly or in the belief that her husband's or relatives' activities were quite legal, it is hardly credible that all of these women . . . set up as the owners of companies or the purchasers of buildings on their own account or on the account

---

* The Rognoni–La Torre law of 1982 for the first time permitted legal access to mafia assets passed on through family business connections and allowed their confiscation. [Trs.]

of relatives who cannot come into the open because of being the object of court proceedings, should have been so lacking in awareness and so naive as to have had no suspicions about the source of the capital which their relatives appeared suddenly to have available to them.[22]

The business of being a front woman can also be regarded as work outside the family, because it implies an individual legal responsibility in the public sphere. Yet the family connection, and subordination to whoever in reality is the active subject to whom a name is being lent, seem to be the principal features of this function.

The diverse businesses of being a go-between or a cover in illegal mafia trafficking in general, although of lesser and subordinate status, none the less are evidence of an active involvement by women, even beyond the strictly familial sphere. In taking on these functions women have autonomous legal agencies whereby they assume responsibility for them. One bitterly satirical text denounces this situation:

> Inside these thriving multinational families the satisfaction of the two sexes is complete and wisely balanced. It may be that feminism has never seen the light of day in these parts, but here the role of woman is fully esteemed. The time-honoured custodian of the hearth has become the wise administrator of the family nest-egg and, contrary to what is rumoured, it is often a woman in whose hands and thoughts the effective management of the most reckless enterprises lies. A silent revolution, without any slogans or hysteria. It's true, there are cases of rape, violence that is the product of a heightened, overbearing machismo, kidnappings thought up in sanguine high spirits, but this happens everywhere. What does not happen anywhere else is this affirmation by a woman that she has been able to combine the virtues of an exemplary wife and mother with her talents as protectress of the fortunes of the Family Firm. From these roots of wholesome, generous attachments can be born the most luxuriant plants, the tallest of trees.[23]

The activities of Giuseppina Falletta Cordovana went far beyond those of front woman. She was accused of having handled and mediated bribes between elected councillors and bureaucrats of the Sicilian region and a Roman entrepreneur connected with Francesco Pazienza. 'Unscrupulous methods, charm and a great deal of professional agility made the fortune of this woman who towards the end of 1982 entered the circle of the Member of Parliament Stornello. She was, one might say, completely at home in the regional administration . . .'[24]

Even the faked kidnapping of the bankrupt Sindona was awash with female involvement, 'for love and for gain'.[25] It was a woman who agreed to hide him in her house at Palermo during the bogus kidnapping, and it was another Palermo woman who acted as go-between in some of the financial transactions at that time.

How is this new reality to be reconciled with the vision of women conveyed by mafioso words, above all by the explicit prohibition on women joining Cosa Nostra? Are there mafia women or not? Can women aspire to some 'equality' in a mafia career, some 'emancipation' within their own world?

One way of understanding the apparent contradiction between the mafia ruling that excludes women and the emergence of certain activities which point to female careers inside the mafia is indicated by certain concepts formulated by Salvatore Lupo, who in turn, refers to Alan Block. Given the importance of these concepts to my argument as a whole, I quote at length:

> We have two different models of organization; we can read these on the basis of the dialectic proposed by Alan Block for the New York situation, between power syndicate and enterprise syndicate, the first 'essentially extortion-oriented, rather than business-oriented', the second 'operating in the domain of illegal businesses like prostitution, gambling, smuggling and drugs'. In Palermo, the label 'power syndicate' can be given to the territorial structure of the families, with their rigid affiliations, formidable long standing, their military strength and therefore their capacity to develop on the basis of functioning vicariously as guardians of public order through the extortion-protection circuit; by contrast the enterprise syndicate is the much more mobile business network which was taking shape as long ago as the last century in the interests of smuggling and cattle stealing, and which now runs the drug and tobacco trade. The fact that the same *cosca* activists are involved in these networks does not invalidate the distinction either conceptually or empirically; Buscetta explains how the families limit themselves to giving their members 'permission' to participate in the various illegal businesses. In any case the network cannot be entirely mafioso; into it come Americans, Neapolitans and adventurers, types from Tangier, Marseille and *women* [my emphasis], men of honour and dishonour, embezzlers and bankers.[26]

In an interview with Giovanna Fiume, where he was asked about the role of women drug couriers, Giovanni Falcone clarified: 'But that is something else! In international drug trafficking we find women, foreigners and so on. Men of honour are also involved in those organizations, but they are intermediate organizations which have nothing to do with Cosa Nostra.'[27]

That is, women are not admitted to the secret mafia organization, to the hard core of power (the power syndicate), while, in common with other groups, although on an individual basis, they can participate in its economic and financial offshoots (the enterprise syndicate). This is the emancipation of making one's way in (illegal) working life, not making one's way inside the mafia.

Mafiosa? No, just a wife

In May 1983 the first section of the Palermo Tribunal, which had been given responsibility for preventive measures with regard to socially dangerous persons, and was presided over by Michele Mezzatesta, with assisting judges Salvatore Scaduti and Giovanni Perrino, gave two judgments which were controversial at the time and which still give pause for thought.

By a line of reasoning which applied in both cases it was deemed that there were no grounds for a prison sentence being imposed on Francesca Citarda, wife of the boss Giovanni Bontade and daughter of the boss Matteo Citarda, and likewise, that there were no grounds for proceeding with the annulment of the mortgage taken out on assets for Anna Maria Di Bartolo, the wife of the construction firm owner Domenico Federico who was connected to the Bontade mafia clan.

Why, after having recognized the objective involvement, so to speak, of both the accused women, did the judges fully acquit them in the end? The explanation is as summary as it is disturbing: the accused are women, and as such cannot be regarded as responsible for their actions. They acted as subordinates, 'lending' their names to financial and real-estate transactions, whose significance they would not be competent to understand because they are women, Sicilian women, what is more, enveloped in tradition and remote by birth from the temptations of emancipation.

Let us hear some extracts from the judgment absolving Anna Maria Di Bartolo; these are almost identical formulations to those we find in the judgment concerning Francesca Citarda:

The family bond in itself is not enough to identify a mafioso subject, although it can be used to qualify particular behaviour or to facilitate the subject's entry into a mafia-type organization. Nevertheless, it must always be the conduct of the subject in its most diverse behavioural manifestations which should be considered, especially when, because of personal character and attitudes, the customs of a milieu and, even more, the lack of emancipation from traditional male power, the person concerned is structurally held back from taking on an active role in family affairs and at the same time has to be subject to or at least accept the decisions of others.

While we make no claim to enter into a detailed and searching sociological investigation, we can turn our thoughts and powers of observation appropriately to everyday matters in order to judge their intrinsic significance, be it within ever-changing social customs. Counsel does not deem that it can unreservedly state – as is instead proposed – that the woman belonging to a mafia family will as yet have assumed such a degree of emancipation and authority as to free herself of the subaltern and passive role which in the past she had always enacted in relation to her 'man', whether in an equal participation or at any rate with independence and autonomous choice in the affairs which involve the male family 'clan'.

So-called 'mafia women' are too remote ideologically, and in terms of outlook and custom, from the women 'terrorists', who sadly have been active participants in the armed bands which continue to attack the security of the state and the democratic order. Theirs is a different cultural and ideological foundation, as is likewise their involvement and personal conviction as well as what they contribute to the criminal organization.

The latter have often operated in the front line or at any rate have made an independent choice of clandestinity and entry into subversive groups. The former, however, not only from longstanding custom which is logically rooted in the conservative and masculinist concept of the mafioso organization, have so far been by their own wishes kept away from the family 'business' and projects, only going so far as to share in certain 'values', underlining their own omertà and, when required, carrying out those actions which will be in the interests of their male relative and covering up for him.

However, although debatable in moral terms, this conduct does not normally fall within the strictures of penal law, being judged non-punishable. . . .

That Di Bartolo furthermore indirectly profited from the alleged illegal activity of her husband, in the form of a high standard of living or substantial purchased assets held by her spouse in her name, is a situation which, regardless, cannot be credited to any independence in the way she leads her life, although it is objectively dependent on her own 'status' as the spouse of Domenico Federico, a position which is in itself not open to criminal charges or sanctions. . . .

Finally, allowing that even a judgment at a purely circumstantial level of Di Bartolo's involvement in undertakings of a verifiably suspect entrepreneurial nature cannot exclude consideration that it is a widespread social custom, especially in our part of the country, and normally a legal one, to register trading licences or joint interests in commercial business or activities in the name of women, wives in particular. From this, however, there can be no incontrovertible conclusion of the woman's conscious and established involvement in the legal or illegal activities of the company for which she has been called upon by her husband to act as a figurehead, especially when, as is usual, either through lack of basic technical-financial knowledge or through a traditional and innate unfamiliarity with the difficult world of business, it is likely that Di Bartolo left it entirely up to her husband to run the company.[28]

This time the 'bewilderment' which Giovanna Fiume had come across in the relationship between the lower orders and the enlightened judiciary of the eighteenth century seems to be the exclusive province of the judges. If we overlook the judges' bad faith, we must still take seriously the commonplaces they come out with about women, which, as always where common sense is concerned, are a dangerous mixture of truth and falsehood. Let us take a look at the aspects most relevant to our argument.

The Palermo newspaper *L'Ora* debated the judgment under the headline 'Mafiosa? No, just a wife'.[29] Indeed, the judges maintained that women's emancipation has not reached the mafia and that therefore the only female way of being in the mafia is to be a wife. Thus far, in view of my own arguments in this book, I might even agree. In fact, I am convinced that the idea of women's emancipation inside the mafia is a contradiction in terms. However, what is meant by the status of *wife*, in the context of what is lawful or unlawful, is quite a different question.

For the judges, the 'natural' status of wife implies complicity, a complicity that goes far beyond the limits of the lawful, and, most of all, a complicity which is seen as innately feminine, the natural outcome of subordination and thereby not something punishable. In this view of the complicit woman, she appears as a being bereft of any will or responsibility, a parasite of sorts, just short of being mentally defective, to the point where she would succeed in 'reaping financial benefits' without having any 'independently determined way of living', even when she 'lends' her name to diverse economic and financial activities. Even when there is the 'substantial purchase of assets operated in her name by the husband', she remains in the dark. What happens 'in her name' has nothing to do with her. According to the lesson handed down by these judges, criminal complicity is not punishable if it is sanctified by the ideology of the patriarchal family. Alas, here, the administration of the law runs up against a deplorable female 'flaw' under the good offices of mafia interests.

We are not told how these judges manage to respect constitutional precepts and the founding idea of our democratic order which puts all citizens on the same level, when they take for granted – in a judgment, not bar-room chitchat – the 'natural and traditional unfamiliarity with the difficult world of business', which is ascribed to women. With this dangerous affirmation there then arises a justification for men having women – especially their wives – register trading licences, real estate, finance companies and diverse enterprises. All of this in the name of a 'social custom which is very widespread, especially in our part of the country'(!).

Rather than a warning to men to give greater respect to the judicial person of their own wives, as should be expected from judges, what we find here is a direct and flagrant invitation for them to continue exploiting this subjection.

This judgment does not represent the only occasion on which the debate about the role of women in the mafia has touched the objective 'complicities' of the judicial order – such as it is – with female criminality in the mafia context. Commenting on the role of Antonietta Bagarella Riina, throughout Riina's years as a fugitive, Piera Fallucca writes:

> Despite having lived with a murderer for twenty years, and sharing his fugitive state, she is not *complicit* in it. She cannot even be prosecuted for being an accessory. I see this as monstrous on the part of the judiciary:
>
> 1) because it gives precedence to family ties before the universality of the law;

2) because it subordinates the definition of individual responsibilities to an 'extraterritorial' idea of the family;

3) because, given the very specificities of how the mafia functions as an organization and Cosa Nostra's own structuring through 'families', not only does this fail to break, but it actually consolidates at a cultural and symbolic level, the existence of 'alternative' laws, the laws inscribed in the codes of 'men of honour'.[30]

Finally, the comparison between 'mafia women' and 'terrorist women' contains a hidden assumption and makes a comparison between women of the South (all hearth and home) and women of the North (greedy for freedom, even at the price of terrorism), which is totally misplaced, from both a sociological and a historical point of view. In the event a comparison with women involved in common criminality might have been fruitful.

By exploiting clichés about women's presumed inferiority, this judgment actually supplies precedents for disempowering the La Torre law which finally allows intervention into the assets accumulated by mafiosi. In my view it is important to stress how, once again, this represents an exploitative use of the distorted image of the feminine in order to facilitate economic and financial manoeuvres of a criminal nature controlled entirely by men.

The Catania Unione Donne Italiane (Catania Union of Italian Women) wrote a letter of protest to the Upper Council of the Magistrature, the Superior Commissioner for the Struggle against the Mafia and the President of the Watchdog Commission on the Application of the La Torre Law, which included the following:

And this is not just something symbolic; is it not apparent that this judgment will encourage the widespread custom of registering mafia assets with the women of the family? Is this not a further dangerous attack on the fundamental principle of the La Torre law, and a way of rendering its application futile in those cases in which it is only through controls and action on family assets that mafiosi can be reached? Can it not also be judged that even 'irregular' involvement in mafia activity can be deemed a crime?[31]

In my view the judges' efforts in this judgment to furnish a sociological framework for the mafia world and women's role within it takes its lead from a received idea as mistaken as it is widely held: the equation between the mafia family and the traditional peasant family. Apart from mistaking the standing of women in the so-called traditional family, this equation reckons neither with the fundamentally petty-bourgeois value orientation of the mafia nor, most importantly, with the cynical manipulation of traditions and values by the mafiosi. Both of these aspects have a profound influence on the functions and scope of women in these families.

This brings to mind, incidentally, a debate on 'the role of women in the mafia', held in January of distant 1977 at the University of Messina. While the invited speakers, most of whom were anthropologists, were explaining the active and central role of women in the transmission of folk culture, and therefore, most likely, also in the 'transmission of mafia values', maintaining that 'the family is an institution which in certain respects depends on the same rules as the institution of the mafia', there was a student (who remains name-less) who kept on stubbornly interrupting and emphasizing the difference between the traditional family and the mafia family in terms of women's role. I believe that this student had already perceived a significant truth. Let us lis-ten to him:

> *Student*: It seems to me that [the speaker] has confused the role of women in Southern society with the role of women in the mafia family. In Southern society women are active protagonists because they transmit the culture; however, in my view, women in the mafia society are no longer protagonists, but are marginalized.
>
> *Speaker*: On this point it seems we disagree completely; I maintain that they have a central role in the mafia family.
>
> *Student*: A woman has a central role only in the blood feud, for when she has been grief-stricken, she can, during the ritual practice, put forward plans for a vendetta to the male. But the fundamental structure of the mafia is not transmitted by women, but by men.[32]

To insist that women do not embody the role of protagonists in the mafia family, that women have no possibility for emancipation within the mafia environment, in no way means that the role of women in the mafia is irrele-vant. Nor does it mean, most of all, that women are deprived of responsibility. Quite the opposite. Women's function, as we shall see further on, seems central to the very functioning of the mafia organization, to the perpetuation of terror and the mafia hold over people. Without the active complicity, so to speak, of women, 'territorial sovereignty' could not exist. But women are of use to the mafia as mothers, as daughters, as wives. The woman as an individ-ual, however, in herself, seems in antithesis to mafioso power and the forms taken by its territorial rootedness.

7

Subordination and Exploitation

The drug couriers

Like bootlegging during the Prohibition era in 1920s USA, international drug trafficking has stimulated mafia activity, profoundly influencing the way power is exerted and forms of control are shaped. If we keep to the distinction between power syndicate and enterprise syndicate we can arrive at some understanding of how the mafia has been able to adapt to the rational necessities demanded by the international drug market in terms of mobility and financial operations, while preserving a strict and detailed check on local territory.

The man of honour plays with skill at both tables: while managing millions and operating on a grand scale, he does not slacken his hold over the corner butcher's shop. Not so much for the sake of money perhaps, as to demonstrate the permanence of his power.

> The fact that the mafia continues to engage in old-fashioned activities like, for instance, controlling small-time gambling or prostitution cannot be explained in economic terms, because the profit accruing from these is not comparable with what comes from the drug trade. However, by controlling small-time gambling, prostitution and the minor infractions of petty crime, it extends its army of militants and accomplices, simultaneously increasing its store of knowledge about what is going on in a particular territorial domain.[1]

And within this balance stands the female figure, the status and the role of women being of fundamental importance. For the sake of preserving its 'territorial sovereignty', mafia hegemony has to freeze and hold back any impulses to change within the sphere of its own territory. It is not only *what* is done that has to be kept in check, but also how it is done and who does it.

Women's absence, therefore, in a sense defines not only their backwardness but the upholding of the local codes which contain their passivity and subordination. It is relevant to observe that the mafia's versatility in linking its own illegal activities with the most dynamic and remunerative sectors of the island's economy . . . involves no alteration in the cultural codes expressed by the groups and individuals of whom it is made up, these for the most part remaining rooted in the socially marginal sphere of their origins.[2]

The fact remains that mediation between the spheres of the corner shop and the 'pizza connection',* for example, which are so far apart in terms of economics, relationships and power, creates constant friction and tensions.

This heterogeneity provokes negative consequences in terms of security, which by contrast is well assured by the compact nature of the power syndicate. . . . More open to treachery and grassing, and in any case dependent on activities which inevitably leave traces (ships, goods, telephone calls, letters, banking operations), drug traffickers are sometimes caught red-handed; they operate at a visible surface level which is ascertainably criminal, while the level of the territorial organization remains mysterious and subterranean.[3]

It is in this setting that women begin to crop up on the scene of mafia criminality, sometimes perhaps unaware of whom they are dealing with. Salvatore Lupo cites the case of the wife of a smuggler from Tangier arrested in 1960; she put forward a claim on behalf of herself and her unborn child for the money owed to her arrested husband by 'Palermo friends': 'There are a lot of you and between you all a little money for one person would hardly be noticed . . . I'm sure that [in my place] you would already have brought out your guns.' Then she threatens vengeance, adding, 'I am not afraid of your mafia.' Lupo comments: 'What stands out here is not just the recklessness of a "foreign" woman who puts the word mafia in writing (which can represent a threat to go to the authorities with information), but the lack of the smugglers' internal group solidarity, in contrast with the care taken to support the families of arrested members which is an internal rule of the mafia group.'[4]

Similar complaints are expressed by women drug couriers, who are arrested and 'abandoned': 'They had told me "Don't worry, there are no problems. You're a woman, nobody will search you. And even if they catch you, what can happen? You have nothing to do with the deal, you're just doing a favour carrying something. If it comes to the worst, we'll pay a fine and

---

* The 'pizza connection' refers to the heroin trade link between the Italian mafia and its US counterpart, and specifically to the big US trial involving Tano Badalamenti in 1987, when he received a 45-year sentence. [Trs.]

they'll release you straight away." But what happened was that nobody turned up, damn them, and I'm still here in prison a year later.'[5]

The fact is that although these women did get involved in mafia trafficking, it was not as relatives of men of honour, but as ordinary people, important – but quickly replaceable – links in the narcotics trade: middle women, couriers and pushers. Their entry into this orbit, at least in Sicily, has been prompted by the mafia's total economic supremacy. Anna Puglisi explains:

> There is then the problem of survival, and it is the mafia which provides the possibility of making ends meet and surviving. Drug trafficking also goes on elsewhere, there are also small-time pushers elsewhere, but the basic fact is that the mafia is the only organization offering work, because nothing else exists. There are run-down areas and neighbourhoods elsewhere too, but here the mafia is the only place to turn economically, and this builds support.[6]

When I read the stories of these women and listened to their words in the few direct interviews available, I realized that flagrant complicity and manifestly sexist subordination closely coincide in their actions. It would be difficult or arbitrary to make any distinct separation between them. However, in order to make the situation clearer, I have in a sense been selective, by means of a broadly subjective form of evaluation. Apart from the facts related, I have tried to understand the tenor of what is being said and the language used, in order to identify complicity and/or subordination, and as a result to grasp the weight of individual responsibilities.

In the eighties, on the Palermo–Rome–New York route, there appeared a particular kind of tourist: housewives, mothers of large families, heavily perfumed (to throw sniffer dogs off the scent), with just one item of hand baggage containing a nightdress and a change of clothes. The purpose of the trip: a few days in a luxury New York hotel, then back to Palermo.

Their stories, 'villainous tales of Palermo housewives', have been told by Marina Pino.

> They were travelling too frequently to America. To New York. A lot of women, alone or in peculiar company. Middle-aged, around forty, housewives, all without a criminal record, most of them burdened with children and worries, most of them living in *catoi** in the hopelessly run-down relics of the centre of old

---

* *Catoi* are like the Neapolitan *bassi*, windowless basement apartments where families live in overcrowded conditions. [Trs.]

Palermo or in the squalid tower blocks of the outskirts. . . . The couriers go off and when they get back the husband and children are waiting for them and there's a big party. In some cases also with a whole gang of relatives, because there's the age-old wish to cause a stir, explaining nothing and leaving the sudden influx of money and cause for celebration still a mystery. Then there's satisfaction to be had from the dumbfoundment of the neighbours, another crowd of hand-to-mouth unfortunates, who see there's a party going on and turn up as well-wishers.[7]

The traffic begins at Torretta, a small town not far from Palermo. The first housewives, their bodybelts stuffed with drugs, set out in the second half of 1985. A precision job, this bodybelt, with its made-to-measure bags of half a kilo and three-quarters of a kilo turned out by Signora Giovanna: 'Inside they have a thin film of plastic, outside they're made of cloth so that they can absorb sweat from the body without slipping on the skin.'[8]

Signora Giovanna is the wife of Salvatore Spina, a Torretta man who counts for something in the organization. So, after a few trips to New York, her husband's position secures her a less risky job at home. At the time of arrest, twelve 'custom-made' bodybelts were found in Signora Giovanna's house.

The business of packaging isn't always done with the necessary precision. Thus it was that Annamaria Cordovino nearly had to be flayed alive when she came back from America, stuffed, this time, with dollars. 'Flesh and adhesive tape had all become one and it was the devil of a job trying to free the woman. Smeared with creams and lotions and put under a scalding hot shower, poor Annamaria ended up literally skinned.'[9]

What are the gains of lending oneself to this very special kind of 'tourism'? Besides the 'all-inclusive' Palermo–New York return ticket, with a luxury stay at the Sheraton or the Hilton, and a daily allowance of $150 for incidental expenses, there is a 25 million-lire reward at journey's end, but the 'courier' also does double duty, leaving with heroin and returning with dollars. It may not be a lot when one thinks of the millions involved in drug trafficking, but it seems plenty to the dreams spawned and fed by advertising which are the stuff of a poverty-stricken life.

In fact, the outcome is that these 'easy, easy' millions burn away in no time.

And at this point the housewife lives out her triumph. Bathroom and kitchen walls tiled all over from floor to ceiling like in grand houses, goodbye at last to the old gas rings and aluminium pots that take so much elbowgrease to shine up, in with the dreamt-of fitted kitchen and the microwave oven, and the stainless-steel saucepan set. Then the dining room all gleaming with mirrors and brass fittings . . .[10]

The temptations are easy to understand, and likewise the outcome can be taken for granted: 'And they went on living in poverty and hopelessness, in the same old ghetto scenario of violence and ignorance. The story of our drug ladies might as well end here.'[11]

I shall stop and linger on the story of Vincenza Calì, not just because her case appears emblematic and typical of other stories too, but also because Marina Pino did an interview with her which allows us insights and perhaps some understanding of the drug courier's own experience.

'On her way to New York with heroin stuffed in her clothes. Mother of eight caught at Punta Raisi', ran the headline in the *Giornale di Sicilia* on 25 May 1986. The mother in question, the 'heroin-running housewife', as another headline inside the paper put it, was Vincenza Calì, the forty-year-old wife of Ignazio Mattioli, forty-three, a janitor in a primary school, who was also arrested. 'With unruffled calm', the woman left with the flying-squad officers. 'There was a different reaction, however, from her husband. When the officers detained him, he flew off the handle. The janitor started screaming . . . saying he had no idea why the police were taking him into custody.'

Later, in the interview, Vincenza was to say: 'I saw how things were at once: bye-bye America. They told me they were amazed because I hadn't reacted, stayed really calm. And what was I supposed to do, if everything was over and done with?'[12]

'Bye-bye America', a fitting metaphor for Vincenza's bitter experience. 'We sold the grey Renault 11 as well and it was a beauty, they just gave me six and a half million lire and we'd bought the car only eight months before.'[13]

Vincenza's is an 'ordinary' story like so many others: at sixteen she went into service and met Ignazio, who was nineteen and a bricklayer; before long they eloped. They went to live with the mother-in-law; 'my mother-in-law is a terrible woman, jealous about that son of hers I married'. Neither the mother nor the son had yet told her that Ignazio was ill with tuberculosis; only when he began vomiting blood did his wife discover the truth.

She went on working as a maid, he as a bricklayer, and 'every year like clockwork a baby arrived'. Eight children in all, while he went in and out of the sanatorium. Apart from that he was just like any other man. 'He's always liked women, he would have the odd fling and then, if I found out, I would have to start a quarrel about it. But Ignazio loves me and the children.'

They made an attempt to leave the South. They went to Milan, then came back; they went to Turin, but were back in Palermo two months later. Then, one day, everything seemed to change for the better. 'When they made me the offer I said yes straight away. It seemed a piece of good luck. There's no point in anybody asking who it was and how it was, because I've got children and I've never wanted to know. I only knew that I had to make that trip . . .' None the less, Vincenza's refusal to reveal the senders' names says a lot about her awareness of the kind of smuggling she was involved in and the mafia character of the entire operation.

In New York she kept to the hotel, waiting to go back to Palermo. 'Why should I be interested in New York? What would I be doing out and about in a place I didn't know with people I didn't know? I would just sit it out waiting for the days to go by thinking about the fifteen million I would take home, and what to do with it so my children could enjoy it. God, what a relief and satisfaction to get that money home.'

Unwittingly it was in fact one of her children who 'betrayed' Vincenza Calì: 'On the telephone, pleased as punch, he tells someone that Mum is going away: "She's going to America and coming back with dollars." '[14]

The dream of 'easy easy' millions was shattered – 'because I've always dreamt of a lovely house, like well-off people have' – the dream of a worry-free life was shattered too: 'Because of his illness, Ignazio ... finally he got the job of janitor at the Cavallari primary school; he'd only been there two months, he hadn't even got his regular wages sorted out yet. ... They say he wasn't even on the computer yet, that he's got nothing coming to him. And now how are we going to make ends meet?'

At the time of the interview Vincenza Calì had been under house arrest for nine months. Her husband was in prison. A cruel punishment and with eight children an unbearable situation. Better off in prison!

I'm grateful to the judge, but it would have been much better if he had let me pay my debt in prison, because I'm going crazy here, the children are running rings round me, eight children, eight children I've got, and they don't realize the scandal, they all feel free as air, they want everything, they fight, they run away from me and I can't catch them. ... And they run away from me. 'I'm going out.' 'Where are you going?' 'I'm going out.' They laugh in my face, I can follow them as far as that door and I can't go any further and they know it, those wretches, they know I can't put a hand on them. I feel as if I'll explode indoors. ... It would have been better if he [the judge] had put my husband Ignazio under house arrest. I'd change places with him in a flash: him as a prisoner at home, me in prison. He'd know how to keep the kids in hand, for they take more notice of their father.

In Vincenza Calì's picture of things, and no doubt also in her everyday experience, men and women have very different powers and capacities. The man is the one who earns respect, 'it needs his father to set him straight'. A woman, as if spellbound, possesses limited faculties. Of the daughter who tos and fros with the lawyers, sorting everything out, she says: 'But she's a girl and maybe she doesn't understand what's involved.'

Simultaneously – and contradictorily – women come to appear as the strong ones, responsible even for men themselves, who are allowed to be thoughtless and immature:

> I'd have been better off if they'd all been born girls because women have more sense of responsibility, they feel more of a duty to help the family, at home and outside it. Whereas boys complain about everything, they expect everything and aren't prepared to give anything. All fun and freedom. They want new shoes, the latest style in trousers, their shirts ironed, their beds made, their lunch on the table. Mum do this, Mum do that, and telling their sisters what to do. Males have no understanding of life.

There is one detail about acting as a drug courier which Vincenza leaves out of her story, one detail which in my view is anything but negligible if we are to understand the role and status of women within this kind of trafficking.

When Salvatore Allegra was arrested he decided to tell Judge Giovanni Falcone everything about the women's trips.

> Totuccio explained why it was better using them. First and foremost there were fewer risks with them carrying merchandise. . . . Then for him, Totuccio, there was the chance to get something out of it personally. Before 'dressing' them, he would 'have' them all. The ritual would be carried out in a villa at Costa Corsara, not far from Punta Raisi. The courier would have to be there the evening before departure to get her instructions, then she would spend the night there. . . . Either that night or even on the morning of departure the courier would pay the obligatory 'lovemaking' toll: a coupling that was over in no time. 'With all of them, every one of them?' the magistrate asked. 'So long as they were women I mean,' Salvatore Allegra insisted, explaining that as far as he was concerned he had no objection to any woman, just so long as she was living and breathing.[15]

But perhaps Vincenza did speak of this, although she didn't give any details: 'They expect everything and they're not prepared to give anything. All fun and freedom . . . males have no understanding of life'. Did she also have Totuccio Allegra in mind?

This is not just about Totuccio, but – how can I put it? – a power relationship highlighted and systematically driven home. 'In America someone would approach the women, make himself known, go to the hotel with them. Here, as at the very start, there would be the ritual of undressing, and here, once again, as was Totuccio's custom in Sicily, the man who would be the courier's connection for eight days would make sure to reinforce the bond by taking her to bed at the start.'[16]

Territorial sovereignty? Just as the millionaire mafia boss neither can nor will loosen his small-time hold on the corner shop, the mafia man neither can nor will give up the open demonstration of his manliness, a myth which needs always and everywhere to be renewed. A compulsion to 'fuck' which is a function of mastery. Territorial sovereignty is both an analogy and a powerful reference: the female body, both materially and symbolically, seems central to strategies of territorial power. ' "When all is said and done a kind of *ius copulandi,*" Judge Ignazio de Francisci commented with bitter irony, although no longer with any capacity for surprise. A ritual which seals a specific alliance, not one between equals, however, given that the compulsory submission of the female to the male master is all too clear.'[17]

Complicity? Responsibility? Subordination?

Another one who paid, so to speak, with her own body was Esmeralda Ferrara, the young singer from Bagheria. Her story is different, but in the end, whichever way you look at it, she ended up seduced, used, deceived and pregnant. And then abandoned.

'She wanted to be a rock star. Instead she met the drug clan': this was the headline in the *Giornale di Sicilia* on 23 December 1982 for the report on the Spatola trial.

When she met Filippo Ragusa, a Sicilian-American tour promoter for singers in the US, Esmeralda was a pretty twenty-year-old who sang in dance halls, nightclubs and open-air gatherings, always accompanied by her doting mother, the secretary who took care of everything. 'She was sweet and shy, she always talked in a quiet voice, almost a whisper. But inside she had a will of iron and she knew what she wanted: she was going to make it.'[18]

The meeting with Filippo seemed like the big break. He 'gave Esmeralda a line that she wanted to hear'.[19] They left for the US, made a record, did concerts in the US and in Italy. What Esmeralda did not know — on appeal at the trial against Rosario Spatola and the drug multinational she was in fact fully acquitted — was that drugs were travelling between Sicily and New York in the boxes for her records.

Esmeralda's big dreams, both for her artistic career and for romance, went up in smoke one evening in Milan at a restaurant called Al Vecchio 400. Esmeralda had been for some days on a 'pleasure trip' with Filippo, but they were quarrelling a lot. He seemed preoccupied, his mind everywhere but on her. That dinner, which would later turn out to be a business meeting between bosses that ranked with Inzerillo or the Adamitas, ended abruptly, and three days later, at a dispatch agent's in Gallarate, forty kilos of heroin were confiscated, found hidden among copies of Esmeralda's long-playing record *Noi due sull'erba*. This was the largest ever consignment to have been seized in Europe.

The young woman went back to Palermo, alone. Four months later she ended up in prison at Rebibbia, six months pregnant, a painful, difficult pregnancy. She came out of prison just before the birth of Giada, Filippo's daughter. 'With Giada there were more troubles: the baby had fluid on the brain.'[20]

For two years Esmeralda's life was hell. Regarded as a 'socially dangerous' person, she was kept under surveillance and there were demands for her custody. Despite countless difficulties she went on singing, while looking after her baby. In the end she was acquitted. 'She never saw Filippo again. He was on the run in no time, perhaps he made his way back to America. He got an eighteen-year prison sentence. He's a fugitive and there's no word of him from anyone.'[21]

Another young woman, Tiziana Augello from Delia, a small town in Sicily, a twenty-one-year-old student with no criminal record, was a middle woman and drug courier between Holland, Lombardy and Calabria. This was at the end of the eighties. She was the friend of another woman messenger, the friend/lover of Leonardo Messina, who has since turned state's evidence. Messina, a man of honour from San Cataldo, belongs to the Madonia clan.

But there came a point when the girl no longer seemed trustworthy. 'She's a young girl, she doesn't come from a mafia family. She finds herself implicated in drug trafficking almost by accident and is not a mafia woman. For this reason Tiziana Augello is not a safe bet.'[22]

When approached by the *carabinieri*, who had traced her through intercepted telephone calls, she finally made up her mind to collaborate. It was listening to one of these tapped calls that persuaded her; the *carabinieri* let her listen in on her own death sentence. 'A recording on which you can hear the Calabrians "bad-mouthing" her and Narduzzu [Messina] replying that he'll see to it.'[23] Narduzzu, being the man of honour that he was, would certainly not have had second thoughts. Had the *carabinieri* not intervened he would of course have eliminated this friend of his lover's . . .

Drug-pushing mothers

Both narcotics trafficking on a national and international level and small-scale drug pushing have features which lend themselves to 'women's work'. When it comes to high-level trafficking, women's involvement makes a lot of operations easier, because it often attracts less attention. As we have already seen, the living room and the home are perfect places for organizing trafficking, and are places where women hold sway. Pushing, dealing in small quantities, demands the existence of a tight localized network, well camouflaged by countless everyday activities: markets, street corners, the hubbub of small shops and, yet again, the home. Who better than the housewife and mother of a large family to take on this new kind of 'work from home'?

131

'She was a housewife with no previous convictions. Arrested in Vucciria, she was pushing drugs in a dressing-gown and slippers.'[24] This case of the lady who peddled heroin among the market stalls just along the road from where she lived seems emblematic. 'The *carabinieri* stepped in when the addict approached her. The housewife's dressing-gown had bulging pockets. In them were seventy packets ready for sale.'

Or: 'Young housewife was dealing in heroin from her home.' And again: 'A woman from Santa Flavia was in charge of the pushers.'[25] Another news item, this time from Mazara del Vallo, has four women as protagonists, 'Michela Casesi, 63, and her girls, Anna, Carolina and Francesca Paola, 24, 27 and 43 respectively'. Once the order was sorted out, 'one of the women would put the packets in a basket which would be lowered down to be taken away by the boys'.[26] Well and truly a family-run organization.

The involvement and use of young boys makes perfect sense, given the inherent features of this kind of activity. Children and youths are fast operators and can go unobserved, often arousing no suspicion.

The description of this 'team work' between mother and children recalls early forms of industrial labour, when the emergent factory engaged the entire family group. But in those days the head of the team was the father. In the case of these families, however, the father is often absent. He has either left, or is in prison, or in some cases has been killed. 'The Zen is female,' Marina Pino points out, 'it is the women who have the market in hand, who organize and run the dealing along with their children, who are always very numerous.'[27]

Pino describes the situation in Zen 2, the wretched tower-block slum neighbourhood of Palermo:

It is easy to keep an eye on comings and goings in Via Giuseppe Lanza di Scalea through the Zen's child 'lookouts', who are stationed at strategic points and well trained to identify whether arrivals are 'natives', potential addicts, cops or suspicious customers. . . . 'It's Beppe,' the lookouts warn. 'Beppe' means the police. The lookout is usually one of the younger children, ten or twelve years old, standing guard in a strategic spot or else riding around on a scooter with no numberplate. The warning is also signalled by a coded whistle sent by the 'go-between' to the supplier, that is, to mum. The go-between is another of her children, usually a little bit older than the lookout, and he shuttles between the drug buyer's car and the point of supply. It is up to him to negotiate the deal; if he settles it he takes the money and goes and whistles under the balcony of the flat. Mum twigs and lowers the basket, or else uses another child as messenger, pocketing the money and handing over the packet in exchange. Payment is always in advance . . . things are always tense . . .

If the warning comes: 'It's Beppe,' the familiar whistle goes round and everything on the market square comes to a halt. The swarm of scooters disappears, the lady of the house hurriedly pulls up the basket or else takes up a position behind the lavatory door in readiness to flush the toilet.[28]

Luisa Prestigiacomo's is a tale of disaster. This forty-year-old woman was arrested in October 1984 along with three of her children, aged fifteen, nineteen and twenty-one. 'They were selling drugs lowered in a basket from the second floor,' was the headline in the *Giornale di Sicilia* on 28 October 1984.

Who is Luisa Prestigiacomo? 'Luisa's is a story of tears, blood and mystery.'[29] She is the widow of Matteo Biondo, a Vucciria smuggler, who disappeared in the summer of 1980, a victim of the *lupara bianca*.

At the time of her misfortune his wife was thirty-five and had six children. She got it into her head that she had to see justice done herself, became an investigator of sorts and, using all the inside information she had come by during her marriage, went searching in the smugglers' milieu, among her husband's friends. That was how she discovered that her husband had been shot to pieces by those very 'friends' and that those pieces had been given to the pigs as swill. 'Everything became clear to her in the end. She went to the *carabinieri* headquarters and told Sergeant Vito Ievolella that she wanted to talk to him in strict secrecy, because she could tell him all about the appalling and dreadful death of her husband, and wanted to do so.'[30]

Her story became the substance of a report on the smugglers of Kalsa and Vucciria and a charge of murder for two of them. But a year later Sergeant Ievolella was killed as he waited for his daughter in his car. The warning hit its mark: Luisa took her children and fled. Her mother spoke to journalists: 'What was my poor daughter to do? She left with all her six children and now she's abroad. She can't come back. You can see why. She talked, she told everything. They couldn't let her get away with it. But now she's had no choice but to leave. . . . She did it all on her own, didn't say a word, didn't ask for advice, just went to the *carabinieri*.'[31]

At the trial a year later, Luisa Prestigiacomo retracted everything and was arrested in the courtroom for perjury, withholding evidence and defamation. Mafia fear had turned her from accuser to accused, at the cost of a *carabinieri* sergeant's life.

She was soon out of prison and for a few years kept herself out of the news. Then she and her children were arrested. 'Her murdered husband had been involved in cigarette smuggling, the wife brought herself up to date and, in line with the times, became involved in drugs. She was known to be a supplier to individual customers with a family organization all neatly worked out.'[32]

Anna Corradi is a friend and neighbour of Luisa's. She too is a strong, energetic and active woman. She has six children, one of whom takes drugs. She runs a street-level drug-dealing operation, but is also involved in fencing a variety of stolen goods.

> The house is lovely, all done up, with tiling on the floors and in the kitchen, enormous bathrooms, furniture with mirrors and gold. Even if Signora Anna gives way to some extravagance and the police and *carabinieri* turn up – because they've never gone for long without paying her a visit – when they get there they're amazed. Things are a bit confused. For example, Signora Anna has three low-fuel cookers, three ovens and four fridges. If you open a fridge you'll find a whole lot of shirts piled neatly on the shelves, just like in a cupboard. If you open an oven you'll find shoes. Signora Corradi has no lack of cupboards, no lack of anything, but obviously she ended up with a few ovens and fridges too many and she's happy doing things this way. A lot of nice stuff comes and goes at Signora Corradi's house: clothes, furs, jewellery, television sets, tape decks.[33]

Anna is at the centre of a family where everyone has been in trouble with the law: kidnappings, murders, drug dealing. 'This whole sordid crowd of brothers, brothers-in-law, children, nephews and nieces gravitates around Signora Anna . . . they call her "the queen" and the scope of her business can only be guessed at.'[34]

Women, young and not so young, and children. But the network of drug trafficking also has room for old women. Aunt Teresa is sixty-four, 'a big dark woman eternally clad in a deep black overall, a huge, untidy person with badly dyed hair, a brick-coloured face and a deep mournful voice'.[35] She has a shop where she sells everything: sweets, sticking plasters, pasta, eggs, cellophane-wrapped cakes, toys. And in the middle of all this there's a syringe ready for use, with solvent or even just water. This at least was the charge. 'When Aunt Teresa had done her time she went back to shopkeeping and complaining: "The police and the *carabinieri* are always on my doorstep, always plenty to say, always keeping themselves busy. But I told the inspector fair and square. Find me an alternative and I'll take it straight away. The thing is, I've got to survive somehow." '[36]

Anna Puglisi relates:

> A friend of mine had to take her children away from a primary school in one of the old town neighbourhoods, because nearly every day some of their class-mates would be found to have sachets of heroin in their pockets that they hadn't managed to sell before getting to school, or else had to sell afterwards (the two children were in the first and third years of primary school). Well, when the mothers of these children were called in by the teachers they said without any beating about the bush that this was the only way they had of getting enough money to make ends meet from day to day. And this is a proven fact; in the

working-class neighbourhoods of Palermo the mafia is alone in responding to people's needs, whatever that may mean in terms of the toll it takes through death, loss of freedom, barbarism.[37]

What kind of relationship do these women have with drugs? Can they really manage to see them as a commodity like any other? They are all mothers, they all have sons and daughters, and day in, day out before their very eyes there are addicts.

The drug courier Vincenza Calì said in the interview already quoted: 'What was it to me that these were drugs? They looked like talcum powder to me . . . I had no interest in knowing anything about drugs.' I believe Vincenza. She didn't mean she thought she was taking talcum powder to New York, but that so long as she was not personally affected by drugs they might as well have been talcum powder for all she cared.

In fact, as the interview went on, she also said:

In prison I found out what drugs were. When I was at Termini Imerese there would be young girls turning up with their eyes glazed and you could see they were in a bad way. Then they would start going crazy, screaming, rolling about, going green in the face, in cold sweats and frothing at the mouth. 'What's up with them?' I asked. 'They're in withdrawal,' I was told. And what's this 'withdrawal'? That was how I found out that these kids were addicts and that when they went without taking the stuff for a bit they would have terrible pains, they'd be in a bad way. They told me they were already dead souls, because you don't get better from drugs and that an awful lot of kids ended up dead like that.

Sooner or later, the drug-pusher mothers get caught in this net which they themselves have helped to weave. Sooner or later one of their children is left as a sacrificial lamb on the altar of easy, easy money.

To add to their troubles the 'heroin mums' all have to cope with the same catastrophe; sooner or later one of their own children will get hooked and become an addict. Mrs Corradi has Giuseppe, Mrs Prestigiacomo has Maurizio, Mrs Chianchiano has Rosario. There's always love and there's always grief because your children are yours, your flesh and blood. But there's also the problem that you can't be sure one of them won't end up like that. How can you trust heroin? Instead of going and selling it, one of them will use it himself.[38]

Murdered women and children

'With three bullets in the face Gilda Passerini, 45-year-old partner of Salvatore Sansone, the well-known jailbird from Vittoria, was brutally shot down in broad daylight as she climbed the stairs to her own home.'[39] Or again: 'cellophane-wrapped packages of heroin and cocaine were found in the handbag of Giuseppina Lucchese, thirty-one, who was killed yesterday afternoon in Via Raffaello.'[40]

Pantaleone Sergi gives the example of Concetta Jorio, 'who was in bed with her four young children when all of them were surprised by a shotgun attack in Santa Eufemia d'Aspromonte', and Francesca Bardo Pellegrino, already widowed in the Seminara feud, 'who was murdered on her way to the parish church nursery school to collect her four children'.[41]

Even if these murders can be attributed partly to the escalation in killings connected with drug trafficking, they are not new aspects of the mafia scene. Anna Puglisi explains: 'We only have to remember Portella della Ginestra!* They just fired into a crowd there, killing women and children at random.'[42]

A powerful element in the social representation of the mafia – which continues always to be defended as the 'old mafia' – is the stereotype of the man of honour who never kills women or children. In fact, this time-honoured image of the mafioso, all protection and family, is badly at odds with the cynicism of the real mafioso who makes no allowances for either age or sex.

As we have already seen, the internal rules of the mafia secret society and the oaths of initiation are unequivocal about priorities. The exploitation of family ties and attachments does not stop short at death. The idea that women and children are 'different' beings, to be respected, protected and saved, is a part of all authoritarian ideologies, and as such time and again is resoundingly belied by events. The mafia is no exception.

There is no evidence that in the past women and children have been spared. The following episode, for example, narrated by Salvatore Lupo, goes back to the twenties:

This period saw the start of the feud between the Barbaccias and the Lorellos over control of the Ficuzza wood, a stopping point for the herds that were

---

* At Portella della Ginestra in Sicily on 1 May 1947, twelve people died and many more were injured when an armed gang led by the bandit Salvatore Giuliano attacked a May Day rally and public meeting of local farmworkers and their families. The massacre was planned by the mafia with the involvement of certain landowners. The CIA also played a now recognized part in its organization, with the aim of eliminating left-wing political leaders and trade unionists. This was at a decisive phase in Italy's postwar history, in the run-up to the first democratic elections since the Fascist period. [Trs.]

stolen between Corleone and Palermo; in the interwar period fifty-eight people in the village of Godrano were to die over this. There were horrifying attacks on the farms, with the cold-blooded slaughter of entire families, women and children included; as at Burgio and Sclafani in 1922 (where there were seven and eight dead). The reason? 'Mafia domination over the area'.[43]

The alleged gallantry of the mafia regarding women and children has a significant bearing on the idealization of the 'old mafia', which was supposedly good, by contrast with the new mafia, which is bloodthirsty. Albeit in measured terms, Antonino Calderone himself puts forward a version of the 'old mafia' which spared the innocents: 'There has never been a rule whereby Cosa Nostra does not kill women. . . . But it is true that Cosa Nostra did not kill innocent women whose only fault was to be the wives or daughters of enemies.'[44]

What can the word *innocent* mean in this context? In mafia language innocence appears synonymous with not knowing, with being ignorant. And are there women who do not know? What forms of complicity are concealed by presumed innocence? And what would the mafia's attitude be to these women whenever there was any doubt?

In this same context Calderone narrates an illuminatingly apposite episode. In Milan, some time around 1973, Luciano Liggio had a rival of his killed, a certain Caruso who lived with a woman who in turn had a daughter with whom this same Caruso also went to bed. Presumably, these two women knew a lot. They were therefore not innocent. In fact, they were treated accordingly. With some excuse or other Liggio had them brought to him. 'The women came at once and Liggio killed the mother, then screwed the daughter, who would have been about fifteen or sixteen, then killed her too.'[45] The women of bosses have also been killed along with their husbands. Giacoma Gambino, Sirchia's wife, died outside Ucciardone prison, as she accompanied her husband who was going back inside. And Francesca Citarda was mowed down at home along with her husband Giovanni Bontade.

In the slaughter of summer 1992* two women were killed, one of them a policewoman, Emanuela Loi, the other a magistrate and the wife of Judge Falcone, Francesca Morvillo. Both these deaths were deliberate and planned. According to Annamaria Palma, a woman magistrate and a friend of Francesca: 'Francesca's death was not a matter of chance; they weren't killed together just because they were a close couple. I think that Francesca knew a lot of things and they were afraid to leave her alive.'[46] A similar view was

---

* The Capaci motorway bombing that killed Judge Falcone and others in May and, in July, the killings of Judge Paolo Borsellino and his bodyguards in Via D'Amelio. [Trs.]

expressed by Fernanda Contri, a former voluntary member of the CSM and also a friend: 'I believe that they deliberately waited for a time when Francesca would be there too, unfortunately. Francesca did not only enjoy her husband's confidence, but she shared in the demanding work of the magistracy. And Francesca probably knew a lot. She would have been a rather inconvenient witness' (cf. the discussion during the ceremony at the Marisa Bellisario Prize, Palermo, 8 March 1993).

Ten years earlier another young woman had been murdered with bullets from a Kalashnikov, paying with her life for her love of a man of state – General Dalla Chiesa. 'What happened to Francesca Morvillo for Falcone, happened to Emanuela Setti Carraro for my father,' said Rita Dalla Chiesa in an interview with *Il Venerdì di Repubblica*.

And what are we to say about the many women and children killed at random, accidentally? But perhaps even their deaths were not so random when all is said and done. First of all because these deaths feed fear and terror and therefore serve the interests of territorial domination. And then because they seem deliberate deaths even if they are perhaps not planned. Let's take the example of the death of Signora Barbara Rizzo Asta and her six-year-old twins Giuseppe and Salvatore Asta. They died, blown apart by the bomb intended for Judge Palermo, at Pizzolungo on 2 April 1985. 'From where they were positioned, the mafiosi who activated the remote device to make the bomb explode were perfectly able to see the car driven by Signora Rizzo Asta with the children in it.'[47]

The mafia's relationship with children deserves particular attention. From two different points of view children seem to be important to the affirmation of mafia power; in the first place within the management of terror, in the second place from an economic point of view, as an especially suitable labour force.

Fears for children and the dread provoked by the thought of their death are a powerful vehicle for the affirmation of mafia power. In one of the stories collected by Danilo Dolci, a farm labourer narrates:

There were five of us children, all boys, and we would go out in the morning, the oldest was twenty-four and the youngest sixteen, and my mother didn't want us to go out, she wanted to come with us; once, my mother locked me inside so that I couldn't go out. For near where we lived there were mafia people who would talk about us labourers: 'We should build a shed (like for cows at night) and put them all in it.' And my mother would shout (for they'd already killed Cangelosi): 'If that's how you want it I'll kill you myself before I let them kill you and have to weep over you in the countryside. Our bellies are only ever half full with the little we had to eat. What if they kill you!' When we got back in the evening she was out at the door and as each of us got back she would ask if he'd seen the others. All five of us slept in the same bed. My mother would kiss us, early in the morning. My father would wake up at four. 'Let's be going, it's getting late, let's go to the square to see if they'll hire us,' and my mother would kiss us before we left, something people don't do here even if they're fond of you, and she was convinced that she wouldn't see us alive again. With every gunshot she heard, for here they kill Christian folk like flies, the land was ablaze with it, she would run into the street because she thought: 'Maybe it's my son.' So she lost her mind and we had to take her to the asylum.[48]

The mafia scares mothers, but the struggle against the mafia also scares mothers. Opposition to the mafia terror also costs human lives. When they tried to set up a police station in the Palermo neighbourhood of Brancaccio-Ciaculli in 1983 mothers mobilized. 'Mothers and children demonstrated against the opening of the police station in an apartment block, carrying signs that read "We are not against the police but we are afraid for our children".'[49] The day after the police station was opened, like clockwork a bomb exploded in the building entrance in broad daylight.

Children, sons and daughters, therefore represent, willy-nilly, a powerful element of blackmail in the hands of the mafiosi. The ever-present threat to their lives promotes *omertà*, promotes obedience to mafioso dictates and, sometimes, also motivates opposition to the workings of the state. 'To Giuseppe Letizia, Giuseppina Savoca, Paolino Riccobono, Giuseppe and Salvatore Asta, and Claudio Domino, children murdered by mafia violence, their future stolen from all of us' reads the dedication prefacing one of the researches of the Sicilian Centre for Documentation.[50]

At the same time children represent an ever more useful resource for mafia-dominated trafficking. We have seen the part played by young children in drug dealing, and newspaper coverage in recent years indicates the disturbing phenomenon of the child-hitman. Children are quick, they can go unremarked and, above all, they are protected by the law. Crimes they commit on adult orders cannot be prosecuted. The parents themselves apparently sometimes send the youngest ones into the front line for precisely this reason.

Luciano Violante, president of the Parliamentary Anti-mafia Commission, writes:

Children are a resource for the criminal world. . . . The child criminal costs the adult organization very little; he risks less; should he come to testify as a prosecution witness he has limited reliability compared with an adult; he can more easily be intimidated or even killed. The child has a changed role in the criminal world; he has entered an illegal circuit that can even be to his advantage; he has become a participant in values of aggressivity and outrage, rather than just their victim; he can draw on money that he would otherwise not have and by means of which he can become an active purchaser finally acquiring an identity of his own.[51]

The men of the mafia are very much aware of the importance of the child, of the collective imagination anchored in him or her and how much children count in the actions of mothers.

A child of eleven, Claudio Domino, was killed during the maxi-trial in Palermo. It was apparent at once that this was a mafia-based murder, carried out by a local clan. The boy must have been an unwitting witness to clan activities related to drug dealing. There were no specific public reactions but, none the less, the accused feared a backlash to this crime. The mafia leaders observed a minute of silence and, speaking for all of them, Giovanni Bontade distanced himself from the murder. 'We have nothing to do with this crime. . . . We have children too.'[52]

In the wake of this the clan leader disappeared and immediately afterwards one of his trusted men was killed. 'Economic reasons are mixed up with "disciplinary" sanctions. Certain solid business connections would have been threatened by the crime and a concern with "image" impelled the mafia organizations to decree death for those who carried out the murder and those behind it.'[53]

The mafia leaders' concern was purely self-interested. The facts show that the mafia has never displayed any squeamishness about children and teenagers.

A lot of people know the story of Giuseppe Letizia, the twelve-year-old shepherd boy from Corleone who was an inadvertent witness to the murder of the trade unionist Placido Rizzotto in 1948. Terror-stricken, the child ran to his mother, in a state of shock. 'The boy was really delirious, and since it was impossible to follow his confused story or to calm him down and stop him from shaking, he was taken to the hospital.'[54]

His mother had taken him to hospital unaware of the head physician's real identity. She took him to Dr Navarra, because he was the head physician there and for sickness cover with the Cassa Mutua. Navarra listened to the child, calmed the mother and admitted her son to hospital. Two days later he returned him to her as a corpse: dead of 'toxicosis'.[55] The autopsy showed the presence of poison in the little boy's body. But 'no one, not even the mother, pressed for investigations to be undertaken'.[56]

In 1959 little Antonio Pecoraro was killed. The murderers, disguised as *carabinieri*, 'pushed open the door of the poor house in Godrano with the intention of killing his father Vincenzo, but the shotgun pellets hit Antonio too'.[57]

Also in 1959 thirteen-year-old Giuseppina Savoca was murdered, 'caught in the cross-fire of the murder of Filippo Drago'.[58]

In 1961 thirteen-year-old Paolino Riccobono was killed during the mafia feud on the Tommaso Natale housing estate.

Women and children have also been killed by the *'ndrangheta* in Calabria.

It is a long list, perhaps a pointless one. But the images of little Domenica who was barely three when she was killed at San Martino di Taurianova, playing in her father's arms, or the two little cousins at Isola Capo Rizzuto who were gunned down with rifle-fire . . . or little seven-year-old Rocco Corica who was killed with his father at Taurianova, and ten-year-old Salvatore Feudale who was murdered at Crotone with his elder brother . . .[59]

And again: 'At Oppido Mamertina, Peppinello, the child of a prostitute, was killed on the afternoon of Easter Monday by a group of youths who had used him as a target in a shooting competition.'[60]

In 1989, Marcella Tassone was nearly eleven when she was killed by the hired thugs of the *'ndrangheta* at Laureana, a small town in the Reggino. The target was her brother Alfonso. 'They brought his car to a halt up in the high part of the town and fired. Perhaps mistaking Marcella for Tassone's young wife, the hitmen shot her first in the back of the neck, then they spattered her with bullets six times in the face.'[61]

At San Ferdinando, a unit of three hitmen shot fourteen-year-old Serafino and eleven-year-old Domenico from a car. With well-aimed fire they killed the two boys outside a crowded bar: a proper execution. Perhaps 'to issue a tragic warning to the father of little Cannatà, or to punish Pasquale Trifaro, the father of young Serafino, or else, an even more horrifying motive, to eliminate one of the boys because he had been an accidental witness of some mafia episode or himself a protagonist in an episode connected with illegal trafficking'.[62]

Calderone describes one incident which is particularly bloodcurdling and at the same time particularly illuminating: the killing of four young boys who were 'guilty' of snatching the handbag of Nitto Santapaola's mother.

> I'll never forget that convoy of four cars that reached the cowshed in the middle of the night to take the boys away. Two of them were made to sit in the car I was driving, and one was so small that he just about disappeared when he sat in the back seat. Their lives came to an end at that same well where the corpses of 'Marietto', the 'scientist' and 'Saro u bau' were thrown. They were strangled, and my cousin Marchese told me that he found it so awful carrying out the order that he hadn't had it in him to pull the noose tight enough around the neck of one boy, so he was thrown in the well still alive.[63]

In recent years, the growing incidence of *pentitismo* has produced vendettas across internal lines. The mafiosi are attempting to break the flow of words which is at last pinning down their culpability, by the indiscriminate killing of relatives – men, women and children. In November 1989 three women fell under fire together: Leonarda Costantino, Lucia Costantino and Vincenza Marino Mannoia, respectively the mother, aunt and sister of Antonino Marino Mannoia. 'The Corleonesi found them in no time. . . . They knew that the women were very close to Francesco; he had used them as back-up; they kept morphine for him when he was mixing and refining. They tailed them . . . Giuseppe Lucchese and his gang killed all three of them in the street below their house which they must have been keeping secret. The father saw everything from the balcony.'[64]

The dull, repetitive banalities of mafia language know no dialectic, no reciprocity. There is only ever one answer to solving every problem, every change: death.

Open Complicities

Granny Heroin

Women's contacts with the mafia seem to be essentially of two kinds: one is a sporadic collaboration, from the outside, as in the case of the drug couriers and go-betweens, the other is what we might call organic complicity.

Women's presence or entry within the mafia orbit is through family membership. Excluded by statute from the honoured secret society and prevented from being an *individual* by virtue of their female sex, women *belong* to the mafia family and the mafioso man. In some cases this belonging may not be sealed by marriage and they remain lifelong lovers, because divorce is forbidden to mafioso men (Buscetta was the first to break this 'law' and he was in fact 'dealt with' as a result of his infraction).

The category of *open complicity* seems best suited to describe the hybrid condition which is the experience of the 'mafia woman'; formally she is a free citizen in a democratic state, becoming gradually more educated, 'urbanized in her consciousness', as Peter Berger would say, perhaps not wealthy but comfortably off; at the same time she is nailed to her fate, her hands are tied, she is tightly bound by invisible fetters and is a participant in a closed, subversive world which is held together by the chilling fear of death. There is obviously no single way of being a woman in these conditions, there must be as many ways as there are women's stories. But the common denominator seems to be loyalty to the unwritten laws of the mafia, and above all a close collusion in her dependency on a violent man, on her absence of responsibility as an individual. Complicity pays. But often complicity also demands a high price.

The story of Angela Russo, who after her arrest was nicknamed 'Granny Heroin', bears witness to the profound wretchedness of family relationships in which 'mafia-ness' runs deep, and at the same time it clearly shows to what extent a woman can be an active criminal in the bosom of the mafia.

'Heroin and old lace' was the headline in *L'Ora* on 15 February 1982. Angela Russo, seventy-four, had been arrested along with twenty-four other people, many of whom were her close relatives. The newspapers immediately cast her in a starring role, which was subsequently scaled down at the trial:

> The granny of the gang was a tough, bossy woman with enormous prestige. She was . . . one of the 'brains' of the operation. From the quiet apartment on Via Abela where she lived with her son, daughter-in-law, grandchildren and paralysed husband, she issued telephoned instructions for consignments of 'shit', 'keys', 'snow', 'junk'. . . . Her business earned a comfortable livelihood for seven people, counting her sons and daughters-in-law.[1]

Angela Russo often took a train to Milan or Salerno. 'She would always travel with the same check overcoat, rather showy for a woman of her age. But she could never take it off. It was the signal for whoever had to collect her overnight case from her at the station.'[2]

Who was Angela Russo?

We have a long interview which Marina Pino did five years after the arrest, when 'Granny Heroin' was nearly eighty.[3] Despite ill health and despite appalling family conflicts and bereavements in the wake of internecine vendettas, Angela Russo appeared a strong, proud woman solidly integrated into what we can call both the world and ideology of the mafia.

> People go around talking about mafioso this, mafioso that. Are they joking or something? It's reached the point where any little fool or other who steals immediately becomes a 'mafioso'. I didn't see any real mafiosi in that trial. It's a lot of nonsense, is this the way to talk about serious things? Where is this mafia these days, these people that talk about the mafia, what do they know about it? I do, madam, yes, madam, I know what I'm talking about because the mafia was there in the old days in Palermo and so was the law. And this law didn't go having innocent mothers' sons killed. The mafia didn't kill anyone unless it was absolutely sure to begin with, absolutely sure that it had to, absolutely sure of the just law. Of course, people who sinned *avia a chianciri*, people who did wrong paid for it, but first there was the rule of the warning. They were warned at least three times: 'Be careful, you're out of line', and then if he kept it up, if he persisted in the error of his ways and didn't straighten himself out then of course he had to disappear and they made him disappear. And if there was some injustice, let's say somebody stole from somebody else and this was unfair, the mafia would intervene and sort things out with everybody's agreement. That was the law and that was the mafia that existed then in Palermo. They were real men. My father, Don Peppino, was a real man and the whole of Torrelunga and Brancaccio stood in fear and respect of him, even as far as Bagheria.[4]

Angela's father was a cattle dealer, a 'man of respect' and at home they never went without anything. Angela was born and grew up in a mafia family, just a pity that she was born female. 'My father's only grief was the fact that he had no sons. Every time a son was born he would die.... I was always like a boy and then I got on well with papà. We would go out hunting ... I liked shooting too ... I was never afraid of anything.... Even as a child, as a little girl I never took fright at anything.'

Unable to be a man, she developed an acute sense of female omnipotence. 'I had all these children but I always worked in the butcher's shop because I was always the boss ... I was strong ... never had any problems with the children either. The births were easy, at home, quick.... I never even needed a doctor, just for the miscarriages.... I had plenty of milk, too much, so as well as my own seven I breastfed three of my sister-in-law's children, for the poor thing was a bit dry.'

This woman's attachment to the world of the mafia seems total; if only she had been born a man she could have been more directly in charge. For her, the law *is* the mafia, and everyone else is in the wrong. Her arrest was therefore a signal injustice.

> I still had everything under my control, respect and command. Damned cops, damned judges. There's no law today, they make up the law, they do it as it suits them. These meddling cops, who can't mind their own business, who wouldn't have a clue about what to do if there weren't any spies, who operate on what the 'grasses' tell them. As if it's gospel, without asking themselves who's telling, what he's telling and why he's telling it. And the same goes for the judges, they make me sick.... And I, who've always told other people what to do all my life, how come I'd be doing this dispatching job on somebody else's say so?

However, at the trial a different picture emerged. 'There were different groups implicated, different mafia families: the Villagrazia clan, the La Noce clan, the Lombardo clan and then a group which was rather peculiar as it was made up of members of the same family, four men and four women: the "Coniglio clan" which took its name from the one who it at once became clear was the *capo*, Salvino, one of Granny Heroin's sons.'[5]

Salvino, the youngest of Angela's children, seemed at first to be the only one on the way to a serious criminal career, with his mother's heartfelt backing. These family dynamics came to light through a telephone tap. Salvino, who was not much more than a cowherd, suddenly went up in the world: the high life in Milan, glamorous women, cars and luxury hotels. But the drug running often led to trouble.

> Salvino would keep on turning up beset with the problems of the drug business. It was at this very point that mum, Angela Russo, would take the leading role. She defended her son, vouched for him, drew the solidarity of the whole family clan firmly around Salvino. On the telephone she would urge:

'We have to help Salvino, he was looking out for all of us and now he's in trouble.' . . . Ma Angela explained that they would need a hundred million lire to cover one of Salvino's debts, but they really only had to get twenty-five or thirty million for the crude stuff for 'cutting'. She is insistent about buying gold jewellery on credit so as to pawn it. She tells her daughter Rosetta that there's no need to be frightened: 'Salvino says that he must have seventy-five million coming from Bubu.'[6]

Salvino works away from home, on the inside of mafia low life; his mother runs things on the domestic front, coordinating the other family members in trafficking, answering the telephone, sorting out the orders and, lastly, acting as a courier no one will suspect, all over Italy, sometimes in the US. 'More a victim of her son than a big *capo*,' maintains Marina Pino.

Involved were her daughter Rosaria and son-in-law Umberto di Cara, her grandchildren Angelina and Alfonso, Paolo, Angelina's husband, and her daughter-in-law Vicenza di Cara, the wife of Mario, who was one of the few family members with no involvement in the drug trade.

At the trial Angela Russo brought all her talents into play. 'Depending on the hearing and other variables, she would come on as a frail old woman bowed down with infirmities, or a woman destroyed and grieving in black, or an implacable and quick-witted accuser.'[7] Moreover, the trial was rich in moments of high drama. A family tragedy on a Greek epic scale was unfolding before the public's eyes: the mother against the son, the son against the mother. Powerful family dynamics steeped in death because they were steeped in the mafia. 'It was called the trial of the dead because there on stage, that is, while the trial was going on, there were two crimes and one of the accused disappeared.'[8]

The turning point was Salvino's *pentimento*. He turned out to have little of the makings of a mafioso compared with his mother, who indeed harangued him as a 'coward, a wretch, a "snitch" and a grass. . . . "He's crazy, he's no *pentito*, your honours, he's crazy. He's such a scoundrel he'll even send his own innocent mother to jail," Angela Russo, swathed in the black draperies of full mourning, shouted to the court.'[9] Granny Heroin responded to her son's *pentimento* with a gesture of maternal knowingness: she asserted that Salvino had gone mad, that he had always been sick and unbalanced because he had had meningitis as a child.

After Salvino's *pentimento* the number of accused doubled, going up from thirty-three to sixty-four. The second *pentito*, the Zisa boss Salvatore Anselmo, who was under house arrest, was killed. His brother and co-accused, Vincenzo, disappeared completely.

A few days after the trap set for Salvatore Anselmo, they killed Mario Coniglio, Salvino's brother and Granny Heroin's oldest child. Mario worked in a butcher's shop and was a quiet man, who had nothing at all to do with the drug dealing in which nearly everyone around him was involved: his mother, his sister, his wife and two of his children. A proxy vendetta killing, a warning to the *pentito*, Salvino. Indeed, Salvino backed out, accusing the judges of having forced him into his *pentimento* and writing a letter to the mafia in which he repented of his repentance. 'I feel like a dead man,' he admitted to the judge.

The death of her eldest was a terrible blow to Angela the mother. 'Mario, my light, the best and most innocent man there ever was and he, blameless as could be, had taken on the burden of this whole sorry family without turning a hair, the only thought he had was to work hard and love us. They killed him because of that scoundrel of a brother. And so now, just like him, I feel I'm a dead woman. . . . I see shadows of the living and inside me there are shadows of the dead,' Angela lamented, years later, in the interview already quoted.

Her hatred for her treacherous son was appalling. She started out cunningly: 'I have forgiven Salvatore, but I don't know whether God will ever be able to forgive him.' Then she continued almost triumphantly: 'They say he's getting out in a year. He knows he's a condemned man, he knows he'll get out and they'll kill him. They don't forgive. He says he hopes first to have time to avenge his brother Mario, who was murdered for his sake. But what does a man like Salvatore think he can do? He should have thought of Mario before. They won't give him time now. Salvino will die now, when he gets out.'

Motherly might in the service of the mafia 'law': 'Salvino watch out, because I made you and I'll kill you.'

Is this a form of flagrant compensation for her exclusion as a woman from mafia command?

The Court of Assizes sentenced Angela Russo to five years and Salvatore Coniglio, her son, to twelve. The Court of Cassation confirmed the sentence on appeal.

The fact that she wasn't a mafia *capo* – a role in which many newspapers did, however, try to cast her – in no way diminishes Granny Heroin's open complicity and responsibility. She was a woman, a female who would have very much liked to be a man, a mafia man.

The bosses' women

'Let's be careful, very careful. We know nothing about them, so let's be careful what we say and suggest, to make no false claims on behalf of people who are really quite unknown to us.'

I would like to endorse these words of Giovanna Fiume's, spoken at the end of a debate in Palermo.[10] The thoughts, fears, desires and dreams of women who live in mafia families are still a grey area for the rest of us. Few of them have dared so far to betray their own world – and those only after unbearable mourning for murdered husbands, children, fathers or lovers. And what of all the rest?

I want none the less to make an effort of imagination and inference, on the basis of those few direct testimonies we have available, to ask myself who these women are and what they think, these women who seem so different and remote from me but are none the less still women who, like me, have loves and hates, dreams and fears.

The great changes which have left their mark on the female condition have doubtless, albeit in a very particular way, also influenced the role of women in mafia families. 'It is certainly a double role: on the one hand it falls to women to act as mute witnesses, as the traditional depositories of a criminal culture which is transmitted from generation to generation, and on the other hand they are obliging accomplices, the ones in whose name assets and property are registered.'[11]

The traditional image seems primarily ideological, as is the distinction between the traditional, kind-hearted mafia and the modern, cynical mafia. Buscetta, who indeed regrets the alleged disappearance of the Honoured Society of the first kind, describes the mafioso's woman in these terms: 'She is made in the husband's mould. She doesn't talk. Because he has trained her to keep silent. She must never know what goes on around the house; she has to stay locked in her world. It's impossible to know how unhappy she is, because she'll never tell anyone.'[12] This image none the less seems more wishful thinking on the part of the mafioso man than reality.

It seems likely that, within a context of unquestionable subordination, these women assume a much more complex role. Above all, and this is the hypothesis I should like gradually to prove, their role is active, their complicity very strong in the continuous reproduction of their own and their daughters' subordination. In ethical terms the responsibility they bear seems strong, very strong, sometimes on a par with that of their men.

There is a widespread dictum that 'women don't know'. In my view this convenient subterfuge should be revised straight away. It is unthinkable that a woman like the rest of us women should not know what is going on around her: the comings and goings of her husband and children, the evidence, in one way or another, of what they are involved in, the amount and source of the money circulating in the house. And the more mysterious the things she notices, the more curious she will be to understand, the more impelled to spy.

Ann Drahmann, the wife of Trigger Mike Coppola, the Italian-American mafia boss, would comb through the various hiding places that her husband had had made in the house for money and documents in the certainty that no one would find them. She tried to work out the extent of her husband's wealth and the source of the money. She was quite aware, even proud to begin with, that she had married a real boss, but tried to discover his secrets so as not to be completely at his mercy. Sometimes she also appropriated his confidential mail. 'A better way to check on Mike was to open his registered mail that sometimes came when he was out of the house.... One day while searching Mike's wastebasket, Ann found pieces of a letter Mike had torn up and thrown away. She put it back together.'[13]

Clearly, knowing does not rule out the possibility that, with understanding, some psychic defence mechanism will be activated: repression, forgetting, some shift in perception, stifling responsibility and any sense of guilt.

That women do know is confirmed by men and women who have collaborated with the law. Piera Aiello said: 'It's not the Partanna people I have anything against, it's the Partanna widows. They can tell you they know nothing, but they can't come and say that to Piera Aiello. A woman always knows what her husband or her son is up to.'[14] And: 'The wives feel everything, whether they are mafiose, Sicilian or otherwise, they take everything on themselves. I was a sponge. If you ask mafioso husbands questions, they won't answer, but if you're nice and keep your mouth shut those guys will tell you, because they're fools like all men and because it makes them feel important.'[15] Giacoma Filipello also bears this out in the interview already quoted: 'The state has no idea how much a mafia woman knows.'

And Calderone explains how hard it is for mafiosi to keep the women in the dark about their business.

> Every Cosa Nostra family lays down very strict rules and punishments for anyone giving away mafia information to his own wife, but I don't know how possible it is to have these standards taken seriously.... Apart from the fact that many wives of men of honour – nearly all the ones I've known, in fact – come from mafia families, they've breathed the air of Cosa Nostra since they were born and for that very reason they know how a mafioso thinks and acts, and it's best not to forget that a man's partner guesses everything in the end, and what she can't work out for herself she gets her own women friends or her sisters and sisters-in-law to tell her, for they're often married to men of honour too.... When my wife ... said 'I do', when we got married, she knew what she was getting into.[16]

Above all there are frequent unforeseeable moves, periods of 'normality alternating with clandestinity', and prison. Antoinette Giancana, the daughter of Sam Giancana, another Italian-American boss, recalls that her father's long absences (he was in prison) were explained to her as his being away 'at college'. 'Secrecy about his life as a criminal was a way of life for Sam.... Never once did he admit to me or my sisters that he was a mafioso.'[17] Obviously the mother was in a different position, on the one hand having to put up a front of respectability with her daughters and neighbours, and on the other being a go-between for communication between prison and mafia (for example through what appeared to be letters from the father to his daughters and which were really coded messages for the mafia) and she also received help from her husband's mafioso friends.

The bosses' women have to be acrobats to keep up a front of middle-class normality in the jungle of criminal life in which the whole family is involved. In the Palermo judges' indictment we read: 'We cease to be amazed, however, when we discover that Santapaola's wife, Grazia Minniti, and his children were accommodated in one of the villas at the La Perla Jonica tourist complex, which is owned by the Costanzo group, from *22 June to 31 December 1982*, namely when Santapaola was wanted for having carried out, with others, the pitiless slaughter on the Palermo ring road.'[18] How did Signora Santapaola manage to explain such a prolonged holiday to her children, just down the road from where they lived?

Sons and daughters, moreover, have tabs kept on them specifically, especially while they are small and could unthinkingly tell strangers things that have to be kept secret. But persecutory paranoia also extends to children's friends.

Whatever the reason [for her father's suspicious attitude], it was embarrassing for me and my sisters. It appeared to us that Sam had a complete resumé on every youngster and his or her parents that I brought to the house. He knew about their fathers and what they did for a living; about their mothers and how they acted; about the families and the friends they associated with. If he decided for some reason that he disapproved of some child . . . I not only couldn't have that child to my home, I couldn't be seen with him or her. I was always amazed at how much Sam knew about my friends and their families.[19]

Both in Joe Bonanno's autobiography and in his son Bill's biography episodes are described which make it hard to believe that the wives were left in the dark about their husbands' mafia activities.

On this day, as on so many others, Rosalie Bonanno felt a sense of loneliness without a sense of privacy; she believed that her telephone was tapped, suspected that her house was being watched sometimes by men with binoculars, that even the sound of her footsteps was being recorded by tiny hidden gadgets. . . . After her marriage to Bill, however, she experienced nocturnal solitude for the first time, and she began to dread the night as she never had as a child, and she remained awake, pondering the uncertainties of her adult life – the fact that when her husband left the house in the morning she never knew what time he would return or *if* he would return; the unexplained origin of her first son, Charles; the mysterious disappearance of her father-in-law. . . . There were rifles among the paraphernalia in the garage, and also a rifle in the guest room behind a bureau on which was a statue of the Christ child. . . . There was an unloaded pistol on top of Bill's bureau in the master bedroom, along with a plastic tube of quarters.[20]

For these women periods of solitude alternate with periods when their homes are overrun with people. Joe Bonanno acknowledges: 'One of the things Fay and the children constantly had to put up with was the conferences at our house between me and other men. Since the conversations often were confidential, I would close the door or take my friends to another room where we could talk in private.'[21]

On such occasions Ann Drahmann Coppola would listen from behind the door.

And Giacoma Filipello relates: 'They were years of dread and fear. And though to begin with I only knew things because I eavesdropped when I was putting their food on the table or serving their coffee, during those years I knew because Natale had been forced to tell me what was happening.'[22]

Calderone told of a trip to Naples, which started out as a pleasure trip with the whole family on which he would become the godfather at the christening of a Camorra crony's son, and turned into a three-month stay on Ischia while an underworld conflict flared up in Catania. 'Pippo and I looked at one another and decided to stay on. The next day we moved into that villa with our families and lived there for nearly three months.'[23] What explanation did he give his wife, who probably ought to have gone back to her job in an office at the University of Catania?

We have already seen that Calderone's wife was aware of and went along with her husband's criminal activities from the moment they were married. All the same, if we pick out a few details of this couple's everyday life the effect is startling. For instance, Calderone talks about Nitto Santapaola's brother, Nino, a coldblooded hitman who had a preference for killing his victims on Saturdays. It should be noted that these were years when the Calderone and Santapaola families were on friendly terms and socialized together. 'On Sunday mornings at my house we would open the newspaper and remark: "The madman worked hard yesterday." We knew some of the people who were murdered. My wife knew them and she was displeased and frightened every time she read about their deaths.'[24]

How did Signora Calderone manage to live a double life as an office worker at the university and as a wife and mother attending parties and lunches with people who kill as regularly as others do the football pools?

Obviously she was adept at making the two worlds fit together; her working career and the fact of being accustomed to deal with people outside the family probably helped her adjust to new situations: from the wife of a boss to the wife of a fugitive to the wife of a *pentito*. Falcone said of her: 'Calderone's wife is a perfect example of "the man of honour's woman", affectionate, discreet, plausible, never saying a word out of place, animated by a boundless devotion. Calderone was arrested in Nice. She called me from there. . . . The two of them had already discussed every last detail of his collaboration with the law.'[25] The constant presence of death, which is central to mafia behaviour, necessarily echoes into everyday actions. Banal, repetitive occurrences assume the character of the exceptional, taking on a heroic aura. Antoinette Giancana remembers what she calls the 'Last Supper syndrome': 'As I think of those moments, it's as if my mother were the wife of a man who was totally involved in combat. Now he was coming home from the fighting, and there she was, looking at him with love and fear in her eyes, cheerfully serving him a sumptuous meal, yet at the same time realizing that when he walked out the door he might never return.'[26]

The need to keep looking over one's shoulder, suspicion, fear and precautions of various kinds tend to become almost routine. Antoinette continues:

> That left a lasting impression on me as a child. There were so many precautions Sam took at home and away from home. . . . Caution seemed to prevail wherever we were. Even as a small child I noticed that before entering a restaurant or any other public place, Sam would always drive around the block at least once or twice to survey the area, see if he saw anything out of the ordinary. Once satisfied things were in order, he would lead us inside, scanning the entire seating area, searching out faces he might recognise. . . . And when we sat down, Sam would never allow us to be near a window, and he insisted that his seat be situated so that his back was to the wall and he could have a clear view of the entrance.[27]

One component of daily life which favours and demands complicity is the telephone. We know from numerous telephone taps that women broadly collaborate with their mafia husbands, answering the telephone and carrying on coded conversations, often between continents. Once more we quote from the Palermo judges: 'This telephone call confirms that Maria Corleo had perfectly understood who her interlocutor was, since she had informed him of her husband's arrest.' The interlocutor was Ignazio Salvo, who wanted to know Buscetta's telephone number. Or again: 'It seems relevant to point out that tapped telephone calls indicate that Mutolo's wife was also in the know about her husband's shady dealings.'[28]

Antoinette Giancana recalls her mother's crucial role in filtering telephone calls. As with the doorbell, the boss himself never answered directly. It was always his wife, however tired or ill she might be, who kept a check on what was involved. 'Sam and Momma were equally careful about telephone calls. They were always screened by Momma. Sam would never answer the phone, only my mother. She would ask who it was, repeat the name loud enough for him to hear, and watch as he nodded his head yes or no, indicating that he would or wouldn't talk to the caller.'[29]

In addition to their domestic involvement, these days the boss's relatives, and particularly his wife, have assumed a crucial function in the management of finances and real estate – the colossal assets that have accrued as a result of drug running and arms dealing. With reference to the 'Palermo judgment',* have already seen the case of Francesca Citarda, the wife of Giovanni Bontade. She would certainly have been privy to many secrets and in fact was subsequently killed along with her husband. 'Not because she was with her husband – Anna Puglisi maintains – but because she too was a mafiosa, and for this reason had to be killed.'[30]

Just as in the days of emigration, when in their husbands' absence the wives would run the entire domestic economy on their own, the bosses' wives carry out many of the functions of husbands who are in prison. But how far does the mafia allow women to take the place of their men? Our knowledge of Cosa Nostra's internal workings is somewhat scant on this point. I am inclined to believe, however, that temporary *financial administration* should not be confused with the administration of mafia *power*. The mafia's apparent distrust of women is such that it is not easy to imagine that men of this kind would let themselves be told what to do by a woman.

Rosa Errigo, the wife and now the widow of the 'ndrangheta boss Paolo De Stefano, carried a certain weight in the financial management of the clan. With huge assets registered in her name, the lady did not think herself above taking personal responsibility for certain illicit dealings. 'The young woman was found in a flat in Rome along with a number of Calabrian and Roman known criminals . . .', writes Gianfranco Manfredi, continuing: 'There is no doubt that the woman had formerly been a phantom in the mafia world, and now changes taking place in the 'ndrangheta are beginning to give corporeal substance, names and faces to these "phantoms".'[31]

The De Stefano couple was also the focus of interest for Judge Cordova in his investigations of a credit given by the Banca Nazionale del Lavoro in Reggio Calabria to Paolo De Stefano and Rosa Errigo, a credit given without the usual guarantee of collateral. The bank clerk who drew up the documents wrote: 'It can be assumed that benefits will be derived from the clients' wide-ranging business connections.'[32]

Is money erotic? Wives and lovers demonstrate their appreciation of unexpected wealth.

The story of Ann Drahmann Coppola brings to mind Brecht's ballads and songs from *The Threepenny Opera* and *Mahagonny*. 'Oh! Moon of Alabama / We now must say goodbye / We've lost our good old mamma / and must have dollars / Oh! You know why.'

Her exploits are entwined with a powerful ambition for social climbing

---

* See pp. 118–22.

153

which is translated into some smart accounting with dollars. (It should be said that in her case we have no autobiography to draw on, but a biographical reconstruction of her life on the basis of documents assembled after her suicide.)

After the death of her first husband, a gambler, Ann set her sights higher: 'When he died she had resolved that when she remarried – and she had no doubt she would remarry – it would be to a top man in the racket. Trigger Mike was as near to the top as a girl could get.'[33] The marriage was a tempestuous one, marked by extraordinary physical violence towards her and psychological violence towards her daughter by her first marriage. But Ann put up with it for some time, spying on her husband with future revenge in mind (she did later collaborate with the FBI) and accumulating dollars to secure her future.

'Money, tons of it. . . . Feeling satisfied with the impression he had made, and perhaps as a reward for her help, Mike gave her $10,000 for Christmas. She put the money away and noted the amount in her little black book. At the end of 1958, it listed some impressive totals: in 1956 . . . a yearly total of $23,200; in 1957 . . . a yearly total of $57,900; in 1958 . . . a total of $68,200.'[34] The harshness, the singlemindedness, the toleration of physical and mental violence and, finally, vendetta – none of this did Ann any good. At the end of the road she was left with no energy and no will to live. Alone, in a Rome hotel, she put an end to her life. In her suicide note she asked for a final act of vengeance against the boss: 'I want to be cremated and have my ashes thrown on Mike Coppola's house.'

The maxi-trial has also opened up some insights into women and money. The Palermo judges write: 'And also the businessman Arturo Cassina has effectively admitted . . . that he paid "protection" to Colletti; a declaration that has been corroborated by the statements of Benedetta Bono, Colletti's lover, who observed that whenever her partner went to the offices of Cassina's company in Palermo he came back with wads of banknotes and gave her some as a present.'[35]

At thirty-two, Benedetta Bono left her husband and moved from Montelepre to Ribera with her four children. Between 1977 and 1983, when he was killed, she was the lover of the mafia *capo* Carmelo Colletti. She then agreed to talk about everything she had seen during this time. 'The story told by Benedetta Bono is a remarkable one, one she never altered, repeating it in the courtroom at Agrigento and also at the Palermo maxi-trial.'[36]

With the death of the lover who had generously kept her and wanted her always by his side, Benedetta's life changed noticeably. 'After Colletti's death I was left with nothing. And I've got four children, one of them in Germany. I couldn't buy anything, just clothes at the street market. I had to go on the game. But I couldn't buy myself any clothes, nothing. I had just one bra that I mended every night. This was my life,' Benedetta relates now.[37]

And the mafia did not forget her. Five years after her evidence at the trials someone shot at her. 'She survived, perhaps by good luck, perhaps because the attack was only meant as a warning, as an intimidatory measure.'[38] But Benedetta denies this: 'God, they shot at me once. But it was for something else. No, they've never threatened me. . . . The thing is, I loved Colletti. He wasn't an easy man, you know. He could be violent, coarse. But I loved him.'[39]

And one thing leads to another. The complicity which is born taking easy money is gradually extended to other kinds of involvement. 'The following day, Cordano Salvina, who lived with Cremona, reported that a fire had broken out in his offices, destroying all the papers that were in it; subsequently, the woman would admit to the public prosecutor in Siracusa that she had started the fire in order to erase any trace of the false invoices that were made up by her partner for his employer's sake.'[40]

In terms of money and status the benefits of complicity are obvious. The position of the mafia man is in part reflected on his women and this clarifies things somewhat because many women seem consenting or complicit in mafia crimes. This obviously goes for the higher levels of the hierarchy, but also has a bearing on local and village situations. Danilo Dolci took down the testimony of a sharecropper who explained:

> Everyone knew that he was the one in charge in the village. . . . These mafiosi are all nice as ninepence, when you see them and talk to them, they're all smiling and good-natured, they seem like the teachers down at the school, they want people to think of them as the fathers of the village, but they're constantly on their guard. And people try to make themselves liked by them, they take them fruit, a kid, cheese. . . . And wives of mafioso husbands have the say-so in the neighbourhood. If, say, you became a mafioso tomorrow, I'd have a different kind of respect for your wife, just so as I'd watch my step.[41]

And Michela Buscemi explains: 'You can tell the wives and daughters of mafiosi right away in local neighbourhoods; they're arrogant, they shout and threaten people. And you can even recognize the children, for the bosses' sons start giving orders to their playmates at a very early age: "You, go and punch him", and the weaker one does it.'[42]

Calderone also said that many women like the mafia: 'Women are well off in the mafia. Being the wife of a mafioso means there are a lot of privileges, big and small, that you can enjoy, and in a way it also has its responsibilities. It can happen that in apparently innocuous circumstances you have to dispose of a person's life.'[43] Here the story continues with the episode of Nitto Santapaola's wife, who was the recipient of attentions from the ignorant owner of a driving school where she passed her driving test and she had to decide whether the unwary man deserved death or something less.

Generously, the lady opted for a compromise and the outcome was that the brother of the designated victim, through mistaken identity, was shot in the legs.

Malevolence? Parisitism? Feminine wiles?

Whatever description we might give to these attitudes, the common denominator is apparently docile submission, an abdication from the individuality of the self in exchange for an illusory participation in male power.

And the mothers of mafiosi? We know even less about them than about the wives. If nothing else, their complicity seems consistent in psychological terms. Endowed symbolically, as we have already seen, with the powerful mafia rhetoric which sets a value on the mother at the expense of the woman, the mothers have obviously styled themselves as 'mother of my sons', sacrificing any possible subjectivity as a woman and as the man's partner. Like the mothers of many rapists, these women abdicate their own gender identities to the point where they justify and support their own sons in the trade of bringing death – so long as it is the sons of other mothers who are killed and not their own.

As we have already seen, in order to 'honour' his own mother, Nitto Santapaola had four young boys killed. 'They were guilty of having snatched his mother's bag and abusing her, she even fell and broke an arm. . . . Had it really been these boys? And did they realize that they were robbing the mother of the Santapaolas? Did they know what they were doing? And even if they did know, was this sufficient reason to kill them? Is this reason to kill a child of thirteen?' the troubled Calderone wondered, having taken part in the execution.[44] And we wonder: what does Santapaola's mother think about it? Does she feel honoured by such urgent filial attention? Is she proud of her offspring? Has she ever wondered what the difference is between her and the mother of one of these boys?

There are as many different women's stories as there are ways of having dealings with the mafia and the men of the mafia. We have already made this clear. On the one hand are women like Giacoma Filipello, who stood by her man, even when he was losing, right up until he was killed; on the other are women like Nick Gentile's wife, who was more faithful to the financial perks than to her husband. When Gentile got back to Italy from America, a loser and a wanted man, his family turned away from him (this at least is the version given by Gentile himself).

> I was given a frosty welcome by all my relatives. . . . In the room next to mine, my wife was with a crowd of neighbours talking about my unexpected return and saying I had come to destroy her home and, after a hysterical attack, she fell to the floor in a faint. By then I had grasped the meaning of those terrible words, which were full of contempt for me and convinced me that the affection so often shown to me was illusory and based only on dollars. . . . [Before]

my standard of living was very high and the family enjoyed comforts that I had won through sacrifice and indescribable risk, with my life always in jeopardy. Then I was regarded as the favourite in my family, whereas now I've become the black sheep. . . . All my relatives saw in me was the gangster who dishonoured them.[45]

Violence that is suffered, violence that is repressed and finds an outlet in a vicarious participation in male violence? The cases in which women themselves have become violent are extremely rare. Perhaps the only relevant episode, reported by the Parliamentary Anti-mafia Commission of Inquiry, legislature V, is that regarding some women from the Greco family of Ciaculli.

In 1947, Francesco Arnone fell into an ambush awaiting him outside his house. Two shots had wounded him badly and he was dragging himself on his knees in an attempt to reach safety when Antonina and Rosalia Greco came out of their house armed with sharp knives and killed him. Francesco's brother, Giovanni Arnone, came outside and fired two shots, killing Antonina and seriously wounding Rosalia: thereupon Mommina and Paolo Greco emerged like furies from inside the Grecos' house, where they had been watching. They disarmed Giovanni Arnone and killed him with his own rifle, firing at point-blank range and blowing half his head away.[46]

Violence in defence of the integrity of the family nucleus, sometimes in defence of the mafia clan of which the family head is a member: a significant example of this took place at Palermo in 1983. When the boss Pietro Vernengo was stopped by the police along with others of his clan, he managed to escape capture thanks to the pandemonium staged by a group of women and children. 'Freed by a swarm of screaming women with their children, by the friends of friends, by relatives and young street-corner loafers. The police had already bundled him into a squad car along with three others after a shoot-out. . . . Crowds of women, children, all seemingly members of the Vernengo clan.'[47]

A similar protest was reported during the maxi-trial. Caponnetto relates: 'I personally recall the violence with which some women – relatives of a prisoner who had decided to collaborate with the law and changed his mind the following day – screamed at the magistrates from the gallery of the underground courtroom, berating them and accusing them of threatening their kin with violence.'[48]

The same episode was also remembered by Giovanni Falcone:

Some women, alas all too many, have not yet aligned themselves with the culture of life. I'm thinking of the wife of Vincenzo Buffa, who had begun to cooperate with me. I made the mistake of letting him talk to her, since he kept

157

on asking to. And she persuaded him to retract and take back his statements. She even organized a wives' revolt of sorts in the underground courtroom of the maxi-trial at Palermo; they were weeping and screaming and protesting loudly, not against Buffa's intention to break *omertà*, but against the judges who had 'forced' him to do so.[49]

Buscetta's sister too denied her brother the *pentito*, after her husband was murdered.

What women get out of supporting the mafia seems to be primarily material gain, of status and purchasing power and comfort. The costs, however, are located at the level of love and affection, at the level of freedom.

The discreet charm of violence

The moment has come to confess, to make known to everyone what I have kept inside for years, tormenting me and causing me periods of deep and intense pain. My sad story began when I met a man, when I fell hopelessly in love and when I discovered that he belonged to one of the Cosa Nostra families, these families which believe that they consist of men of honour, following the rules and laws made by themselves and hazardous to transgress against. I was changed by this love, I had accepted everything I had come to know and nothing mattered to me at all; but when I was alone in my room a veil of sadness fell over my eyes when I thought of the evil and the terror and how these people are indifferent when they talk of crimes and getting even. All this made me pretty sad, but I could not free myself from this man; first because I loved him and I would have done anything, second because deep down I was a bit afraid, because I had got to know about certain things that had happened. I am still living this nightmare today; I'll never be able to free myself from it, however much I want to. Memories keep coming back to me, I feel I am dead, without any strength to take action, most of all when I think that I shook hands with a guy who was killed a few minutes later. Sadly, even though I know all these things I still love that man, I can't live without him . . . Palermo, 7.3.1988.[50]

Female fantasy does not scorn violence. Manly attributes such as shows of strength and predatory attitudes certainly have a hold on many women's erotic fantasies – when placed in the service of courtship and seduction.

'Mary felt attracted to me because of that terrible past she had heard about and the way it drew her. The abyss has its appeal and for Mary I was the abyss, the incomprehensible, the mysterious,' says the mafioso Nick Gentile.[51]

Giacoma Filipello was also attracted by the abyss:

At first he didn't attract me. He was forty-four and he seemed coarse. And I was only nineteen. Then he won me, he satisfied my every wish. He was jealous, he was unfaithful, but then he would get down on his knees in front of me and become a little lamb. I was drawn by that deviant, reckless life. . . . I loved Natale. . . . I felt I was different from the other girls. I have always been a rebel.[52]

In 1964 Luciano Liggio was captured at Corleone. 'He was captured in that very house where by any human logic he should never have been able to find shelter.'[53] And Gellert writes:

There's still a murky background to the story of Liggio's arrest: he was hiding in the house of the Sorisi sisters, one of whom, Luchina, had been engaged to Placido Rizzotto before Liggio killed him and threw his body in the gorge. 'We'd thought of everything, but not of that,' said Colonel Milillo. How did he manage to get on the right side of that woman who had been wearing mourning for years because of him?[54]

Enzo Biagi mentions other details, but the whole picture is still something of a mystery.

Placido's 'girlfriend', the lovely Leoluchina, swore that she would tear the murderer's guts out. Later, however, she welcomed the young man who had suspicions and arrest warrants hanging over him, giving him shelter and safety in her home, where no one would suspect, because the human heart is mysterious, and she took care of the fugitive. They say that when the police captured Luciano and took him away in an ambulance, the tender and loving Leoluchina Sorisi stroked his hair and kissed him and burst into uncontrollable tears.[55]

According to other versions 'she said nothing, just lowered her eyes in shame'.[56] There are known stories of women who became the lovers of a murderer with vendetta in mind. Could it have been that Leoluchina was stopped before she carried out a plan of revenge?

Could it have been that she set out to know more and that then, as things went on, became attracted and dominated by the man she set out to dominate?

Or, more simply, that some dialectic of passion developed between the victim and the butcher, along the lines of Cavani's film *Night Porter*?

The attraction of evil. Attraction and repulsion, the forbidden, the perverse. Here we are dealing with fantasies and the imaginary. Falling in love in its nascent state, intoxicating, transgressive and effervescent. Usually violence takes a hold on the mind, but this is not to be confused with reality. Its enactment, however, is often equivalent to a non-elaboration in the psyche. The world of the psyche tends to be enriched by the very measure in which enactment is suspended. But what occurs when material violence impacts on it? What happens to these women when something that is in us all, that erotic and violent effervescence of the nascent state of falling in love, what belongs in the realm of the imaginary, is transformed into an everyday routine? Fantasized violence is usually sublimated in love, tenderness and companionship. But the mafia man exercises violence in earnest, as an everyday routine, as a trade of killing.

I am guessing, trying to understand, to put myself in these women's shoes. I think that where violence is concerned there is rupture, not continuity, between fantasy and reality, the intrapsychic world and the real world. Fantasizing and enjoying fantasies of violence have the function of defusing the aggressive drives within us. It may even be that the material exercise of violence atrophies the capacity for fantasizing and dreaming. The 'banality of evil' which Hannah Arendt talks about engenders and is in its turn engendered by an incapacity to imagine.

This speculation is supported by the 'compulsion to fuck' and the genital fixation which is found in many mafia men and which has already been discussed in Part I of this book. The psychic elaboration of violence and the sublimation of aggression put a check on violent action, whereas violence that is constantly carried out blocks the capacity for sublimation. If this were true, violent men would be found dull and disappointing in intimate relations. Obviously, the truth is that things are far more complex.

It seems possible from this to discern some kind of schizophrenia in relation to violence and death, a doubling of inner worlds, which are parallel and disconnected: on the one hand intimate attachments, love and passion, on the other a fierce, cynical and bloodthirsty insensitivity. This schizophrenia is characteristic of women and men. The former seem able to love even while knowing that the object of their love is a ferocious murderer, while the latter seem capable of tenderness and love, even despite the murderous ferocity which characterizes their social dealings.

Falcone said: 'We can derive a lot of insights about relations between husband and wife from reading the transcripts of telephone conversations recorded by the police. We find enormous affection for their children and an incredible warmth in family relationships, all of which are surprising in ruthless people for whom the use of weapons is routine.'[57]

It is as if women who fall in love with murderers had, in the process of individuation, failed to develop an ego strong and mature enough to be able to reconcile intimacy with the social world, inner worlds with the world outside. Perhaps there are no emotional resources for judging reality, either internal or social, with any ethical coherence. Also lacking is a capacity to see the other as an individual. The 'emotional trap' muddies the view of the total person beyond the relation of intimacy. Love does not feel reason. This is the dilemma which is well exemplified by the letter quoted above from the young woman in love with a hitman.

Reflecting on her childhood and how she grew up, Antoinette Giancana shows a very shrewd grasp of the difficulty, not to say the impossibility, of making a coherent assessment in ethical terms of family ties of affection on the one hand and bloody ferocity outside the family on the other, in relation to many mafia men she knew.

She writes of her father: 'When I was a small child, Sam had cuddled me in his arms, bounced me on his knee, and spent hours decorating our Christmas trees and putting toys together for me. And as he did those things . . . those loving and thoughtful acts . . . he was also deciding whether men should live or die on the streets of Chicago.'[58]

And then there were her father's friends:

Some, like Rocco Fischetti, Willie Potatoes Daddano, or Chuckie English, were more than business associates, they were like members of the family. . . . Publicly their names had become synonymous with the crimes of Al Capone, but for me, they were second fathers – kindly, generous older gentlemen who treated me with affection . . . I have to admit that for many years I didn't believe Willie Potatoes was capable of such cruelty. He got fifteen years on the case and died in prison, but accounts of Willie's brutality, like those of so many of my father's friends, bore no relation to the Willie Potatoes who ate at my parents' table and whom I grew to love as a child and as an older woman. . . . Despite his reputation for violence, Willie was a pussycat at home.[59]

And she adds: 'I guess that for as long as I live I will never forget that moment or the fact that the man in the red [Santa Claus] suit was Fat Leonard. He had bought those skates for me. He had rented the red suit and played Santa Claus so that a little girl wouldn't lose her belief in Santa Claus. It is hard even now to realise that Fat Leonard was one of Sam's professional killers, a man who lived by the gun and eventually died by it.'[60]

Antoinette knew these men as a child and as a daughter, and this makes her dilemma more understandable. But what of adult women who can make no distinction between love and complicity and rather than be alone become the accomplices of murderers and terrorists?

There has been recent discussion in the newspapers about 'top-ranking' women of bosses: Saveria Benedetta Palazzolo Provenzano, Antonina Bagarella Riina and Grazia Minniti Santapaola, strong and, at least as it would appear, ruthless women. Women who are emblematic in their open, altogether female, complicity with the mafia. Holders of secrets, accomplices from love? From fear? From self-interest? We know little or nothing about their lives at the side of ruthless criminals like Provenzano, Riina and Santapaola, but we know for sure that their psychological and material support has made a substantial contribution to these men's conquest and holding of power in Cosa Nostra.

Provenzano is still at large, or perhaps dead. After twenty years of being on the run, his wife has returned home to Corleone. 'No one has been able to rob her of the secret of her husband's fate. Not one clue, not even a tear.'[61] Saveria Benedetta Palazzolo seems an educated woman, responsible and fully aware. She speaks Italian without any hint of dialect, she dresses elegantly and her children speak English and German. 'She was officially a shirtmaker, but in the sixties she controlled assets of over two hundred million lire. She had been put in charge of the Latoia estate, an estate in the Alcamo countryside which has now been confiscated. The judges gave her a year and a half for laundering, but the sentence was suspended.'[62]

Antonina Bagarella grew up in a mafia family; her brothers Leoluca and Calogero were on Liggio's side. Calogero was killed in the Viale Lazio murders in 1969, in which Riina was involved, but as became evident from bugging devices in the Bagarella household, the women of the family only discovered this twenty years later. Antonina went to the *liceo* (secondary school) in Corleone between 1959 and 1964. One of her old schoolmates now recalls: 'Ninetta was pretty. She was full of life. We knew she came from a mafia family, but they were poor, people without much money.... We all knew that she was promised to a mafioso, and nobody had the nerve to court her. We would ask her to the parties but she always refused.... She was a good student, clever, industrious.'[63] Another of her schoolmates, now the local councillor for arts and culture at Corleone, says: 'She was a beautiful girl. She studied hard and she was ambitious. She wanted to get a degree and teach. She didn't confide in anyone.'[64]

There is an interview with Ninetta Bagarella, given to Mario Francese, the law reporter for the *Giornale di Sicilia* who was later killed by the mafia. The interview was in 1971. Here Antonina furnishes an image of herself which is in many respects a credible one, both from a subjective point of view (a young woman's wish to make good, having been born and grown up in a poor and illiterate environment) and from a social and environmental point of view (a priori identification with a mafia ideology of rebellion against the state). Ninetta relates:

> I lived in poverty and for this very reason I dreamt and felt the need to become independent. I wanted to go on with my studies. I wanted to achieve a place in the world. Not only culturally, but also in financial terms. That was when I began reading books from the school library and the municipal library. Books of criticism and fiction. At that time I was particularly struck by novels that spoke about the oppressed and oppressors because it was like seeing the life of Corleone in those books. Machiavelli interested me a lot. And do you know why? Because his guiding principle, the end justifies the means, was applied to the letter by the local police. When it came to achieving the ends they had in mind they never bothered about the means.[65]

With hindsight, it seems, those very qualities of intelligence and will to autonomy point to her guilt and confirm her responsibility.

After the *maturità* exams Antonina enrolled in the Faculty of Arts and Philosophy and attended the university assiduously for a year. She was a member of Azione Cattolica and held office as an assistant in the diocesan charitable body at San Giuseppe Jato. She abruptly left university, took a teaching diploma, and began teaching physical education at the Sacro Cuore school in Corleone.

It would seem that Ninetta had been in love with Salvatore Riina ever since she was a teenager, a love that was returned and probably made more passionate by the very impossibility of its fulfilment. The hero of her dreams spent six years in prison for murder and was subsequently on the run. This meant there were few opportunities for the two to see one another, to get to know one another. With the solid family attachment to mafia codes behind her, Ninetta must have seen in Salvatore a man proud of wielding the gun and unjustly hounded by the law. Was there really any harm in this love? Especially when the controversial, not to say scandalous administration of justice gave her carte blanche: 'I love him because the Bari Court of Assizes has also told me, with the 10 June sentence [1969, in Bari], that Riina is fully acquitted of all those crimes and has not stained his hands with blood.'[66] Did Antonina really believe this?

When Salvatore Riina went back to Corleone after being acquitted in the Bari trial he celebrated his official engagement to his Ninetta. 'A formal gesture of love which at the same time, however, spells out once and for all to police and *carabinieri* her role as a mafia woman. For this she would be accused in 1971 in two separate investigators' reports of deliberately seeking to make connections between Luciano Liggio, already a notorious fugitive, her father, her brothers and her man, whom she swore she did not see on the night of her official engagement.'[67] Everything in Ninetta's story seems to have prepared her for this role of messenger and bearer of orders: her family background, her intelligence and education, the man with whom she was in love and the climate of hostility to the authorities in which she grew up. 'And she was smart too, shrewd and intelligent. Most of all, she was entirely to be trusted.'[68]

The trial in which she was accused of complicity took place on 16 July 1971. Ninetta appeared self-assured, she defended herself skilfully and presented herself as an honest woman whose good name was being unjustly impugned. 'I am a woman and I am guilty only of loving a man whom I respect and trust. I have always loved Totò Riina, I was thirteen and he was twenty-six and he has never left my heart. This is all I am guilty of, Signor Presidente.'[69]

The self-portrait drawn by Antonina Bagarella at this point is the version which in essence was to remain unchanged over the years and would be put forward by her again when Riina was arrested and she re-emerged from clandestinity twenty-two years later.

> Don't I have the right to love a man and follow the law of nature? I know you will ask me why my choice of the man in my life had to be Totò Riina, who is said to be so many things. I chose him first of all because I love him and love disregards so many things, and then because I have respect for him and trust, the same respect and trust I have for my brother Calogero, who was unjustly involved in so many things that happened. I love Riina.[70]

There it is: 'love disregards so many things'. The invocation of romantic love to legitimize the woman's loss of responsibility as an individual is undoubtedly a winning card in the courtroom debate and for public opinion in general. And Antonina Bagarella puts firm emphasis on this image: 'It's true, I could have chosen a teacher or a highly educated man. But what is a piece of paper worth in love? You know Riina through police reports; I know him intimately and I can tell you that he is neither the bandit nor the bogeyman that everyone has described. What he is, is a normal, good man with a capacity for feeling, able to love and to care,' she told journalists.[71]

Ninetta presents herself as 'a citizen who respects the law', offended in her basic rights as a woman in love. She even risked a comparison with the heroic and, so to speak, sacred couple of the Italian imaginary: 'After what has happened I can only marry in the light of the sun. I am not a character in the *Promessi Sposi*. I am not interested in taking on the part of Lucia in her secret wedding to Renzo.'

Words that were effective, but hardly prophetic.

On that occasion Antonina Bagarella avoided a spell in prison, and instead was sentenced to special surveillance. For a number of years she would not be able to leave her house before seven in the morning or after seven at night. In February 1974, shortly before the end of this period, Ninetta disappeared. She became a fugitive and joined her anti-hero.

Soon after, on 16 April 1974, the marriage – a secret one – was celebrated by three priests of the Monreale diocese, one of whom undoubtedly was Don Agostino Coppola, in the drawing room of a villa near Cinisi, as some have it, and, as others suspect, at a little church in the San Lorenzo district of Palermo. Totò Riina was then forty-four, Ninetta was thirty. Of the honeymoon in Venice there is a photograph which was found by the police during a search, along with some of the little cards that went with the wedding confectionery.

In the next ten years Ninetta gave birth to four children, all of them born in an exclusive private clinic in the centre of Palermo and all of them duly registered in their own names. 'All four of Salvatore Riina's children were vaccinated at the USL number 58. Each of the certificates bore the signature of Antonio Rizzuto, the doctor in charge.'[72]

We know little of her clandestine life, except that she was always by her husband's side. 'I have spent all of these years just being a mother. And my husband too has been a good father' – this, once more, is her version.[73] According to some reports, the children led an almost normal life in Palermo. 'Every morning the Riina children would be taken to school by someone closely attached to the family, obviously without any criminal record. These would be shopkeepers, small traders, artisans – the network of respectability which also rendered the godfather's family invisible for so many years.'[74] According to other reports, however, the children's upbringing was almost exclusively in the hands of Ninetta: 'After Riina's capture . . . the mother was to say that their education was always and only her concern.'[75]

Clandestine, yes, but comfortably so. 'Summer holidays at Mazara del Vallo, in a villa owned by Mariano Agate, the local boss. Christmas and Easter in the country, at San Giuseppe Jato, in a farmhouse put at their disposal by the Bruscas. At Palermo they lived in a fine villa in Via Bernini, number 54, in a residential complex thickly surrounded by greenery, among palms, umbrella pines and geraniums.'[76] There was also a swimming pool, a gardener and a chauffeur.

Forty-eight hours after the boss's capture Antonina and her four children returned to Corleone – like emigrants going back to their village after many years of absence.

Michela Buscemi, a woman who paid a high price for her courage in breaking the silence imposed by the mafia, regards women like Antonina as 'cornerstones of the *cosca*':

> Take Bagarella, Riina's wife. Hers was a caste marriage, in the mafia nobility. A conscious choice. She has enjoyed the material benefits of the blood spilled by her husband, whom she arrogantly persists in defining as a saintly man. She has had twenty years to redeem that butcher, and she hasn't done it. Yet she was able to use her love as a weapon. . . . If I were to meet her? I would feel disgusted. I might ask her how she has been able to let that slimy hand caress her for so long, how she has allowed him to touch her children.[77]

A few days after Antonina Bagarella's return to Corleone, Simona Dalla Chiesa, the daughter of the general who, according to the charges, was killed by personal order of Antonina's husband, wrote her an open letter. In this letter Simona sets out questions, seeks understanding and asks for some act of rupture. But she also takes into account Antonina's full responsibility.

> I need to understand by what complicated tangle of feelings a woman as strong and well educated as you are could have got to the point of making such a choice in life. . . . You know, Signora Antonietta, I just cannot think of you in terms of the classic canons of subservient, silent femininity; no, yours is rather

the figure of the second-in-command, a woman capable, also because of her superior education, of exerting a lot of influence over her partner. In other words not a victim of the milieu, predestined from birth and family connections to breathe the air of crime, more a clear-headed observer of her own world, whose rules and conduct she has chosen to share in. A real mafia woman.[78]

Not even Grazia Minniti, the wife of the Catania boss, Santapaola, seems a victim of the milieu. Grazia does not come from a mafia family. Antonino Calderone, a friend of the family before his decline as a boss, speaks of her in these terms: 'Nitto Santapaola isn't married to a mafia woman. His wife comes from a very modest family and until she got married she worked as a corset-maker, making corsets. Then she found her place in the mafia very well. She is as mafiosa as him!'[79]

She is elegant, educated, and the proprietor of a travel agency in Catania. In better days she would appear by her husband's side at public functions, in the company of prefects, police commissioners, businessmen, politicians, magistrates and policemen. In worse times she acted as a precious link between clandestinity and normality. 'What would become of a big boss without a woman who was able to see him through his griefs, cheer him up when the going gets rough? . . . Would Nitto Santapaola have been able to lay down the law for eleven years moving around in the shadows from one end of Sicily to the other without the protective mantle of his wife?'[80]

No, these women do not really seem victims of their environment. It might be more apt to speak of a deep-rooted and conscious loyalty to the mafia world, with its iron, albeit unwritten, laws. The key to understanding the life they have chosen, aside from the obvious factor of material wealth, is to be found in intimacy and fidelity to the man who is loved. How much this love and passion is fuelled by the discreet charm of violence remains unknown, but a well-founded suspicion remains.

Even public fantasies of 'mafia women' must embody a certain fascination. We can hear the heroic tones in the words of one columnist on the *Giornale di Sicilia* of 20 May 1993: 'A boss and his woman. Faithful, patient, silent and discreet. A woman who can understand her man with a look, a glance. Who can share with him the terrors of a life lived on a razor's edge. Many women have stood out by this choice of a life that is hard, brave and full of risk, deciding to "sacrifice" their own lives in the name of an ideal that consists of flight and fear and living in hiding.' An ideal in other words, a real example!

So, are they women like us? I think it would be too easy to make an instant denial, perhaps out of indignation. Certainly they are like us, they feel love, passion, fear, the need to be protected. But at the same time they are not like us, because they consciously lavish these affections on men who are violent criminals and murderers.

When it comes to violent death there is no sitting on the fence. Either you

166

are with life or you are with death. Often, however, this awareness comes late, too late, as the letter quoted on p. 158 seems to suggest.

A great deal of the same ambivalence can be seen in the story of Carla Cottone, the wife of Aldo Madonia, the youngest son of one of the most powerful mafia families in Palermo. Carla was the young daughter of pharmacists who were well known in Palermo and she met her future husband during her pharmacology studies. They got married because, in her words, 'you can't lump everyone together in this family'. Her family consented. 'My parents made allowances because Aldo as a person deserves to be seen for himself.'[81] The questions asked by Carla Cottone provoked a rather interesting public debate.

Carla went on the Maurizio Costanzo show to make a public confirmation of the innocence of her husband, who had been sentenced to twenty years for drug running, along with his father and brothers, and to insist that the only thing Aldo was guilty of was his name, his membership of the Madonia family.

When Maurizio Costanzo asked her: 'Do you really mean that your husband wants to dissociate himself from his family?' Carla answered: 'No, my husband has no need to dissociate himself because he has never been associated.... He has always lived a different life, because his family has always lived in turmoil . . . his father and brothers have been in prison and he lived with his mother . . . there is already dissociation in the fact that my husband led a completely different life.'[82]

The ambivalence in Carla's attitude was made plain by the issue of dissociation. While her discussion with Costanzo inclined her to agree with a condemnation of the mafia and of the Madonia family, in a later interview broadcast on RAI 3 she backtracked: 'I was not dissociating myself from my husband's family, absolutely not.'

Here is a thorny issue which goes well beyond this individual case. No blame can be attached to the fact of being born into a mafia family. However, the pervasive presence of death makes individual decisions inordinately radical. Anyone born into a mafia family, whether man or woman, would seem to bear the mark of fate. While, on the one hand, the way is already paved to a mafia career, or at least made easy, on the other the choice of any 'normal' life seems extremely difficult. What for any other person is a simple matter of no consequence, can even involve the risk of death for the sons and daughters of these families.

And the same goes for acquired relatives, like Carla Cottone for example. In dealing with the mafia naivety certainly involves risks; it is not possible to count yourself out, insisting on your own good intentions. Moreover, Carla's case introduces the issue of the historically compromised relationship of Sicily's 'good society' with the mafia. In a situation so unremittingly polarized between belonging to the civil sphere and belonging to the mafia sphere of society, as in Palermo where Carla Cottone lives, a third, neutral way seems to offer no recourse.

> Truly, I live in dark times!
> The guileless word is folly. A smooth forehead
> Suggests insensitivity. The man who laughs
> Has simply not yet had
> The terrible news.

> What kind of times are they, when
> A talk about trees is almost a crime
> Because it implies silence about so many horrors? . . .

Bertolt Brecht wrote these lines in the poem 'To Those Born Later', a commentary on the dark times of Fascist totalitarianism.[83]

Carla Aleo Nero and Angela Lanza interviewed Carla Cottone Madonia and their conclusion was: 'Dissociating oneself without taking a position is therefore not enough. Reality has to be taken into account. You cannot be truly innocent if you are not truly free. And you cannot be truly free if you do not take up a position against the mafia. . . . It is the illusion of "neutrality" which contributes to the perpetuation of the mafia's supporting fabric.'[84]

What then is the role of women in the mafia domain? It seems beyond dispute that women do have both material and moral responsibilities and that they embody an extremely important role on a number of levels.

First and foremost as wives or cohabiting partners, women represent an irreplaceable material and emotional support for the man of honour. Especially in periods and places marked by conflict with the law, women function as invaluable mediators between clandestinity and legality, providing logistic support and turning the home into a centre of operations. As guarantors of a normal everyday routine, women give a cover to the mafia crime which allows mafiosi territorial mobility like fish in water.

Moreover, because they are covered by the protective shield of the law which regards them as 'not responsible' because they are subordinate to men, these women function as important channels for the laundering of dirty money, the concealment of sudden wealth and a variety of financial operations to which they lend their names. Sometimes, when their man is in prison they cease to be mere front women and are temporarily transformed into the direct administrators of the wealth accumulated through crime.

Others, for the most part poor women, not necessarily related to mafiosi, live off drugs at a variety of levels, from that of small-time dealer in dressing-gown and slippers to that of trafficker at an international level with luxury hotels and compulsory escorts thrown in.

There are even cases where a woman can also play a direct part in some violent operation. Calderone talks about Nitto Santapaolo's sister: 'Nitto's sister is even more mafiosa than his wife, and Nitto would even take her along on heists. They would do the surveillance together in the car, pretending to be two lovers.'[85] And in his reconstruction of the story of the *'ndrangheta* from Unification until today, Ciconte found traces in court proceedings of women who were 'armed and dressed as men' and took part in theft and robbery.

> These instances are exceptional, the only ones known of in the mafia picture. But they are significant, because they mark an active presence by women in the different *'ndrine* which until now has been completely obscured or unknown. We still know very little about this presence. The evidence we can recover from the court proceedings suggests that women in the *'ndrine* did not always occupy a passive, background role.[86]

I take the view, however, that none of these activities is to be seen as a sign of 'parity', or a sign of female 'emancipation' within the illegal economy of the mafia. In the mafia domain women's presence is, by the mafiosi's own definition and wishes, admissible and strongly desired only under conditions of subjugation and dependence. The mafia and emancipation are mutually exclusive. This was what was written in 1979 by the women of the feminist Collective of Cinisi and Terrasini, after the killing of Peppino Impastato: 'By passing on mafia culture women are effectively reproducing their own slavery, perpetuating their own subordination to the male, given that mafia culture is strictly masculinist and based on female subjection.'[87]

It is that very mixture of strength and subordination which endows the women of the family with a central importance for the mafia. Not as individuals, but as wives, daughters, sisters and mothers, women are indispensable for mafia men. In the mafia strategy of territorial sovereignty it is women who function as an echo chamber for blackmail and threats and the terror of death created by *omertà*, complicity and obedience to mafia law.

None the less, mother love is a double-edged weapon. It is for their children's sake, so as not to put their lives at risk, that many women play along with the mafia, but it is for the very same reason, out of despair at the death of a child, that women then 'betray' it. 'It is a conflict without a solution,' says the film maker Margarethe von Trotta. 'Women must leave behind their protective sense of persecution. Perhaps now they are beginning to understand that they cannot bring children into the world while letting others be killed. It is foul.'[88]

Open complicity, which seems the female form of participation in the mafia, can therefore be expressed on two parallel levels. On the one hand complicity 'pays' in terms of wealth, social mobility and status. And on the other hand complicity is fuelled by emotional dependence and to a large extent can be explained by a close and very strong bond with the mafioso man as partner.

It is their own subordination, within a dialectic of oppression, that gives women a potential power, some possible way of undermining the plan. 'But they must be able to tell their husbands: if you commit that crime I shall leave you.'[89]

Women as wives of mafiosi, women as mothers of mafiosi – this close complicity can be broken, transformed into its opposite. At the Marisa Bellisario Foundation prizegiving on 8 March 1993, the lawyer Fernanda Contri spoke:'I remember the testimony of another woman who had spoken out and given evidence at a trial about the intimidation she had been subjected to by the whole milieu, perhaps even by the lawyers: "I'm afraid of nothing, because they took away my son and now that they have taken my son away I have nothing left, so they can't take my life away. My life ended with his." '

In this context, an emancipatory gesture can only be a gesture against. 'Why not regard real emancipation as belonging to those women who turn to the law, when the wish for legality is converted into a break with *fidelity*, an open *betrayal* of the system to which they [the *pentite*] belong?' Rosalba Bellomare wonders.[90] This is a step which is subjectively very hard, a choice which means total rupture and isolation, one usually only taken after the death of the man or the son who is loved. And the domination over women which was exercised in life seems not even to dissolve after death. 'I don't know if I've done the right thing, it feels like a lack of respect for my husband. If he came back to life he would destroy me.' These are the words of a mafia woman *pentita* spoken at a debate in Palermo.[91]

As yet, alas, mafia culture and judiciary practice have a mutual tendency to confirm the negation of women's personal responsibility. The following episode, reported and commented on by Rosalba Bellomare, is significant:

> The retired sergeant-major at Corleone stated: 'The *capos*' women would give support to men evading the law; Liggio's sister bought land at Piano di Scala, Antonietta brought orders, Provenzano's wife, Saveria, looked after business. They said it wasn't right to bring the women into it. So that was the end of the inquiries.' But wouldn't it have been worthwhile to try and understand the new part played by women in the mafia set-up? The old sergeant-major just lets slip this memory, but why didn't he go on with his inquiries? Who said it wasn't right to bring the women into it? These are questions that ought to be answered.[92]

And it is no coincidence that the defence of Sicilian women as an alleged special case, all family and tradition, is put forward by men with an interest in the status quo, and tends to obscure the workings of mafia domination. Dario Fo and Franca Rame recall a comic sketch they did on the 'notorious *Canzonissima* of thirty years ago' which had a mafia woman as a character. 'We got death threats. There were questions asked in Parliament. Malagodi wrote an article stating that the mafia did not exist and threatening both of us. And he ended the article like this: "You are besmirching the honour of Sicily and Sicilian women, shame on you!" '[93]

It seems instead that it is women's dignity that is 'besmirched', as their individual rights and duties, their civil rights and responsibilities continue to be negated.

It is important that we as women demand that the equality guaranteed by the Constitution is respected by judiciary practice, both to give women's responsibility as individuals its full weight, and to combat the mafia as necessary. Maria Falcone, the sister of the murdered judge, says: 'We've had enough of the kid-glove approach with the women of mafiosi, for fugitives' little helpers, enough over-sensitivity to the relatives' civil liberties, and therefore likewise the women of the bosses. If there is an intention to undermine Cosa Nostra, then the law as it is is inadequate.'[94]

I think that if some tangible sign were to come from judiciary practice it could also represent an element of hope for young women in mafia families who would like to free themselves from this fate. This 'message in a bottle' was found on a thousand-lire note:

> I am a girl from Reggio Calabria with parents and brothers who are mafiosi. I have lost two brothers who were murdered. On holiday at the seaside I met a nice, decent boy who wants to marry me. He doesn't know about my family, I would like to go and live in his town, but my parents are giving me an apartment and won't let me leave Reggio. He has agreed to move here, but he doesn't know anything about my family and I'm afraid to tell him the truth.[95]

What hope can we give this girl, if the democratic state does not even recognize her right and her duty to take responsible care of herself because she is a woman?

That this girl's worries are well founded is demonstrated by the case of Concettina Labate, who was killed in Reggio Calabria on the evening of 5 October 1982. Only now, twelve years later, through the testimony of a *pentito*, does it come to light that Concettina was killed at the instigation of her own brothers because she had left the husband that the clan had forced upon her and chosen a new companion.[96]

Breaking with the mafia, then, also seems particularly hard for women. 'When a woman becomes a *pentita*, she is risking much more,' says the magistrate, Liliana Ferraro, 'because she then becomes aware of how delicate her position is, a position that makes it much harder for a woman to live at odds with the structure that forms her life. It is much harder, takes greater resources, especially in certain social contexts in Sicily.'[97]

PART III

Women against the Mafia

Emotions as a Resource

Words are stones

Nothing else exists of her and for her other than this trial which she alone is preparing and undertaking, sitting on her chair beside the bed. On trial is the feudal system, her servile condition as a peasant, the trial of the mafia and the state. She identifies herself totally with her trial and she has her own qualities: she is sharp-witted, alert, suspicious, shrewd, skilful, imperious and implacable. Thus this woman has become in a single day: her tears are no longer tears but words, and the words are stones.

In the fifties this was the portrait given to us by Carlo Levi of Francesca Serio, one of the first women to have challenged mafia arrogance by recourse to the law.[1]

Francesca Serio was the mother of Salvatore Carnevale, a trade unionist and secretary of the Sciara trade union headquarters, who was killed by the mafia on 16 May 1955 at the age of thirty-two. Salvatore Carnevale had founded the Sciara Socialist Party branch in 1951 and had set up the trade union centre. He fought against the feudal system that still prevailed on the estate of the Princess Notarbartolo and organized the quarry workers' trade union struggle to have the contractual eight-hour day respected instead of the eleven hours that were worked in the quarry which also belonged to the princess. 'The quarrymen's strike brought the double-track laying work to a halt on the railway because of the shortage of stone, thereby damaging both the interests and the prestige of the Sciara mafiosi (who had a stake in the quarry workings) and of the Trabia mafiosi (who had a stake in the track-laying).'[2]

Salvatore Carnevale was strong and self-confident – 'strengthened by the law' – and was impassive in the face of attempts to corrupt him. He was stopped by neither the mafia's threats nor their bribes. 'The mafia was offended and its prestige, its very core, was wounded, not so much by the trade union issue in itself but by the proud and intransigent way in which it was conducted,' explained one of his comrades.[3]

They killed him on the sly, at dawn, not far from the quarry. 'The murder was signed, so to speak, with the symbolism of mafia killings: the blows to the face, to disfigure the corpse, as a sign of contempt; and the next day the theft of forty hens for the traditional banquet.'[4]

When his mother came running, the *carabinieri* would not let her near, telling her that it wasn't her son, pushing her back.

> When they told me it wasn't my son I took a step forward and I saw the dead man's feet; he had been placed face down and covered with only his feet sticking out but I saw the white socks, the socks I'd washed yesterday for my son, that my son put on those feet, and those feet were just like my son's feet, so . . . 'I won't touch him, I just want to see him; he's my son, he's my son from his legs, he's my son from his feet, he's my son from how he is, I want to see his face.' I slipped between them three times so as to see his face – it was hidden. Those *carabinieri* had placed themselves beside me and they held me back, watching me.[5]

The shock of encountering her dead son brought an immediate and irremediable clash with injustice, with a keen perception of values being the wrong way round. 'When they came to murder my son there was no one there to watch [meaning, no surveillance], and now they are watching me. I didn't kill anyone, I looked after him for thirty-two years, and now when I want to go and see him they watch me, they watch *me* and they let those men go free.'[6]

In the early days Francesca Serio had been a newcomer to Sciara. She had come from a village in the province of Messina, alone with her five-month-old son. Her husband had left her, a disappearance followed by his death. And so for this woman the whole sense of her life was invested in her son. 'I went out to work to make ends meet for this little son . . . I had to hoe in the fields because I had the baby and I didn't want him to starve, and I didn't want anyone to look down on him, not even in my own family. . . . I sent him to school for five years, he got his certificate and went out day-labouring, and we did our best to make ends meet until he went into the army.'[7]

So Salvatore had grown up with a lot of pride. He did not accept the condition of servility: 'The peasant movement spared him from the individual protest, the revolt of the bandit, and he became a trade union organizer.'[8]

To begin with Francesca Serio did not at all share in her son's choices. She wept and begged. 'I didn't want it; but now that I was the mother of a socialist what could I do?' Warnings of death, threats and offers of bribes were not foreseen. She too was directly approached by the mafia to act as an influence on her son. Until the death sentence.

'I was making bread when my son died. . . . I can't stop seeing him; I can't remember any more how he walked, how he would come in, I can only remember him face downwards on the ground, on the path.'[9]

Carlo Levi was fascinated by this fifty-year-old woman, 'with her harsh, withered beauty, violent and opaque as a stone, merciless and seemingly inhuman', by this mother who 'talks as if she must never cease to talk until Judgment Day'.

Francesca Serio's words like stone strike at the killers and those who sent them, and at the injustice of the so-called law. The son left it to the mother to bear witness; the trade union, the party and the peasant movement were the legacy which enabled her to confront denunciation.

> Even the terms she used sounded new and strange in the dialect: legal and political words, law, reform, sharecroppers' percentages, struggle, organization, opportunists and so on. But in her mouth, in the face of death, this language, this flat, conventional language of party politics, became a heroic language, as if it were the first way of affirming her own existence, the dry song of a rage that exists for the first day in the new world. The new existence is born, formed by tragedy, it is dark and fastidious, opaque and fierce. It is a revelation, in the theatre of the courtroom of conscience, and of the real courtroom in Palermo; a point of truth arrived at which gives life and impulse to everything and keeps being tirelessly repeated, in a rendering that is now fixed, never to be lost, as that certainty reached is not lost. The death of her son has opened her eyes.[10]

This was 16 May 1955 and Sandro Pertini was in Sicily to bring the electoral campaign to its close. Within days there would be a new Assembly; only Sicily was still to vote and that inconvenient corpse was hurriedly taken to the mortuary of the cemetery. 'As the national leader of the Socialist Party, Pertini managed to get the coffin set up in the funeral chamber, wrapped in a red flag, making sure that there were full honours.'[11]

Salvatore Carnevale's funeral sealed a pact between these two people who were in some respects so distant: the mother of the murdered trade unionist and the Socialist leader. It was Pertini who defended the interests of Francesca Serio, both in the trial at Santa Maria Capua Vetere against four mafiosi, who were given life sentences, and in the appeal case heard eight years later in Naples, when all four were acquitted on the grounds of insufficient evidence.

Defending the mafiosi was another future President of the Republic, Giovanni Leone. 'These were years when the word mafia could not even be uttered. And Leone had the "mafia motive" dropped.'[12]

'Mamma Carnevale' had asked for justice not only for her own sake, but for those who had believed in the same ideas as her son Salvatore. She was defeated and those waging the struggle at that time were also defeated. Vera Pegna, who was a local councillor in nearby Caccamo for a period, recalls:

It was an act of tremendous courage for the mother to have named the murderers, who in the first instance were found guilty and later, on appeal, were acquitted on the grounds of insufficient evidence. From then on terror reigned over Sciara and Caccamo and anyone who had the temerity to forget this was reminded by Carnevale's murderers themselves, who had just come out of prison and were going around with rifles slung over their shoulders and no one to stop them.[13]

Too much blood, there's no love here

Hands off Rosaria! It can happen in a city like Palermo that the visible grief of a young woman who has seen her husband cut down is regarded as 'self-dramatization'. Whether they are shy or self-confident, screaming or silent, passionate or calm, radical or conservative, these women . . . are *in the way*! It's fine so long as they stay in the *background*, pigeonholed in a pre-given role to match other women's individual tastes, setting themselves up as judges without appeal. Why? Do we want to impose yet another torment on these women, on top of their grief? 'Without justice I cannot die,' says Rosaria Costa Schifani. Without expressing myself, without expressing my grief I am dead. There are the usual hypercritical types (the 'kinder' ones say 'How naive!' when they see Rosaria) looking strictly for what reflects their own version of *relative of the victims*. The right to be oneself is denied, genuine self-expression is found tedious. . . . In the face of female freedom! Testimony and grief have to conform to the rules of representation ('but she doesn't even know how to talk') and politics ('she's letting herself be used'). GO FOR IT ROSARIA; don't let them silence you. Don't let them shut you up. Do what you think is right. And do it as you think fit.[14]

Young Rosaria Costa, married at twenty-one and widowed at twenty-two – with a baby only months old – left a mark that cannot easily be erased when she spoke out at the funeral for those who died in the Capaci killings. Her husband, Vito Schifani, was one of three bodyguards who were killed along with Judge Falcone and his wife Francesca Morvillo.

Her spontaneity, along with her great grief and the desperation and directness of her words to the mafiosi, broadcast on television throughout the country, have well-nigh turned Rosaria into a symbol of the rage, the grief and upsurge of revolt going on at that time. Her speech departing spontaneously from the text she had prepared with the priest so that broken sentences erupted as if seeming to rise up unbidden and uncontrollably in her mouth, regardless of protocol, Rosaria was able to convey the emotional depth of her desperation, while making a terrible moral condemnation. 'My Vito Schifani . . . the state, the state . . . because there are mafiosi there too . . .

I forgive you, but you should get down on your knees . . . they don't want to change, they don't change . . . too much blood, no love here, there's no love here, there's no love here, there's no love at all.'

The eruption of these 'night thoughts' into the clear prayer of 'daylight' was like the breaking of a taboo. Rosaria expressed a primordial and violent 'nostalgia for the abyss'. 'The widowed Signora Schifani misses her Vito in a physical way, she misses his beautiful legs.'[15] 'Nobody had the right to destroy his body. This is what I always think, simple as can be, without thinking about it at all in any clever way.'[16] With a minimum of words and gestures, Rosaria was able to say the unsayable, to give voice to what many of us feel but find it hard even to think about. 'It is the pagan despair of someone with the painfully reached understanding that *never again* really means *never again*.'[17]

Keep it up Rosaria, we mean it!

But who is Rosaria Costa Schifani? She herself tells us in the account of a 'journey' undertaken with the help of a journalist after that terrible explosion which split her life into a before and an after. A journey into memory 'so as not to forget' and, at the same time, a journey exploring the future; and also a kind of pilgrimage taking her to meet so many other women who have already experienced what is happening to her.

From the Capaci killings to the Via D'Amelio killings; this same summer so many people known to Rosaria died: from the bodyguards who were friends of her husband to Judge Borsellino. And he was the one who had consoled her after Vito's death – along with his wife Agnese and his children Manfredi, Lucia and Fiammetta. And now she is the one consoling them. . . . 'The six coffins in the Palace of Justice mirror the defeat of a life which is not worth living. It is a mistake to think this. My life is always worth living, but when I see the six coffins, in the same place where I had cried over Vito's, my spirits are cast down immeasurably.'[18]

Rosaria is first and foremost a young woman like so many: school, unemployment, irregular jobs, romance, dates at the discotheque, riding around on a scooter, a dream wedding, a honeymoon in the Maldive islands, commemorated in photos and home movies. 'It was as if I was living in a television commercial, looking at somebody else's life as if it was too beautiful because I was the one it was happening to. And the fact is it was the only holiday I've had in my life.'[19]

And now these images really do seem to testify to someone else's life. 'I've got the photos of the wedding and the video of the Maldives. My son will know his father from these. And he will know all about this suffering and about the mafia who tore his father away from him. We need to tell our children everything.'[20]

But all the same, Rosaria also seems a bit special, a young woman not altogether like the rest. She has a strong character, an exceptional tenacity and great civic courage. At fifteen she encountered the Mormons. 'I discovered the

Bible with them and learned to believe. . . . A God that I began to see and feel inside me. I gave myself rules for living, setting myself to do some good for others every day. . . . I am just a Christian . . . I don't do any harm going to the Mormons as well.'[21]

It is the intelligence of her emotions that sets Rosaria apart. The courage to express her most intimate feelings and to convert them into plans, knowledge and curiosity. This is how Rosaria approaches the 'monster' that killed her love.

She wants to find out, she wants to know, she wants to struggle against it. Before it touched her Vito she knew little or nothing about it. 'But I can't do it alone. I can't remember, or know, or understand. I need help and in search of the truth I travel around this city looking for anyone who even knows a little piece of it. . . . I'll try to understand, and make up for lost time.'[22] Within a few months she became familiar with the criminal entanglements between the mafia and the state – through reading and discussion, but most of all through direct acquaintance with many victims. Women and children most of all, mothers, wives and children of men killed by the mafia.

Rosaria also addresses women and children on the other side:

> I say to you, women of the mafia . . . they are murderers. Let's say it loud and clear to their children so that they can look them in the eye and see what murderers' eyes are like. I imagine them all sitting at home round the table. . . . I think about them: the little one, who is three and the big one, who is ten, convinced as I am that mafia *capos* also get pestered by little misses who grow up fast and are quick to ask a lot of questions, going to school and coming home, like all their classmates, with little essays to write against violence.[23]

Murderers too get asked questions by their sons and daughters, even murderers who have kept silent. Children haven't yet learned the basic rule of common sense: there are some questions that you don't ask.

With passion and tenacity Rosaria set out to meet many women, and a few men, who are joined to her life by a shared bereavement, in order to ask practical questions and find an answer to her inquiries: what can *I* do? Her conversations with these people are very beautiful and also very illuminating. A book within a book.

> Displaying one's own emotions and claiming one's rights as a citizen means you must bring things to light and make things plain, make others see you, do not use the words of others, but let your own presence speak for itself. Then there is understanding between victims, between the injured, a recourse to a basic vocabulary which is none the less deeply embedded in history, and has an underlying complexity wherein emotions themselves are inherent. With the knowledge of grief, key words emerge 'spontaneously'.[24]

All of them received her with generosity, letting her share in their own grief, their anger and memories; they encouraged her to continue along the same road. Here are some testimonies.

'I advise you always to ask for justice because it is not pointless. And I advise you also to speak, to speak a great deal. Don't think only of forgiving. Ask, claim justice and speak most of all to those who live in this place.' (Rita Bartoli, widow of the State Prosecutor, Gaetano Costa)[25]

'What I really appreciated in your prayer at San Domenico was the mistrust woven into those words "the state, the state". Well done, Rosaria, make your scepticism a lever for knowledge. And remember this is a state that has signed a blank cheque for the mafia.' (Giovanna Giaconia, widow of Judge Cesare Terranova)[26]

'Speak, speak, speak, dear Rosaria. For years I stayed at home refusing to take part in meetings and debates. I didn't feel ready. Then one day I found myself in Bologna involved in a demonstration. I spoke. The words I said were simple. But they were effective. Word got around and from that day on I got invited all over the place, even to consulates abroad. I have even written a bit.' (Giuseppina Zacco, widow of the Sicilian Communist Party secretary, Pio La Torre)[27]

'The words I heard you speak on TV, Rosaria, are the same words I spoke then. I saw myself in your image. I saw myself as a very young woman, struck in the face by the monster. Be strong, Rosaria. And strengthen others because it really seems to me that you have it in you to give hope to people.' (Marina Pipitone, widow of Michele Reina, Christian Democrat Party secretary in Palermo)[28]

'I feel such regret about Rita [Atria]. We could have helped her. But we didn't know about her and Rita didn't know we were there. We have to try to make it known that we are many, that we are prepared to defend and protect women like ourselves.' (Michela Buscemi, sister of Salvatore and Rodolfo, both killed by the mafia)[29]

'What you're saying is marvellous. You are coming to see us in our homes in search of words, ideas and hope, but as you can see you are the one to give them. I would never have been able to do what you did in the church. You are teaching us something. But I don't know if you will manage to reach the hearts of the mafiosi. And don't expect too much from anyone, least of all from people.' (Maria Leotta, widow of Boris Giuliano, Palermo Flying Squad Chief)[30]

'Rosaria, how was it that you remembered me? Thank you for coming . . . Rosaria, I am tired, very tired.' (Emilia Midrio, widow of Giovanni Bonsignore, regional civil servant)[31]

'We are all in low spirits. When I was in the car with my husband, they spared me, my daughter and my mother-in-law. It's all different now with the bombs. . . . I don't know what I can say to you. I can't help you. Nobody can help you, Rosaria.' (Irma Chiazzese, widow of Piersanti Mattarella, Regional President)[32]

'In some ways my husband's case was straightforward. But they still didn't solve it. The doorman, the petrol pump attendant, the neighbours . . . there were leads to follow but nothing happened. . . . I've already said this to a journalist and it's been written in a book. I feel as if I'm coming out with gossip, things that are dead and buried that no one wants to hear any more. . . . There is nothing to be gained.' (Laura, widow of Ninni Cassarà, Vice-Superintendent of Police in Palermo)[33]

'Certainly, we need to speak and fight against the mafiosi. But, as you can see, here the battle has to take in those who pretend not to see, those judges who are in the wrong and so many politicians. . . . You see, Rosaria, what has to be defended in this city, if we are to try and save it, are work and education. I know you would like to penetrate the minds of the children of the mafiosi to undermine that way of thinking, and this is what I hold in highest regard about you, and what we have to succeed in doing.' (Pina Maisano, widow of the businessman Libero Grassi)[34]

'Rosaria, help me to move the mountain. . . . Now they listen to you. Make yourself heard. But don't fall into the trap of playing the heartless media game, with newspapers giving you a headline today and tomorrow forgetting to dig, to go in deep and give those in power no let-up, asking questions, asking the same questions again, making the questions echo and resound until they get an answer. Don't get pulled into their game.' (Vincenzo Agostino, father of Antonino, police officer killed along with his pregnant wife)[35]

'Dear Rosaria, my son ended up in an ugly trap. . . . In this Palermo of shady goings-on, I, the mother of a son I have not been able to mourn, am afraid of shaking the hands of mafiosi. I'm afraid of the mafiosi coming here to my house to show me solidarity. And I am suspicious. I am suspicious of everyone. Even people I know. Those murderers took everything away from me. Tears as well. There was no mourning in this house. No one here has died. We didn't even have a funeral. But Emanuele is gone.' (Signora Piazza, mother of Emanuele, Sisde officer, disappeared)[36]

'You have the courage to speak and to shout like me. And we must shout also for those who do not have our courage.' (Saveria Antiochia, mother of the bodyguard officer Roberto, killed along with Ninni Cassarà)[37]

'I started from nowhere like you Rosaria, standing up to all the people around me who were criticizing, or, rather, not giving a damn. . . . I know that they had me down for a fanatic, as if I was using my position to show off, get special treatment, go on television and be interviewed. I don't listen to them, I just keep going, living and shouting. Because silence is the same as death.' (Rosetta Prestinicola, widow of the police doctor and university teacher Paolo Giaccone)[38]

'At the beginning you would like to change things, you fight, you feel angry. . . . Then you look at your son growing up and you don't know what's best. He's still small but he understands everything: "I know why you won't take me to the country, Mum. It's not just because you're sad. You're scared they'll kill me too there." ' (Tiziana Poplowsky, widow of Baron Antonio D'Onufrio)[39]

'I admire you Rosaria for having such a will to know. It is important that women don't stay at home when they've got something to say, when they are prepared to fight. We must go out there. I've been saying it again and again for a long time.' (Father Ennio Pintacuda)[40]

On her heartfelt, multifarious and contradictory anti-mafia 'journey' Rosaria travelled a long way towards consciousness-raising and understanding, a long way in working through her mourning. 'Coming together with others who are stricken by the same grief can also be read as a modern form of working through mourning.'[41] But at the same time this helped to construct a piece of the future. Rosaria swung agonizingly between the hope excited by her decisive actions and the emptiness of the outcome.

Rosaria Schifani wrote:

I always end up confusing and being confused, because I get the investigative tack mixed up with my impulse to raise people's awareness. In fact successes are so rare on the first front and it's ghastly, even if in the end some big-time fugitive winds up inside. What is important is that there should at least be results on the second front, the only one where we grieving relatives can attempt to have an effect without prompting tears because that doesn't help us and because each of us weeps for our own, but turning grief into a springboard for collective pressure. Words? I hope they're not just words.[42]

'Moral familism'*

In these dark years in Italy the subjective experience of loss, bereavement and grief has become the stimulus for a powerful ethical and political argument. Issues which are private on the surface have assumed a public weight.

We deliberately speak of bonds, connections and relationships as being familial but never strictly family, because in terms of values and behaviour there are new things being engendered in the realm of personal relationships rather than the family as an institution. It is not the family as such that is rallying and making

---

* The term 'moral familism', as opposed to 'amoral familism', has its origins in Edward C. Banfield's book *The Moral Basis of Backward Society* (The Free Press, Illinois 1958), which has stimulated much debate over recent years in Italy. [Trs.]

its presence felt, but always an individual as part of a dyad, that closer bond that sometimes joins brothers and sisters, or fathers and sons, or mothers and sons.[43]

This distinction is all the more pertinent – as we shall see more clearly further on – in the case of women who come from a background which, if not strictly mafioso, is none the less subordinate and dependent on territorial mafia domination. 'Moral familism' is enacted by *individuals*, which might appear a contradiction in terms. Yet, the innovatory potential of this civil and political resistance, rooted in personal emotions, comes precisely from this: someone stricken by the loss of a person they love takes it upon himself or herself for the sake of a familial bond of affection – but always as an individual – to prevail upon justice and claim the right to life for his or her family; not as an abstraction but as the time and space of its closeness, of its ties of love.

This is a brand-new phenomenon of recent decades. Victims of acts of terror, victims of drugs, victims of the mafia and victims of disasters of different kinds are 'brought together by love'. Increasing numbers of citizens whose dignity has been trampled, and who have been neglected by those official bodies which should have been concerned to protect their rights, have chosen to speak out. 'The voices of many other citizens have joined the chorus of relatives, and other associations have been formed with this same common denominator: the choice of self-representation in every sense, the rejection of delegates and mediations and the assumption of responsibility for one's own actions with the aim of fulfilling one's own rights.'[44]

Consciousness-raising, through the experience of bereavement and the absence of redress, and a progressive loss of rights along with access to new resources, has given rise to demands of an ethical nature which are identified with a new form of political demand: a political demand with the issue of dignity at its heart. In the words of Giovanna Terranova, president of the Association of Sicilian Women against the Mafia:

After a tragedy of this kind the first instinct is to lock yourself away in your own grief, howling with anger at yourself, and the last thing you think of is making any public protest. But I felt I was not just the protagonist of a personal tragedy, but of a collective tragedy, and the danger threatened a whole society, not just me. This is what drives people to speak publicly, at the point when you tell yourself that this isn't just your business, but the business of every citizen. Whenever they lose the part of the city which is most alive and most vital, each and every citizen should feel injured and hurt. So I have tried to make that tragedy less personal, that was what I set out to do. It was something I did instinctively. Otherwise, if we lose the means to take action, we have not only lost our husbands, those dear to us, we truly lose the thread that connects civil society, that connects us to one another in a civil society, the thread of connected action. It is this which ultimately impels us to say: 'I can never resign myself. Nor should anyone else, and I have to push the others not to resign themselves and not ever to forget what happened.'[45]

As the genesis of this new way of asking questions about rights, justice and citizenship, injury at the level of emotion and the most intimate feelings involves new forms of protest and political representation. Traditional customs and convictions are being overturned. What belonged to the strictly personal sphere is made public from the outset by the death of those one loves and by this grief.

> There is a kind of 'deviation' from the emotional norms which regulate the expression of mourning. . . . Socially acceptable behaviour as a consequence of respecting those norms should therefore mean accepting the misfortune with which one has been stricken and cutting oneself off from the rest of the world for a period of time which is also preordained. Grief and mourning ought therefore to lead to separation from the public. Conversely many relatives of mafia victims have made a choice . . . exploding into the public sphere. . . . A kind of 'deviant' behaviour has come about, be it in the formation of emotions or their expression.[46]

There has been a similar development of rebellion and public testimony against the extortion racket. 'To begin with, opposition to the racket was motivated by a defence of self-interests: defending the fruit of one's own labour. But values are also involved. With concrete experience of opposition there is bound to be a meeting point between the level of interests and the level of values,' explains Tano Grasso.[47] In 1992, this assumption led the association of shopkeepers against the racket to ask for the offence of extortion to be regarded as a crime subverting public order, as an attack on the Constitution. 'The aim of this was to stress that extortion not only strikes at assets and property but at the person in his or her totality as an individual and a citizen. It is the dignity of the person which is offended.'[48]

'A deathly silence enfolds the economy,' said Libero Grassi, who paid for this denunciation with his own life. 'Leoluca Orlando wanted to head the procession. And I said no. Because it was the women workers from the factory who should have been at the head of the procession. He died for them, to defend their jobs. That was the important message to give. The defence of work. Work as a means of freedom and enfranchisement from slavery and conditioning. As far as the rest went nothing mattered to me,' Pina Maisano Grassi told Rosaria Schifani.[49]

In these moments of extreme grief, words and gestures become stones.

'Grief thus becomes one way of creating new behaviour, because there is never any rhetoric in the words of stricken relatives, there are truths it is hard to overlook.'[50]

It ought to be remembered, all the same, that the struggle against the mafia and women's participation in it have a long history beginning in the last century and also involving men and women not directly affected by the death of close relatives. Anna Puglisi writes:

> Can this be a long silence or is it a long deafness? Since the struggles against the mafia in Sicily between the end of the nineteenth century and the late 1970s are almost completely unknown, likewise it is not known that women were also involved in those struggles: peasant women who struggled beside their relatives against the landowners and, later, women who were militants in parties or movements, in the knowledge that this struggle for freedom also implicated – and still does – the struggle against the mafia, which violates our lives even if it does not affect us directly with murder.[51]

Today, however, rather than political programmes and parties, it seems to be subjective experience, enlarged by the mass media, which is the point where political and associative connections coalesce, and it is subjective experience which furnishes elements of identification as a basis for mobilization. (There none the less always remains the danger of disinformation and manipulation through the mass media.)

In the words of the victims' relatives, words that derive their force from everyday experience, the distance between private and public is reduced to nothing. Official discourse is instead based on the repression of emotions and when this is made impossible it aims to diminish their political and civil scope – 'the denunciations of Dalla Chiesa's children are merely "the result of an understandable filial display of feeling"; those of the relatives of the victims of the Bologna massacre* are merely irritating'[52] – the new message based precisely on the claims of grief and the emotions points to new forms of politics and representation mistrustful of proxy actions. The issue of ethics, arising from private indignation, invades the public sphere.

Women have shown themselves to be particularly involved in this process, both because they are often affected through their attachments, by the death of a man, be it father, son or husband, and because they are 'naturally' (that is to say through the process whereby the female gender is socialized) impelled to give more importance to the actual human beings and material circumstances of everyday life than to the institutional structures and formal conventions of politics.

---

* A reference to the bombing of Bologna railway station in August 1980, when over twenty people died. This is thought to be the responsibility of neo-fascists, although investigations were never conclusive. [Trs.]

It is women primarily who are changed by the experience of moral familism; their eagerness to insist on their own visibility transforms them from victims to accusers, from passive onlookers into protagonists. Contacts with magistrates, politicians and journalists set them on a stage outside the domestic theatre. Thus they undergo a peculiar emancipation from traditional roles, almost professionalizing their lives as managers of the everyday, and changing from being their own and their relatives' custodians, nurses and social workers into liberators who open family life into society. Having set out as mothers and sisters, they discover themselves to be social individuals and citizens. The specificity of their customary sphere, when projected into the public sphere, is revealed to be a source and a resource for redefining roles, subjects, limits and principles.[53]

Such a way of looking at things, both in terms of society and combativity, seems particularly relevant to opposing the mafia. Indeed, the mafia makes an exploitative show of family values and the mafia indeed has long since abolished the difference between private and public. And, through terror and pressure, the mafia keeps an eye on the small acts of the quotidian; its 'territorial sovereignty' encompasses the minutiae and the material and symbolic aspects of everyday life. Its domination seems domestic in the extreme. And, presumably, the mafia is also especially vulnerable on this terrain.

For example, the way sheets were used after the Capaci killings managed to 'give a voice' to many terrified citizens. 'The question now being asked is: how can we be less useless? The majority of Palermo people have no doubt that the contest with Cosa Nostra is lost. The business of the sheets has the merit of barring any further paradoxes. They shoot with heavy guns and we answer by hanging a sheet out on the balcony.'[54]

Emotions as a resource, words that turn to stone, grief freeing itself from traditional modesty and becoming an ethical question and a political issue. The women whose stories come next are linked by this thread. Beyond the single stories, beyond their evident diversity of class, status and age, of biography in other words, they are all *equal* in terms of courage, civil commitment and grief. And they are equal in terms of the esteem, recognition and *gratitude* which all of us owe to them for what they have chosen to do.

I believe that it is only by first recognizing what *unites* them that we can, in the event, reasonably consider what separates them. For example, to make a distinction between women 'of the lower classes' and 'well-bred' women as does the following passage taken from the preface to the memorial of Giovanna Cirillo, the widow of the police representative Stanislao Rampolla del Tindaro who killed himself 'because of the mafia'. This was courageously addressed to the Minister for the Interior back in 1889. Pasquale Marchese's preface dates from 1986, alas. 'This is why Giovanna Cirillo brings us back to the well-mannered but firm testimony of the "widows" Terranova, Giaccone, La Torre, rather than to the hot-headed Serafina Battaglia or the ravaged mother of Salvatore Carnevale.'[55]

Why are Giovanna Terranova, Rosa Giaccone and Giuseppina La Torre not allowed to be 'ravaged' or 'hot-headed'? Why, conversely, do Serafina Battaglia and Francesca Carnevale appear incapable of 'well-mannered but firm testimony'? I do not regard these as legitimate divisions. The wounds are too deep and the stakes are too high to let these experiences be categorized within obsolete schemas which still set out to create divisions where something new is being given life by the very things that have united these women.

10

Mothers, Sisters and Widows in Mourning: Women Alone

The mafia 'in my house'

Starting with the basic fact of grief and loss that unites the women who, over recent years, have taken a public stand against the mafia, it seems altogether appropriate to tell their stories, bearing in mind the diversity of their family backgrounds, the socioeconomic context of their everyday lives, their educational affiliations and the nature of the conflict which has brought them into head-on opposition to the mafia. They are all women who have spoken out and struggled on the basis of what has happened to them personally, exposing themselves directly through open denunciation, as the plaintiff in trials, and by cooperating with the law at various levels. There is of course a fundamental diversity in their relative distance from or closeness to the mafia world itself prior to their rebellion. Those who were close to it, or even lived within it, have of course taken very extreme steps, whose costs have been particularly high, both materially and psychologically.

Since, by statute, they are outside the mafia organization, its command structure and decisions, women from this background seem particularly flexible in situations of change and conflict. Giovanni Falcone's experience confirms this:

> In the past the women seldom played a decisive role in the life of the mafiosi, who were satisfied with a matriarchal-style family where the wife, though never told about anything, knew everything, but kept silent. But I've come to believe that the women have now assumed a shaping role; they are forceful and self-confident, and have become the symbol of everything that is vital and joyful and pleasant in life. They are on a collision course with the world of Cosa Nostra that is closed and dark and tragic, withdrawn and always looking over its own shoulder.[1]

Although they are privy to a lot of secrets without officially being entrusted with them, and are frequently enmeshed as accomplices in serious crime, they are liable to be swayed by their own strong feelings in matters of conflict. Indeed, the mafiosi see them as 'not trustworthy'. This feature is apparent in the so-called *pentimenti*. 'The women are the first and the most willing to come forward, for instance . . . at the point when a decision has to be made about changing sides they display a more open-minded attitude than their men.'[2] Moreover, perhaps for the very reason that they are strangers to the logic of the organization and are more bound by feelings and attachments, the women tend to go all the way in their demands for justice. Besides, these demands are nearly always made in the wake of a bereavement, the extreme nature of their demand for justice deriving from the extreme trauma inflicted on them by death.

'The truth is that violence is age-old and age-old too is the custom of suffering in silence; what is new is the courage and awareness of the women who ask for justice for themselves. While the barter of *pentimento* in exchange for protection and a reduced sentence is something male, it is certainly the women who desire truth as an end in itself.'[3]

The case of Serafina Battaglia shows how a woman 'of the mafia' can come to think of turning to the law – after exhausting all possibilities for private vendetta. In April 1960, with the killing of Stefano Leale, the mafia man with whom she had lived for more than twenty years and with whom she had a son, she set out on the usual route followed in her world to try and save her son from the same fate: she turned 'to boss Torretta, who promised protection and instead allowed the Rimi family from Alcamo to kill him. Then the woman denounced the murderers and in the Catanzaro courtroom confronted Torretta, throwing her contempt in his face: "And you're pleased about calling yourselves men of honour. . . . You are a man worth half a lira." '[4]

Despite her negotiations with boss Torretta, however, her son, Toti Lupo Leale, had the intention of avenging his father. At the time of his death he had 'a 38 automatic in his raincoat pocket and a "machine pistol" under his arm' and his mother 'hired a "minder" on a monthly basis, whom she had provided with guns and ammunition'.[5]

In the light of these facts Serafina Battaglia would seem to be a mafia woman who stuck to the rules, up until her son's death. She sought out alliances within the ranks of the mafia and had her sights on vendetta.

Let us hear one opinion of her from inside the mafia itself. The *pentito* Calderone put it like this: 'Battaglia was a nasty woman, the kind that bears grudges and stirs up vendetta. . . . From the moment her son was killed, Battaglia changed from being a villain to an informer, a grass. And she told the law everything.'[6]

When Serafina Battaglia went to the law for support she had burnt her boats and had 'nothing left to lose'. She became an implacable and reliable accuser. She turned to Judge Cesare Terranova, who was killed in his turn in 1979. His widow, Giovanna Terranova, recalls:

I know that she trusted Cesare enormously. When she was asked: 'Do you trust the law?' she answered: 'I trust Judge Terranova.' That's exactly how she answered. I don't think she was a woman who had a good relationship with the law, but she had heard people talk about Judge Terranova and she went and told what she knew. Cesare said that it was very sound information, that there were a lot of important details of fact that were the basis for a lot of work. But then, at the Catanzaro trial, they talked about her being half-senile and so they didn't take all she had said into account.[7]

For Serafina Battaglia, as for many other women in her circumstances, the law, alas, did not turn out to be a sound alternative to private vendetta. None of the many cases brought to trial with her indictments is in any way an encouraging example for someone wanting to change sides. Her long, singleminded odyssey through the courts ended in 1979, after twenty trials and nearly twenty years, with all the accused acquitted on the grounds of insufficient evidence. 'The sentences were at odds and often disconcerting. Between one hearing and the next a good fifteen years went by. Finally, in 1977, the Court of Cassation annulled all the sentences, brought the different trials together and referred the whole affair to the Court of Assizes of Appeal.'[8] This was the final acquittal.

It may be that over these long years Serafina Battaglia did really fight for justice as well as to avenge her dead. She denounced mafiosi and traitors, including relatives. She helped to throw light on a chain of bloody crimes carried out between 1958 and 1962, which were connected with a war between two mafia *cosche*, and whose final victims were in fact her partner and her son. Judge Caponnetto said: 'This brave woman told the judges the story of twenty-four murders, involving thirty mafia bosses. . . . The fact is that this woman did not see justice done. . . . Now she is over seventy and lives shut up in her house in Palermo.'[9] In the early days she had a bodyguard of sorts: *carabinieri* and plainclothes officers would watch her every move. 'The mafiosi are straw men and they act big only with those who are afraid of them. But if you're brave enough to attack them and cut them down, they turn cowardly: they're not men of honour, just nonentities,' she told journalists.[10]

Serafina Battaglia's words express hatred and contempt, perhaps even a touch of disappointment when she accuses the mafiosi of cowardice. The way she talks about these men brings to mind similar words, expressed in a somewhat unusual way by another woman whose man had been killed by the mafia. In April 1978 the husband of Maria Mignosi, who was twenty-eight and had five young children, disappeared; an instance of *lupara bianca*. In July she decided to challenge the mafia in a letter to the daily newspaper *L'Ora*. The letter's aim was to make a public statement of her contempt. She defined the mafiosi as 'half-men . . . string puppets . . . cowards and wild beasts disguised as respectable people'. And then she wondered: 'How can their women be intimate with them; don't they feel disgusted when they go to bed with them?'

There is no doubt that Maria Mignosi touched on a crucial point – the way in which the men of honour bring the infection of death to everything around them – and her anger and desperation are very direct and connected to the corporeality of both the butchers and the victims.

> I want to know where my man's body is. I am tortured at night. I dream about Aldo, I feel himself beside me alive, on the edge of the bed. We kiss and he tells me he is coming home. It is as if he was there, present. I can feel his body, his hands, his breath. . . . Then I wake up and it is dreadful! I look for him all the time, I even think I can smell him.[11]

(Maria Mignosi's case is an episode that has been completely forgotten. Simona Mafai recently drew Anna Puglisi's attention to it.)

Women like Maria Mignosi and in other respects Serafina Battaglia are very familiar with the mafia world and therefore know how to target it. When she was asked, at a hearing of the Palermo tribunal, how she came to know all the things she was denouncing, Serafina Battaglia answered:

> My husband was a mafioso and the mafiosi of Alcamo and Baucina would often gather in his shop. They would be there talking and arguing and this was how I would get to know each one of them. I know what they're worth, how much they count and what they've done. Anyway, my husband would tell me everything, so I know it all. If the women of men who'd been murdered made up their minds to speak out as I'm doing, not out of hatred or revenge, but from a hunger for justice, the mafia in Sicily would be long gone.[12]

While Serafina Battaglia's story shows how much women in her circumstances know, it also blatantly illustrates how little the law has wanted to know of this, until now. The contempt in which the mafiosi hold women – who are not to be trusted – has its counterpart in the law, which frequently will not acknowledge women's authority to act as witnesses to the truth. 'Mafia trials are full of female characters, like the wife of Comaianni, who was killed by Liggio; after much hesitation she worked up the courage to accuse him and had a meeting with the Public Prosecutor, who opined that there was no need "to pay heed to a little woman who first said one thing and then another".'[13] At a trial where one after the other the key witnesses withdrew their statements, because sticking to them would have been tantamount to suicide, the judges were not prepared to understand the fear of this woman, who, 'hearing shots outside the house, had pushed open the door and seen Liggio running off'. The three children confirmed their mother's words. But it was all in vain. 'The Bari Court of Appeal . . . fully acquitted Liggio.'[14]

Judge Caponnetto recalls another case, that of Agata Fregale. This woman, who lived in one of the most run-down districts of Palermo, reported the disappearance of two brothers and a sixteen-year-old nephew.

She recognized and named the well-known hitman Gino Abate, alias 'the Sub-Machinegun' who had made them get into his car for a one-way ride. The judges did not believe her, even although the *pentito* Marino Mannoia confirmed all of Fregale's accusations. When Mazzola went to interview her, she screamed: 'We want justice, my mother is going crazy with grief, we want to shout out our rage.' She urged all the women not to cover up their relatives' crimes: 'If there is a murderer in your family hand him over to the law. Otherwise get rid of him yourselves, since nobody believes us.'[15]

In Calabria, the detailed accusations of Anna Maurici met a similar fate. As an eyewitness to the murder of her brother-in-law Benito Corica and his seven-year-old son Rocco, she identified five of the seven assassins. 'The star witness unwaveringly pointed out the alleged assassins, thereby shattering the iron law of *omertà* which in such cases keeps everybody's mouth shut,' wrote the *Giornale di Calabria*.

The crimes charged were links in the chain of murders which made up the bloody 'Taurianova feud' which, in the first half of the 1970s, saw the Raso and Corica clans in opposition for local mafia domination. Anna Maurici's sister, Giuseppina Maurici, also joined her as a plaintiff, having lost her husband and son in the attack.

Anna Maurici is a woman marked by this chain of murders. The reporter at the trial wrote: 'At this point the witness got up from her seat, raised her arms and said: "I am telling the truth scrupulously and conscientiously. We have had five dead in my house." The presiding judge, Lombardo, adjourning, said: "We know that you belong to a suffering part of humanity." '[16]

The trial was interrupted by a startling drama: Anna Maurici disappeared, having given her lawyer to understand that she had accused innocent men. 'The woman has left the country and is at an unknown location in France.'[17] Notwithstanding the flight of the star witness, the trial went on, with the widow remaining as plaintiff. Let us hear an extract from the Public Prosecutor's statement of charges demanding life sentences for the Raso brothers:

The tragedy was swiftly executed in ninety days with the death of all five people in a climate of terror. Only the women have made statements. . . . A great deal has been said in condemnation of Anna Maurici. But it should be made clear that there has been an attempt to destroy this despised woman. At eighteen, Anna Maurici lost her husband and her father and she has not only lost the support of those who sadly died, but the support of her husband's relatives. . . .

She is a woman living in fear of the opposition . . . but she acted well when she went to the *carabinieri* all covered in blood after having brought back the corpses of her brother-in-law and her little nephew; she acted well when she handed herself over to the law for protection. . . . I questioned this woman with a degree of humanity, and when I met her later in the corridor she told me: 'If I'd known it was so hard to convince you I would not have spoken out.'[18]

Two days later all five accused were acquitted, some on the grounds of insufficient evidence, like the Raso brothers, others in full.

None the less, with the historic experience of the anti-mafia pool,* and the new attention being given to 'those who collaborate with the law', something has changed for ever. These women now seem a bit less alone.

'The first time they shot my husband Natale, one day in the street I came across one of the men who wanted him dead. I was in the car. "Ratface", that's what I called him. "You've made an attack on him, but wait and see what happens if Natale dies, I'll make you pay for it." That was in 1984. I've kept my word,' said Giacoma Filipello in the interview with Silvana Mazzocchi, already quoted. She too, as a true 'woman of the mafia', aimed, first and foremost, at vendetta. 'I saw Natale naked. For the identification. He was on the ground, with all that blood and those holes from the machine-gun bullets that had torn him apart . . . holes so big I could put my finger in them. A blood-bath. I waited several days for his friends to avenge him. But nothing happened. Then I talked. It's true that I did it for revenge. But not only that.'

Hers too was a very 'corporeal' grief; love and affection for her man, for his body – already cut to pieces after the first attack – prevail, even when the contest seems to have been lost. 'I felt a strong compulsion to speak. I wondered if I could have protected him by doing that. Breaking that chain of vendettas and murders. I knew that I could never have persuaded him. Of course, I could have done it without telling him. But in one way or another I would have had to leave him. And he was blind in one eye now and he only had me.'

It's true, perhaps, women are the first to come forward, in an awareness that the chain of murders will break; but they only rebel after death has got really close. It is not just a matter of courage. 'I think women are braver than men,' affirms 'Za Giacomina. Most of all it is the romantic idea of love which the women are afraid to shatter. It is the will of the other, the man, his identity which is not to be touched, and that is what counts, and there can be no doubt that plans of one's own must take second place for its sake.

---

* The pool of anti-mafia judges in the maxi-trial of 1986–7. [Trs.]

Though strong when it comes to action, these men seem somewhat frag-ile when it is a matter of working things through and changing at the psychological level. It is at this level that the women seem more courageous, whereas the men would often rather die than embark on a journey back through their own certainties. 'Paolo Borsellino went to see my husband in hospital and he said to him: "L'Ala, do you really want to wait until they kill you?" He sighed and answered him: "Let me die as a man of honour. It's how I was born . . .".'

And his woman is with him. 'I've been through everything with Natale. Being stuck in hiding, being on the run. I've stayed locked up at home because of his jealousy, and other times because he was in jail. I've been backwards and forwards to different prisons. I even chained myself up outside the Town Hall when they wouldn't let me see him.' Even after his death her actions were inspired by fidelity, her courage and individuality invested in keeping faith with her image of him. She threw herself on her man's killers, careless of her own safety: 'My well-being will be their misfortune. Tell them. Because so long as I've got a thread of life and courage, I'll do everything to cut open the breast and eat the heart of Natale's murderers.'

And yet the final and furthermost step she took in her vendetta – collab-oration with Judge Borsellino – meant an overturning of priorities, an explosion of new values, an existential revolution. Giacoma, now forty-seven, admitted:

It isn't easy to start out again in these circumstances, but I grit my teeth. I've got my poetry, my little rhymes. I've written about eighty of them. I started after 1990, out of anger and loneliness. But it's a few months now since I've been able to take up a pen. Perhaps later I'll be able to again, I haven't lost heart. When I absorb myself in these thoughts my mind turns to Rita Atria, the young woman who was giving information to Borsellino, who felt lost after his death and killed herself. I've written a poem for her. As for myself, I'll get by. Of course if I were to go back I wouldn't do what I've done again. Not because of the tragedy I've lived through, but because of the question of morality.

It is as if that element of gender difference which characterizes women – a more elaborated psychic life, internalizing and sublimating drives rather than acting them out – while making them for the most part more flexible, also fixes them in their own romantic idea of love even beyond all reasonable limits.

The turnaround made by Maria Saladino caused little stir. She was the daughter of a Camporeale mafioso, in the Belice valley. When her father was killed she turned her back on her own world and devoted herself to social work. They called her 'the good mafiosa'. She turned her own house into a children's refuge: 'It was my idea to set up a project to give a better upbringing to children who were the sons and daughters of mafiosi or were children at risk ... and give them a roof over their heads, a safe place, a better background and a job to get them out of the mafia "spiral",' Signorina Saladino told a woman interviewer on the RAI. When the mafia tried to get hold of her house and land after her father's death, Maria Saladino made the shrewd move of donating everything to the Salesian Brothers of Don Bosco.

'The mafia in my house': the most deeply harrowing and conflictual story is that of Felicia Bartolotta Impastato, who was both the wife of a mafia man and the mother of a left-wing militant committed to fighting the mafia. In both her heart and her home there was a struggle with no way out, one part of herself against another.

In their preface to the long conversation Anna Puglisi and Umberto Santino had with Felicia, they write:

> The home, which before was a space seared by conflicts, where a father who was a domestic tyrant asserted his disputed authority and a son who was physically frail but totally unshakeable proclaimed his autonomy, in an intolerable challenge which went beyond generational conflict to take on the significance of cultural apostasy, at a terribly severe cost (of nerves, of denied emotional attachments, of life destroyed day by day before the explosion at the station platform), has now become the prison in which Felicia Impastato has 'voluntarily' locked herself away, where she speaks and remembers, accuses and condemns, expresses chagrined tenderness and implacable harshness, a prison from which she cannot step out, cannot release herself.[19]

As a young woman her life was 'naturally' bound up with rules and codes governed by the mafia, which ruled without question at Cinisi, the village where she was born and where she still lives. We can take for example her memory of the mafia *capo* Cesare Manzella who was her brother-in-law on her husband's side.

> Cesare Manzella? I can't speak ill of him. Once, my husband took up with a woman.... I had this child, I was really young and he couldn't care less. And he went to bed with her. Her husband and relatives knew about it; when they went and knocked on the door he came out in his underpants. Then I left, I took my son and I went off to my family. I said: 'I don't want to see him again.' Then this Cesare Manzella came; he was nice as can be, because he respected me, and he said: 'So, what do you want to do?' And he came and went back and forwards, and he went to my mother ... and then, then they must have given the woman money to settle things with her. He even talked to my brother: 'You're responsible for your sister.' 'Why is that?' 'Because you must get them to make things up.' 'It has to be her who makes things up, what have I got to say about it?' 'No, you are responsible.' My brother said: 'Look, Felicia, go back, for there's not

much else you can do.' But I was still sick to my stomach, the bad feelings didn't go away.[20]

The mafia peacemaker re-established order, but a bitter aftertaste remained. Yet it was Felicia herself who wanted to marry Luigi Impastato: 'Yes, I was engaged to someone else. It was what I wanted. . . . Then I got engaged to him, he attracted me, I have to admit.'

The marriage conclusively sealed her cohabitation with the mafia.'I didn't understand a thing about the mafia at the time, otherwise I would not have taken that step. . . . As soon as I got married it was hell.'

Her daily life was drawn into clashes between rival clans, and the Badalamenti, and even Liggio as a fugitive are very vivid memories. For a time the family had to hide out in the mountain village of Contessa Entellina. In the mafia war fought out in the early sixties between the Greco and La Barbera clans her powerful brother-in-law was killed.

And in her memories, Cesare Manzella's death seemed like a premonitory event:

> He went to open the car window and he was blown up, that other poor fellow too. It had quite an effect on Giuseppe. That was when he started saying: 'So, they really are thugs then.' He understood more and more. He realized that they really were thugs, and he hated them. . . . My son Giuseppe said to me (he was fifteen at the time), Giuseppe was struck by this: 'You know when they kill a lamb? They found shreds of flesh hanging off a tree.' I wanted to tell him: 'Son . . .'. I knew he would meet the same end. . . . And he went and asked: 'Uncle,' he said, 'what would he have felt?'[21]

This was the same question that Felicia constantly asked herself, after they killed her son Giuseppe, blowing him up with a TNT charge on the platform of the Palermo–Trapani railway line.

Why such savagery, and, what is more, against the son of another mafia man?

Giuseppe, 'Peppino' to his friends, had engaged in a head-on struggle against the mafia, on several fronts: at the level of generation and family against his own father, at the political level against the 'historic compromise' between the Communist Party and the Christian Democrats, against property speculation and against drug running, against the building developer Finazzo, and against the powerful Badalamenti clan. And he had joined battle against the mafia's slippery seriousness with the terrible, desecrating weapon of irony and satire. His private radio station, Radio Aut, brought into every house, behind every lowered shutter, the sacrilegious message: the emperor has no clothes. On Crazy Wave, Peppino Impastato uttered the unutterable name, giving visibility to a phenomenon that was by definition invisible: the mafia of Don Gaetano

Badalamenti, the boss of Cinisi and the *cosca* which ran the international airport of Punta Raisi, and thereby the international traffic in drugs. 'Don Tano Seduto,* an adept with the shotgun . . .'.

Visibility, solidity and naming seem the most feared enemies of the mafiosi, who have built their power precisely on suggestion, silence and actions that are ambiguous. Vera Pegna tells of an apposite story from the early sixties which amply illustrates the disruptive force of an outlook, in this case her own, which is inspired by good sense and directly shuns the mafia alphabet:

> Opposite the door of the Party office, five metres away, there was a butcher's shop where Don Peppino or some other Panzeca would be sitting, without fail, in clear view, so as to intimidate anyone wanting to come to us. Being seen by a mafioso as you entered the Communist Party office was no small thing, which meant the presence of the Panzecas there was intended to ruin our meetings.
>
> The comrades were telling me all this, just as Don Peppino was taking up position on a chair brought to him by a boy, and settling himself down in view of an open meeting they had called by going from street to street. At that very moment they were setting up the loudspeaker, with someone saying: 'Hello, hello, testing.' I took the microphone out of his hand and said: 'Testing, testing, for Don Peppino. If he stays there sitting across the road from us then it's true he's a mafioso; and if that's the case then I'm asking him to look up and smile so that I can take a photograph of him.'
>
> No one can imagine what a dramatic effect these words had. The comrades who were with me on the balcony disappeared inside as if whooshed away by sheer terror. People in the square were flabbergasted. Don Peppino rushed into the butcher's shop and disappeared through a back door.[22]

Peppino Impastato's clash with his father had as its starting point the clash between the 'culture' of mafia bullying and the culture of learning, interwoven with the libertarian impulses of the sixties. His mother remembers: 'My husband would say: "If a son of mine didn't want to study and they failed him, I'd shoot him." . . . He would take this badly, coming back with: "Shoot", right away . . . you see. Giuseppe would say: "I'd like to put it to the test, I'd like to fail for a year and see what . . ."'[23]

And, as time went by, Felicia increasingly became her son's accomplice, sharing his ideas, trembling at the consequences of this commitment, and still trying to persuade him not to expose himself publicly. 'Yes, I always talked about things with my son, but not with my husband. Giuseppe said: "What is society, what is . . .". And that was Giuseppe's starting point for reacting.

---

* A mocking pun on Toro Seduto, Sitting Bull. [Trs.]

Giuseppe would talk about injustice and abuses of power, that was his starting point. And I would say: "You're right, son, but there's no point in talking about it." '[24]

Torn between the old law of *omertà* – 'there's no point in talking about it' – and the discovery of new horizons – 'you're right, son' – Felicia pursued an impossible family compromise.

The situation became exacerbated as time went on. The mother tried to smooth things over as much as possible – 'he was involved in politics and I would be everywhere . . .' – but mafia pressure mounted fast. They threatened the father who, in turn, threatened the mother. 'I heard them, I heard them from behind the door: if I had a son like that, they said to my husband, I'd dig a grave and bury him. Shut him up or else we'll shut him up! We'll have a package for you outside your door,' Felicia told Ferdinando Scianna in an interview.[25]

When Peppino spoke at public meetings his mother stayed at home, filled with dread – 'tell him not to talk about the mafia. Don't talk about the mafia' – while his father went off to the country, enraged and powerless, so as not to hear. Finally he threw his son out of the house. Yet the mother secretly let him back from time to time.

> Then my son would come and I would get a bath ready for him, always without him knowing. I would say: 'Hurry, Giuseppe.' He would take a bath and put on clean clothes and then he would leave. He would come to me for meals, always without his father knowing. I would set the table and serve him pasta, and meat, and fruit. 'Hurry, just in case your father comes in.' He would eat and leave.[26]

The other son, Giovanni, shared Peppino's political ideas as he grew up, and also became a left-wing militant. The situation became more and more tense, until, all of a sudden, the father left for America, without leaving any trace.

> With a suitcase he had to fill with clothes because he had to leave, because this son, he said, was even worse than the older one. He said: 'I can't stay in this house any longer. It's shameful!' 'How is it shameful? It's not as if your sons have stolen or killed, they don't have no-good women. So what shame is there for you?' He answered: 'I can't stay any longer, I have to leave.' But he didn't tell us where he was going, he wouldn't say, the mafiosi and his brother knew.[27]

Did he leave to punish his family? Did he leave to give the mafia a free hand? Did he leave to seek help among other mafiosi in America? His wife will never know for sure, but the 'American' relatives were later to describe that on a number of occasions the father had said: 'I told them: before you kill my son, you have to kill me.'[28] So there had probably been a meeting where the father had had his back to the wall: 'Either with us, or against us.'

Shortly after his return from America Luigi Impastato died in a road accident whose circumstances were never entirely clear. 'Some people say it was an accident. Now, I don't know. . . . There should have been an autopsy. But for the sake of not drawing it out any longer . . .' said Felicia, for whom, all the same, this death had the resonance of a verdict. 'Everything was falling apart for me. I would look at my son and say: "Son, who knows how this will end for you." '[29]

Giuseppe Impastato was murdered on 9 May 1978, the same day the body of Aldo Moro was discovered, and a few days short of the local elections in which Giuseppe himself was to stand as a candidate. He was thirty years old. After his death he was elected as a local councillor with an unprecedented number of votes for the Proletarian Democracy list in Cinisi.

The mafia staged the farcical scenario of a failed terrorist bombing action, and for a long time the investigations strictly pursued this lead; it was only thanks to the investigative work of Giuseppe's comrades that the mafia basis of the crime finally became an officially credited hypothesis. But the investigations did not get far. After being shelved, they were taken up again by the investigating judge Rocco Chinnici, but there was no time for him to reach any conclusion, because he too was eliminated by the mafia in a dynamite explosion in 1983. In 1984 the investigations were resumed, targeting Gaetano Badalamenti, who was suspected of being the man behind the murder. Yet, in 1992, even with the mafia basis of the crime established, the Prosecutor asked for the files to be closed. In an appeal for the inquiry to be reopened we can read:

> After the statements of the former Minister for the Interior, Gava, who could not give Peppino Impastato's family the assurance that he was a victim of the mafia, although this emerges unmistakably in the prior investigatory documentation . . . the closing of the inquiry is a cruel blow to civil society's demands for justice and truth for all those within the magistrature and the forces of order who fight against the mafia.[30]

'The man who ordered this murder was him, Gaetano Badalamenti,' states Felicia Bartolotta Impastato, with quiet courage. The man behind it is known to her, but those who carried it out remain unknown.

But beneath this unflinching accusation the mother harbours harrowing images – or imaginings, rather – of her son's final hours.

> How can I ever know? Maybe two or three of them forced him to stop. There must have been two or three of them, armed, or he wouldn't have had to get out. Did they take him there in his car, or did he walk? Did they get into the car and take him there? Did he only go because they said: 'We want to talk to

you'? No, he wouldn't have gone. Especially there. Which means they must have had to stop him on the road themselves, put him in the car and take him there. They must have knocked him out and stunned him, and with him stunned, off they went. They put the car there, because the car wasn't touched. Then they laid him down where that seat was, inside that house, because there was blood on it, then they took him there and left him there. But I can't know who did it.[31]

Like Salvatore Carnevale's mother, Francesca Serio, Felicia took on what her son bequeathed to her: a legacy of political commitment to freedom and dignity against cowardly mafia tyranny.

I screamed, just one scream that left me speechless. They had found Giuseppe blown to pieces by TNT near the station platform. They wanted to make it look like a terrorist bomb. Or a suicide, maybe. Then I realized that there was no time to weep. Because first and foremost I had to deny this, I had to defend my son's memory and explain even to the *carabinieri* that it was the mafia who had killed him. And that being on the left as he was didn't mean he had anything to do with terrorism.[32]

Her break with her relatives and the majority of her fellow townspeople was total. She took sides unequivocally. The time for impossible compromises was over. 'I sent them all on their way. Maybe if I'd wanted revenge they'd have given me the chance. But I wanted the truth for Peppino as Peppino had wanted. And the truth was against them. And I screamed it out: the mafia murdered my son. And I'll go on shouting it everywhere as long as I'm still breathing. Anyone who comes to talk to me about my son honours me.'[33]

Coming up with the right names, not forgetting, keeping her son's memory alive: 'I want justice to be done, I want these people to be punished, this is what I want. But vendetta against vendetta is no good to me,' Felicia said in a television interview.

Her reaction, along with the public demonstration against the mafia, meant something totally new in Cinisi. Many were at Peppino's funeral and at commemorations of his death in the years that followed. Umberto Santino said:

There were more than a thousand of us at the funeral, it was a big demonstration. I agreed to speak, and they told me that names should be named. Cinisi has a long straight road running through it, and when I looked up, there was an endless row of closed windows. So then I decided to speak to those closed windows: 'I know perfectly well that you Cinisi people are there behind your closed windows, and you know perfectly well who Peppino Impastato was and the work he was doing, and you know perfectly well that Peppino named the names of the mafiosi of Cinisi, and these are names that you do not utter. You know who Gaetano Badalamenti is and you know that drug running is going on here. . . . If these windows do not open then Peppino Impastato's work as well as the work that we want to continue is in vain.'[34]

Felicia only ever leaves her house for visits and demonstrations concerning her son's memory.

And I heard them shout 'Badalamenti murderer' right outside this house. It was a new sign, the first one. There's no doubt that my life changed after Giuseppe's death. I learned to speak out, and not to be afraid. I go on the radio, I tell the whole story, even if people think badly of me. When the TV came they filmed me outside the house and I felt the whole village watching me from behind the blinds. But Giuseppe left me all his courage.[35]

This recalls the public meeting held in the early sixties by the young comrade Vera Pegna at Caccamo. 'No one ever came, none of the windows were ever opened, often they would be deliberately closed in fact, but I took Scazzone's advice and I spoke all the same. . . . Every time we went back into the party office after a meeting, Scazzone would tell the comrades that it had been terrific, because there had been so many women behind the lowered blinds.'[36]

With the strength and intelligence of her feelings, Felicia Bartolotta Impastato broke down this invisible wall. From being 'their woman' she became her own mistress. Corrado Stajano writes:

This was perhaps the first time that a Sicilian woman spoke like this . . . not as a frustrated Mediterranean mother, not as a vengeful Fury, but as a woman who wants to use good sense, who looks into herself, who can hide her passion so as to preserve the memory of her beloved son. Felicia does not wail and groan, her voice comes from the depths of a complicated and difficult reality. She has not resolved her contradictions, but she made a straightforward choice, across however many violent options, to stand against her bullying husband, a mafia man and a friend of mafia *capi*, against the society of injustice and *omertà*, to stand with her rebellious son 'who got himself murdered because he wouldn't tolerate all this'.[37]

In the wake of Giuseppe's death, Felicia radically revised her relationship to both domestic space and public space. The defeat of her desperate attempts at mediation to save her son's life made her choices radical ones, completely erasing all respect for social conventions, which were revealed as hypocritical. And with this she shook off the subaltern status which made her one of 'their' women.

She shut the door in the face of her relatives who, despite also having lost a son through a mafia vendetta, 'wept and kept quiet. For them Jack's death was in the nature of things.'[38] Her rejection is directed at her relatives and the people of Cinisi, the ones behind the shutters: 'I don't want to look any of the Cinisi people in the face, with one or two exceptions. First they didn't know him. During the funeral the journalists were asking. . . . Tell us the truth about what happened to my son! Now they do know him, that he was good, and there's no end to their compliments! I've got no time for them.'[39]

The priest, too, is part of this silent majority behind the shutters. Even more, he was openly a friend to the mafiosi. 'I could have wrung his neck! Talk, say something to these people! Not a single word. And then when they killed Nino Badalamenti, he absolutely had to say Mass for him every month. They killed him on 19 August, and every month anything else had to take second place.'[40]

At the same time, however, Felicia opened herself to the world. Although she hardly ever left the house any more, she relished the visits of journalists and scholars. 'Because I like talking, because what happened with my son is getting bigger, they understand what the mafia means. And they come for this, and what a joy it is for me when they come! They imagine: "This is a Sicilian woman and she'll keep her mouth shut." But no.'[41]

Outcasts in their own world

From the day when I became a plaintiff at the maxi-trial we lost nearly all the customers from our bar. No one came any more, except the kids from a nearby school. Some days we took in less than forty thousand lire, which wasn't even enough to pay the overheads. Why did this happen? Because people regarded me as a spy; yes, a spy for the law. This is how they think. My mother and my sisters are no exception. Even now they disapprove of my having become a plaintiff. 'Do you want to take on the mafia on your own, my girl?' my mother said. I've broken off all contact with her and with my sisters. I pretend they're dead. My mother has cursed me. She said: 'I'd like your children to end up just like my son Rodolfo, then you'd understand how a mother should act.' What does she mean, wasn't Rodolfo my brother? Didn't I suffer just like her, when they killed him? And anyway, how can a mother talk to her daughter like that, wishing the death of her grandchildren?[42]

These are the words of Michela Buscemi, one of the two 'ordinary women' who were plaintiffs in the maxi-trial. The other is Vita Rugnetta. Michela said at the opening of the trial:

I admit that I'm frightened. But I realize that what's needed at this point is an act of courage. I'm still thinking of my brother who's lying at the bottom of the sea. And I would like to find not just those who strangle and shoot to kill, but also those who've become rich with their drug millions, who have bought houses, villas, blocks of flats. I look at the cages and I wonder: are these the ones, or are the ones with the money still outside?[43]

Michela was the sister of Salvatore, who was killed in a drinking joint in 1976. He had a reputation for violence, he did small-time smuggling, and had perhaps come into conflict with neighbourhood bosses and their followers. Another brother, Rodolfo, disappeared along with his brother-in-law in 1982. He was on the trail of the killers, perhaps even involved in small-time crime 'unauthorized' by the local mafia; he was tortured, strangled and thrown into the water out at sea. Rosetta, Rodolfo's young wife, pregnant with her second child, brought the pregnancy to full term and then refused any food and let herself die of despair.

Michela's life as a child and a young woman was full of small dramas precipitated by a father who was as odd as he was irresponsible, perhaps seductive in his egocentricity, but also tremendously authoritarian. He was a jack-of-all-trades who had several tries at emigrating. He squatted and then rented out empty houses, went in for small-time smuggling, started up a number of businesses that did not last, was a hanger-on at the fringes of the Christian Democrats, a rag-picker, did the football pools. . . . All in all he acted like a wayward child, oblivious to the fact that he had meanwhile become the father of ten children. 'My mother didn't want him, he made a show of throwing himself off the Oreto bridge, and everyone came running, so she felt sorry for him and they got engaged, then they *eloped*.'[44]

The mother was perpetually busy reproducing, so busy she didn't even have the time or the desire to be a mother. Soon Michela, who was the eldest daughter, was taking on the role of mother to her little brothers:

> My mother had ten children as well as twenty-eight miscarriages. . . . I was very fond of my brothers and sisters, because they were my children and the first one they called Mummy was me, not my mother, because my mother made them then handed them over to me. The obstetrician would leave and she would put them in my hands, because she was already thinking about producing the next one.[45]

Michela's memories readily dwell on her little brothers and sisters. The little surprises, the presents, the parties, the sweets — she tried to give them everything that she herself had not had from her mother, despite the poverty in which the family lived.

Michela liked school, but she was not allowed to go; her domestic labour was too precious. 'In the evenings, without fail, when my father got home he would put me over his knee and take the belt off his trousers and hit me on the behind with it because I had gone to school.'[46] At twelve she went out to work; in one of the little salt-fish factories, at basketmaking, dressmaking. After work the housework was still waiting for her, however.

Despite all the turmoil, the instability and the beatings, Michela remembers hers as a 'united family': 'Me and my brothers and sisters would joke and play, and if one of us needed something another would be there, that kind of thing. . . . Sunday was always a special day and my father liked to have all his children sitting around him, and we would sing . . .'[47]

These few glimpses can give us some insight into the dreadful, devastating power the mafia exercises over hearts, feelings and intimate relationships. There is no reason to doubt that her brothers and sisters were equally fond of Michela, especially since she had brought them up. Yet, when Michela brought charges against the mafia, as the murderers of two of her brothers – Salvatore and Rodolfo – they all turned their backs on her.

It caused Michela a lot of pain, to the point where she in her turn had to 'kill' them in the depths of herself, in order to make this suffering bearable. 'Now, when I see them from a distance, they seem like strangers. It leaves me cold. But I have to say that I did suffer to begin with . . . I overcame it, I pretended that the mafia had butchered them all, killed them all. Over and done with,' she confided to Petra Bonavita.[48]

After the revelations by the *pentito* Sinagra, giving the macabre details of the execution of Rodolfo, it became possible for her to act as a plaintiff at the maxi-trial. Michela made up her mind, but her brothers and sisters one after the other insulted her on the telephone. Her father was dead by this time and her mother cursed her:

Her answer to me was that there was no way she would act as a plaintiff, because she was afraid for herself and her children. When we got to that point I told her: 'What kind of mother are you then? There are two children with neither a mother nor a father, and three others who have lost their father, yet you won't be a plaintiff. Rosetta died over this, and we've had a whole heap of grief, yet you won't be a plaintiff, when they've killed two of your sons!' And then, with a voice cold as ice, that made my blood run cold, chilled me, she said: 'You should feel the same grief, they should kill your children, and then you'll feel the same grief!' And that's what she said. And there was no way I could steel myself to go into the other room where my husband and children were. I locked myself in the bathroom and broke down in tears, and I swore that from that moment on this family no longer existed for me.[49]

Having been rejected by her blood relatives, Michela was also cold-shouldered in her own neighbourhood. People snubbed her. Customers no longer came to her bar. 'One of the customers told me he had been approached by a gang member; he asked him if he wasn't scared to go to the Del Sole bar, where the owners might be killed and him as well,' Michela said in an interview with *Venerdì di Repubblica*. The mafia sealed the whole thing by placing a bomb.

> None of the customers came any more . . . yes, people round here are scared. And then they think we are spies because that's the expression they use, *spiuni da quistura* [police station informers], it's a dialect phrase they use a lot. It's not acceptable for someone to bring charges, it makes you a spy, as if I'd gone and said: 'Signora so-and-so went and stole from such and such a place.' Things that are no concern of mine, things other people do. What concerns me is that they killed my brothers and it's right that those who killed them should pay.[50]

But there was more to come. Another bitter surprise awaited Michela. Both she and Vita Rugnetta were excluded from the funds collected through a national subscription to pay legal costs for plaintiffs, because they were not relatives of victims who were 'servants of the state'. Umberto Santino wrote:

> The maxi-trial involved defendants for ninety-two murders. The only plaintiffs were the relatives of the 'servants of the state' from Dalla Chiesa to Boris Giuliano, from Giaccone to the bodyguards. The only ones who came forward demanding justice for the other victims – and they were numerous – are these two women (Buscemi and Rugnetta). Their actions should be regarded as an event of importance, a precious example to be encouraged, so that all the others who have not done this can feel prompted to do so in the future. Yet they were isolated and turned away.[51]

This point is so serious that I want to go into it in depth further on.

The decision to make a public stand against the mafia and to name names utterly changed Michela Buscemi's life. Though many of her relatives ceased to have any connection with her, others – her husband and her five children – showed their courage, understanding and love for her. They supported her: 'Be brave, Mum, don't get downhearted, we are with you,' the children told her. Her close family connections diminished in number perhaps, but grew in quality. And within the environment inhabited by the family, it cannot be easy to display an outlook of this kind. Michela:

> Two days before I went into the courtroom, at the street market where the bar is, a stallholder who sells woollens said to me: 'I saw you on television.' . . . I'd spoken with this gentleman before. He told me: 'I come from Kalsa, I'm known there and I know how these people think. Your brothers are dead now, it's better if you keep out of it. *Ma so maritu nenti fa, 'u ci stocca i ammi?* [But what's your husband doing, he should have crippled you by now?] You mustn't take offence. I'm telling you for your own sake.'[52]

After seeing her on television, one daughter's fiancé took to his heels, not without a display of hypocrisy first: 'He telephoned my daughter: "You make me ashamed. You're a mafia family." What? With everything I've tried to do and he tells my daughter that we're mafiosi?'[53]

Her family connections have changed, her friends have changed and her work has also changed. Now Michela plays an active part in the anti-mafia movement, speaking in schools and centres and at public meetings. She is a member of the Association of Sicilian Women against the Mafia, is involved in the Giuseppe Impastato Sicilian Centre for Documentation and has joined the PDS.* She earns a living doing cleaning jobs paid by the hour and her husband is unemployed.

At the appeal hearing Michela was finally compelled to withdraw from her action as a plaintiff. The threats had become too serious, her children's lives were in danger. 'I had to tell my husband. I've never seen my husband weep, but he was weeping when he begged me to withdraw. The lawyer told me: "Signora, we can't take the risk." '[54]

But Michela Buscemi withdrew with her head held high, accusing and denouncing the threats, and explaining the reasons for her action to the court.

> The night before I went into the courtroom I had a dream. I was driving along and they were following me in one of those big long cars. I was alone, I was inside the 500. There were four men. Once we got to a deserted street they forced me to get out of the car and they took me to a clifftop. They were beating me. They pulled out my tongue. As I bled I thought: 'Better me than my children.' Withdrawing as a plaintiff is like my brothers being killed all over again. It makes me furious. It means they always win.[55]

Vita Rugnetta, the other woman who took action as a plaintiff in the maxi-trial, lost her only son, Antonino, who was forty. After separating from his wife he had gone back to live with his mother, with whom he ran a furniture shop.

Vita Rugnetta made up her mind to follow things through to the end. Her hatred for the murderers was much stronger than her fear. 'They murdered my son, they tortured him by flaying his skin, and I looked in the murderers' faces in the dock, I heard from the lips of the *pentiti* the whole story of the tortures they inflicted on him. . . . And what do these murderers think, that I'll forgive them? Never. Never! And if they have children, I

---

* Partito Democratico della Sinistra, the Party of the Democratic Left, which replaced the PCI, the Italian Communist Party, after its dissolution in 1989. [Trs.]

hope that they too will suffer the same agonies my son went through. I know no pity.'[56]

Antonino Rugnetta, who was involved in cigarette smuggling, disappeared one November day in 1981. From the testimony of the *pentito* Sinagra it could be reconstructed that he was kidnapped and tortured in order to extract information about the hiding place of the mafioso Salvatore Contorno, who had escaped an attack by the Corleones and was a friend of his. Rugnetta was taken to the same 'torture chamber' at Sant'Erasmo where Rodolfo Buscemi died – a room fitted out for torture and with sound-proofed walls so that no one would hear the screams of pain from outside.

After lengthy torture Vita Rugnetta's son was strangled.

Vincenzo Sinagra then saw one of the torturers cut the cords binding the corpse to the chair and pushing it to the ground before taking a long hempen rope. He had to hurry before the corpse stiffened. The body was swiftly trussed up in the simplest way, with the hands and ankles tied together at the back with a metre or so of rope which was then twisted around the dead man's neck. . . . This horrendous procedure had even been given the name *incaprettati* [literally, trussed like a goat] . . . in fact the corpses were treated like this in order to make transportation easier, just as if they were ordinary pieces of baggage.[57]

The corpse was eventually left to be found in the boot of a stolen car, in the centre of Palermo.

Attempts were made to conceal the grisly details from the mother. 'It was at the funeral that I found out the truth. I overheard something an acquaintance said . . . I believe that even if I had never known about the torture I would not have forgiven my son's murderers, but since I found out about it, not only can I not forgive them, but I hate them through and through, I curse them and I wish them the same torments they inflicted on my boy.'[58]

On the first day of the maxi-trial Vita Rugnetta came forward in court, without having been called. With a steady step, and holding up a portrait of her son, she walked towards the cages where more than a hundred mafiosi were in custody and 'uttered a sentence harsher than any a judge can write'.[59] Suddenly there was total silence. 'I walked past the bars of the cages and looked at them one by one. As soon as they met my eyes they lowered their gaze, as if they feared a poor old woman. What kind of men are these? They had been brave enough to torture my defenceless son, but they did not have the courage to look me in the face.'[60]

Vita Rugnetta lived in a neighbourhood with a high mafia density. Besides, her son was also very caught up in this milieu. 'I know . . . he died without winning any medals. But this doesn't matter to me. If they are the murderers they must pay,' she said.[61] And so people in the neighbourhood turned their backs on her. 'I have had to close two of the three shops I had, because I couldn't pay the rent on the premises. I kept the smallest one. But from then on I didn't sell a single chair or coatstand. I come here every morning and roll up the shutter, but I know that nobody will turn up. I keep the shop for the sake of dignity.'[62] Not even her daughter-in-law is on her side. 'I understand her though,' says Vita Rugnetta. 'But I lived alone and I've got nothing to lose.'[63]

But it is not just fear that drives away the customers. It is clear that some people speculate on the misfortunes of others:

> We sold furniture on hire purchase. People would come, take the furniture home with them and sign agreements with us for payment in instalments. Since Antonino died customers who were still in debt to us have refused to settle what they owed. They say they have already given the money to my son, in cash ... but the outstanding bills are still at my house. So far, there has been no way of getting the money, even with legal action.[64]

Signora Rugnetta ended up virtually alone. The Sicilian Centre for Documentation announced a collection, a private television station opened a subscription, and the San Saverio Social Centre sent her an invitation. But, in the meantime, Vita Rugnetta also closed the last shop and is no longer seen in the neighbourhood.

On 17 October 1984, in a shed in the Brancaccio neighbourhood of Palermo, eight men were machine-gunned to death in what became known as the Piazza Scaffa massacre. Four of these men were relatives of Pietra Lo Verso, the woman who acted as a plaintiff in the trial naming the alleged murderers. The four were her husband Cosimo Quattrocchi, a brother-in-law, the husband of a niece and a cousin. Those who wound up in the dock accused of having ordered the massacre were the Palermo boss Pietro Vernengo and the Catanian meat trader Antonino Fisichella. Also accused, but at large, are the bosses Nitto Santapaola and Carmelo Zanca. Two other meat traders, La Torre and Amico, were accused of perjury. 'The men behind it are from Catania,' Quattrocchi's widow had alleged from the start.

All of them were acquitted after a lengthy trial. 'If you say you don't know anything, they accuse you of not wanting to cooperate with the law. If you talk ... this is the outcome. You accuse and the law lets them all go free. . . . I've become a different person since Monday. I don't trust anything any more. Because it was pointless. I told the truth and they didn't believe me. As if I had just told a heap of lies' – this was Pietra Lo Verso's bitter comment after the verdict.[65]

Who is Pietra Lo Verso? She is a woman who grew up in a poor background, in a neighbourhood that lived off cigarette smuggling, she had little schooling and had to go out to work from the age of ten. Pietra 'lived until the birth of her first child in an agglomeration of *catoi*, those little cellar-level houses which consist of a single room full of beds and household paraphernalia where a whole family would be crowded in (however big it was), known in Palermo as "minimal houses", in Via Tirassegno, in the Sant'Erasmo district'.[66]

Sant'Erasmo is a high-risk neighbourhood, and her parents were aware of this. 'It mattered a lot to my father and mother that we kept out of prison,' Pietra narrates.[67] But her sister 'eloped' with a young ex-con who spent the first eight years of the marriage in prison. And her other siblings also 'eloped' with their partners, 'as a prelude to spur-of-the-moment marriages embarked upon almost in adolescence, and therefore without any capacity to maintain a family'.[68]

Her father, an upholsterer, died when she was nine. Her brothers work as dustmen, her sisters went into service and, at ten, Pietra started work in a hairdresser's. 'I got six thousand lire a month, in those days we thought that was something. . . . We were always at home. On Sundays we did the housework, the ironing, cleaning the floors, that's to say we divided up the chores between us. Sometimes we went for lunch to my father's sister's.'[69]

Before long she met her future husband Cosimo, but Pietra's mother didn't want him for a son-in-law; Cosimo was the son of a smuggler who had been in prison for a number of years and his brother had also been arrested for stealing a car. 'We thought my husband was like them. . . . So my mother didn't want him and she said: "No, you can't have him." '[70]

But Cosimo was different; he started work in his grandfather's butcher's shop at Ballarò and after an engagement of two and a half years the lovers eloped. But there was also another woman with her eye on him and when she saw him go off with her rival she reported him to the police (for violence?), with the result that he served three months in prison.

Through the marriage Pietra finally managed to achieve some relative contentment; the horsemeat butcher's, which was passed on to her husband after his grandfather's death, did well, giving work to six families. Her husband worked in the shop but also went to the villages to buy the meat. The children went to school.

My husband was an easy-going man, he got on well with people, he was a sociable sort, but we didn't like going out with friends that much because he kept himself to himself. I mean he was a home body, he spent his time at the shop and at home. He would come home at two o'clock, have lunch, rest for a bit, I'd call him at four and he would go down to the shop, and if they needed me he'd say: 'You come down as well.' He'd take the kids out, and we were a very close family: husband, wife and children.[71]

The massacre hit the family like a bolt from the blue. None the less, Pietra straight away targeted the Catania lead. For over ten years her husband had been getting supplies of horsemeat from a Catania dealer, one Fisichella. But for a number of weeks, for a combination of reasons he'd been trying to change supplier. At this point two things happened at once: the Catania trader would telephone at all hours of the day and night, insisting that their connection not be broken off, while another wholesaler, La Torre in Bari, to whom Quattrocchi had gone instead, refused to supply the foals. When Cosimo called the Bari trader the latter was adamant; this was in Pietra's presence: 'The answer he gave was: "I won't do the dirty on Fisichella...". My husband had an inkling...' she relates.[72] Quattrocchi went to Bari all the same, finally buying a wagonload of foals which he had trouble getting back to Palermo, however. When he finally arrived, late in the evening, the trap was sprung. It was dark by the time the men brought the foals into the stable; all eight of them were mowed down and the massacre was only discovered the following morning.

Pietra Lo Verso was never in any doubt.

The police chief at the Carini barracks said: 'Your husband did something or they wouldn't have killed him.' They questioned me like this and I told them: 'It was Antonino Fisichella, the one from Catania.' And all my statements, just like what I'm saying now, were made at the Carini. And they told me: 'You'll have to identify the dead bodies.' So they took me to the hospital. They took me down there to the basement, where all the dead bodies were. What was it like! A real slaughter! I recognized my cousin Cosimo right away. I didn't entirely recognize Schimmenti, because they got him in the mouth. They got my husband in the shoulder and the back of the neck. From behind. My brother-in-law in the heart. My cousin Cosimo here, under the ear. Another fellow in the eyes. My nephew Marcello in the temple. Butchery, I'm telling you! Butchery! The skin was hanging off my husband's neck. I said: 'They shot my husband in the head!' *Suoru mia, vitti cosi chi* ... [My dear, the things I've seen ...] And I made the statements straight away, there and then. Because I'd seen what had happened in those two weeks with that Fisichella in Catania. I made the same statements to the investigating judge, to everyone involved. Whoever questioned me I always made the same statements. I didn't take anything away and I didn't add anything. Always the same statements.[73]

The other relatives were prepared to act as plaintiffs, until they knew the content of these statements. When they realized how far the charges went they disappeared. 'And when they were called to the trial, they all declared that they knew nothing. And so I took on this whole massacre of eight people. And I put my life at risk, and my children.'[74] It was the same old story. Pietra was isolated. And she didn't even have the support of her children. As if by magic the butcher's shop emptied when the newspapers and television started talking about her position in the trial. 'I would go and do my shopping in Piazza Ballarò and I would see all my customers in the other butchers' shops and I thought: "I've done the trial and I've thrown myself out on the street." . . . And my children held it against me.'[75]

The business of the lawyers deserves a special mention. When she still had the support of the other relatives Pietra went in search of better lawyers. She tried everywhere, but she found no one available! 'And I went to see more than ten lawyers, the best there were in Palermo, the best lawyers, because I wanted justice for my husband. They told me they were defending Fisichella. I knew I was in trouble, because nobody would take on my defence and the trial was very close.'[76] These are the same gentlemen who, during the trial, accused Pietra Lo Verso of 'wanting the limelight'. 'During the trial she got telephone threats. Not even the defence lawyers treated her well, but accused her of "wanting the limelight".'[77]

It was only the help of Judge Borsellino that enabled her to find lawyers in the end – these were Galasso, Gervasi and Nadia Alecci.

Alone, with four children, the widowed Signora Quattrocchi went through a terrible time. The eldest son left school to help out in the shop. Pietra had no pension, nor any savings. The neighbourhood was hostile towards her and her relatives stayed away. She had thirteen million lire in debts to a meat trader, who continued supplying her.

> There came a point when he said: 'I'll butcher the foals for you, but I can see that there's nothing you can do with them.' And the wretch went on butchering until I had to throw the meat away, because it went bad, because with no one coming to the shop, the meat that was taken out of the fridge every day went bad. In October 1986 the trial began and in January 1987 I shut up shop. I kept the shop for nine months and I paid the rent. I had to pawn all my gold jewellery to pay the rent.[78]

The only people who were close to her in this terrible period were the women of the Association of Sicilian Women against the Mafia and the members of the Impastato Centre. 'They did a lot for me and I've always had them close to me. I've had none of my relatives the way I've had them.'[79]

At the trial Pietra was the only relative of the eight murdered men with the courage to speak out. Dressed in black and sitting with a large handbag in her lap, she repeated the statements she had made from the first, firmly and implacably. 'It's Fisichella from Catania who's behind it, the only person with whom my husband had had a conflict of interests because he had decided not to buy any more meat from him.'[80] In the public gallery sat the women from the Association. The television report shows how Pietra looked up at the gallery and how the women signalled encouragement to her. 'These women were very close to me at the time. When I was going through

212

all this they were really the only ones who helped me. They give me a feeling of protection.'[81]

The relatives were nowhere to be seen. 'None of my relatives helped me. Nobody. My relatives don't come to my house any more either. . . . My brother doesn't speak to me any more, and none of my sisters speak to me, because I brought this case. I've been deserted . . . we haven't spoken for five years.'[82]

From being comfortably off, Pietra was made poor by her decision. She lost the butcher's shop and because of her husband's prison record she was excluded from the regional funds set aside for the victims of mafia crimes, and has had to pawn all her possessions in order to pay her debts. In the end the Town Hall found her a casual job as a cleaner at the Biondo Theatre.

Meanwhile, however, there occurred a serious event 'rich in emblematic significance': her two eldest sons were arrested for drug pushing. 'The truth was that she had been defeated in her battle against her husband's murderers and her boys saw an unwelcome guest come into their house: poverty.'[83] Clearly, the male children set themselves up as the men of the family, and, from their point of view, by becoming a *pentita*, their mother had brought about the loss of their butcher's shop and reduced them all to poverty. 'They are protecting her from the slanders of the neighbourhood. They must rebuild the family's shattered honour in other people's eyes.'[84] This meant that Pietra was effectively forced to hide her own convictions and her anti-mafia activities in her own home. During one interview there was a ring at the door. Pietra was worried: 'Let's hope it isn't my eldest son. He doesn't want me to meet any strangers and start talking again,' Pietra whispered, 'because now he's the man of the family.'[85]

Pietra had nothing left but her memories:

My husband was everything to me. We were happy. I can't resign myself. Every night, when I go to bed, I take his photograph and kiss it and I talk to him and I always fall asleep crying. And then I dream about him. Last night I dreamt about Cosimo. He was looking into my eyes and talking to me. But I don't remember what he was saying. It's always like that: he talks to me and I can't remember.[86]

Commenting on her interview with Pietra Lo Verso, Giovanna Fiume raises the issue of what Pietra's actions meant, or rather how her struggle against the mafia, which has turned her into a kind of symbol for the anti-mafia movement, can be reconciled with her background, which bears the unmistakable marks of subordination. 'Any ideology of emancipation [is] foreign [to her]. . . . Education is superfluous and not thought of as a form of social redemption, work is a necessity.'[87] Pietra appears to have a 'natural' place in a division of behaviour and rules which is bound up with protection, dependency and subordination. Her convictions appear to be deep-rooted and, one might say, unconscious.

Giovanna Fiume concludes:

> Pietra plays a part in political exchange, exchanging symbols for resources. For us there remains the problem of understanding how much these symbols belong to her personal 'background'. Since she gave up her husband's butcher's shop because people had stopped coming to buy meat (provoking indignation in the foreign press), she has pawned all her gold to survive while she waits for a casual job to supplement her meagre income. She stands as the woman of the people demanding justice against the mafia, a banner for the anti-mafia professionals. Dignified and combative, she takes part in public meetings and gives interviews. What she asks for in exchange, rather than work, is a civil servant's job for her son and some help from the state.[88]

Yet Pietra's demand for justice was a sign of breaking away, and not just that – such cases, I believe, are out and out acts of emancipation. Challenging the mafia claim to life and death means putting oneself at extreme risk. This is the step which in the first instance – and justly so – is taken for concrete and personal reasons: bereavement, grief and anger – and only later can what is known as asking for *justice* become identifiable. Each one of the women whose story is discussed here – and probably, in the event, each one of us – ties different meanings to the idea of 'justice', on the basis of her own story, and the background and culture in which she has lived and continues to live.

Whatever happens later, the act of breaking away changes things. None the less, there are ways and ways of experiencing justice. Thus, an extreme choice, at the subjective level, like Pietra's and that of other women like her, which does not encounter an 'objective' counterpart within the practices that give a material connotation to what we call justice, and which does not find a counterpart in the *experience* of justice, remains an isolated act of emancipation, an open wound. An isolated act certainly cannot be enough to provide an overall vision of the world in emancipatory terms. The aspect of emancipation to do with the trial requires a collective correspondence. It is here that the slow-witted response of the institutions appears doubly serious: towards the woman who is repudiated by the environment which denies her actions any value, and towards the environment which becomes further encouraged and confirmed in its negation of any overall prospect of emancipation.

> They've acquitted them now on the grounds of insufficient evidence; the massacre was at half past eleven at night and no one saw them. What is this law? Please. Since the trial I've stopped believing in the law, completely. Fisichella attacked me on the day of the plea. He told the Public Prosecutor that he didn't

know me. How come, didn't he come to my house for a meal? *Ci cuntavi tutto cosi, puru chiddu ca si manciò . . .* [I've told them everything, even what he had to eat in my house . . .] They all said the same thing, even though that one came and ate with us . . . but now that they've all been acquitted what have I to hope for. Even in the Cassation Court in Rome they were acquitted. Where am I to go now? I'm screwed, excuse my language, I've nowhere to go.[89]

An open wound and a burning disappointment, but also an inner victory and a message for anyone who'll listen: that she kept faith with something vital, that she did not give in to the murderers' bullying. 'I'll still fight for my husband until I die. Because I want justice for my husband, because my husband died an innocent man. . . . I loved him.' The victory of eros over thanatos. With the battle lost in the courtroom Pietra has none the less won an internal war. And this is a gift that she has given to all of us. This is where something new can begin to be born and this is where mafia arrogance will begin to be crushed.

Deserted by the authorities

But it is also here, from the gift of their strength of mind which these women have given us, and from their open wound for want of justice, that the struggle against the mafia – a struggle which concerns us *all* – must draw arguments and strengths.

The isolation which women like Vita, Michela and Pietra suffer in their own environment is a part of the mafia stranglehold of threats and crude bullying. 'Territorial sovereignty' allows the mafia to threaten relatives and friends, to take customers away, to point the finger at women who have wanted justice for their dead as bearers of bad luck. The mafia also recruits most of the best lawyers, so that a paradoxical situation is created whereby the ordinary citizen who wants to have recourse to the law against the mafia finds it difficult to take legal measures. And finally, as we have seen, the judges often attribute scant evidential weight to the testimonies of women against mafiosi, even if these are detailed and circumscribed.

It seems really reductive to talk about problems with the law in these cases. What is at issue is the very quality of our civil society.

In a letter to the press, Vita Rugnetta wrote, among other things:

I remember that the day the trial began I was in the courtroom and a number of lawyers, among them *avvocato* Galasso, and other people, including the sons of General Dalla Chiesa, came up to me and asked me if I wanted to act as a plaintiff. I said I did, but I pointed out that I didn't have the money to pay the lawyer. The lawyers and these other people told me not to worry because there was a subscription for the plaintiffs. In March 1987, a year after the start of the trial, I discovered from the newspapers that Signora Buscemi and myself had been excluded from any possibility of using funds from the subscription, because my son and Signora Buscemi's brother were not 'servants of the state'.... Now the lawyer has given me a bill for ten million lire. I have no means of finding such a sum, because people have stopped coming to my shop and I'll soon have to close it down. So I am wondering what I am supposed to do ...[90]

What had happened? The daily, *La Repubblica*, had sponsored a subscription to meet the costs of the plaintiffs in the maxi-trial; this had been launched by a committee which included trade unions and the Committee for the Monument to the Victims of the Mafia. A year after the start of the trial some four hundred million lire had been collected; when these funds were being awarded, the President of the Committee for the Protection of the Plaintiffs in the maxi-trial made it known that the beneficiaries were strictly families of 'servants of the State' who had been murdered by the mafia, because this 'is the code of procedure which has been accepted unanimously by the nine wards of the Committee'. This meant all of the plaintiffs with the exception of two: Vita Rugnetta and Michela Buscemi.

The decision aroused consternation in various quarters, but it was irrevocable. The fifty million lire from the regional authority, likewise administered by the Committee, subsequently also ended up in the grip of the same questionable set of constraints. *La Repubblica* did not write even a single line about this exclusion, and there was silence from the press and television. It was an unfair and narrow-minded decision, wrote Umberto Santino, the President of the Impastato Centre.

> Signora Rugnetta has been isolated twice over: by the world in which she lives, a world permeated with mafia culture, but also by those who should have encouraged her and supported her decision. It seems incredible that it should be the so-called swamp-clearers who are creating this swamp. In the wording published by *La Repubblica* before the maxi-trial there was no mention of making distinctions between the plaintiffs. This questionable decision was taken later on, using a criterion that I do not understand. It is my personal opinion that anyone who shows a will to break away from mafia culture should be encouraged even more than anyone else.[91]

It appears that the courageous decisions made by Michela Buscemi and Vita Rugnetta were not understood even by those who profess the wish to combat the mafia.

But do we know the opinion of the anonymous supporters – who are probably in the dark about the Committee's decision? And what the other plaintiffs really thought about the exclusion of two of their number? We do know that nobody protested.

Sandra Rizza comments:

> It is an ugly business, particularly because the story of this limitation has only come out now, after thirteen months of hearings in an underground courtroom. And those women acting as plaintiffs were counting on the help of the Committee.... Are there class-one victims and class-two victims? ... Is it legitimate to marginalize the only women who, in order to enter that courtroom, have had to shrug off an age-old tradition, an atavistic culture of toleration that is the ground on which the mafia has freely grazed for centuries?[92]

Rather than 'class-one and class-two victims', the issue here has to be addressed in terms of class-one and class-two plaintiffs. It matters that these women are not regarded as individuals, as singular and responsible, but always as something other than themselves. Of what relevance is it to any woman's freedom and sense of responsibility that her husband was a petty thief or a policeman, a mafioso or a magistrate or an ex-con? She is the one exposing herself, taking the risk, assuming the freedom to act like a responsible citizen.

Pietra Lo Verso was treated in a similarly discriminatory fashion. In her case it was not a matter of the costs of the trial, because her action as a plaintiff was not a part of the maxi-trial, but a regional contribution, allowed for by the law as it stood. Pietra was excluded on the grounds that her husband had a previous conviction. So what? Does the fact that she herself had no convictions count for nothing? When she put herself on the line in the courtroom only Pietra Lo Verso herself was responsible for the statements she made. Outside the courtroom, does she no longer count as a responsible individual?

Class justice? But can people really believe it is possible to fight against the mafia in this manner?

The only help that has come to these women has been from private organizations, collecting funds and expressing their concrete solidarity: the Impastato Centre, the Association of Sicilian Women against the Mafia, the local Members of Parliament of the Communist group and a private television network.

But behind the discriminatory and apparently merely bureaucratic moves there undoubtedly lurks an interpretation of the mafia, a specific way of seeing the social conflicts with which the Italy of these years is riven. To undervalue or misjudge the disruptive power of these examples of resistance to mafia might is at the very least to undervalue and misinterpret the specific nature of mafia domination: its creeping hold over perceptions of the world, which goes hand in hand with its economic and financial power. Mafia power is authoritarian and totalitarian in nature. It is a danger to democratic society as a whole. To separate opposition to the mafia into first class and second class is to regard the mafia as 'their' problem, something to be settled 'between themselves', without understanding that this would be a way of pushing huge sections of the population deeper into the deadly embrace of the mafia.

'When a woman like Vita Rugnetta, a real Mother Courage, succeeds in finding the strength to point the finger at her son's butchers, only to see herself deserted in this way, the message that comes back to her is: who made you do it anyway? Go back where you came from.'[93]

Within this context even low-key gestures take on importance or at least demonstrate scant sensitivity. While Pietra Lo Verso was struggling to survive, psychologically even more than materially, one of her little nephews, a son of the sister who did not cooperate, wrote a composition at school in which he forgave the murderers of his father, who, as we recall, was also a victim of the 'Piazza Scaffa massacre'.

> The composition by the little Piazza Scaffa orphan 'got reported', was taken up by television news and the Regional President met the child and his mother, presenting him with a bicycle. Different treatment from Pietra's which says it all: a prize for the 'forgiving' child and the mother who stuck to *omertà*, and a door slammed in the face of a woman who spoke out and did not forgive.[94]

The lawyers provided the one exception here – that is to say, obviously, those who took the decision to represent people at odds with the mafia. According to Michela Buscemi: 'When I went to testify, on 20 July, the lawyer said: "Signora, have you heard that Signora Rugnetta and you have been excluded from the money collected to pay the lawyers?" I said: "No, I don't know anything about it." . . . Then I said: "So what am I to do now?" The lawyer told me: "Signora, don't worry, it means that I've worked for you at no charge." '[95]

The subject of questionable official attitudes towards the mafia phenomenon recalls the stories of other women who come from families and backgrounds which are connected neither to mafia culture nor to the culture of anti-mafia struggle. These stories illustrate the terror which can be unleashed by merely incidental contact with the mafia world, arising for professional reasons, physical proximity, or business matters. More or less anyone may come into contact with the mafia and then be unable to break away from it. These stories demonstrate that mafia and anti-mafia are not in a 'professional clash between cops and robbers'[96] but that the danger of the mafia lies precisely in the ever-present potential threat to the individual freedom of everyone within the context of civil coexistence. Opposing the mafia is therefore not just to do with experts and professionals.

In October 1986, in the main square of Locri in Calabria, the nineteen-year-old student Rocco Zoccali was killed. His father, who worked for the regional administration, and his mother, Giulia Bova, a teacher, had rented out a warehouse to members of the powerful Cordì *cosca*, who did not pay the rent but refused to give the building up. Unknown to his parents, Rocco tried to sort the matter out, but he got beaten up. At this point he got hold of a weapon, threatened one of the mafiosi with it and wounded him in the leg. A week later came the exemplary execution in the square. But by then the boy had told his mother everything.

Giulia Bova became a plaintiff and spoke to the court about threats received even after the murder, and about the climate of intimidation that had formed around her family.

Signora Bova's experience of the law could not be worse. The trial took place with a delay of eighteen months with respect to the committal decree; the first two hearings, which were moreover lengthy and painful, were declared void on a technicality, and when Giulia Bova wanted it to go on the record that she intended to say everything she knew, adding: 'But if as a consequence of this something should happen to one of my children, let it be known that it was their relatives,' naming members of the Cordì family of Locri – the President of the Court silenced her with the words: 'We're not on television here.'

'I would never have thought', said Giulia Bova, 'that having started out as the injured party asking that justice be done for such a dreadful crime, I could have ended up being virtually the defendant. And yet that was just what happened.'[97]

When it finally came to the trial, the two accused were fully acquitted; at the appeal one of the two was still on charges, the one whose forensic tests had been found positive. Yet this defendant too was acquitted. The law had absentmindedly neglected to make a correct record of the tests, which, therefore, could not be regarded as admissible.

Anna Pecoraro, also a teacher, works in a secondary school at Prizzi in Sicily, where she was born in 1949. She lost her husband to the *lupara bianca*, his body never being found. 'A murder without a corpse. This is the worst, because you never give up hope. You aren't even left with a grave for the loved one. It means that for the whole of my life I'll have to live with suppositions and imaginings. As well as grief this brings an incredible impotent rage,' said Anna with tears in her eyes.[98]

Hers was an energetic and forward-looking family. Her husband, Ennio Alongi, succeeded in building up his own construction firm, and as well as teaching, Anna was active in the Socialist Party; she was the first woman to be elected as a local councillor in Prizzi. The children were looked after by Anna's mother, who lived nearby. They were a self-assured couple who were respected locally, and in their different fields were committed to working for democracy, she in the local council, he in his work and in sporting activities.

We made the mistake of speaking out publicly against corruption. . . . I think he felt very confident about this. It didn't even enter our heads that things could have turned out the way they did; professionally, my husband had widespread recognition. Even people who weren't intending to work with him came to see him to ask his advice. Ennio was very independent. He wouldn't let anyone get the better of him, he was convinced that he was competent enough to do everything on his own. Other people would have taken this confidence as a challenge.[99]

But as time went by they both felt they were being surrounded 'as if an invisible wall had been built around us', said Anna.

They struck a month before Christmas; this was in 1983. That day, Anna had flown to Rome on a visit with her youngest child. When she got back to Punta Raisi in the evening, she found no one at the airport. She waited, rang up relatives, but to no avail. 'I waited for seven hours, practically the whole night, with the child sleeping, waking up now and then and crying. Ennio didn't come.'[100] The following day the *carabinieri* found the car burned out in a ditch, and that was it. At the time Ennio was forty-one, Anna thirty-five; the elder boy was twelve and the younger one five.

A few months later Anna Pecoraro took action as plaintiff against five members of the two Prizzi *cosche*. In the courtroom she told everything she knew about corruption in public contracts, but the few witnesses who were prepared to speak were not taken seriously.

The judge asked one Prizzi police officer who confirmed my suppositions: 'But then, why didn't you simply arrest the mafiosi?' The statements were just ridiculed, the witnesses regarded as unreliable, and these were people with the courage to speak out in spite of being frightened. Nor was my own testimony, which I had prepared for weeks, taken seriously; it was pushed aside as the misguided suspicions of a grief-stricken widow.[101]

The five were acquitted and the investigation was shelved. The murder remains unsolved, and unexplained. 'Sometimes either I or one of my sons runs into one of these men on the street in Prizzi. Each time it happens I feel sick. That out-and-out acquittal was a humiliation to me, after I had collected so much evidence.'[102] Her party suggested that she should no longer stand for office, her mother begged her not to put her life any further at risk.

But Anna was left with her friends, including some from the party. She threw herself into her children and her commitment to education. She even set up a private vocational school which was a way of developing her aims in public life. 'This is how I want to go on fighting. I would like to do everything I can to develop new ways of thinking in Sicily.'

Also in the eighties, Dr Vincenzo Gentile was killed in Gioia Tauro in

Calabria. He was a municipal doctor and rebel Christian Democrat who was a popular leader and the town's mayor. Even the mafia boss Piromalli had always been one of his patients. 'He was our doctor and a great friend of my whole family. I was particularly grateful to him because he had treated us for thirty years. It's as if they had killed a brother of mine, it really is, a member of my family,' said the shrewd 'Don Peppino' Piromalli, serving a life sentence, immediately after the murder, just as the investigations were targeting his own clan.[103]

This tribute is ambiguous, just as the doctor's relationship with the mafia in general, and the Piromalli clan in particular, had always been ambiguous. 'The fight against the mafia was not something he was committed to. Quite the contrary. For Vincenzo Gentile the *'ndrangheta* was even an invention, a "slander" against his people.'[104] And his wife, Marianna Rombolà, explained: 'He tried to play down the seriousness of the mafia presence and put it in a different perspective, only so as not to discourage public investment in the area or dampen hopes for industry.'[105]

Whatever the case, Gentile was killed as he returned home after a session of the local council, on 8 May 1987. He left his wife Marianna and a daughter of fifteen, Natalina. 'Perhaps it was some secret torment, or maybe a weariness at living under the mafia heel that made Dr Vincenzo Gentile, the Mayor of Gioia, refuse, on the morning of 7 May 1987, to sign a payment order for an invoice from Carmelo Stillitano, the nephew of Peppino Piromalli. They killed him the next day, and the day after that the ruling group approved the payment order.'[106]

With ample knowledge of the world in which she was born and had always lived, Marianna Rombolà pulled herself together and set out alone to investigate who was behind the crime. In a long interview with Gianfranco Manfredi she described the events that followed.

> For years I lived with a public man, one of the most popular men in this area, but now I am the one and only person defending him. Apart from my daughter who, despite her age, understands and shares in my decision, I can only trust the police and some of the magistrates in Palmi. It's as if I had nobody, neither friends nor relatives. The mafia holds absolute sway here and it suffocates everything and everybody, parties, social organizations, even the Church.... See how the council didn't even stand as plaintiffs, not just in the trial for my husband's murder, but also in the trial where former council administrators were accused.[107]

The trial to which the widow referred was based mainly on what her private inquiries came up with. It was thanks to her that the investigating judges in Palmi were able to take out a warrant for the arrest of the fugitive Carmelo Stillitano, Don Piromalli's favourite nephew, and she was also the key witness in the trial of 1988 that brought charges against three Christian Democrat mayors who were successors at the head of the Gioia Tauro Council, six former heads of committees and Christian Democrat and Social Democrat councillors, and another thirty-seven defendants including businessmen who were 'friends of friends', bosses and henchmen of the powerful Piromalli *cosca*.

What were the investigations that enabled Marianna Rombolà to formulate these massive and yet well-detailed charges? 'I can only say that immediately after the crime I was motivated by one single hope, the hope that I would be the one to find out who and what exactly had killed him. I trusted nobody to begin with, which meant I acted only on my own initiative.'[108]

Marianna had a hunch about which direction to look in: contracts, the administration of public funds, the relationship between the mafia and politics. On a pretext, she invited to her home the Christian Democrat mayor who had succeeded her husband and wheedled him into talking about what had happened. 'I invited him here, into the living room, where I had hidden a tape recorder at the back of a shelf, and I made him talk. The investigators now regard that tape as a document of significant value, perhaps even more so than I myself had reckoned. They only complained about the quality of the recording; because, without my daughter's knowledge, I had used the tape recorder from her English Language course.'[109]

There emerges a sorry picture of council management: public works worth hundreds of millions granted to companies run as fronts, or directly to mafia members with skilfully piloted contract tenders. At the centre of the murdered mayor's final administrative actions were the municipal sewers, 'a truly bottomless pit' from which the young nephew of the Piromalli boss, Carmelo Stillitano, in hiding, extracted hundreds of millions in contracts without lifting a finger. The mayor had refused to approve an umpteenth 'contract' of this variety, hence his death sentence. 'Gentile, long given to favouring the Piromalli clan, would not, however, accept the role of mere onlooker, and the result was that, after a series of pressures followed by heavy warnings, he ended up crushed by the very mafia machinery which he had deluded himself into thinking he could keep under control.'[110]

From then on Marianna and Natalina, mother and daughter, lived shut up in their house under high-security protection, and on their rare outings were accompanied by a bodyguard. Marianna put herself on the line. As well as her testimony at the trial she was a committed activist in the Association of Women against the Mafia and Violence of Every Kind, which was based in Reggio Calabria. In 1989 she was awarded the Femmes d'Europe prize, conferred on her by an international jury of journalists for the bravery she had shown in the fight against the mafia.

What was the outcome of so much courage, at law and in the quality and credibility of our civil society? All the accused acquitted, once again. And Marianna and Natalina no longer live in Gioia Tauro. They have had to move to a location known to very few people, giving up home and family. Paradoxically, they are 'on the run'.

'Three years of investigation which led to a legal limbo, and now the last straw ... the murderer wasn't Carmelo Stillitano ... nor that poor dustman called Giovanni Loprete who decided to emigrate to America with his whole family a few months after the crime.' Paradoxically it was the well and easily documented friendship between Gentile and the mafia bosses which in fact weakened the charges made by the widow, in the eyes of the judges. 'A few months before he was killed Gentile had been a godfather at the christening of one of Don Peppino's grandchildren; he had made it his business to take an eminent clinician into Palmi prison to have the boss's heart trouble checked out.... The medical Mayor sat down at table with important bosses not just in Gioia Tauro,' wrote Pantaleone Sergi.[111] As if to say: they were too friendly with him to kill him.

Recent statements by a *pentito* of the *'ndrangheta* reveal that the man behind the Gentile murder was, however, Piromalli's nephew, Carmello Stillitano, but without the say-so of the boss. He, unable to punish his own nephew, had had the two hitmen killed in the meantime. Could it be that some day a court will give this *pentito*, a man, the credit it denied to the grief-stricken woman?

The story which perhaps more than any other highlights the terror and routine persecution which can be unleashed through undesired proximity to the mafia world is that of Maria Benigno. In this secret war between neighbours she lost her father, her brother and her husband. On the other 'front' a mafioso died. The whole thing only makes sense perhaps when it is known that to begin with the Benigno family was unaware of having anything to do with what we now know is one of the most ferocious mafia clans.

Maria came from a family that was fairly comfortably off. Her father, a shopkeeper, sold his properties in the country in the interwar period and bought land in the Corso dei Mille area in Palermo, a district which was then being built up. The family lived in a different part of Palermo, a residential district physically distant from the mafia. But after the Second World War, for a variety of reasons, they moved to Corso dei Mille. 'And that was how we got caught up in a mafia environment.' Besides the houses, the father owned a stable, also in Corso dei Mille, which was rented to the Marchese family, which, in turn, sublet it. After disagreements and threats, the stable was finally restored to them. This precedent from the start weighed heavily on relations between the Benigno family and the Marchese clan. And Maria's family only really had a vague idea of who the Marcheses were. 'We minded our own business and we really didn't know anything about the kind of dealings they went in for. We only thought that they were determined to make us leave, but then we didn't know about all the things they were involved in ... they were all relatives in the neighbourhood . . . so nobody gave anything away. We were the fish out of water, we were the only outsiders, so nobody talked to us.'[112]

In the wake of the controversy over the stable, Maria's father died in mysterious circumstances. He was standing beside his moped, very near his house, when he was run over by a car which drove off fast. But the traffic police got the registration number. Her brother Antonio set about tracking down the driver responsible for the accident. It turned out that the car had been rented from a garage where Salvatore Marchese worked. Once the driver had been tracked down, threats became so serious, both against the Benigno family and the eyewitnesses, that charges were not even brought. 'My father's death, then, was not an accident. It was a murder.'[113]

But this was just the start of interminable harassment. Her brother's car was burned, then, after this was reported as a crime by persons unknown, there were intimidating telephone calls during the night; in the middle of the night too there would be loud knocking at the door and loud noises could be heard outside on the terrace. 'Once, they even tied a chamberpot filled with faeces to the handle on the other side of the door.' They threw stones at the puppy, crippling her, they swore at the mother whenever they met her on the stairs. 'Us being there was a nuisance for them, we couldn't stay there, because we weren't people who belonged in their world,' Maria explains today.

An act of vandalism carried out by the Marcheses on a landowner's property, and which they tried to pin on Maria's brother, was cleared up so that the Marcheses were contacted for damages. 'From that day on, every time my brother went by they would call him "canary". They would say: "Did you go and sing? Canary, snitch," every time my brother went by.'[114]

One New Year's Eve, as Maria was greeting her mother at the door, there was gunfire. 'Just like that. One of them was just firing wildly, as if shooting in the air for New Year's Eve, and all the lead landed outside our door and we screamed and took cover underneath the balcony.'[115]

By now Maria had married Salvatore Alimena, a lorry driver. One of her brothers had emigrated to America and her mother now lived just with her son Antonio.

At this point things happened thick and fast. Filippo Marchese, who had been given a custodial sentence and suspected that Antonio Benigno had been behind the charge, stood in the middle of the street and shouted threats. 'It was obvious that they wanted to be rid of us, they wanted us to go because they thought we were connected with the local police,' said Maria. Shortly after Filippo Marchese's departure there was a serious intimidatory incident when the Benigno family's front door was pushed in with a heavy girder during the night. Antonio now went to the police again and made a charge against persons unknown. When he got back from the police station there was a fight.

Maria Benigno remembers:

There was a circle of people who had come from all over the place. . . . When my brother made a greeting as he went by, Angelo Rinella's father . . . , instead of answering good morning, answered him by spitting on him and saying: '*T'amu a scippari a testa* [We should rip your head off].' At this point, after the distress he'd gone through during the night, and what they had said to him, my brother just lost his head. There was nobody at home to hold him back and stop him going too far and doing things we wouldn't have let him do. Because if we had been bad people we would have done it with a feeling of being 'right', and not like that. He went into the house and got the rifle.[116]

In the shooting that followed a number of people were wounded and Salvatore Marchese died, hit by a bullet that ricocheted off a car.

Antonio, who was then twenty-six, was not fully aware of what had happened, but he knew that from then on he was a marked man. His feelings of persecution only increased. 'At the police station they were concerned that those people would take revenge, and we were given police protection night and day, with a bodyguard to take the children to school. They themselves had taken precautions, because they knew how dangerous the Marcheses were and they had realized who we were. We could only fear the worst.'[117]

At the trial Antonio was recognized as being not of sound mind and was sentenced to five years in a criminal asylum. While he was in the prison at Barcellona, he was found hanged but was saved at the very last by the guards. 'We thought he had wanted to kill himself. But now I've read in the newspapers that one of the things Calderone has said was that Filippo Marchese had given his brother Giuseppe, who was also in Barcellona, the job of killing my brother.'[118]

Antonio is a broken man. According to his sister: 'When he got out he came to live with me, and my husband was named his guardian. Do you understand what I mean? Antonio had gone mad. Fear of being killed by the Marcheses had driven him mad. He wouldn't leave the house.'[119]

Vendetta arrived some nine years later, on 17 December 1976, with careful attention to anniversaries: this was the date of the trial for Salvatore Marchese's death. When Maria, her brother and her husband got out of their car, outside the building where they lived, they were held up by three armed individuals:

As soon as I got out of the car, still holding the door open, I saw that we were surrounded by a lot of people. One of them, whom I later identified as Angelo Rinella, pointed the pistol at my brother, another one was hunched down behind the 500 and another was at the front, facing the steering wheel where my husband was. The first to fire was Rinella, who shot my brother in the throat. . . . The other one fired on my husband, who was hit in the chest, and he went right round the car firing all the time. . . . I was screaming, screaming. I too was targeted on the throat with the pistol. I don't know how I stayed alive, just the terror of it. The one who fired on my husband, who had a high-calibre pistol, aimed it at my breast, the centre of my breast, because I had gone round the car screaming, with my hands up.[120]

In the photographs submitted to her at police headquarters, Maria immediately recognized Rinella, who was on the run and was only arrested in 1981. She also provided a detailed description of the other two, one of whom she identified three years later as Leoluca Bagarella, after seeing his photograph in the newspapers.

Maria Benigno stood as plaintiff and at the trial Rinella received a life sentence and Bagarella was acquitted on the grounds of insufficient evidence. On appeal Rinella's sentence was reduced to thirty years and Bagarella was again acquitted on the grounds that the identification took place too late. The Court of Cassation confirmed this. In debate the defence tried, with a degree of cynicism, to imply that Maria too was not of sound mind, given the precedent of her brother. 'It's true that my brother was declared not of sound mind, but it was the Marcheses' threats that made him sick with persecution mania,' the key witness retorted.[121]

After Calderone turned state's evidence Maria's charges were further confirmed. 'Calderone says this consistently . . . and he also talks about Rinella and him getting orders for the double murder from Filippo Marchese. Just as I told the magistrates and wasn't believed. The magistrates should have done what I said from the first day, arraign Marchese. Instead they made the trial go on for nine years.'[122] And she confided to two women interviewers: 'They trust Calderone right away, even though he was arrested as a criminal, but they don't do the same with a woman. . . . Perhaps now the judges finally understand that you can also trust the testimony of a woman!'[123]

How did Maria live through all those years?

> Alone, completely alone. My relatives deserted me for fear of vendettas. I would look in my rear mirror, from fear of being followed. I sold what little I had to cope with the trial and I was left without a lira. I try to sew, but my eyes aren't up to it any more. The damages that were later awarded in court are a joke. Rinella has the cream of lawyers, even a university professor, but on paper he's poverty-stricken so he can't pay any damages. My husband's pension is sixty-seven thousand lire a month and I have an unemployed son. But I'll manage all the same.[124]

Her relatives are frightened and her husband's relatives have even snubbed her because they blame her brother for the death. Only her children are on her side. But they are terribly fearful. She told Antonia Cascio and Anna Puglisi:

They were happier when you came to us from the Association of Women against the Mafia. They were more trusting, they were braver. But when I had to go alone with my son to the trial, he was very dispirited, because he didn't feel up to facing them directly, and he told me: 'Mum, I'm getting sick. I'm not going, I can't go to the trial and you should write a letter to the President and tell him that you're withdrawing as plaintiff. Because I haven't got the strength to go with you. Can you understand that I can't look them in the face!' This was the son who's at home with me. Then, when you came along, he was heartened and more willing to come, and he would always ask me about you, he felt you backed him up.

But to begin with Maria also felt rejected by the Association; her first contact was not a happy one:

> The first time I turned to these women to ask for help I came across the widow of a judge. Her husband had been killed by the mafia too, and she was full of hatred. She suspected that we were in cahoots with the mafia, because we had lived a long time at Corso dei Mille, an area with a bad reputation. What's more, my brother had been sentenced for the shooting. 'If someone fires a gun,' she said, 'he can't be an honest man.' . . . Later when I later met Giovanna Terranova, the relationship was different.[125]

For years Maria was branded in this way by Corso dei Mille, along with the prison sentence served by her brother. At a hurried glance, as might happen with some journalist, her life can be mistaken for that of a mafia woman. She was even forced to write to the newspapers to set things straight, as for example on 9 February 1985 to *L'Unità*, which had addressed her as a 'mafioso widow'. Maria wrote: 'I was both upset and humiliated. . . . I wish to bring it to your attention that my husband was anything but mafioso, he was an honest working man, a democrat respected by everybody. He was murdered by the mafia above all because he was an inconvenient witness who was a danger to the hitmen. . . . I myself was spared . . . and I have felt a full duty to tell and report everything I knew and had seen.'

Maria also took action, kept going and stuck out in her demand for justice in the name of a strong inner imperative: not to forget. The image of the two dead bodies beside her seems to have a double significance: on the one hand it torments her by its cruelty, on the other it stirs strength in her. 'It nearly drives me crazy when that picture comes before my eyes, when that happens it's enough to make me say: "But why must I go on living?" . . . There's a big difference between seeing someone killed and not seeing the killing, a big difference . . .' The proximity of death gave her rootedness and strength. 'Now I see killings and I don't care. If they kill me, I've already fought my battle. . . . All the decisions I've taken in my mind, alone: to sell, not to sell, to work. I've always found the way by myself. Often with a lot of confusion, because it wasn't easy knowing the right thing to do. Because at such a dangerous and important time, a person no longer knows how to take life, what to do.'[126]

David against Goliath: the little dressmaker of Corso dei Mille against Filippo Marchese's clan. Not surprisingly, Maria Benigno is tired. For years she has worked as a travelling saleswoman, driving round small towns – 'I'm scared, mind you, I'm scared. Because I've had dealings not with decent people, but with bloodthirsty, really ruthless elements who take pity on nobody' – but in the end she received the regional award for innocent victims of the mafia and her sons have been given jobs. Maria has had no regrets about her decision. 'How could I keep quiet? If we all were to talk we would not be reduced to this level in Palermo, where we leave our homes in the morning but we don't know if we'll return alive.'[127]

11

The Women of 'Men against
the Mafia'

Living under siege

The first thing I did was bend down towards my husband. No, before that I saw that two other people had stopped in front of my husband, who had fallen on the ground on top of our little girl. They were both armed with pistols and were aiming at his head. At that moment I guessed that they were on the point of finishing him off and then I threw myself on my husband, covering him with my body to protect him and I looked the two murderers straight in the eye. One of them stared back at me as the other ran off and fired at me from a short distance away. Instinctively my hand went to my breast as if to find the spot where I had been wounded and I was amazed that I was still alive. As he ran away too I turned towards my husband and since our little girl showed no sign of life I released her from his arms which were still clasping her, then I took her and I realized that her left cheek and her arm were all bloody. I tried to wipe the blood away with my hand, then I realized that luckily she wasn't wounded. The blood on her was her father's . . . [1]

These are the words of Silvana Musanti, taken from her testimony at the trial for the murder of Captain Emanuele Basile, her husband. The captain was murdered as he was on his way home with his wife and their little girl Barbara. They were walking down from a reception at the Town Hall for the local saint's day and the little girl had fallen asleep in her father's arms.

Silvana's testimony gives us an 'inside' look at the everyday fears that creep into the smallest details of the domestic life of a 'servant of the state' who is caught in the gunsights of the mafia. The killing was preceded by a variety of threats, particularly aimed at the daughter. The captain told his wife, but not everything, trying to play things down while at the same time taking precautions. Early on the nursery was warned to keep a special, close watch on Barbara, and not to let her leave with strangers. A bit later the little girl was taken away from the school altogether. As always, the mafia aimed to put a check on its enemy's every movement so as to paralyse and make its presence felt in private life through terror and persecution. 'So for a while now the Basile family has been unable to live with any peace of mind....The little girl stopped going to the nursery, the family went out as little as possible and he himself weighed up every move. The widow's testimony has drawn a picture of a family compelled to live in fear of retaliation.'[2]

When Captain Basile died bodyguards were not yet much used, but the life of his family was already tending towards siege conditions. The disturbing mafia threat produces a profound alienation, an inner sense of siege that affects relationships even before any concrete experience of it.

Whenever we talk about living under siege we must therefore always make this effort of imagination: not drawing the line at what seems obvious and visible, the bodyguard for instance, but sensing the distress of an apparently normal everyday life lived behind a protective shield. Protection suggests a degree of security, but it keeps tension constantly high, stressing the existence of danger.

With old-fashioned courtesy, Judge Caponnetto put his finger on this sacrifice for family members, who lead a life at war in time of peace. At his farewell ceremony, when he left Palermo in 1988, he addressed them. 'On that occasion, I felt I had to express thanks, something no one had thought of, to all the wives, mothers, sisters and children of Palermo magistrates, for the wonderful way in which they had helped the work of their relatives. Of course, as I uttered these words, I was looking at my wife.'[3]

The film maker Margarethe von Trotta has made this particular effort of imagination. Her film *Il lungo silenzio* (*The Long Silence*) gives us a brief flavour of the impossibility of living under siege: no holidays, no normal social life, no cinema, no shopping, no going for walks; the impossibility of any spontaneous activity, like wandering off, admiring a sunset, having an ice cream. A life with compulsory security, no way out, everything tensed against death, at a cost of giving up life itself. An indirect staging of the totalitarian rule of the mafia.

In such a context, what meaning is there in love and sensuality, in the gestures of everyday life? In an article in *L'Unità*, Dacia Maraini wrote: 'Is it right to sacrifice one's life for the sake of an undiscovered truth? Of course this is a film without hope, but it has a high moral charge. If only political writers were to follow this path, where news reports are faced fairly and squarely and turned into a universal sense of the tragic.'

This 'universal sense of the tragic' is inspired by the story of Francesca Morvillo, the wife of Giovanni Falcone. Francesca was born in Palermo in 1945; she graduated in jurisprudence and, at a very young age, entered the magistrature. For sixteen years she worked on the Minors Tribunal in Palermo, and was subsequently made a Judge at the Appeal Court, still in Palermo. Shortly before she died she was pronounced a member of an

Examining Commission in Rome so that she could be closer to her husband.

Francesca Laura Morvillo is remembered by friends and colleagues for her remarkable personality as a woman and a magistrate, for her dignity and modesty. 'She had an exhaustive knowledge of the Penal Codes. She studied every trial punctiliously as a perfectionist. She was extremely reserved and unassuming, she never let her tiredness show, and she would never show off her knowledge.'[4]

The woman director of the district office for minors wrote:

A woman who was not a mother, but a magistrate 'of minors': this is why on *Samarcanda*[*] I shouted for all I was worth, 'Francesca was a judge of minors for sixteen years,' for this was how she wanted to be remembered in the midst of the multitude.... Francesca loved young people, the street kids of her city, her region, and she well knew what road to take to get 'true justice' at the heart of a society riven and wearied by so many contradictions and by *omertà*.[5]

Annamaria Palma, a magistrate and a friend of Francesca, stresses her commitment to young people. 'You should have seen her dealing with minors ... and these kids adored her. Even when she upheld the charge, she knew how to talk to them, and she would go and see them in prison; she wasn't just a working magistrate with them, but a personality who tried to understand them, who got close to them.'[6]

In May 1986 Francesca married Giovanni Falcone. Both of them had a failed marriage behind them and these were difficult years for Judge Falcone. In the early days, when they were both waiting for divorces to go through, their relationship had even been opposed by wagging tongues at the Palace of Justice. 'It was His Excellency Giovanni Pizzillo who made an issue of it. He summoned them, saying that two magistrates, who were furthermore in the same district, could not behave in that way. He said that their relationship was a cause for scandal and that some solution had to be found, or it would be a case of falling foul of the Superior Council of Magistrates.'[7]

Francesca was aware that she was about to marry one of the most threatened men, and she never made it any harder for him.

She seldom went anywhere with Giovanni. If they were going to the same appointment she would get there with her own transport. Those were the days of sacrifice. For years to come the judge would be denied the smallest of everyday activities: enjoying a walk, going to the barber, choosing a new tie, having

---

[*] *Samarcanda*: a current affairs discussion programme on Italian television. [Trs.]

an aperitif with friends. He would get used to delegating a lot of things to
Francesca and she would be his contact outside the bunker.[8]

During the drafting of the committal proceedings order against 475 defendants at the maxi-trial, at little notice the judges and their families were taken
to the high-security prison at Asinara – 'yes, just like convicts' – to be out of
the way of a mafia attack. Francesca managed to bring her mother as well.
Maria Falcone, the judge's sister, recalls:

> It was the first time he [Giovanni] worried about us too, about me, my sister
> Anna and our families. He told me he had talked to the Police Commissioner
> about the question of our safety. . . . Those words made quite an impression on
> me. . . . What terrified me was the certainty that my brother was in such imme-
> diate danger that he had to go into hiding, along with the consequences there
> might also be for us. I thought about my children most of all . . .[9]

Shortly after this Francesca and Giovanni got married, almost secretly.
According to his sister: 'He was trying not to be conspicuous, even on a day
that was so important to him. So that nothing got out about it, on the morning of the wedding he went to the office as usual.' And his fatherly friend
Caponetto: 'He arrived that afternoon without a bodyguard, driving the car
himself. The newspapers wrote that the wedding had taken place at night, and
someone actually wrote that Giovanni and Francesca had got married like
two thieves. Yet it was on a sunny afternoon. There was something furtive
about it though . . .'[10]

Her love and regard for her man, together with a strong personal and civic
identification with the struggle against the mafia, persuaded Francesca
Morvillo to accept a siege life of the most extreme kind. After an attack on
Addaura, Falcone's seaside home, the situation became grimmer and more
tense. In a desperate attempt to protect the woman he loved, the judge insisted
on their living partly separate lives.

Maria Falcone relates:

> It was only then that Giovanni realized how much danger Francesca was in,
> perhaps he hadn't ever thought about it before. For this reason he decided to
> create some distance between them. Of course, she could not be happy with
> this situation, and she insisted on making every effort to be with him as much
> as possible. But Giovanni demanded that his wife should at least not spend
> nights with him; it was a way of protecting her.
>
> I also understood why he hadn't wanted children. He had said so, to me and
> to Francesca: 'I don't want to bring orphans into the world.' He was so fearful
> that he thought about separating from his wife: a fictitious separation whose
> only purpose would be to safeguard Francesca by showing the outside world

that she was separate from him. He revealed this plan to Fernanda Contri, a friend who had been close to him during the argument with Meli, but she dissuaded him, saying that some scams work well enough for avoiding income tax, but not for making the mafia forget you . . .[11]

The long shadow of the mafia was cast over every aspect of private life, obviously beyond professional life. From major life decisions, like having children or not, to everyday habits, and the act of love, even in the intimacy of the night; the siege conditions of those who oppose the mafia is the extreme result of the deadly attack made on the whole of our civil society by the whole weight of the mafia institution. An evening visit made by the journalist Francesco La Licata to Addaura, not long after the attack, gives us a tangible picture of this situation, a negative one, almost like a science fiction scenario: 'The villa was lit up by extremely powerful electric eyes which illuminated the way out on to the beach. It was night and it seemed like the middle of the day. This very powerful light attracted all the mosquitoes in the area.' At the end of the evening, when the journalist was getting ready to leave, the dazzling beams of the floodlights outside metaphorically invaded the inside of the house as well: 'He called Francesca, who had no intention of leaving him, and told her to get ready to go to the house in town. She ventured a mild protest, but Giovanni called the bodyguard to escort her. "She won't get it into her head", he told me, "that these gentlemen really mean business now." '[12]

Francesca Morvillo was killed, along with the man she loved, in the Capaci massacre, on 23 May 1992.

On 8 March 1993 the Marisa Bellisario Foundation awarded a special prize in her memory. 'The prize awarded to Francesca Morvillo is meant to be a prize in honour of life, in the sense of consistent commitment and courage,' said Lella Golfo, the President of the Foundation.

In that burning summer of the Palermo massacres, Beatrice Monroy came up with these fine thoughts on lives lived under siege:

The whole city is on the move to get some fresh air. Except for some. Some have to stay hidden away at home or they'll be killed. Others are protecting them and have to stand guard on the streets, submachine guns at the ready, to make sure that things are as they should be. The city is empty and they must be afraid. It is human to be afraid. Oh, Sunday in Palermo! I dedicate this Sunday to the little soldiers in my street. Five roadblocks. Here it's the *alpini* who are protecting us from a bomb that those cannibals could easily place, could set off all of a sudden, without warning, without giving time for any lives to be saved. That's always how they do it. They're professionals, those guys. The little soldiers had asked to join the *alpini*, young boys from the mountains, children of the Alps, feathers in their felt hats, and they've ended up in Palermo's forty-degree heat making sure that no more bombs explode. Besides, if a bomb goes off they'll be the first to go up. Sunday morning. A day off for us. A day like any other for them. Stuck on street corners in a city they don't know, submachine guns slung over their shoulders to save their country. Like protective Rambos, they are already at war; we aren't, yet. I dedicate this Sunday morning to them as I make the sandwiches to take to the beach.[13]

Living between a 'before' and an 'after'

We had woken up together that morning, we had had coffee and croissants. We said goodbye till later. Not even two minutes had passed, I'd say, then I heard a crash that I couldn't identify immediately, it was as if there were a thousand shutters all coming down at once, a great big lorry unloading stones; it wasn't the sound of a revolver, not distinct gunfire, it had been a submachine gun. But I didn't even have time to wonder what it had been when I heard five revolver shots, clear and distinct. I was still in bed, it was twenty-five past eight, half past eight. I got up just as I was, I didn't look out of the window, I think I grabbed a dressing gown, put it on in the lift, and I remember that as the lift was going down I said to myself: 'What will they think when they see me like this? They'll take me for a madwoman, a lady going down to the street in a night-dress.' I got to the point of thinking that if they took me for a madwoman I'd be happy, because it would mean that nothing had happened. My head was buzzing with momentary, split-second thoughts, but when I got to street level, from the way the concierge said to me: 'Stop, stay there', I realized that something awful had happened. I said: 'What's happened, tell me what's happened right now.' But there was no need to say anything. Then I went towards the car. They caught me, I think my legs buckled. I have a distinct, precise memory up to the point I'm describing to you. Then I sank into a bottomless pit, and I don't know if I'm even out of it yet. The shock brought on a kind of block, and I've wiped out, forgotten the first few hours, I think, and then for forty-eight hours I had a time lag of five or six hours. I had no sense of time. I don't remember the people who came, I didn't see them. Therefore I can't have any clear memories. Yes, this darkness was the end of everything for me. Yet, later, life began again, rather slowly.[14]

For Giovanna Giaconia Terranova time stood still in that terrible moment. As if her psyche had wanted to mark out a caesura between a before and an after. Even though at a conscious level, after a time, Giovanna readjusted to the reality principle, that displacement of five or six hours marked the end of a life. In the time that followed, in the life of 'after', metaphorically, that displacement conferred a particular tonality, a specific quality on her identity. I take the liberty of giving this interpretation, in the hope of not seeming invasive.

234

Giovanna's life with her husband, Judge Cesare Terranova, had been a happy one.

As the daughter of a landowner, who, however, spent little time in the country and lived in the city a great deal, Giovanna Giaconia had had a carefree childhood, in a well-off family with little interest in politics, though with anti-Fascist tendencies.

There were eight children, seven girls and one boy. After attending an exclusive French private school in Palermo – 'I should tell you that I never had any sense of being kept down at the Sacred Heart; they never used the word forbidden, at worst they glossed over certain topics' – Giovanna took an Arts degree, and for a few years gave private lessons. 'I've never used my degree . . . I was shy, diffident in a way that I've always been since I was a child,' Signora Terranova now says.[15]

Giovanna met Cesare in August 1950 at Petralia, where she had gone to spend a holiday at a friend's house. It was love at first sight. 'And straight away, I think after just a month, we talked about getting married, because Cesare was at the Magistrates Court in Rometta whereas I was in Palermo, and though we were writing it seemed impossible to live so far from one another.' The wedding was six months later. The couple lived in Messina to begin with, then, from 1958, in Palermo.

While Giovanna had hardly ever heard the mafia mentioned during her childhood, when she was with her husband the Honoured Society became a constant presence. Terranova was an impassioned and courageous judge, so that all the mafia trials got piled up on his desk. At first Giovanna saw the mafia briefs as work like any other: 'No, I wasn't really worried, I was proud in fact. It was something he very much liked doing, he got more and more absorbed in it as time went by and I didn't have any worries about it.'

It was only little by little that pangs of doubt crept in, also because before the murder of the prosecutor Scaglione there was a widely shared belief that the mafia wouldn't touch the representatives of institutions.

He was quite serene. But Cesare was serenity and strength; he emanated strength and he possessed that serenity at every point in his life. He may even have been a little bit worried, but he never communicated it to me, never. I'll tell you, in fact, that when they arrested Di Cristina and he confessed things, including what he said about Liggio having sentenced Cesare to death, I got worried sick. Cesare, who obviously knew the whole story, said: 'Don't worry, this is all press ballyhoo.' If he had any worries he never let me know about them. And he must have had them, because in the drawer of his desk he left a letter for me, written a whole year before he died. He told me not to worry and he too in a way was unworried. Until there was a change and that came when they killed Boris Giuliano. The thing was, as I've said, that Scaglione's murder had been a totally isolated event, and when they killed Colonel Russo, Cesare did get worried, as well as being terribly sorry about it, there's no doubt. But when it was Boris Giuliano, for the first time I saw something different in Cesare's eyes, I can't really explain it, something indefinable. But that was my alarm bell . . .[16]

Giovanna Terranova's story is steeped in tenderness for her husband. Over the years they had obviously reassured each other and hidden their fears from each other, in a mutual attempt to ward off the danger. For one period of legislature Terranova agreed to be an Independent Left Member of Parliament and worked on the Anti-mafia Commission, but at the end of his term he wanted to return to Palermo. It would seem that neither he nor Giovanna thought about the danger.

> But these worries he had because of Di Cristina's statements had been there for six months, maybe a year. Cesare left me that letter as a testament, and I compared the dates: he went to police headquarters to talk about those things on 28 February, although he told me that he had gone to pay a visit to the Commissioner. . . . And then a lot of people have told me that they had warned him there was grave danger. And on 1 March he wrote me that letter. I knew nothing about it, I found it after he died. So Cesare was worried, there's no doubt, but whenever I showed any sign that I was he would immediately dispel it.[17]

On 25 September 1979 Judge Cesare Terranova was killed outside the building where he lived. His bodyguard, Warrant-Officer Lenin Mancuso, died with him. Terranova was about to be named head of judicial investigations in the Palermo Tribunal, and that morning he was on his way to the Palace of Justice for the first time after his return from Rome. This was a clear and powerful message to the Palermo magistrature from the mafia. Many years later Terranova's widow would explain to Schifani's widow: 'Rosaria, this was where war broke out for the takeover and annihilation of the magistrature's power of jurisdiction.'[18]

With him died a part of Giovanna.

> To me he was life, life. Cesare was strength, my strength, in everything, for his advice, for the protection he gave me, in every sense. To me he was a special person. He was exceptional, he was very open to things, all in all he was someone who really deepened love. . . . Perhaps with me he was too protective, even about the most trivial things. I was so used to leaning on him that I was really sure I couldn't live without him.[19]

How did Giovanna Terranova's life take shape in the immediate 'after'? Most of all by keeping faith with the memory of the man she loved, by telling other people how he was. In an interview with Marina Pino, given just nine days after the attack, Giovanna said:

> He loved the countryside, even though he couldn't distinguish between a daisy and a rose, between a poplar and a lime. He loved the green everywhere, the silence, the fragrances, the home-made bread, the hens he kept. He loved chewing the fat with the farmer; he would go to the village festival and come back with a paper bag full of *calia e semenza*,* pleased as punch, as if it was a treasure.[20]

But that first period was very, very hard.

> I had nightmares, I'd hear those revolver shots and I would start up from the bed. And then terrible dreams, the kind of thing you can only understand if you've been through it. Losing him like that was just indescribable. Then on top there was anger and indignation. Then I wondered: 'Why? And who?' as well. But knowing who it was was less important. . . . Well, it's like this, it triggers something in you and you say: 'It's not just a tragedy that's struck me, it's a serious threat for the whole society.'
>
> All of this pushed me to step outside the private, to overcome those instinctive feelings of shyness and embarrassment which I have as a woman without any political activity behind me, with no experience of social commitment, strong only because I lived at the side of a man of substance. For me the real shift, the right pledge to be made for the sake of the tribute paid by my husband, was to confront a new reality, to throw myself into problems that were quite different from my landowning-family roots, and to join many other people in taking on the challenge that has been handed on to me and overturning the age-old image of the grieving woman hidden in the shadows of her home.
>
> When there is the strength to take it, the transition from the private to the social is a deeply felt choice, dictated by an awareness which is gradually achieved that the tragedy whose victims we have been, the bereavement which has stricken us, are no longer just personal matters, but that our mourning and our grief have a collective place.[21]

With rage and at times with incredulity, Giovanna became aware of the way in which she was isolated, both by friends and by institutions, whenever she expressed the least wish to know. 'Around me there was a lot of talk about Cesare, about what he was like, what a good, affectionate man he was, about what kind of magistrate he was, and for months on end I heard people say all this. But very little talk about what really interested me when

---

* *calia e semenza*: roast chickpeas and pumpkin seeds, a common Sicilian snack. [Trs.]

all was said and done: about why he had been killed, about this mafia that called the shots, I heard very little talk about these things.'[22]

What most upset her were the reactions, or rather the lack of reactions, from the institutions. 'My blood froze at the Palace of Justice.' On the first anniversary of the death 'no one came to represent them. It made my flesh creep. It was a bitter disappointment.' A study grant was established to commemorate the murdered judge, but it was only after sundry refusals and a lot of awkwardness that Giovanna succeeded in getting permission to use the great hall of the Law Courts. 'I was furious, furious.' One high-ranking magistrate who had stood in the way of the ceremony took the liberty of making this cynical remark to Giovanna: 'Signora, remember that Cesare belongs to history, not news reports, and history takes time.' There was a strong impulse to erase and forget this inconvenient judge.

Giovanna recalls: 'Later, however, there was outrage after outrage and things changed. But at that time there were two strangely different things going on, for a lot of people wept over Cesare and remembered him, with the unofficial part of the city being very very close to me, in an extraordinary way, but officially there was nothing.'[23]

The scant commitment of so-called justice – or it might be better to call it complicity – was crudely highlighted at the trial for the murders of Terranova and Mancuso. Investigations were entrusted to a judge who enjoyed a reputation as the friend of mafiosi. In Reggio Calabria the prosecutor Bellinvia was known as Don Ciccio and he owned a bar in partnership with a mafioso, the 'Roof Garden', also known by the nickname 'Truf Garden'.[*] Despite the protests of Signora Terranova, who had brought an action as plaintiff along with the Mancuso family, this judge took his investigations in only one direction: Luciano Liggio's personal blood feud. 'It was an eloquent crime in a very clear language, a message to the Law Courts that magistrates of that kind do not enter here, those magistrates are not wanted, they are in the way. This was very plain and the Liggio trail was too reductive. That was when I really came into conflict with Bellinvia. . . . It was one of the most important trials going on at the time and he dealt with it as if he was up against a chicken thief.'

The trial itself, which took place in Reggio Calabria at the end of 1982, confirmed Giovanna's worst fears: Liggio's arrogance, the lack of sensitivity towards the injured parties, the increasingly obvious shortcomings of the investigation. The injured parties didn't enter the courtroom on the first day. 'I felt sick at heart when I heard these things and the magistrate let him say them. . . . Perhaps he couldn't silence him, but after all, to tolerate going so far

* The reference is to *truffa*, a fraud or swindle. [Trs.]

as insulting a man's memory in that way. Liggio said that Judge Terranova was witless or half-crazy, because it wasn't justice he was after, he only had a fixation on persecuting him.'[24]

And the trial ended badly. The request from the plaintiffs for further investigations was rejected and they left the courtroom in protest. 'I didn't come to this trial just to get a conviction for the sake of it, but to prompt the law to seek the truth about this and other outrages. This aim can be served if the court widens the scope of its reflections,' stated Terranova's widow.[25] Liggio was acquitted under reservation, a judgment against which Liggio himself sought to appeal, because he wanted a full acquittal.

'At one point there was debate over whether Liggio had looked at Cesare with hatred in his eyes. They were saying the kind of thing that made you wonder if you were really in a law court, at a trial, or if this was street-corner gossip,' Giovanna Terranova indignantly recalls.

For this woman, events around the trial marked the start of that public commitment which for so many other women has embodied hope in the midst of the terrible bereavements which have characterized these years. She wrote to the President of the Republic, Pertini, to ask for more intensive investigations, and denounced the slowness of the law in a number of interviews. For Giovanna Terranova it was not an easy thing to become a public figure.

> Things as extreme as what goes on in this city cannot be forgotten. This is not a demagogic decision, but something really heartfelt, because it's clear that you have to make an effort. For a shy and reserved nature like mine, you see, taking a step like this from being a private person to speaking out has been very difficult. As I've told you, I wanted to do it, there was no one pushing me to do it, but I felt it deeply, and it wasn't something simple.[26]

A social and civil commitment deriving from personal events, from deep wounds and grief. The awareness that the evil which seems only to have struck a few individuals does in fact have a bearing on the collective whole. A need for justice which goes beyond anger, beyond hatred, beyond revenge.

> It's something different from what drove Serafina Battaglia to turn to my husband. There it was a desire for the death of her husband and son to be avenged, a desire undoubtedly moved by deep feelings, probably the feelings of a mother rather than of a wife, which had been violated and which released that strength which has destroyed centuries of fear, of traditional silence and omertà. That's a different thing, though it's understandable too. . . . Of course, if some day I discover that the man responsible for my husband's murder has been found, I'll be pleased, not so much because they'll put him in prison, but because justice will be done, because finally a mystery will be solved, because it will be the start of

dismantling something big and important. I can't understand how people can be indifferent and resigned. I want to be respectful though, because I realize that people all have their problems, but it wasn't in my nature, it's been impossible to resign myself.[27]

It was in this spirit that Giovanna Terranova then took action, with no preconceptions and open to other people's experiences; by overcoming her own shyness she encouraged other women to come forward. Later on, in her role as the President of the Association of Sicilian Women against the Mafia, she turned to women like Anna Pecoraro, Pietra Lo Verso and Maria Benigno, offering them solidarity and inspiring courage. But not all women bereaved at the hands of the mafia opt for visibility. 'The reason is that they are afraid of being conspicuous, they are fearful of being manipulated, but I think that we have an obligation to speak out. After all, even Falcone and a lot of magistrates were accused of seeking the limelight. We have never been active in politics. I've been contacted many times and I have never wanted to be a candidate . . . there's not a lot we can do. But the little we can do we must do, we absolutely have to do,' Giovanna Terranova told Rosaria Schifani, when she asked her to follow the route she herself had taken.[28]

This commitment has not always been properly understood, not even by close friends, who have sometimes seen public appearances as transgressing a role, indeed as a kind of self-promotion. 'I would tell them: "You clearly haven't understood." But what does it matter? Let them talk. Showing off your own grief! Can it be showing off when you are waging a struggle of this kind?' is another of Giovanna's responses.[29]

Strictly speaking, joint political activism by women against the mafia began in 1980, when signatures were collected for a petition to the President of the Republic with the aim of speeding up anti-mafia legislation. The initiative had been taken by Communist women, with Rita Costa as the first signatory and Giovanna Terranova as the second. Giovanna was one of the group of women who were received in Rome by Pertini.

'After that first initiative it occurred to us that we could continue anti-mafia activism as women, realizing that when all was said and done it was the right way to go about things, and we had worked it out, so we decided to form a committee. I remember that the first meeting was in a room at the Regional Assembly and there were about thirty of us. . . . That was the first committee of women.'[30]

Giovanna Terranova approached the mafia threat from a woman's perspective and, as a woman, had contacts with other mafia victims, in particular those from a social milieu quite close to the mafia itself. 'It was a difficult process from the point when the group was opened up to these women too. Many were afraid of working with them, because of prejudices. None the less they recognized that these women too were victims of the mafia.'What linked them all was a determination not to forget. 'Perhaps women are more passionate than men. It's clear that a woman cannot remain unperturbed, cannot forget, when she has been hurt in what are her innermost feelings. There's no doubt that women fight in a different way from men.'[31]

What joins the 'before' to the 'after', what preserves and reworks the 'before' in the 'after', is the work of memory. The utopia of happiness is anchored in memory, Marcuse said. Individual memory being offered and threading its way into the fabric of something that goes beyond the limits of the personal. In a newspaper interview Giovanna said: 'If I had stayed at home I would have felt guilty. I would have thought that Cesare died for nothing. Because being murdered is a terrible thing, but being forgotten is even more terrible. It is like dying twice over.'[32] This density of memory, an integral part of working through mourning, was even deeply embedded in her home, so that the interviewer wrote: 'Cesare Terranova has never really left this house. There is something of him still in the little study with its flower-patterned wallpaper, in among collections of paper-knives, corals and shells, on the desk cluttered with papers.'[33]

Within the woman's identity the 'before' overlays the 'after', and the intricate play of memory, forgetting and self-awareness becomes a background to working through mourning. Giovanna Terranova says: 'I couldn't stand being called a "mafia widow". It gave me a sensation of physical violence, as if they'd shot me too.'[34]

Less than a year after the murder of Judge Terranova, on 6 August 1980 the mafia killed Palermo's chief prosecutor, Gaetano Costa. He too fell just outside his home, on the point of leaving on holiday with his family, as he was looking at the books on a street stall. His wife, Rita Bartoli, recalls: 'We were doing the packing together, making sure we didn't overlook anything. Then he stretched out on the bed, there wasn't a breath of air. I sat in the armchair. We chatted away about this and that. I went into the kitchen, he washed his hands and said: "I'm going out but I'll be back right away. I'll just take a turn as far as the newspaper kiosk." Usually I would go with him, but that night I didn't.'[35]

'While I was watering the flowers, my husband was dying. The TV screamed out the news and I was in the kitchen getting the cheese. He'd gone out saying he'd be back in five minutes. Instead my daughter came in, her face distraught and hardly able to speak. "Something has happened to Dad. Don't be frightened." That was how death entered my life.'[36]

'At the hospital my husband was under a white sheet. I knelt down. Maybe they thought I was praying. No, I wasn't praying, but I was promising justice. . . . It's not something you're prepared for. It wasn't just death there, but the violence which humiliates and annihilates someone.'[37]

It is as though, from the very moment of the death of her beloved partner

Tano, Rita had felt she was invested with a moral duty, with the task of completing an itinerary they had begun together. 'I had lived in my husband's shadow. After his death, a death that made me feel the weight of unimagined cruelty upon me, I couldn't hide away in a corner sobbing my heart out. My silence would have been submission and complicity. It was my duty to come out of my shell, so to speak, and look people in the face.'[38]

Theirs had been a very strongly shared commitment, when they were young and were both activists in the clandestine organization of the Communist Party against the Fascist regime. Rita joined at seventeen, the only woman in Caltanissetta. Her anti-Fascist convictions came from her family background. 'The family, a famous name, landowners, who had been promised baronetcies at a dinner with King Ferdinand . . . the mother, "a fierce anti-Fascist. A danger. In public she had to be kept quiet." The uncle who spoke ill of Garibaldi.'[39]

Childhood in Mazzarino, adolescence in Caltanissetta. Rita cherished vivid and lovely memories of her city:

> Caltanissetta was a provincial city, but lively and full of anti-Fascist ferment. The mines and the countryside were its life. The miners weren't sub-proletarians, but working-class . . . I can still remember the silence that fell over the city when the bells rang to warn of some calamity, a death at the mines. The miners were a symbol for us young intellectuals. . . . My first anti-Fascist book was given to me by Pompeo Colajanni; I took it home as if it were a bomb. It was a book by Piero Gobetti. . . . And Vitaliano Brancati* was there teaching at the teacher-training college. . . . That was the Caltanissetta where I met my husband, the finest thing that life has given me. The relationship between him and the children was wonderful too.[40]

Rita met Gaetano, who was a student in Palermo, when she was in her fourth year at secondary school. Their engagement and, in 1945, their wedding, besides sealing a love story, was also stamped with a collective dream: 'We thought that now we would be able to live as free citizens in a democracy. I never dreamed of this bloodstained Republic.'[41] And on the altar of this dream both of them sacrificed their commitment as political activists, he to become a magistrate and she to become the wife of a magistrate.

---

* Pompeo Colajanni was a militant in the PCI and a leader of the partisan group which liberated Turin at the end of the Second World War. Piero Gobetti was an early anti-Fascist writer forced to leave Italy and live in Paris, where he died in 1926; his books and journalism investigated the relationship between politics and culture. Vitaliano Brancati (1907–54) was a Sicilian writer who had a distinguished career as a novelist. [Trs.]

I had to choose. In those days at Caltanissetta you couldn't be a magistrate or the wife of a magistrate and be involved in politics. I could have gone on with it, leaving him. I married him. I gave up politics. Between politics and love, I chose love.... But staying at home doesn't mean you don't see what's going on, or that you don't think, or that you have surrendered understanding. Even buying one newspaper rather than another is political. The way you bring up your children is political. Choosing all the time how you build your own life and what relations you'll have with other people, with your neighbours.[42]

It was in the political key, by returning to active, militant politics, that Rita Bartoli Costa reacted to her husband's murder. 'Then the reasons for giving up politics were greater, while now the reasons for going back to it are greater,' said Rita in 1981 when she stood as an Independent on the Communist Party list for the regional assembly elections. She said in another interview, with Roselina Salemi:

Of course, those pistol shots changed everything. If Gaetano Costa's private life belongs to me and my children, his death belongs to the violent life of this land. I have tried not to lose my head and instead to fight for justice. I turned to the Superior Council of the Magistrature, I saw the inquiry slowing down and coming to a halt. I was burdened with grief and I protested: my husband was not a private citizen, but it's on my skin alone that the blood burns.[43]

For the old Communist militant, ideally, personal life and political life are, and should be, two different things. But she was not always able to keep grief separate from politics.

I went back for a meeting to Mazzarino, the town of my childhood. Beneath the platform there were men and women whom I'd known as children. They were weeping. I wasn't saying emotional things. I didn't talk about how it had been for me on that 6 August. To me it's a private matter. On the platform I talked about politics: mafia, maladministration. They were weeping. And in the end they came and embraced me. A lot of people. Not just Communists. A lot of young people. And at that point I couldn't hold back the tears. And for the first time in ten months I wept.[44]

But even before she stood in the elections, along with Communist women in Sicily and Calabria, Rita undertook to collect signatures for the petition to Pertini which was signed also by Giovanna Terranova. She was won over and inspired by sharing a political commitment with other women. A few years later she would say: 'Because in Sicily women have been able to rally this theme of civil society, this eagerness for freedom that is continually denied by violence. We kept quiet, we were ashamed of exhibiting our grief. Then we dried our eyes and told ourselves: why not? Behind this "women's thing" there's a great desire for change, for refusing to be resigned.'[45] Thirty thousand signatures were collected and taken to Rome by a delegation of women dubbed by the newspapers as the 'mafia widows'.

As well as the petition, Rita Costa also wrote a letter to Simone Veil, in her capacity as President of the European Parliament, asking for the European Parliament to intervene with the Italian government to 'request extraordinary and urgent measures by the state against the mafia'. 'I wonder', Costa's widow wrote, 'what prospects there are for a state to educate its children if it has surrendered to the mafia after losing all the battles.'[46]

Guarding her husband's memory and preventing any distorted account of his work as a magistrate are among Rita's constant commitments. Only one of the alleged murderers stood trial: Salvatore Inzerillo, who was accused of having been the look-out for the attack. The trial, which took place in Catania, ended with his acquittal. Schifani's widow went to see her after the massacres of the summer of 1992 and Rita Costa told her: 'This trial, dear Rosaria, is a milestone for Palermo. It marks out the time when the magistrature woke up from centuries of torpor. With Mattarella* killed there was a prosecutor prepared to investigate, not just to catch the murderers but to analyse the political and business context in which this had clearly taken place. That was the danger Costa represented in a Palermo where people are dying over contracts.'[47]

Like Giovanna Terranova's, Rita Costa's experience of the institutions could not be worse. There was the seemingly emblematic episode of the plaque to commemorate Costa's murder, with the word mafia missing from it.

> This is an absurd city. It was a mayor who went to crazy lengths to make sure the word mafia wasn't engraved. What it says is 'treacherously murdered'. By whom? Why? The plaque doesn't speak. I ought to publish the correspondence I had with the mayor at that time, Nello Martellucci, the mayor who didn't want that word because that's what he was like. One day he came to my house with Simona Mafai, the Communist Party leader on the council. If it weren't a tragedy it would be laughable, my dear. He told me that any reference to the mafia on the plaque in Via Cavour could degrade this city. To cut a long story short, we had to take off the word mafia and the fact is that from this plaque you get no idea who killed my husband. . . . When the plaque was put up, on

---

* Piersanti Mattarella, a Christian Democrat president of the Sicilian regional authority, was killed by the mafia in January 1980, after attempting more open and less corrupt forms of regional government. [Trs.]

the first anniversary of the murder, the Vice-President of the CSM was there. It was ruled that nobody was to speak, with the obvious exception of the mayor, whose speech did not make the faintest reference to the mafia. I broke this condition and, as soon as he had finished, I said something pointedly about the mafia. But without a microphone. There were a lot of people but nobody heard why it was better not to risk the unexpected by giving the microphone to a woman out of control.[48]

Just as Do Not Forget is an ethical imperative for the victims, the institutions seem to have an interest in forgetting – with the complicity of broad sections of the population who are indifferent. Giovanna Terranova had the same experience: 'I had to move the stone in remembrance of my husband because the block of flats next door, all respectable people like engineers and doctors, didn't want it there. They had a meeting and a majority of them voted against it, for "aesthetic" reasons.'[49] And Rosi di Salvo, the widow of Pio La Torre's chauffeur, has this to say: 'After three years of bureaucratic delay, Mayor Elda Pucci honoured my husband and Pio La Torre with two street names in the most horrendous part of the ring road area, without telling anyone. I went to see. Via Rosario di Salvo is an appalling run-down alleyway, and the street name on the wall was done by hand with a paintbrush. I was so angry . . . I want the name dropped.'[50]

But the Costa family, Rita and her two children Valeria and Michele, point the finger primarily at the Palace of Justice. Michele said:

Any serious inquiry into my father's murder, if it was ever meant to be a serious inquiry, would have to begin from inside the Palace of Justice and with the deputy prosecutor who exposed him to the mafia vendetta. The drug runners and certain political groups with involvement in the Mattarella murder were worried about the moves being made by the enterprising new prosecutor, but when word went out that he was isolated within his own office, the death sentence was triggered.[51]

Because, in fact, in May 1980, a few months before he was killed, the general prosecutor, Gaetano Costa, remained the only signatory to the arrest warrant for fifty-five mafiosi of the Spatola, Inzerillo and Gambino clans, whom his deputies wanted to release. It was a long, fraught meeting. Rita Costa explained to Rosaria Schifani:

When the door was opened Sciacchitano [the deputy], flying in the face of other testimony, pointed out my husband as the sole author of the warrant for these measures to two journalists and a lawyer whom I later encountered as the defence for the only accused at the murder trial, namely Nino Fileccia, the same criminal lawyer who, when defending Totò Riina, said on TV that in Palermo he had met with this client of his who had been wanted for twenty years. There was Sciacchitano throwing cold water over everything on Saint Dominic's Day when, after reading out his psalm, on TV he stressed the idea of falling out between 'families' and thereby belittled the value of my father's initiative as well as ignoring the isolation that made his execution easier. I didn't sleep that night, I got a pen and paper and wrote to Pietro Giammanco to the effect that as a prosecutor of the Republic he should rebuke that man so that he would never utter the name of Gaetano Costa in public.[52]

And what about the inquiries? Two days before the attack, outside the house of the 'red judge', the police had detained Totuccio Inzerillo, a youth belonging to one of the families affected by the arrest orders. Although the officers had some suspicions, he was immediately released. After the murder he disappeared. 'Nearly a week later, he presented himself voluntarily in the prosecutor's office, accompanied by a legal representative. This time he underwent forensic tests on his hands. Something even more curious followed: they released him without waiting for the results. And Inzerillo disappeared once again.'[53]

Guarding the memory of her partner Tano, the general prosecutor Gaetano Costa, in the difficult and painful 'after' Rita Bartoli has rediscovered a political and public commitment that was fundamental to their love when they were still young underground militants.

Paradoxical though it may seem, it has been left up to the relatives, and the widows especially, to ensure the remembrance – beyond private memory – of what their men did in defence of the democratic state, against another part of this same state which seems rather more concerned with obscuring these memories.

It has become a bigger scenario. This is no longer the mafia of corrupt contracts. Today there's something bigger. The money mafia. How does it get its hands on this money? Through politics. The other mafia, the straightforward criminal variety, lends a helping hand. And perhaps this hand is lent to some 'arm' of government. I'm not just playing with words. What I mean is appallingly serious: that these are crimes willed by the state. I'm saying this loud and clear so that history won't say tomorrow that these were mafia crimes. They were all crimes of the state.[54]

These are the words of Giuseppina Zacco, the widow of Pio La Torre, the secretary of the Sicilian Communists, who was killed with his driver Rosario di Salvo on 30 April 1982, while they were on their way to the Party Federation. 'First I missed the world around me, then I realized I had a debt towards my husband who had not been served by justice at the trials.' Nine years after the murder, Signora La Torre agreed to stand for her party, now known as the PDS, and she entered the Sicilian Assembly, taking over the seat left by Rita Bartoli Costa. She was a member of the Regional Anti-mafia Commission. 'It cost me a lot to go back to Sicily ten years after Pio's murder. . . . Going back to Palermo, as the party had asked me to, meant reopening all the wounds. . . . But anyone who thought that my role would be limited to a formal presence on the Anti-mafia Commission was wrong.'[55]

Giuseppina and Pio's story began in 1948, a tender love stamped by a great revolutionary commitment. 'We met at a party meeting. At the end of it he asked me if I'd read Lenin's writings on women's emancipation. I said I hadn't. So he gave me the book. . . . Pio was never a private person. It may seem inconceivable, but his whole life turned around politics,' said Giuseppina in an interview with Bianca Stancanelli.[56] A Communist wedding at the town hall in 1949, with a partisan leader, Pompeo Colajanni, officiating, then their short honeymoon on Capri was interrupted by events in Sicily: peasants' struggles for the land. 'We hurried back. He went off somewhere and I somewhere else. In 1950, at the height of the struggles, Pio was arrested, at Bisacquino, when I was with other comrades at San Giuseppe Jato.'[57] 'And when our first child was born, Pio was locked up in the Ucciardone prison for his part in the peasant struggles.'

Giuseppina Zacco came from a bourgeois family, whereas Pio's background was poorer.

> I admired my father, who was a medical officer running the hospital and the Red Cross, who broke with his snobbish family when they criticized my marriage to Pio, a boy who didn't have a lira and who was totally involved in the party and the peasant struggles, with saving this land of ours. . . . One day, after a public meeting, I was arrested. At that time any girl would have feared not just the police but her parents' wrath. . . . I had gone to a building site for the meeting and I had been arrested for threatening behaviour. They took me in the van to police headquarters and sent an officer to my house. When he turned up with this news my father couldn't resist the opportunity to make a joke: 'Damnation, Giuseppina just put on her new coat this morning.' The policeman felt he was being mocked and he was right. He got into his car, went to a bar near police headquarters, called a lance corporal and had a cappuccino and some brioches sent up to me.[58]

From 1969 the La Torre family lived in Rome. Yet Pio was a passionate man and he missed Sicily a lot. 'Every time he saw things going badly he was tempted to go back. So when they asked him to go down there and be regional secretary he didn't waver for a moment; he felt he was able and strong enough to handle the job. And he felt it was a duty.'[59]

From that time on, throughout the nine months Pio had left to live, fear and foreboding crept into their everyday life. Giuseppina relates:

> That pistol he carried around, and him left-handed. I said to him one day: 'What good is it to you, you don't even know how to use it.' He answered that you never know what can happen. And he would lock and double lock the door in Palermo, it was odd. And one day when we were on the beach at Altavilla with a little crowd of comrades, he kept looking over his shoulder. And in the last week there were the telephone calls to the house, no one speaking, regularly, in the morning, the afternoon, as soon as he went out. I'll have them put a trace on calls, he promised me. He didn't have time.[60]

Giuseppina looked on and feared for him.

> My husband was very concerned with two stories and two men who seemed part of a single plot: Calvi and Sindona. . . . Pio saw a single hand behind a developing pattern of crime. The organization of the Red Brigades, the Black Brigades, P2* and the great upheavals shaking Italy he saw as being bound up with a single economic strategy for the country. . . . Pio came out with all this in articles, interviews, at rallies and public meetings. Always naming names. One day at a press conference I begged a journalist I knew not to mention all the details Pio had given. In my own way I was trying to protect him. But the journalist looked taken aback: 'He'll be furious if I don't write it up.' . . . One day, as we were driving back to Palermo with one of our children he thought we were being followed; he braked to a stop, got out and walked towards the car he suspected, by himself. Perhaps a way of making sure he was the only one who died.[61]

For Giuseppina La Torre the shared life of before was separated from the after by shock, by the 'private grief which belongs to me alone, not to others'. Her biography is marked by a kind of amnesia, a 'small death': 'I can't remember anything about the first year now. It's a matter of time. I can't even

---

* P2 was a secret masonic lodge, exposed in May 1981 when its membership list was shown to include a number of prominent politicians and senior civil servants as well as generals in the armed forces. Its head, the financier Liceo Gelli, had mafia connections and used his banking contacts to recycle mafia money. Roberto Calvi, with whom Geli had connections, was the Italian banker later found hanged under Blackfriars Bridge in London; Michele Sindona, head of a financial empire which collapsed amid the banking scandals exposed with P2's discovery, was arrested and died in prison. The Red Brigades was a terrorist organization with roots in the extra-parliamentary left of the 1970s. In March 1978 it kidnapped and killed the Christian Democrat leader, Aldo Moro. The Black Brigades refers to neo-Fascist terrorist organizations. [Trs.]

remember the day of Pio's funeral, except being up there on the platform, like a robot. Apart from that, before and after is a void. What have I done, who have I seen, what have I said? . . . Things are better now. I go on living with Pio. I see him about the house. I'm aware of his presence. I hear his voice.'[62]

Little by little she has begun her life again. 'You can't just look on without doing anything. I'm talking to the young people in particular, it's long-term work that I'm interested in. . . . I work, but I'm not optimistic.'[63]

Pio La Torre was not the only one to die. He was with his driver Rosario di Salvo, a Communist militant who had given up a good job as a bookkeeper so as to be useful to the party. He left behind his wife Rosi and three little girls of eleven, eight and three.

'Life is very important, but many of us haven't realized yet. . . . In religion we are all brothers and sisters but for people who aren't near relatives or close friends of the victim bereavement ends after a couple of days,' the eldest wrote in a school composition, just ten days after her father's death.[64]

Rosi came from Caltanissetta. Her father was a bricklayer and a militant in the Communist Party. As a little girl she was always at the local party office, and was given lots of cuddles by the comrades. At thirteen there was her first job; as time went by she worked in different factories, and finally worked as a travelling representative, selling books all over Italy. That was how she met Rosario, fell in love and got married. After one try at emigrating to Germany they ended up in Palermo, he a bookkeeper, she a young mother. 'I didn't want Rosario to join the party. I had my sisters' experience, their loneliness on those Sundays at home with the children while their husbands were at the party office,' Rosi said in an interview with Claudia Mirto.[65]

But their story did become bound up with the party, as if by fate. Then, when Pio La Torre arrived, it was like a moment of truth for Rosario. As well as the pleasure of party involvement there was his almost filial relationship with the secretary: 'He adored Pio, loved him like a father.' They were to die together. They saw the first signs of danger. Rosario armed himself, but he didn't know how to shoot; he hid everything from his wife, however. There were strange telephone calls, like some kind of surveillance. 'I wasn't alarmed, he was calm. Only later did I find out he had confided to a friend that he felt he was being tailed by a 128. Only later did I find out that he changed the route he took to the party office every day. Then that 30 April . . .'[66]

Around Rosi and her little girls there was much affection from the comrades; many people would embrace her in the street or at the supermarket. But, yet again, there is disappointment in the institutions. 'Will there ever be justice in a city that just a month ago saw Basile's hired killers acquitted?'[67]

In another interview, two years later, Rosi seemed resigned, bitter and marked by mourning that showed no sign of abating:

It isn't true that time heals wounds. The seasons go by and it gets worse. To start with it's a nightmare and you deceive yourself that you'll come out of it some-how. Instead, you realize that it is reality. There's been no light shed on a single mafia crime. People die and there's a state funeral. People in black ties file by and the big shots take their hats off. Then everything goes back to how it was before.[68]

This bitterness, this sense of desertion, is something pronounced in a lot of women, the wives or mothers of 'servants of the state', who have suffered at close quarters from the collusion between the state and the mafia.

In the killings at Razzà di Taurianova, in Calabria, in April 1977, the *cara-biniere* Caruso and Lance-Corporal Condello died. Despite serious threats, Caruso's mother and Condello's widow took action as plaintiffs in a trial which skidded from one postponement to another. Condello's widow was forced to leave Calabria, but the threats followed her. ' "So, this is the line you're taking, aren't you forgetting that you have two young children, don't you care about your children's skins?" But I wasn't scared, nor am I now! Who are they? The same ones that are here, the ones on trial,' she told Gianfranco Manfredi.[69]

Even the lawyers backed out because they were threatened. Yet the two women persisted. Signora Caruso emphasized:

> I want justice for my son and I don't intend to give up ... here the mafia is everything, it's not the law that's in charge but the mafia. But my son has already been deserted; why aren't the state lawyers, who will stand as civil plaintiffs just for a damaged car, here in this trial? What's the point of a funeral with so many big shots, guards of honour, wreaths from the state if the state lawyers won't act as plaintiffs for him?[70]

One woman who seemed particularly embittered was Maria Leotta, the widow of Boris Giuliano, the head of the Palermo Flying Squad who was killed in 1979. She became hostile to public demonstrations. She came to reject the press, explaining on the telephone: 'Too much disappointment, too much bitterness. It was my personal inclination to say nothing; I spoke out. I went to give testimony at the CSM. The outcome humiliated me.'[71] She refused to sign the petition of Sicilian and Calabrian women to Pertini, and not even Rita Costa managed to persuade her: 'She told me: it's a political thing and I don't like that. ... I couldn't persuade her.'[72] Maria made no bones about it to Rosaria Schifani:

> Where am I to turn? To the judges who were a disaster. They did all but dis-courage and impede the investigations. I spoke out about it at the CSM but nothing happened because some of the magistrates at the time who were at odds with my husband are still active in Palermo, in key jobs. ... In these few

years I've had a bitter sense of there being complicity, widespread gaps and silences. And how do you get to the bottom of it now? I've been watching and waiting for twelve years but I can see that the state has made little effort. It's not revenge I want. I'd have hoped that at least the death of one just man might help to shed some light on the dark years of this city of ours.[73]

The 'men of the state' – as Maria Giuliano prefers to call them rather than 'servants' – have been left all alone. People like Boris Giuliano, Beppe Montana or Ninni Cassarà were odd men out within the state. 'My husband would do an investigation and present reports to the magistrature, and these reports would often just not be acted on,' Giuliano's widow told Claudio Fava in a television broadcast.[74]

With the death of Ninni Cassarà, the Deputy Police Commissioner of Palermo, in August 1985, killed along with his young 'guardian angel' Roberto Antiochia, serious suspicions increased that these men were being killed through some colleagues' treachery: suspicions which shed an even more sinister light on those years, particularly since the recent arrest of the commissioner Bruno Contrada. After the murder of his friend and collaborator Beppe Montana, Commissioner Cassarà spent six days and nights at work in his office carrying out interrogations and sleeping on a camp bed. 'How did the murderers come to know that Cassarà would return home on the sixth day at 3.15?'[75]

In the open letter that the officer Antiochia's mother sent a few days after the attack to the then Minister of the Interior, Scalfaro, we read: 'Let's have no state lies, you accept the theory of mafia infiltration, perhaps within the Questura, perhaps in the Squad itself. So what are you going to do? Will you make do with having been smart enough to see how things are? If these spies are indeed there will we catch them? People have been on to them for years, think about Boris Giuliano's death, the warning of Rocco Chinnici's death . . .'[76] Signora Laura Cassarà no longer trusts anyone and repels all intrusions. Saveria Antiochia, however, fights like a lioness. 'None the less, we should never weary of demanding justice. If we haven't yet had it it's because in all these years there hasn't been the political will. I don't know if we'll get to the truth but it's important to fight for the truth.' And then she added: 'Laura Cassarà isn't fond of talking. They threatened our lives when our investigations built up again because they didn't want those investigations going on. But Laura will talk at the trial. . . . We shall be plaintiffs.'[77]

Don't forget, keep your son 'alive' in the battle for justice, which is simultaneously a battle for memory. Individual and collective memory. Antiochia died at twenty-three by the side of Commissioner Cassarà for whose protection he had voluntarily returned early from his holidays. His mother says:

I can't sleep at night. I talk to Roberto. I tell him he will have justice. . . . As well as weeping for them, we women also have to be a bit out of the ordinary so that we can go on with what they were doing. . . . I know that a lot of people are afraid. We need to understand them too. . . . Sometimes it's our own relatives who are the first to get scared. Take me, I have no relatives left. They were frightened. And when I began demanding justice they asked me why I signed myself as an Antiochia. It's because I'm defending my son Roberto Antiochia. Afraid? My son wasn't afraid so why should I be? This was my son, my life, torn away from me one afternoon in Palermo.[78]

Saveria kept her ties to Palermo, even though she was from Turin. She comes often, and for nearly a year she accepted the post of local councillor. 'Palermo is a big part of my life . . . love and grief . . . it's as if Roberto were calling me to seek out a trail that he somehow left behind.'[79]

The legacy of professional ethics

If you want to do your job it becomes a problem here. This is something intensely difficult in our environment and it's the measure of how much the example of a businessman like Libero matters when he manages to pass on an element that's usually ignored, the dignity of work. . . . We took it for granted that we wouldn't succumb to the racket. Libero and I have always had the same views on these things. Our family had no religious background. We'd never been under anybody's thumb, never doffed our caps to anyone or kowtowed to any power. Instead we've always preserved and upheld the dignity we got from work.[80]

The dignity that comes from work, the professional ethics and abilities which are in a sense its tangible expression, are outlooks which appear radically 'different' within the system of patronage and favours. In this context those who do their job well, with competence and skill, are easily shut out, regarded as dangerous and even arouse suspicion.

By its mere exercise, professionalism lays bare the fraudulent poverty of mafia-political double-dealing. 'It is the mafia itself which operates as an element in inefficiency and corruption, and holds back any planning for efficiency.'[81]

If you do your own job well this indirectly unmasks all those who do it badly. The system implicitly requires, even puts on pressure for jobs to be done badly and this is an offence to those who do have professionalism and the dignity that comes from it. The inherent logic of the principle of professionalism is directly opposed to that of the personalized system of patronage. . . . The professional ethic is not just degraded by being asked to give deferential treatment, but it is frustrated by the failure to acknowledge it as a source of raised status and economic advancement.[82]

Pina Maisano, the widow of the Palermo businessman Libero Grassi, who was killed in August 1991, argues for this independent professional ethic against the custom of patronage which is a fundamental prerequisite of the mafia's ingrained place in the social fabric.

The individual dignity which comes from work is closely bound up with the different cultures of work which, in turn, are the basis of both individual and social identity in industrial society. Professionalism confers independence from the expectations of clientelistic power and is not easy to reconcile with the unwritten rules of being a hanger-on. Pina Maisano says again:

> What little industrial culture we had in this city has been destroyed. . . . Little by little over the years the system wound up destroying this industrial culture and converting everything into public and semi-public, at any rate into subsidized concerns, because the more subsidy and public funds you put into something the more the powers-that-be can pull the strings. A real industrialist backed up by his capital can take or leave the politician. The dependent industrialist who is obliged to ask for public contributions will be subordinate to the party, the political current, the committee head, and since politicians need to build consensus by handing out privileges and livings like some feudal lord, it becomes a vicious circle.[83]

The 'territorial sovereignty' which coalesces mafia rule disputes the state's monopoly of violence, the individual's freedom and civil rights, and society's general organization designed to ensure a satisfying quality of life. It is this last aspect which relates particularly to professional ethics: a criterion of skill and merit nullifies mafia intent to conduct decisions and management solely on the basis of tyranny and armed threats. While mafia clientelism promotes ignorance and incompetence in order to rule undisturbed, professionalism radically threatens clientelist dealings. The mafia, therefore, is liable to destroy, sometimes at birth, any initiative inspired by this ethic.

Just how far mafia-political pressure has undermined the very bases of the dignity of work is shown by the battle waged by Pina and her children Davide and Alice to keep their Sigma factory going and preserve the workers' jobs after Libero's death. Two years after the murder Pina Grassi observed: 'I have the impression, for one thing, that the business and entrepreneurial classes have no great motivation to win back control. What I do see is an eagerness to be protected. Either by the regional authority, by the mafia, by some bank or politician.'[84]

Those in charge have given no indication of official recognition of Libero Grassi's sacrifice. Pina said:

I wanted to resume production during the transition [with the intervention of the GEPI, a public fund to assist private industry in crisis, Sigma had become a new company, Dali, combing the names of Davide and Alice] but they preferred to keep everybody on unemployment benefit with the machinery shut down. There were some trade unionists who had the nerve to say that it would be better if the company went out of business because the workers would immediately have become the responsibility of the GEPI. But our victory would be symbolic and this seemed to be of no interest to anyone, starting with the Sicilian regional authority, which was ready to take on the women workers as caretakers and put them to work shining up the image of public employment.[85]

But it was the women workers themselves who wanted to go on working in the factory, against the wishes of the mafia, the public authorities and even the trade union. 'I'll never forget the CGIL* leader who followed through the "Sigma case" saying with disarming ingenuousness: "Our problem is that the women want to work," ' Pina recalls.

Her life with Libero had been lived in terms of independent secular choices. They got married in the Town Hall 'when doing that wasn't as easy as it is today'. Their marriage lasted more than thirty-five years. From the age of seventeen Pina worked in the curtain and carpet shop in the centre of Palermo which Libero's father opened before the end of the war. For years she was active in the Radical Party, and now works with the Greens. At the last elections she won a seat in the Senate. 'I agreed to stand for the Senate in Turin where, throughout the electoral campaign, I never spoke of Libero's struggle against the mafia because I was afraid of exploiting a man and his story. . . . After Libero was murdered I couldn't have endured being voted in in Palermo just because I had become the widow of the businessman who had been so much ignored when alive.'[86]

Women, politics, professional ethics. This beautifully clear statement by Pina Grassi brings to mind another comparable one by Maria Falcone, the sister of the murdered judge. Proposed as a mayoral candidate in Palermo, Maria wrote a letter explaining the reason for her refusal:

Everything I've said and done during this year of my life which has been so tragic sprang only from the need not to squander that immense legacy of values which Giovanni left behind. This wish to feel he is alive, by trying to see that his ideas go on living in all of us, should not be mistaken for any desire on

---

* CGIL, Confederazione Generale Italiana del Lavoro, the Communist-Socialist-affiliated trade union. [Trs.]

my part to enter political life by exploiting a name which is great because he, and not I, made it so.[87]

Libero Grassi was killed in the street outside his house at 7.30 in the morning when he was setting out for his factory. Not only had he refused to pay protection money, but in newspapers and on television he had publicly denounced the notorious 'building surveyor Anzalone' who was making phonecalls asking for millions of lire to support the mafiosi in prison. Pina recalls:

> The morning they killed him before he left the house we had coffee together on the terrace. The morning was still cool and there was a bright sun. Coffee cup in hand, Libero noticed that a plant had put out its first bloom: 'What a victory: it's flowering.' ... They were his last words. With the emphasis on 'victory', a word that says it all. It strikes me as a strange and beautiful coincidence. Yes, we did win. Davide said it with that gesture he made, his fingers shaping the V sign as he supported his father's coffin on his shoulder, the coffin of a man who had never yielded, who didn't want to lose his battle.[88]

And independently, without any rhetorical wavering, Pina and her children kept careful watch over Libero's memory, from the funeral ceremony onwards. The remains were honoured at the factory, with the women workers at the head of the procession. 'Everyone wanted to make speeches that day, from Pannella to Spadolini,* but my children and I looked at one another and decided that no one was to speak. My friends made a cordon around me, Davide and Alice stopping everyone from coming up to the front with the coffin and us, stopping anyone from getting to the front for the photos, because we realized that they were all trying to do that.'[89]

Cardinal Pappalardo's representative also had to withdraw. 'Libero had always made it clear to me that he wanted a secular funeral. . . . But the representative intimated to us that it was never too late even for the lost sheep. I remarked to him that if there really was a God up there above us all he must have quite different standards of judgment.'[90]

And the factory reopened only four days later. 'It was a way of saying that we weren't giving in, that we were starting our work all over again.' Some months later, however, the factory had to close because of restructuring – the conversion from Sigma to Dali. Pina Grassi believes that companies which have been damaged by the mafia should be assured ways of staying in business.

---

* Marco Pannella and Giovanni Spadolini, politicians, leading figures in, respectively, the Radical Party and the Republican Party. [Trs.]

Sigma is one example; for two years now we have been struggling to relaunch the company. . . . The provision for allocating 1,700 million lire for restructuring the premises where Sigma-Dali will operate was disputed, although only in part by the State Commission. . . . Yet I wonder whether we Grassi aren't just fools? If we had been asked to be taken on by the regional authority, perhaps our problems would have been solved earlier and to greater personal advantage, but we would no longer have been an independent concern.[91]

The stand taken by Libero Grassi, which Pina and her children are in some way continuing, peculiarly struck home. This, at least, is one reading of the embarrassed silence among the people of Palermo which followed his death. Libero's courage and his death effectively assert a generalized responsibility; faced with his example, it is very hard not to take sides. After the funeral Pina and her children wrote an open letter in which they said: 'Even if the state had been there and even if the state had guaranteed our protection nobody would have been able to defend us from the mafia nature of the people.' Pina explained:

In Palermo people almost end up justifying the killings of judges, policemen and *carabinieri* because, some way or another, because of their work, policemen, judges and *carabinieri* have direct contact with thugs. And therefore somehow people find a reason for it. Libero's murder, however, struck a chord with people because they didn't expect that some poor guy who did a different kind of job could also come to the same end.[92]

The make-believe that the struggle against the mafia is some kind of game of cops and robbers, as Umberto Santino would put it, patently doesn't hold water in the case of Libero Grassi.

A good number of those who did not follow the Grassi family and the cordon . surrounding the hearse simply felt to blame. The man they were accompanying to the cemetery was a hero made by circumstance; in any other part of the world nobody would ever have heard of him. But in the context of Palermo, Grassi had done something amazing. He had shown the path for everyone to follow in order to fight against Cosa Nostra, but first and foremost against the crushing abuses amid which Cosa Nostra can breed. . . . Grassi was a man unlike the rest of us, a hero without armour. Falcone did have armour, as well as a horse and a bodyguard. He was a blameless and fearless knight. And they killed him all the same, in an underhand way. He is now a clear symbol who does not weigh on the conscience as does Grassi, deserted by everyone and left to die in sandals and a tunic.[93]

It was Libero's, then Pina's, very insistence on professional ethics which

256

created the embarrassment. In June 1991, two months before he died, Libero took part in a conference held by Pina's Green friends, with the involvement of the Impastato Centre, on the market economy and its self-regulation. The conference, titled 'A peaceful background to economic development', took place in the Town Hall council chamber. No one was attracted by the topic. Pina recalls:

> Now they're all talking about Libero Grassi, but that day, apart from the six speakers, there were twenty people in the room, and by chance, for perhaps half an hour, a school group on a visit to the Town Hall came and sat at the back of the room as they were curious to hear what this man was saying about fighting the villains of Palermo, and they stopped to listen and applaud. That's one of the few nice memories. But where was Palermo?[94]

Moreover, a few months before the Catania Judge Luigi Russo had caused a stir by pronouncing that the payment of mafia bribes was not a crime. And the head of the Industrialists Association, Salvatore Cozzo, stated in an interview that *L'Ora* published on 11 April: 'Grassi is undermining the image of the businessman. . . . What would Libero Grassi have us do? Should we tell our members to refuse to pay protection money? . . . We would be stripping our association of its institutional goals and doing a different kind of job. Our activity has quite different objectives.'[95] The president of the Industrialists Association has a peculiar notion of professional ethics when subordination to mafia blackmail is deemed to be irrelevant to the development or otherwise of industry. Yet, before Libero Grassi, eleven other businessmen had been killed in Palermo. None the less, President Cozzo's vision of enterprise is shared by the majority of regional entrepreneurs; only one business leader had turned up to the debate mentioned above, although Pina had personally sent out two thousand invitations after obtaining the register of names for all the associations.

Pina Maisano continues the battle initiated by and with her husband. But her life has changed too. 'We are not rich and powerful, we thought we had no reason to be afraid, and yet I am afraid. Of course I'm afraid not so much for myself as for my children. I should say that I am not driven by the spirit of personal revenge, and my revenge is and must be collective,' she said in a television broadcast on RAI.

She derives a lot of comfort from the women workers in the factory and from customers in the shop, from ordinary people.

> I've discovered human warmth in people, the customers who come to the shop aren't oddballs, they don't pretend nothing has happened – they come to me and say: 'Signora, we've been loyal to you and we always will be.'. . . A woman from the working-class Borgo neighbourhood, whose husband was killed a few

months ago, told me almost in tears: 'Believe me, you were lucky, your husband died instantly. Mine was three weeks in hospital hanging on to life, and then he left me all alone . . .'[96]

A year before Libero Grassi another man, Giovanni Bonsignore, was murdered. His death also provoked embarrassment and the same kind of repression. 'He was an honest civil servant and he should not have been a man at risk. But these days being an honest civil servant means being a man at risk,' wrote Emilia Midrio, his wife, who came originally from the Veneto.[97] She went on: 'It happened on a Wednesday, at eight in the morning. . . . He went downstairs and five minutes later I heard the shots; I looked out and there was no one there. It occurred to me that he should have got as far as the newspaper kiosk by then and I feared the worst, then I told myself that nobody's going to shoot an office worker.'[98]

Indeed. But Giovanni Bonsignore was a civil servant who took his job seriously, going so far as to refuse to sign a document that he found suspect: 38,000 million lire for studies and projects related to works amounting to 500,000 million lire in the food and agriculture sector. 'My husband died because he stood in the way of large-scale interests and because he insisted that the big market sums would have been swallowed up by the studies,' Emilia reiterated. But few people heard this version of the facts. '*For three years I've been fighting for justice* and I'll go on doing so, because I've sworn on my husband's coffin that I would seek that justice that was denied him when he was alive.'[99]

After flatly withholding his signature, the honest and professional office worker was transferred to the department for cooperation with local businesses, 'by order of the Socialist committee head Turi Lombardo, who was furious because my husband was making him drop a scheme for plans and contracts linked to the development of substantial markets, a deal in which Giovanni could see some dirty business', Emilia affirmed.

But the honest worker did not give in. He presented a detailed statement to the prosecutor, in which he named names, and, somehow trusting the workings of bureaucracy, like a true Don Quixote, he waited. He waited in vain. His wife recalls:

I cried at the time of the transfer. I told him, 'Gianni, take retirement.' . . . 'Do you think that I've fought so hard so that they can win now?' I answered: 'Well if nobody will listen to you at the prosecutor's office, give a statement to the administrative tribunal.' And he said: 'No, the law should tell me that I'm in the right . . .'. Making a great unforgivable mistake, he kept on saying at home and at work: 'I have other things to say but I can't write them down. I must tell them directly to the magistrate . . .'. If the judge had summoned him perhaps the worst wouldn't have happened. But my husband made the mistake of having complete trust in the magistrature.[100]

258

Bonsignore was killed in May and his statement is dated the previous November; yet, somehow, this statement had never reached its destination and ended up in a drawer. After the murder and the 'rediscovery' of the statement the only thing noted was an abuse of powers on the part of the committee head, Lombardo, and the judge carrying out preliminary investigations shelved everything.

> This is penal justice. But Lombardo felt he was being hounded, he complained about me on the grounds that I was ruining the public life of an important Member of Parliament and I was charged, accused by a man who meanwhile is looking out for his career. They put him on the Anti-mafia Commission, in other words the organization that should have been making sense of the political and administrative implications of my husband's assassination.

Here again there's something pulling the strings.

In the Bonsignore case, more than any other, the distorted vision of the institutions becomes flagrant to the point of absurdity. And Emilia experiences these contradictions in a way that is painfully acute.

> With its decision to shelve the case the magistrature absolved itself from having ignored the statement presented by my husband and absolved the committee head who transferred him as a punishment because 'everything was in order'. But a month after this decision I was sent the President of the Republic's gold medal for civilians because, as the judgment upheld, my husband 'denounced irregularities, incompetence and mafia infiltration into the vital nerves of public administration'. Who is right? The judge on the preliminary investigations who shelved the case or the Head of State? Or are they all making a fool of me?

She went on:

> At the pension office, without Scotti's signed order, they won't accept that my husband was killed by the mafia. I go up to the counter and I have to listen to some idiot saying: 'What evidence do we have that your husband died in the line of duty?' Listen, I'll give you the certificate from the Minister of the Interior with the gold medal, is that not enough? No, they want the official order. Well, get it yourselves! What are the offices for? Don't you see that I can't take any more?[101]

Emilia Bonsignore's travails bring to mind the battle waged, exactly a century ago, by Giovanna Cirillo, the widow of the police representative Stanislao Rampolla del Tindaro. He too had been transferred for the untimely professionalism and excessive zeal he had displayed in finding and reporting powerful and compromising links between politicians and mafiosi at Marineo. Such was his sense of humiliation that he killed himself. His widow, Giovanna, in a petition sent by her grandson to the Minister of the Interior Crispi, had denounced those morally responsible for the suicide, invoking justice against the mafia. She had in her possession documents and observations, perhaps even things her husband had told her in confidence.

The trial that followed acquitted the mayor who had been incriminated, intimating the mental instability of the police representative and condemning the grandson who presented the petition as slanderous. 'The mafia does not exist in Marineo, Stanislao Rampolla is a mad old man and his grandson Luciano is a young careerist who talks nonsense. . . . Rampolla was defeated twice over: the first time when he was alive, by the transfer, the second time as a dead man, with the acquittal of the mayor and the verdict of slander inflicted on his grandson' – and thereby, symbolically so to speak, on his widow.[102]

Let us hear Emilia Bonsignore once more:

My husband didn't die the day they shot him but the day they transferred him. In moral terms it was a dreadful thing for him. He kept saying to me: 'Do you realize? What will people think of me?' He spent the last months of his life in a terrible state of anxiety. After the murder I hoped that people would at least understand that this was the death of an honest and capable bureaucrat. But no! Because the judge's verdict more or less said that he was an incompetent. It had to be one of them. If the committee head did everything above board it meant that the one in the wrong was my husband. Is it right that one verdict should categorize Gianni as a man who wasn't up to his job while the Head of State regarded him as a hero?[103]

Emilia seemed tired, disheartened and very much alone. But she stuck it out. 'If people are still talking about the "Bonsignore case" it is because I keep it alive. And maybe I niggle them a lot. I can't walk away. That's also because Palermo is my city now, not Venice. Of course, it's a city that has to get by on its own efforts, but it's also brave and generous.'

As time went on I was getting worried and he would calm me down: 'What are you worried about Rosetta? I'm just a doctor.' He managed to soothe my anxieties even though I later made connections between a lot of things that happened and realized that he wasn't calm at all, quite the contrary. . . . The moment I heard I thought it was a mistake, because I thought nobody could kill a doctor. But in Palermo this does happen and ordinary men, office workers, professionals, bureaucrats, become dangerous men, become targets and martyrs, just because they do their duty without making compromises.[104]

On 11 August 1982 two hitmen killed the police doctor and university teacher Paolo Giaccone in the neighbourhood of the Palermo Policlinico; he had refused to falsify his appraisal of some fingerprints that nailed a mafioso. His wife, Rosa Prestinicola, recalls:

> Whenever I think about that August morning I feel I'm going crazy. Paolo and I had left one another at 8.15. He had gone to work at the Policlinico, I was busy with various appointments, children and solfeggio lessons. At half past eight I heard a police car and I thought: 'That'll be today's first death.' Then the phonecall came and I rushed to the Policlinico, hoping for the impossible and discovering it was all over. . . . I can remember clearly that feeling of paralysis that seized up my muscles and stopped me even from screaming.[105]

At the trial Rosa spoke about telephone threats and anonymous letters. 'At that time Signora Giaccone had two further proofs of the pressure on her husband, I heard him shouting down the phone: "No, *avvocato*, these are things you shouldn't ask of me!" . . . A few days later, listening to her husband's answering machine she happened to pick up a threatening message: "Professor Giaccone," said an unfamiliar voice, "don't be a smart aleck, or you won't live long." '[106]

Two different ways of interpreting professional office: on the one hand the police doctor who refuses to falsify a report despite mafia threats, and on the other the lawyer for the mafiosi who does not hesitate to interfere with a doctor so as to persuade him to overlook his professional duty.

Rosa met Paolo in Paris, where her father was the director of the Banco di Roma. Paolo was a young blood specialist on a research scholarship and was already very interested in forensic medicine. Rosa's father invited Paolo to lunch. 'But I was at the lunch too and we fell in love . . . I was twenty-one and he was twenty-eight. We soon got married and I followed him to Palermo. . . . I watched him working like crazy for thirty years,' said Rosa.[107]

They led a pleasant, quiet, 'almost frivolous' life according to Rosetta. There were tea parties with her women friends, poker games, conferences that she went to with her husband, and the children. They had four, one boy and three girls, now young adults: 'The youngest is twenty-three now and is a violinist. The second eldest works at the USL as a specialist in forensic medicine. She wanted to do the same work as her father but I was afraid. The oldest girl was in her fourth year studying medicine when my husband died and now she's an assistant at Villa Sofia and the boy works in regional government.'

But she always found Palermo disturbing, rather frightening: 'It's a city full of memorial stones, crosses and memories of killings. But the mafia seemed such a remote thing, something to do with other people, not us.'[108] This perception is now tragically altered.

Terror rages here now. You leave the house in the morning and you don't know if you'll come home at night. Because if somebody thinks you're in the way they wait for you on the corner and eliminate you, wipe you out with a bullet or a bomb. So human life is reduced to nothing, to some cheap bit of rag. It's something a lot of people in Palermo have on their minds all the time, always on the alert for some danger that keeps you perpetually tense, mistrusting everybody, even your friends.[109]

'So at forty-five I found myself without my man and with my four children. Without them I would have killed myself.' Paolo's death disrupted and changed Rosa's life and her relationship with the children. 'You can't take the place of a father. And I became a sister. We're not so much a family now as a boarding school. Nobody had the heart to set the table without the sixth place. We have casual meals, we sit in the kitchen and talk. As Pirandello says, you get used to living with a blade stuck in your heart, without feeling the pain of it.'[110]

After the first year marked by deep depression and feelings of death, it was the children who gave her a new anchor in life.

I seriously thought of ending it. . . . I seriously thought of taking the little pills that a doctor always keeps on his shelves. . . . And I came within a hair's breadth of it because death doesn't frighten you the first time . . . if you decide to go on living as I did, then you have to come out of your shell. I realized I couldn't just sit looking at a photograph ready to feel bad. I still can't look at a photo where the two of us are arm in arm, or a photo with us and our children. I go crazy, I start crying, I feel bad. . . . I was just a crumpled heap in the first year, I let myself fall apart, I got by on tranquillizers. Then one day I woke up and said to myself: either I do away with myself or I make a new start. So I decided to live and to fight. I washed my face and braced myself and went out to do battle.[111]

Rosa Giaccone joined the Association of Sicilian Women against the Mafia, became involved in the investigations, which at that point were at their height, and, most of all, involved herself in her children who were in great need of help.

Rosa is one of the very few women who in a sense have achieved justice. Giaccone was killed by Filippo Marchese, who in his turn was later murdered, and by Salvatore Rotolo, who was given a life sentence at the maxi-trial. None the less, in March 1991, Judge Carnevale released dozens of mafia leaders from prison, including Rotolo. Only an order by the then Minister of Justice Martelli annulled Carnevale's scandalous decision.

I found out that Rotolo had come out of prison when I saw the news on television in the evening. I was in the kitchen with my daughter Amalia. My husband's murderer appeared on the screen as he was leaving the Ucciardone prison laughing and hugging his wife and daughter, while I and my daughter were alone in our house, powerless as we watched this scene of happiness. It was dreadful. Amalia was fifteen when her father was killed and ten years later, poor girl, she couldn't bear to see a murderer who'd been given life walk free. She got into a terrible state. I had a really bad night. I couldn't sleep. I couldn't cope any more. I thought about that beast in his home. And me alone. And Amalia alone. . . . But the Court of Cassation bypassed Carnevale and went back to the original line held by Falcone and Borsellino.[112]

Words, memory, justice: 'The Policlinico is now named after my husband. This is also a way of seeing justice done. So long as people walk past that plaque and wonder who Paolo Giaccone was, he will live on.'

In one way or another all of these women have spoken out and broken the silence. According to Chicca, the wife of Mauro Rostagno, who was killed by the mafia in September 1988 near Trapani, outside the therapeutic community of Saman where he lived and worked: 'The mafia is afraid of everyone who speaks out, because it is silence that keeps it alive, words that bring it death.'[113] Mauro was killed for the very reason that he spoke out, using a private television station because, as his daughter Monica said on the same broadcast, he came forward as someone 'who every day gave voice to the Trapani that does not speak out, that cannot speak out'.

Silence is that great soft cloak that envelops politicians and mafiosi and gives a halo to the powerful. 'In Sicily the less recourse you have to words the more *powerful* you are, thereby showing that the exercise of power has very ancient individual roots and is not subject to any verbal reverses, which are by definition elusive.'[114]

The solidity of the words of grief and mourning, the demystifying relation to the powers that be, the great charge of emotion and the utopia of memory – these are the elements which characterize the women who are in rebellion against mafia terror. On the basis of an ethical standpoint, be it social, political or professional, left to them by their dead, and through great personal stress, these women have 'invented' a way of making visible and audible the terrible damage that the mafia inflicts on us. Their demand for justice lies beyond the limits of the private and overshadows the awareness of every one of us.

Dacia Maraini said after a seminar in Palermo:

I have heard it said that what is being said and done will be futile, that it is all an illusion, a superficial thing. But I don't believe this is true and I want to be optimistic. No, there really is a need for optimism; there are moments in history when optimism is necessary, when it is a kind of engine and it's my impression

I can hear it around us, beneath that leaden thing, that pessimism which says that nothing really changes, everything is pointless, because those people are so strong. . . . I want to say that optimism is also an extension of desire. If you don't have the desire to change you don't even have this optimistic projection.[115]

I want to end this chapter with a few words from Chicca Rostagno, a kind of interior dialogue which moved me very much:

At the start you have to tell yourself – no, death is never in vain, because it makes you strong, it makes you find meaning, you say . . . so what! . . . Then you cling to everything that can give a sense to death, and you find that this death must have had a meaning for that person, for him and, yet at the same time you think that he was someone who loved living.

12

Women and Kidnappings

Lives as currency

Although kidnapping is not a criminal activity exclusively associated with the mafia or the *'ndrangheta*, its intrinsic features convey that arrogant contempt for life, for the deepest and most intimate feelings and emotions, which distinguishes the mafia. The kidnapped individual, whether man or woman, child, adolescent or adult, is in the most ferocious way reduced to a thing, is commodified and made an object of exchange, of an unequal exchange which once again exposes the totalitarian nature of the criminal organizations of the mafia and the *'ndrangheta*. The apparent but misleading rationality of the so-called negotiations for ransom often tend to obfuscate the uncivilized nature of this 'economic' transaction which is by no means one of redistributing wealth, but of a criminal hegemony over life and death. A form of slavery, a violent invasion of rights, once again by a power based on arbitrariness and brute force. Kidnapping is one of the greatest challenges to the state; what it does is lay bare the state's incapacity to guarantee one of its absolute premisses, the basis of its legitimacy: the safety of its citizens.

I want to stress this aspect because kidnapping is often 'tolerated' by public opinion, distanced or displaced with the convenient pretext that these are 'the poorest of the poor' taking revenge on the rich, or else are presumed to be acts of vengeance between mafiosi and people at any rate rumoured to be so. These commonsense assumptions are mistaken; kidnapping, like all other aspects of mafia activity, is a direct attack on civil rights and individual freedom: *our* freedom and *our* rights.

Kidnapping and the mafia go together throughout history. This is not a recent activity by the *cosche*.

Frances Elliot, a nineteenth-century traveller, related her impressions of Sicily in 1880, writing with ironic charm:

We will suppose orders are issued to 'sequestrate' a particular individual for a ransom. Certain of the lower affiliated are told off to do it. They may be the person's own relations; but they are bound, at the risk of their own lives, to obey.

The person disappears. Where is he concealed? . . . The Mafia knows, and commands precisely what shall be done to him. You naturally ask what the police are about? Where is the prefect? The troops? The commander-in-chief? The generals?

Until the affair of the ransom is arranged, they can do nothing. The blood of the sequestrated man would be in their hands. The authorities would be branded as murderers.

Such is Sicily!

It is utterly useless to apply to the family. It is a risk of life – a certainty of death, to divulge the smallest clue during the negotiation of the ransom. You might put the whole afflicted family into a mill and pound them into powder, and you would get nothing out of them!

When the ransom is paid, then the authorities can act, and the family will furnish particulars.

. . . Now, it is no use to say these things are out of date, when only last year, in the spring, a Sicilian duke was sequestrated at Trapani. . . . People, excellent people . . . go a step further, and actually submit to pay a sort of black-mail.[1]

The words of this 'lady in Sicily' clearly illuminate the paralysing dilemma whereby the kidnappers constrain both the authorities and the family of the victim; in some respects it is impossible not to react, in others every action risks endangering the life of the hostage. And, as we shall see, this dilemma still strongly conditions civilized collective responses today.

From the late seventies on, the mafia and the 'ndrangheta have played different roles in the so-called kidnapping 'industry'. These differences derive from considerations of practical convenience and contingent factors, and are by no means the outcome of ethical imperatives.

In Sicily, after a number of highly publicized abductions like that of Pino Vasallo, the son of the construction magnate and friend of the bosses, and of Luciano Cassina, the son of the businessman Count Arturo, the mafia decided to ban this activity from the island. Tommaso Buscetta revealed to Judge Falcone:

It was decided that in Sicily there should be no more kidnappings – this wasn't for humanitarian reasons, but was the result of a straightforward business calculation. Kidnappings actually create a generalized feeling of hostility on the part of the population towards the kidnappers, and this is counterproductive if it happens in parts of Sicily where the mafia is traditionally established;

266

moreover kidnappings draw greater attention from police forces towards organized crime.[2]

None the less, the Corleones broke this rule a number of times. After Liggio's transfer to Milan in 1972 both he and Riina allied themselves with the Calabrian *cosche* to usher in a new season of kidnappings. Often the victims were abducted in northern or central Italy, then transferred to prisons in the Aspromonte. One of the best-known cases was the abduction of the young millionaire Paul Getty. Simultaneously the *'ndrangheta* made an alliance with Cutolo's Camorra. 'Certain hostages taken in Campania were immediately "sold" to Calabrian gangs which were more "specialized" in negotiations and the custody of kidnap victims, thereby allowing the *'ndrangheta de facto* control over the coordination of this sector throughout national territory.'[3] And then there were the many, many Calabrian kidnap victims: pharmacists, doctors, teachers, farmers, men, women and children. Second-class hostages, as it has been said, because there was not a lot of talk about them as they happened to be Calabrians like their jailors.

'I was in a pit in a cave. I was stretched out and could hardly move. I was chained in three places: on my neck, on one foot and one wrist. Once there was a downpour and the cave was flooded. I lay in the water for several days. They'd given me a stick as a defence against rats and snakes' (Carlo Celadon, held by kidnappers for over two years).

'It was a hell. A hell I despaired of ever leaving alive. They were animals, they tortured me. I was tied up like a dog with a chain round my neck and they kept me barefoot in case I tried to escape; I was hidden in a pit dug in the ground with one of the kidnappers who was hooded and would beat me with a stick every two days' (Giuseppe De Sandro, held for 199 days).

'The fear of being killed grew in proportion to the endless term of my imprisonment. A few days before I was freed fear gave way to resignation; with every hour that passed I expected someone to put an end to a torture that had gone on for too long. They kept me tied up with a chain round my ankle, and I was blindfolded. I suffered a lot from the heat in summer and from biting cold in the winter. They would sporadically allow me to wash after taking off my blindfold, under threat of death if I opened my eyes' (Vincenzo Guarhieri, held for a year).

'The people who come out of the Aspromonte prisons are often no more than human ghosts. Men, women and children who are shocked and marked for life as a result of being deprived of any human closeness. They suffer constant nightmares and find it hard to re-enter the world of free men.'[4]

Newspaper reporting offers us some indication of intolerance towards kidnapping atrocities within the kidnappers' own milieu. Pantaleone Sergi talks about 'women who have collaborated in revenge for the wrongs done to their men': 'By means of a revolt among mafia housewives (at least four wives

267

of known criminals spoke out) the Palmi Prosecutor was able to reconstruct the story of a gang of kidnappers.'[5]

There have been many women kidnapped and many children. Enza Rita Stramandinoli, aged seventeen, and Maria Graziella Belcastro, forty-six, both from Cinquefrondi; Angela Mittica, twenty-five, from Oppido Mamertina; Rocco Lupini, aged ten, along with his mother Fausta, forty-two, from Molochio; Vincenzino Diano, aged eleven, from Lazzaro; and Raffaella Scordo, the unfortunate schoolteacher from Ardore who was beaten to death with a hammer by an unnamed gang because she resisted capture.[6] To mention only a few of the less well-known victims ...

I personally give little credence to the various anthropological or psychological interpretations which view the apparently inexplicable cruelty of the jailors as features of social rebellion, as some desire for revenge or else as the rough ways of shepherds. What I see is a transparently clear strategy of physical and psychological terror, in order to achieve the maximum profit within the shortest time and at the minimum cost. Only the 'banality of evil', which is to say insensitivity and an incapacity to think and imagine what you are doing, can produce this kind of damaging treatment. The disturbing question arises: what on earth was inflicted on these people as children that they should have so little empathy for the sufferings of others?

The courage of Angela Casella

One foggy night they turned me into an animal. It was 18 January 1988, I was eighteen and I thought life was wonderful. That night they dragged me away from my home, from my town, Pavia, from my people, and for 743 days and 743 nights I was a dog tied up with a chain, a rabbit in a cage, a mouse under a cat's paw. I was an animal to be ransomed or butchered. . . . It may seem crazy, but knowing where I was, even if it had been hell, would have made that nightmare more bearable. What I couldn't stand was not knowing what was happening to me, who I was with; that was the violence I could not get used to.[7]

Cesare Casella's kidnapping was one of the longest: two endless years buried alive in the dens of Aspromonte and, like all those kidnapped, deprived of the most basic respect for his human dignity. Even in this 'branch' of its activity the mafia displays its character as a total institution; the kidnap victim is stripped of his or her personality, gagged and allowed not a single moment of privacy, tied up, moved around and kept like an object. The victim is placed in a limbo outside time and space. From the commodification he endures by becoming an object of exchange there is a correspondingly experienced form of subjective alienation which often leaves ineradicable marks on the victim.

The progress of Cesare's kidnapping, the 'routine' of negotiations which a perverse reasoning would have had take place in silence and *omertà*, was disrupted by a woman's arrival on the scene, Cesare's mother, Angela Casella. Such was the stir provoked by her shattering initiative that even her son found out about it:

In June 1989 my humdrum days were dramatically disturbed by a bombshell. I was looking through the most recent issue of *Panorama* slowly, page by page, and looking forward to reading Pansa's *Bestiary*. When I finally got to my favourite page, I had a shock: in the middle of the *Bestiary* there was my mother, chained up outside a tent. I was momentarily stunned, unable to grasp what that little photograph meant and why my mother was tied up and where the photograph had been taken. Then I threw myself on the article and read it to the end. This was how I found out about my mother's protest in the villages of the Locride area, and became quite certain that I was being held a prisoner in the mountains of the Aspromonte, and that my father, as I read, had already handed over a thousand million lire. . . . 'I have an exceptional mum,' I thought. 'I knew that she would turn the world upside-down to have me back.'[8]

In June 1989, seventeen months after the kidnap and the payment of a thousand million lire, in agreement with her husband but breaking all the unwritten rules that assumed a certain silent 'complicity' between the victim and the perpetrator, Angela Casella arrived in Calabria. She arrived with her mind made up to break that silence, and indeed to provoke the widest possible mobilization both at the mass media level and at the level of social participation. Although impelled by desperation, her action represented a civilized and collective response to the mafia challenge which was altogether new. And it was accepted as such by broad sections of the population. Her action was both revolutionary and extremely simple. 'And what am I supposed to fear? I'm doing nothing wrong, I'm defending my son. I was tired of standing still and waiting. How could I do nothing knowing that Cesare was in some cave, in the dark, tied up with a chain. I didn't expect so much warmth. These people are wonderful, I was right to believe that the malicious are a minority in this part of the country,' she said during her first few days in Locri.[9]

Right from the start Angela Casella acted as a mother and as a citizen, taking care not to let herself be used by political forces. Her goal was to build solidarity around an unbearable wound that was purely personal only on the surface. Her protest brought civil society face to face with itself and laid bare the many shortcomings in the institutions, in politics and in the state. Angela turned first of all to the women, who were likely to have a more deeply felt understanding of her grief.

I'm not acting out some staged drama, this is a decision I have thought through and been tortured by, and I'm asking for the help and solidarity of all Calabrian mothers, and I'm not leaving without getting my son back. Whatever anyone says, I'm convinced that motherly feelings are stronger than violence and stronger than the mafia. If the mothers of Calabria, of Locri, of San Luca, give me a hand I'm sure I'll be able to save my son and take him home with me.[10]

The empty words of the politicians, the ineffectual shows of strength by the forces of order, the fruitless secret negotiations were counterposed by Angela Casella with her woman's body, her completeness as a person. A tiny body which became from the start a hard obstacle to move. She chained herself up in the square at Locri, slept in a tent, went day after day to the Locride villages, chaining herself up in their squares and going from door to door to talk to the women in her search for help and solidarity. She was thin and slight, distressed and alone, but also very determined to make a fuss whose disturbing effects would teach the top. She had journalists and public opinion on her side. 'If they won't give me my son I'll let myself die. I'll go on hunger strike. Which in the state I'm in would be like suicide. But I won't leave Locri by myself. Either with Cesare or dead.'[11]

From the very first day a number of victims of mafia violence and their relatives came to embrace her and be with her. There was Giulia Bova, whose son, the same age as Cesare, had been killed by the mafia; Francesco Morgante, who had been abducted in 1978 and Giovannino Furci, abducted in 1979 when he was just eight. She was embraced by Signora Fausta Rigoli and her son, who had both been abducted in the past. Later the President of the Association of Women against the Mafia in Reggio Calabria, Marianna Rombolà, came to meet her, along with some of the members. And Angela Casella visited Signora Concetta, Signora Campisi, 'whose husband had been kidnapped four months before and who now weighed only thirty-nine kilos'. They sent a message of solidarity to the parents of Roberta Lanzino, the student who had been raped and killed the year before.

Other people, mostly women, came to form a widening circle around the victims and their relatives, organizing an impromptu street procession, or bringing small gifts, or leaving signed written messages in the 'solidarity notebook' which Angela Casella always carried around: signing your own name in full with your address is an important and also perilous act, because it means breaking *omertà*, bearing first-person witness to a dangerous transgression of mafia law. 'To declare your own opposition to the *cosche* around here out in public is a symbolic act that counts for a lot. Even if later some suspicion arises that the very people who went to clasp the hands of the mother who had come from Pavia and is bewildered by so much unexpected solidarity might also include Cesare's kidnappers,' wrote Luca Villoresi.[12]

A committee sprang up to support Angela Casella and a manifesto was drawn up and signed by all the associations that were active in the Locride area. The protest widened. The mayors of the Locride local councils threatened to resign in support of the struggle of 'mother courage' and in protest against the running down of the region. 'We see Signora Casella as a dynamo. We want to join her so that we can all get out of this desperation,' said the Mayor of Siderno.[13] The Locri shopkeepers decided on a lock-out against the mafia, which was observed by nearly everyone. Party delegations arrived. The president of the Anti-mafia Commission, Chiaromonte, arrived with his two deputies, Vitalone and Calvi; Nilde Jotti telephoned, Occhetto wrote.* The ruling parties fearfully remembered the spectre of the Reggio revolt.† But Angela Casella hung on. 'I can see that they're beginning to use my presence here. It's election time; but I want to make it clear that I'm not interested in the politicians who are coming to get themselves seen here. I want solidarity, nothing else. That's why I'm turning to the women most of all; they are less involved in political disputes and disagreements.'[14]

Angela went looking for solidarity in the very places where her abducted son's proximity could most be felt and imagined, but probably where his abductors also lived: in the tumbledown villages of the Aspromonte, San Luca, Platì, Cimìna, Bovalino. She had been there once before, ten months after the kidnap, quietly and without making her name known, in the wake of a woman journalist, in search of some contact, some trail that would lead her to her son. She had knocked on doors, implored, searched, but to no avail. This time she went with the whole weight of her desperation and her public protest. When Angela chained herself up in the squares, the women would go up to her, somebody would sign, somebody else would bring her a cup of coffee or a glass of water, or a home-made cake. The men kept their distance on the other side of the street. They watched in silence and did not sign.

'A signature, signora, will you sign. . . . For my son Cesare.' The woman, who is old, dark and wrinkled as one imagines the women of the Aspromonte must be, shakes her head. She is trembling: 'The truth is, I don't know how to write my name.' But it's not an excuse. The old woman comes close and embraces Signora Casella. And then she gives her a long hug, stroking her with her illiterate hands,

---

* Nilde Jotti, currently a PDS MP, is a veteran parliamentarian and one of Italy's most prominent female politicians. Achille Occhetto was also a leading member of the PCI and was its deputy general secretary for a time. In 1989 he founded the PDS. [Trs.]

† In 1970 riots erupted in Reggio Calabria over the issue of the city's rejected claim to the status of regional capital and seat of regional government. This was a popular protest fuelled by frustration and anger about prevailing economic conditions, but its direction was manipulated and controlled by the neofascists. Violence escalated, the army intervened and a siege situation lasted for several months. The outcome was a compromise division of regional responsibilities between Reggio Calabria and Catanzaro. [Trs.]

to tell her what she cannot express in written words. 'Poor downhearted mother' . . . . A woman of around thirty comes out of one of the houses carrying a tray. She goes up to Cesare's mum: 'I admire your courage. Anyone with children understands. What's happening to you is worse than an illness. Forgive us if we're not able to put things into words.' And she holds out a cup of coffee, with two little home-made cakes on the saucer.[15]

Weighty representatives of the Church also take up Signora Casella's initiative. Don Riboldi, the Bishop of Acerra, was in daily contact with Angela and offered himself as a hostage to take the place of Cesare, probably also acting as a mediator for a new contact with the kidnappers. Don Riboldi was critical of the authorities: 'It seems to me that either they don't have time or they're inefficient. When they're talking about motorways it's fine. But when it comes to human beings, in often extreme cases, I get the impression that they are still relying on rather bureaucratic procedures.'[16] Monsignor Ciliberto, the Bishop of Locri, also intervened decisively, with a pastoral letter and a vigil at the cathedral. The bishop said: 'The arrival of Signora Angela Casella has stimulated a sense of awareness among these people who live under repression. Citizens have found the courage to demonstrate in public. . . . A mother in tears has brought out all the good there is in the people. And this is not a small amount.'[17]

The abductors clammed up and the authorities got nervous, putting pressure on Cesare's parents so that 'mother courage' will stop making a fuss. But Angela didn't give way.

> I don't want to move people to tears, I want to make everyone think for themselves. . . . I know that they all prefer silence. . . . But it's clear that silence is not always useful. And then it's better to shout and call on the compassion and the helpfulness that I can see here in Calabria, surrounded as I am particularly by the motherly solidarity of women and by this community which is asking for justice for me and for itself.[18]

Perhaps for the first time, Angela Casella's actions removed the crime of kidnapping from the half-light of rivalry between two powers who contest the monopoly of violence – the state and organized crime – and brought to everyone's attention the concrete implications for the lives of the victims, by demanding the right to fight directly for release. And this was a message that came from afar, that touched all citizens on the basis of straightforward feelings of empathy. 'There came a time when we realized that reality is not "normal" as resignation compels us to pretend we believe it is. For a moment, thanks to Signora Casella, we felt that it is really deeply unacceptable. Perhaps this at least means something to all of us.'[19]

Perhaps Angela Casella had been helped by her own past. 'I'm not frightened of a future without any money. I was born poor and I've worked all my life.... Work doesn't frighten me and I don't give myself airs.'[20] Both she and her husband came from a working-class background, he was a mechanic and she was an engineering worker. A life of hard work until they ran the Citroën concession. In the words of her husband, who had stayed in Pavia:

> I have worked hard for thirty years, only thinking of building something for my children. But if I had imagined that this could mean Cesare having to spend a year and a half shut up in a hole, I would have done things differently.... When I see Angela on TV she seems a different woman. She has changed, she's stronger, she's obstinate; she won't give in. She's spent too long at home in despair, knitting jumpers and waiting.... Life changed the day they kidnapped Cesare.[21]

After a week of highly public protest, however, Angela Casella was compelled to give in. The 'experts' suggested to her, with extreme insistence, that to continue her protest might put her son's life in danger. 'How can you carry on when they tell you that your son might even die and it would be your fault? ... I'm not leaving defeated, I'm going to my relatives in the Cosenza area. We need some time to think. I'm not letting go. . . . Nothing has changed. The state is not helping me. I'm leaving because I need to think about things, that's all.'[22]

It was as if Angela's departure had left a void in Locri. People kept converging on the Town Hall where 'mother courage' had pitched her tent. 'There's a small table left there and on it are dozens of messages and notes, newspaper cuttings with things written in the margins. A lot of people leave their calling cards, nobody touches anything. "Don't give way", "Thanks for everything you've done", "You've spoken for all of us", "You've given a voice to the Calabria of decent people".'[23]

This spontaneous response from the people would be repeated in Sicily with the many messages left on the 'Falcone tree' and outside the house of Borsellino's mother in Via D'Amelio in Palermo.

After Angela had gone the women's associations of Calabria held a big demonstration in Locri. The Association of Sicilian Women against the Mafia sent a message of solidarity in which it emphasized that the 'time of rupture and rebellion' that has taken shape in Calabria must be used 'to conquer fear'.

Against reasons of state

Angela Casella's vociferous and desperate protest was born of exasperation and frustration in the face of the blatant failings and shortcomings of the institutions and the state. 'An atypical social subject is emerging, "the family citizen", that is the person who is impelled by personal feelings to shout and speak out for himself or herself and for others with the same problems, to participate and protest instead of being contained and remaining weak with the family inside domestic walls.'[24]

Angela Casella is a woman who described herself as a mother and a house-wife, a woman who in the past had never undertaken public duties and had never been active in politics. None the less, when the terrible situation that came about for her family required it, she acted without faltering, with simplicity and in a very practical way. Her protest too belongs to that phenomenon of 'moral familism' which we have already discussed.

> Conquering embarrassment, breaking with isolation, discussing things with others who are affected by the same problem, as a form of consciousness-raising, perceiving oneself therefore not as victims of individual disasters or to blame and responsible for this situation, but as members of a wider collectivity which demands public, social responses to problems that are neither private nor individual.[25]

And people understood this, identifying with her, and glimpsing a new and different means of relating to the *res publica*. 'There is no such thing as a private sphere and a public sphere, nor any border zone between the two, but rather the intermediate zone is itself the refoundation both of the private and the public.... Feelings then become words. And words are public, are representation,' Gabriella Turnaturi writes.[26] This different way of confronting what is public takes on special relevance in the Mezzogiorno, where civil society is weak and citizens tend to live in a permanent, direct antagonism with the state – with a state of which this weakness is also an expression and something that is exploited. Its power, and the resulting abuses with which the history of the Mezzogiorno is marked, is very much based upon this weakness both of the citizenry and in the public, civil sphere.

Indeed, politicians in government, as well as those in the institutions, did not look kindly on Angela Casella's initiative, going so far as to evoke the threatening spectre of the Reggio Calabria revolt, although it was certainly quite different. The angry words of the then Prime Minister, De Mita, in a television broadcast, speak for all of them: 'She is to be admired, but she is making a big mistake.... The impression is that things are being handled, I wouldn't say reprehensibly, but handled oddly by the family.... The last thing we want to do is dispute the right of parents to protest against such appalling occurrences. But ...' And then the politician intimated that Signora Casella's protest threatened to jeopardize some behind-the-scenes but effective work by the police and the *carabinieri*, alluding to the fact that making too much fuss could even entail risks for the hostage. As if to say: it's your fault if things end badly.[27]

If De Mita did at least allow relatives the right to protest, Claudio Vitalone, then Vice-President of the Anti-mafia Commission, proposed much more radical measures to stifle at birth the bothersome 'moral family action': 'Since it is not possible to entrust the handling of negotiations to the independent initiative of the kidnap victim's relatives, we must envisage some legislative mechanism to prevent any contact between the family and the kidnappers.'[28] But the Commission was split over the question. Indeed, its President Chiaromonte retorted: 'Excuse me, we are here to express solidarity with this mother, I don't feel it's up to me to say what a mother should do to get her son back, nor did I do so at the time of the Moro kidnapping.'[29]

With regard to politics and politicians, Angela Casella expressed that mistrust with which so many citizens identified: 'They treat me kindly to my face but they demonstrate great irritation with everything I do.' In opposition to the twisted logic of reasons of state she set a vision that was disarmingly practical and concrete: 'From tonight on I'll sleep in a tent and I invite ministers Gava, Craxi, De Mita and the Chief of Police to do the same. That way they'll understand what it means to be a prisoner for seventeen months.' And in Pavia her husband responded:

> I can only say that a few months ago I sent the honourable De Mita a registered letter begging him to intervene and do something for my son who had been held hostage by the bandits for over a year. I got no reply. I wrote to Craxi, with the very same result, and I wrote to President Cossiga who sent me an extremely formal answer that he shared in our grief. This is as much as we have had from the authorities who now criticize us.[30]

If a 'mother's reasons' have the might to resist reasons of state, it is a lot harder to take no heed of the insistent advice given by so-called experts. It was they who halted her progress with a concerted action conveying how much the Casella family was getting in the way of the image of the state and the authorities, especially in the run-up to elections, for elections to the European Parliament were coming up soon. 'What more can you achieve?' Prefect Sabatino wondered with irritation. 'It's experts who are needed. Have you ever seen a surgeon letting a child's mother be present when he's being operated on just so as she can hold his hand?'[31] And one of the biggest experts, Luigi Rossi from the central headquarters of Criminalpol, put it like this:

> Good heavens, with all respect, but these actions are complicating things. . . . Do you know what's the hardest part of keeping a kidnapping under control? You don't know? I'll tell you. It's making the hostage's relatives behave. It's method that's needed in managing a kidnapping. And without any false modesty I can state that in Italy we have a lot of skill in this area. You find that surprising? Well,

it's the truth. You only have to think that 70 per cent of cases are solved and those responsible sent to prison. For no other crime is there such a high success rate.[32]

The expert has a truly individual way of looking at things. By some partial logic exclusive to his profession, he loses sight of the context. And so, instead of admitting that it is difficult to keep the villains in check, it is the relatives whom he turns into objects of surveillance. And the eulogy of Italy with regard to hunting down kidnappers overlooks the fact that it is virtually only in Italy that kidnappings take place. His modesty, indeed, is false. The skill of the investigators needs to be put in perspective and the occurrence of kidnapping denounced, and as something all the more shocking given that we are talking about a modern state like Italy.

The belief that the mother's continuing stay in Calabria could put her son's life at risk is thus not surprising, it is as if to say it would be the mother's fault if they killed him. What way is there of resisting such blackmail?

It is worth mentioning that not all those within the institutions share this view taken by experts. Carlo Macrì, Deputy Prosecutor at Locri, gave a cautious appraisal: 'There have been around four hundred kidnappings carried out in Calabria, but it is the first time the relatives have reacted like this. It's a new and disruptive element that has unsettled everybody. I'm not able to say what it means.'[33] And Rocco Lombardo, State Prosecutor in Locri, said: 'In my view Signora Casella's presence in Locri and the stir this has caused can't jeopardize young Cesare's life. It may perhaps jeopardize future contacts, but nothing else.'[34]

This silence, which in the case of institutions is called 'reasons of state', and in the case of criminals is called '*omertà*', seems very hard to break. And it's understandable, given that what is at stake is always life or death. Milady Frances Elliot had marvelled at it on her sojourn in Sicily in 1880. And we should all of us marvel at it. Yet Angela Casella demonstrated that what seems immutable does not necessarily have to be so. It is just one strong woman's voice, for all this mother's outward vulnerability and frailness, that has taught us many things about the potential of civil society in Italy.

After 743 long days and 743 endless nights, Cesare Casella was released in January 1990. Whatever may have been negotiated in the end to influence his release, let us congratulate Angela Casella.

=13=

'Between Killing and Dying There's a Third Way: Living'

The centres and associations

For complex reasons that cannot be discussed in this book, civil society's response to the mafia has been heterogeneous and without any continuity over time. All I can do here is reflect generally on the overall question of the 'anti-mafia problem'. However, I should like to dwell somewhat on the most significant aggregations and initiatives of the last few decades and the last few years in particular, which have been articulated by women only or else which have at any rate had a strong internal component of work by women, around women and for women.

The words of Christa Wolf which give this chapter its title well express a tension which has fuelled all the initiatives, however diverse, that I want to talk about: a call to life which identifies in the mafia that negative, deathly force which is deeply rooted in the social fabric and that presence which is to be fought against even in the smallest activities, in customs, in material everyday culture, obviously as well as in its direct articulations of criminal, economic and political power. I give by way of example for this tenor of work against the mafia, Letizia Battaglia, whose words radiate that sunlit vitality imbued partly with experience of pain, which seems the most radical negation of the spectre of death which accompanies every mafia act. At the time of the Palermo Spring* Letizia was the local council committee head for the quality of the environment: 'Until now the trees were just there; we lived alongside them, or else they died. Now we know that if these trees are to grow and stay healthy they must be looked after. We have begun again to talk about trees in the city, not just about blood and corpses, and the palms give us pleasure.'[1]

---

* The Palermo Spring refers to the period in the late 1980s when the city council had a ruling group headed by Leoluca Orlando of the Rete Party. La Rete was then a new party and its anti-mafai platform rallied strong support. [Trs.]

The Sicilian Centre for Documentation (CSD) has been functioning in Palermo since 1977; in 1980, it became a cultural association and was renamed after Giuseppe Impastato.

> The Association's aim is to collect materials of a political, economic, historical and sociological nature; to conduct studies and researches; to promote cultural initiatives (conferences, seminars, debates, screenings, exhibitions, etc.); to publish books, pamphlets and diverse materials; to make known in Italy and abroad the realities of Sicilian experience.

So it is described by its working team in a leaflet explaining its activities and listing its numerous publications over the years. The Centre has a specialized library that is among the most outstanding of its kind, as well as an archive and a newspaper and periodical library. The Centre is almost exclusively self-financed and over the years the distinguishing features of its outlook and activities have been intellectual rigour, political independence and concrete solidarity as effective practice. Besides the rigour perhaps, another fitting legacy from Peppino Impastato is expressed by the irony and satire which inspire some of the publications originating at the Centre. The Centre is also part of a broad pacifist movement and its team take part in conferences and demonstrations both nationally and internationally. Working with schools is a significant part of their activity.

Their commitment against the mafia is distinguished by courageous denunciations and practical, sometimes even hazardous actions, like for example the challenge to the Badalamenti boss whom they charged with responsibility for the murder of Giuseppe Impastato in his 'domain', Cinisi, or their solidarity with Libero Grassi before his death and the campaign in support of his company, Sigma, after he was killed.

The research project 'mafia and society', which was launched in 1984, represents a thread that runs through the theoretical work of the Centre; this project brings together different monographic researches which have been carried out at one time or another in collaboration either with organizations, universities or single researchers, some outside the Centre itself.

What is the Giuseppe Impastato Centre's link with women? I would say that the question of women and the mafia has always been and remains a component of the Centre's interests and activities on two levels. At one level are research and understanding. One of the sub-projects in the mafia and society research concerns women's contact with the mafia. Anna Puglisi, sometimes working together with Umberto Santino, both founder members of the Centre, has assembled life stories and interviews with women who have been victims of the mafia, like Felicia Bartolotta, the mother of Peppino Impastato, like Michela Buscemi, Pietra Lo Verso, Maria Benigno or Giovanna Terranova; women from extremely diverse social backgrounds, with personal histories that have little in common, but united by a shared grief, mourning and anger. Women 'against'. The dossier *With and Against* was produced in collaboration with the Association of Sicilian Women against the Mafia.

Underlying this research which has developed over the years, there is a relationship of trust between these women and the Centre's team, without which the research work would probably not have been possible. This mutual trust is the fruit of the Centre's other level of activity, its material solidarity, the fact that it is there, and has always been there, with steadfast commitment, at protests and during the testing experiences of what happens in the high-risk neighbourhoods, at trials and in the battles over the legal actions and financial support for plaintiffs. The Centre has fought firmly against the exclusion of 'ordinary women' from the funds gathered for the actions of plaintiffs in the trials, on the basis of a conviction that a serious struggle against the mafia has to begin there, in concrete solidarity with those who break *omertà*. The closer someone is to the mafia milieu the harder the choice to break with it obviously is and it demands respect and support. Umberto Santino wrote in polemical vein in his preface to the stories of Michela Buscemi and Pietra Lo Verso, assembled by Anna Puglisi:

> This hasn't been a simple matter of 'chance' or 'accidental oversight', for this policy [of exclusion] has been the logical, we might even say *natural*, outcome of one notion of the mafia (as a gang of thugs, as a criminal, bloodsucking counterpower to the state) which can only be matched by one notion of anti-mafia (the indignation of the party of 'decency', the stifling of the 'democratic state', cops chasing robbers) which ignores the fact that the mafia is a piece of the bourgeoisie, which is to say of the ruling class, that the intimate bond between legality and illegality is the keystone of the mafia economy and the mafia system of power, to be counterposed by a thoroughgoing strategy whose central goal is to break the circuits of interconnection and build a mass mobilization of the people to bring them out of their economic, political and cultural subjugation, rather than just being a matter of occasional public protests.[2]

In this spirit Anna Puglisi is a constant presence at public debates, in schools, at demonstrations and in courtrooms, specifically as a representative of the Centre, but also as a woman belonging to the Association of Sicilian Women against the Mafia. Her work on 'women and the mafia' has gone further than research and become a kind of permanent survey of all the issues that concern women in this context.

> In our midst there is a world of people we sentence to death. At times, it is this plight that impels them to rebel; they are answered with submachine guns and prison bars. Let there be an end to siding with the strongest and giving them a chance to suffocate the rest, systematically, in broad daylight. I don't think we are

all so cruel as to want to go on killing like that. I don't believe it. Let it also be known that the flow of life cannot be stopped.

The words are Danilo Dolci's, as published in a leaflet from the San Francesco Saverio Social Centre in the Albergheria district of Palermo, words that epitomize the spirit animating the activities of this Centre, which also carries out joint initiatives with the Impastato Centre. This social Centre originated in 1986, in the wake of a series of mass meetings held by those who live in the neighbourhood. As documented by its founders, this is 'a *non-sectarian* and *non-party political* association of citizens who aim to work together for the sake of one of the most blighted districts in the centre of Palermo'. The Centre operates in four primary sites: the eighteenth-century church of San Francesco Saverio, which as well as being used for worship has a role as a multi-purpose neighbourhood venue; the San Pietro Hermitage, an ex-monastery which houses a variety of services, including an after-school centre for children, a 'peace laboratory', a women's space and a day centre for elderly people; the Edison Cinema and the Al Vicoletto trattoria, which is run by young people in the neighbourhood.

Former Catholic militants and former Marxist militants have come together at the Centre, united by a new political and social will which goes beyond any ideology and aims 'to organize the people of a particular district so that they become the main characters in their own rescue', as Augusto Cavadi put it.[3]

The Centre has a multiplicity of activities: it functions as a children's activity centre, has an outreach team with a doctor, two social workers and two women community workers; it carries out local research and assists elderly people; it gives training seminars and refresher courses, sponsors adult prisoners on parole and youths with a criminal background; and its women's space sets up projects to promote a more active social participation and civic sense among the women of the neighbourhood.

It was not easy to reach the women. According to Maria, who has been involved in the Centre for years:

We began by organizing an after-school centre with activities for children and so this enabled us to get in touch with the families and with the mums, the women, certainly in a way that made them considerably less suspicious about us.... We set up a cutting and dressmaking course ... loads of women from the district came along ... we let things rest there, taking it easy and because while you're cutting and sewing you build up a contact that's relaxed and friendly and has some give and take, so you talk. So maybe while we were cutting and sewing we would natter away about things in our lives, about our relationships with our husbands and children.[4]

Little by little, people start talking. Anna Puglisi recalls:

And this is when we started looking at the mafia. Compared with other aspects of the project, the mafia side of things turned out to be the most unpleasant, the most unpalatable for these women. . . . And then we discussed drugs, small-time dealing, mafia responsibility. Even though these aspects of it were closer to their lives, it was still very difficult.[5]

And just there, practically opposite the Centre lived Vita Rugnetta. 'Cosimo, the priest who we work with at the church, invited Signora Rugnetta a number of times, he invited her to come as a person around whom some halo of solidarity could be formed. But instead, there had been a void formed around Signora Rugnetta, nobody went to buy furniture at her shop any more. Signora Rugnetta has shut the shop now, and we don't see her around any more,' said Maria.

In her view, 'poverty is a fundamentally cultural thing'. It's tremendously hard to get through to these women. It's the male who is dominant everywhere, even in the home. Of course, widespread crime does result in consumer gratification. But consuming what?

I'd take you around some parts of Albergheria that are mind-boggling: you see the kids who go in for bag-snatching going around in leather jackets with new cars, but they live two families to a room, with one big bed where everybody sleeps together and rain pouring in through the roof. . . . Not a single one of those we've sponsored is at liberty. . . . Look, the first prisoner we had was a guy who nicked cars which got flattened for scrap, well this guy had children . . . and he would tell us that he used the money to buy himself a gold Rolex that cost five million lire, that he bought a motorbike and then sold it, he'd bought a horse and then sold it. There was no notion of supporting the family. He even said that he bought things and then sold them just to show off that he was able to do all these things. In my opinion there's some kind of compulsion to keep doing the same things, almost.[6]

The harder it is for these women to confront the mafia issue, the more this seems a sign that their everyday coexistence with the mafia is a real problem and source of tension. And when Michela Buscemi was invited to the Centre there was a great deal of interest. 'This was a meeting that meant a lot to them, and a lot of the questions they asked were personal ones. They asked her a lot about relationships between her and her family, her and her children, her and her husband, this was the topic they were all keen to know about. And the mother who had rejected Michela.'[7]

It takes a commitment to something solid, something grounded in reality, to engage these women who are grappling with such great contradictions at a day-to-day level. A course in fabric painting, part of a project developed by the Impastato Centre and financed by the EC, was welcomed with enthusiasm and a lot of involvement. 'These were women who were happy at getting together and learning these techniques, being able to express their creativity, but also learning something useful. And it was also an excuse to get together and talk about the mafia.'[8]

> We actually started out with the idea that there was a specific female component in the struggle against the mafia. This was in the late seventies and at that time the women's movement and feminism had a conception of women as naturally pacifist, particularly because of being mothers. The line we took then (ideologically too, I can see now) was that 'the mafia is violence, women are against all violence and therefore must have a particular part to play in the struggle against the mafia'. And this was our starting point.

These are the words of Elvira Rosa, one of the nine founding members of the Association of Sicilian Women against the Mafia – along with Silvana Giuffrè, Antonia Cascio, Giovanna Giaconia Terranova, Anna Costanza, Anna Savagnone Pomar, Vincenza Catalano Barillà, Giuseppa Ferraro and Maria D'Amico. This initial conception clashed with the reality of the mafia milieu, within the concrete experience of the trials, for example. Being by the side of Maria Benigno at the trial of Rinella and Bagarella is an experience Elvira recalls with some apprehension:

> I remember that when we went into the courtroom it was really scary; there were about ten of us; in the dock were the men she was directly accusing . . . the way they looked at us! . . . and behind us were the relatives of the accused – they were mostly women like us (this was the eighties, when we still cherished the utopia of some great 'instinctive' solidarity between women) and it was the first time we came face to face with the women of the mafiosi, and with the fact that these women were defending their sons and husbands, just like in rape trials.[9]

This experience highlighted a significant problem in the discussion of equality and difference between women, with reference specifically to the mafia milieu. Consideration of this issue on the basis of concrete experience has gone on at the heart of the Association over these years, drawing on a more elaborated and problematic notion of difference, one which seems extremely relevant. Elvira Rosa again:

> Since working-class women in particular are not aware of their rights they have no consciousness either of themselves or their own strength, and this lack of awareness becomes a kind of grey area, where everything happens. . . . We have

thought a lot about this idea of awareness of self and one's own rights. Since the mafia prevents you from being a citizen of this state, if you take on the concept of citizenship you are fighting the mafia and are no longer in a grey area. Finally, the most recent idea we've been working on this year in fact is that since the mafia is anti-democratic and undermines the idea of democracy, we are stressing that women must be more sensitive to democracy than men nowadays.

The Association was formally established in 1984, but its activities and the grouping of women began a few years earlier, around the protests on behalf of the widows of magistrates, politicians and police who were killed at the end of the seventies. They like to think of themselves as being linked with women even further back in time. According to Anna Puglisi: 'I want to recall the involvement of women in the peasant struggles of the nineteenth century and the period after the Second World War and it makes me glad to see a connection between the commitment of those women and the establishment of the Association of Sicilian Women against the Mafia.'[10]

Giovanna Terranova, President of the Association since it was founded, recalls the early days:

> It started with that petition in 1980, when we collected thousands of signatures for an appeal to Pertini. It was the Communist women who took that initiative and I was the second signatory, with Rita Costa as the first. When the signatures were collected we went to Rome. There was me, Rita Costa, Marisa La Mantia, Teresa Noto and there were Calabrians, Nadia Alecci, and representatives from all the parties, and we went to see Pertini. We were received and we presented the petition for the laws to be speeded up – there were two at the time, the Rognoni law and the La Torre law.* They were only being drawn up at that stage. We asked for discussion to be speeded up and for a special supervisory commission to be established. Pertini gave us a good reception. . . . Then we went to Rognoni, who, naturally . . . promised . . .[11]

More than thirty thousand signatures altogether were collected in Sicily and Calabria. Besides Giovanna Terranova and Rita Costa, among the first signatories were the widow of Mancuso, the daughter of Costa, the fiancée of Beppe Valarioti and the daughter of Giannino Losardo. Valarioti and Losardo were two Calabrian Communist militants from Cetraro and Rosarno respectively, who had recently been murdered by the 'ndrangheta. This initiative did not end up as a one-off; immediately in its wake it was decided to set up a committee of women against the mafia, which aimed to make links at diverse

---

* See notes pp. 6, 115.

social levels, through debates, testimonies and public declarations; a commitment to civic development, which was advanced particularly in schools.

In 1983 a conference approved the establishment of a Joint Committee of Women from Sicily, Calabria and Campania and launched the idea of a national demonstration to be held in Rome the following year. There was also subsequently established in Calabria an Association of Women against the Mafia and Violence of Every Kind, based in Reggio Calabria, which, for example, gave support to Angela Casella.

The activity which perhaps more than any other has engaged the Committee and subsequently the Association of Sicilian Women against the Mafia has been participation in trials against mafiosi. The physical presence and moral support of women from the Association at crucial points in courtroom testimony has heartened those brave women who were prepared to break the silence. One suitable example is the case of Maria Cangialosi, a Sicilian woman from Lercara Friddi who grew up in Liège in Belgium. She came back from Belgium and married Antonino Messina and was an eyewitness to his murder right outside their house. Maria had recognized and reported the murderer. Anna Puglisi recalls:

> She called us for the day when she had to give her testimony in court, and I went there with Antonia Cascio and Giovanna Terranova. When we arrived we signalled to her that we were there. She wrote to us later, telling us that after we turned up women from the village had gone to see her and that she had had a lot of solidarity and supporting testimonies from them. Now she was no longer so isolated, so our presence had been helpful to her. To a degree.[12]

Subsequently, however, Maria Cangialosi had been compelled to withdraw; she had had serious threats made against her children. Enrico Deaglio writes:

> I went to see her again and she explained to me, without mincing her words, what had happened. . . . She wanted to live and she didn't want to clash with things bigger than she had imagined. . . . She offered me some coffee and when we said our goodbyes she added, with a smile: 'I'm sorry, because I got on well with the other women on the committee and I'd have liked to continue going around speaking out against the mafia.'[13]

At the first big trial, the Spatola trial,* the Committee of Women applied

---

* The Spatola trial in 1983 was the first big investigation – headed by Judge Falcone – into the assets of those with mafia connections. The Spatola family was prominent in the construction industry and had contacts with Michele Sindona (see p. 248). [Trs.]

to take action as plaintiff, but the application was refused for the reason that the Committee had not suffered direct personal injuries. 'It obviously isn't enough for the judges that there are many widows of magistrates and police killed by the mafia who are members of the Committee, nor is it enough that the women feel that their right to live in a city without violence is injured.'[14] The same process of application and response was repeated for the trial against the murderers of Judge Chinnici, his bodyguard and the doorman at his residence. The atmosphere in the courtroom was tense. According to the newspaper reporter:

> At the back of the courtroom, around the widows, the women who fight against the mafia were gathered. The action as plaintiffs was signed by Silvana Giuffrè and presented by the Socialist Member of Parliament Maria Magnani Noya, who has several times been an under-secretary, is a practising lawyer in Turin and would like to introduce some 'Savoy ritual', as the lawyer Veneto caustically quipped, though he was soon on the receiving end of the repartee. Magnani Noya referred to the commitment of the Sicilian women and applied that they be admitted to the trial in order to defend the 'vital interests' of a society threatened by the mafia: 'an action which aims to testify to the high price paid most of all by women'. The defence opposed this. . . . 'We too are fighting against intimidation and especially against fear,' retorted Magnani Noya. The presiding judge did not appreciate the tenor of her words and invited the women's legal representative 'to stop talking as if she were addressing a meeting'.[15]

This time, however, the women did at least uphold their request for the state to act as a plaintiff.

Given the precedents, the Association decided not to present itself as a plaintiff in the maxi-trial. The women wrote: 'The Association considers it none the less more appropriate to make a commitment to help all of those who have been directly stricken by mafia violence and whose actions as plaintiffs may become more than a secondary component in the progress of the trial and its conclusion.'[16] This led to the collection of funds for the plaintiffs, which we have already talked about, and the practical solidarity given, particularly by accompanying women at the hearings, being close to them in these difficult, often extreme circumstances.

In 1984, at Milan, the Association received the Carlo Alberto Dalla Chiesa prize, 'for having been able to combine human feelings with civic passion, two spheres which are almost always kept apart in our collective culture, and often in our individual cultures'. Those present were Giovanna Terranova and Rita Costa. 'The most solemn moment in the ceremony came when Ambrosoli's widow and Rita Bartoli Costa embraced and then Rita was again embraced by Maria Leotta, the widow of the Palermo Flying Squad

Chief Boris Giuliano, who was killed one month after Giorgio Ambrosoli.'[17] These two men, Ambrosoli and Giuliano, had brought an exceptional professional and civic commitment to their confrontation with a single powerful enemy, the link between the mafia, politicians, high finance and Freemasonry, and are dead because of this commitment; their widows, two women, one from Milan, the other from Palermo, spanning the years in an embrace.

I feel that this scene symbolizes an important piece of the history of the First Republic in Italy. And it poignantly raises the issue of the 'widows' and the victims' relatives in general. The use of the denomination *widow* is ambiguous. The way in which the mass media reiterate the term 'mafia widows' seems like pigeonholing, reification. Often the widows themselves do not identify with it. I have already quoted Giovanna Terranova saying: 'I couldn't stand being called a "mafia widow". It gave me a feeling of physical violence, as if they had shot me too.' 'We are not the Association of Widows,' asserted Elvira Rosa. She said: 'It also happens to me whenever I go somewhere to speak on behalf of the Association, I'm asked whose widow I am, because it becomes extremely hard to imagine that I might want to fight against the mafia unless I've had someone killed.'[18]

And yet, it is precisely this wound, this grief, this loss that have conferred strength and ethical value on this movement of women against the mafia. This was stressed by Rita Costa after the preview, in Palermo, of the film *Il lungo silenzio* (*The Long Silence*):

Thank you Signora von Trotta, for having given this extraordinary film to Palermo; Palermo cannot forget, nor should it.... My husband, our murdered husbands should not remain just a bundle of blood and shame for this city and its young people; they must teach those who come after them and all our children about the meaning of dignity and courage . . . forgetting is the most powerful tool in the service of power . . . our grief so as not to forget.

Rosaria Schifani said: 'Grief must be shown; let everyone show it and say it and scream it out in their way. Otherwise none of all this that we're living and suffering through can have a meaning.'[19]

It was in October 1993 that the Association of Sicilian Woman against the Mafia, together with the *Mezzocielo* editorial group, proposed setting up a House of Memory in Palermo. Piera Fallucca wrote:

Memory is difficult, and yet with Warsaw's Jewish cemetery, 'the wood of memory and death', Berlin's Museum of the History of Nazism in Germany, and in Jerusalem, people have been able to create sites for working through intolerable feelings of unease and our inevitable shame, transforming individual horror into a warning and a consciousness for everyone.[20]

It is perhaps through the shared will *not to forget*, through memory as commemoration, and at the same time through asking persistent ethical questions in the present, that the widows and all the other women with them discover that kind of unity which respects diversity between different women.

There is one thorny issue, however, that undoubtedly arouses debate between the women who belong to the Association. This is the difficulty, sometimes impossibility, of contact between members who are the widows of men killed in the struggle against the mafia, and others who come from that very background, and are sometimes themselves the widows of mafioso men.

> We members of the Association of Women against the Mafia have also had great internal anguish. We have our origins with a number of eminent widows, the widows of men who died because they were fighting against the mafia. When we decided to help Signora Rugnetta or other women whose families were connected with a milieu close to the mafia, conflicts erupted within our organization. Some of our members could not tolerate being in the same room as these women. There are widows who have cut themselves off from the Association. These were reactions that are perhaps understandable in human terms, but very short-sighted from a political point of view. . . . Even if a mafia woman were to turn state's evidence and come to us she ought to be supported with every means we have! It would be a huge step to take and we would have to help her, back her up, give her our solidarity.[21]

Maternal thinking and public protest: the sheets . . .

> We tried to come up with a symbol. The sheet that newspaper photographs show stained with blood covering lifeless bodies, a veil over the mess of violent death; we washed it, bleached it and hung it out over the balconies of our houses. A sign of cleanness, a flagrant first-person condemnation of the most high-risk neighbourhoods in the city. It's there to say: 'I, who live right here (my name is on the doorbell!), am not on your side. Don't count me in. I belong to another Palermo.'[22]

The bloodletting of summer 1992 irreversibly marked public opinion in Palermo, and beyond, in relation to the mafia – with the murder of Judge Giovanni Falcone, of his wife, the magistrate Francesca Morvillo and the bodyguard Vito Schifani, Rocco di Cillo and Antonio Montinari; and later, the massacre of Via D'Amelio in which Judge Paolo Borsellino died along with the bodyguards Emanuela Loi, Agostino Catalano, Vincenzo Li Muli, Walter Cosina and Claudio Traina. Many people realized that the days of leaving it up to others and not making a fuss were over. The tragedy and the appalling outrage of those bombs touched individual consciences. A process was triggered whereby old ways began to be torn apart: indifference, silence, *omertà*. Single individuals may not be able to do much, but they can at least do something. Giovanna Fiume wrote:

> The sheet became a symbol of a new way of acting, something tangible rather than envisaged, something centred on the ethic of personal responsibility. ... No one is in doubt that the mafia has to be fought not just on this level and we're well aware of the need for complex, coordinated resources at the judicial, economic and social levels. But the significance of this process rules out any grounds for hesitation and scepticism.

Throughout that summer which stained Italian history, the dismay and desperation, the anger of people in Palermo were enormous. The very ordinariness of everyday life was cast in doubt. 'Somehow you have to go on doing the same things you always do: getting up, going to work, coping with road traffic, everyday life. But it's not the same everyday life as three days ago. People can't concentrate on work. You notice people in the traffic looking anxious, troubled, everyone wondering, asking themselves, probing: what can I do? what can we do?' recalls Marta Cimino, writing in *Mezzocielo*.

This time the state funerals were not followed by the usual curtain of silence. This time people waited, looked about, eager to stay on the streets, gathering in the squares, to be with others. 'What if we hung out sheets from our balconies with protests written on them? What if everybody "exposed" their own sense of outrage? I said this in the silence, in an undertone, speaking to myself at the meeting in the hall where our eyes were lowered on our shared grief rather than on the newspapers,' Marta went on.[23]

The idea of the sheets worked like a spark, a perfect intuitive correspondence with the mood of so many at that moment of emergency, of disordered collective ferment. It was a simple idea, a suggestion within everyone's scope and perfectly in keeping with the condition most people feel themselves to be in: alone, but yearning not to be so. The sheets talk to one another:

> I hung out my protest sheet from a balcony overlooking Via Marqueda and as I was knotting it to the railings I got to know Elisa, Cettina, Gabriella and Maria, students from Acquedolci. There were people on the balcony opposite mine looking at my sheet curiously, and we exchanged nods of understanding. This had never happened. Half an hour later they too hung out a sheet which had written on it *Falcone today. Who will it be tomorrow?* I was very moved, because this meant that the message, the sign, the need to abandon anonymity and take a small step forward was working and could spread.[24]

It was an invitation to be creative, enabling people to express themselves in their own way, and accessible to men and women, children and old people.

It didn't surprise me that Laura Miccicali did it – she studies pedagogy and is a primary school teacher; it did surprise me and it moved me that an 85-year-old aunt of mine who had in the past been a president of Catholic Action did it. 'I don't care whether they're called mafia or cut-throats,' she told me, 'I'm hanging out a sheet against these thugs who don't give us room to breathe. I want them all to know that they can't count on me! And I don't need anybody's permission to hang that sheet out!'[25]

A fine thread of belonging is formed between people united in a shared opposition. Marta Cimino told Enrico Deaglio that people displayed a vast range of reactions to the tiny inch-square sheet she had pinned to her blouse, with *Enough of the mafia* written on it:

It was a very useful and very instructive identification mark. . . . Once I went into a bar in a very mafia neighbourhood and I got dirty looks. At the cash desk there was an old woman who whispered to me, hardly moving a muscle: 'I pray for you people struggling for those of us who can't.' It is hard to imagine how strong the chains must be. . . . But you realize that there's a whole section of this city that lives under mafia rule and it has finally grasped that there are other ways possible. And it's asking you in the most rudimentary of terms to free it.[26]

Paolo, a university teacher, talked about his seven-year-old sons:

They too played a part in designing a big twelve-metre-long sheet that was spread over three floors on the outside of our building. They wanted to write: 'In memory of the mafia dead'. Then, they decided it would be more solemn to write: 'The mafia deceased'. They went along with other kids from the building to make up the big sheet in the playground of their primary school, where they could spread it out full-length. The school, the building, the playground, the street. For them society and institutions have taken on a post-mafia character. . . . You hear people saying that it won't be sheets that defeat the mafia. Of course not. But they will be imprinted on the collective memory of a generation now growing up. Those who spread them out to paint them in the school playground, those who saw them filmed on television and photographed in the newspapers.[27]

The Sheets Committee sprang up. Other forms of activism, scattered across the city, joined in. A diffuse civil resistance, from the workplace to the home, by way of streets and squares, found a voice and a means of expression. It was not a movement of women. Yet in its structures and forms of expression, and in its genesis it is closely linked to women's ways of thinking and acting; you can see in it the legacy of feminism. Giovanna Fiume said: 'Feminist awareness of the connection between individual women and wider history has since then become generalized; individuals, "militants on their own behalf", feel themselves equally bound to take on civil responsibilities, so that they are not represented by those who can wield strong powers within a weak civil society, those who in the South are mafiosi and outside institutions.'[28]

It is the *way* of relating to rebellion, to grief and to political and social perspectives on the future that characterizes the sheets movement, a way alert to concrete gestures, to the individuality of each and everyone and to communication between people. In this sense, even though it is not advanced only by women, it seems an expression of what Sara Ruddick has called 'maternal thinking': 'For me, "maternal" is a social category: although maternal thinking arises out of actual child-caring practices, biological parenting is neither necessary nor sufficient. Many women and some men express maternal thinking in various kinds of working and caring with others.'[29]

The sheet is first an object, then a symbol that belongs to the world of women. It reaches other women, and men with the courage not to fear their own feminine side, men who place themselves on the other side of the divide from mafia phallocracy.

> The creation of a symbol like this had to come from women, the reproducers of life, within the forest of symbols of death which crowd our everyday lives and in which we are as if 'lost'.... Mafia vocabulary and symbology abound in signs which allude, evoke, threaten, promise and magnify death. . . . The sheet is a symbol of the visibility of female difference and women have used it to effect a displacement of meaning and value: the shroud, which they have used to cover their dead, in a tender office historically reserved for women, becomes the flag of a new resistance for which there is no intention of surrendering responsibility, altering the sign, uncovering, affirming, 'in letters of fire' that are ironically hung from a clothes peg.[30]

The sheet can take on different meanings, according to who is using them to communicate, according to the message they want to convey, and according to the address of the message. One group of artists painted ten large sheets that were then exhibited. Franco said:

> Here the sheet, which in daily use embodies the meaning of covering up, has been taken over and had its symbolism reversed: it no longer covers but reveals, it is no longer a blank white, therefore not silent; it speaks or even screams. The struggle against the mafia has been passionately expressed through a plurality of interpretations out of which issue grief, indignation, hope and a horror of violence, all in a tumultuous flood of colours.[31]

Old household sheets won't do any more, we have to go and buy new ones. 'The shop assistant unrolls the cloth and tells us the price, but from the back of the shop the owner interjects: "A discount of thirty per cent for anti-mafia use," ' recalls Gabbi.[32]

Concrete gestures of solidarity, practical suggestions for giving everyone a sense of shared opposition to the mafia: these include a proposal to display photos of important long-time mafia fugitives in all public buildings, a proposal to leave untouched the crater blown out of the motorway until the hitmen and those who sent them are tried and sentenced; a proposal to toll all the bells in the city in mourning on the anniversary of the killings, and to offer gestures of friendship towards the army 'sent to Sicily to struggle with us against the mafia. We suggest that families might invite the soldiers for an ice cream, a pizza, for lunch at home.' Then there are the 'nine pieces of uncompromising advice for the citizen who wants to fight the mafia', ranging from how to bring up children to contacts with institutions and services and political voting, printed on leaflets and circulated.

Since the authorities, yet again, kept quiet, it was ARCI* that printed forty thousand posters with photos of the most important wanted men to be put up in all the localities.

The Cartello di Palermo came into being with the by no means easy task of coordinating the efforts of the voluntary anti-mafia movement. Weeks of great collective excitement were followed by a human chain, a demonstration by a hundred thousand people who had come from all parts of the country.

> What those taking part in the demonstration were most struck by was the exhibition of sheets with anti-mafia slogans. . . . This 'sign' in Palermo stood for something very powerful, the people of the mafia capital expressing its own anger, *the sign becoming a symbol*. This symbol wasn't a flag or a party logo, no sickles or crosses, no party colours or flower emblems, the sheet symbol was a blank space, and everyone turned it into something personal, expressing what they felt, without paying any advertising charges, without any leaders or sponsors.[33]

But here I feel it is important to remember that what came out of the enthusiasm of that moment in 1992, what came to be known as 'Year I of the anti-mafia movement', though certainly an important shift in awareness of the danger of the mafia, was not new as a movement. As recent history shows, it was extremely hard to coordinate the diverse efforts of the struggle against the mafia,[34] and Falcone himself had had bitter experience of this. Moreover, in the long term the strength of a movement is measured by its

---

* ARCI, Associazione Ricreativa Culturale Italiana, a national leisure and cultural organization established by the former Italian Communist Party. [Trs.]

capacity to engender acts of practical solidarity which are tangible and well-defined and which can then take on a potent symbolic value. A previous example is the help given to 'ordinary' women who have acted as plaintiffs in the big trials against the mafia. It is therefore to be hoped that the 'Year I' Movement continues to give the present and future struggle maximum impact and range.

On 19 July 1992 that climate of mobilization and civil solidarity was violently shaken by the second slaughter of the summer. The demonstrations of those particular days have already entered history. Gabbi recalled:

> We discovered less than two months later that we didn't count for much, since the Via D'Amelio killings were planned and carried out in the same city that was spanned by the human chain. That courage and that remarkable strength I was talking about were swept away by dynamite. Then, when the wreckage was gathered up, another more desperate form of courage was reinvented. You see why I think of the human chain as a dream or a childhood memory.[35]

. . . And the fast

'Another, more desperate, form of courage': by upping the ferocity of its intimidation in the Via D'Amelio killings, the mafia thought yet again that it could rely on the resignation of the majority and the complicity of a significant proportion of the institutions. Yet, as never before, it found it had a vast section of the population against it.

In the immediate wake of the massacre of 19 July 1992 women were able to draw around them a form of radical resistance to match the situation, using an exceptional means of protest to stress the extremity which civil coexistence had reached. Simone wrote:

> From a distance I can see the silhouettes of women friends moving about around a small table, lifting the trestles. I am overwhelmed by a feeling of tenderness and love. Dear, dear women. So unrealistic, so improvident and unpredictable, so stubborn. Their desperation is of a different kind from men's to start with. There is no leader, no secretary, just friends and then the rest. Between the women there is a constant sense of egalitarianism, of interchangeableness ('I started, why don't you finish', 'take my place for a minute', 'you go on'), of being a linked circle reaching out to strangers. It is the steel chain of a virtually unbeatable unanimous resistance.[36]

We read in a 'Manifesto for Rebel Citizens', signed by The Fasting Women:

It suits the plans of the killers and those who sent them, those who connive with them and are complicit, those who are indifferent and incompetent, to be on people's minds when they are vacant in the torpor of August. And later, as usual, the time will come for forgetting and putting up with things. Grief and loneliness, disarmed and impotent rage will weigh only on those who have loved, on those who can never find anything to justify so much suffering. We say: *It is unjust*, this time it won't happen.

The Fasting Women was a group that came into being on the evening of 21 July, after the funeral of the bodyguards, when the friction between the population of Palermo and those in power had reached its worst. 'It was soldiers from the Veneto, from Emilia and Valle d'Aosta who had been put in place as a human barrier with rifles aimed to shut out the ordinary people of Palermo from the ceremony commemorating the dead. Beneath a burning sky, their uncontainable fury exploded,' Simona recalls.[37] Bice Mortillaro Salatiello wrote: 'What we did primarily was give some meaning to our emotions, so as to understand and communicate, even if just with our eyes, in the middle of the crowd at the funeral of the bodyguards on 22 July, where we gathered . . .'[38]

The following day a press release announced:

> *This afternoon there will be a meeting in Piazza Castelnuovo to announce the start of a hunger strike we are undertaking as women citizens of Palermo who do not belong to any parties or associations. The strike will go on until resignations are offered by Prefect Jovine, Chief of Police Parisi, Prosecutor Giammanco, Senior Anti-mafia Commissioner Finocchiaro and Interior Minister Mancino.*
>
> *We know that this is just the start, but the extreme nature of the situation, the responsibilities of the power system which has governed us for more than forty-five years and the rituals which follow every murder while waiting for the next victim call for weighty and significant action.*
>
> *Our minimum demand is that those who occupy institutional roles should finally assume appropriate responsibility.*
>
> *This is the only course we feel we can take.*
>
> *We want to go on living in this city.*
>
> *We will welcome anyone who wants to join our strike in Piazza Castelnuovo beginning this afternoon.*

The argument is clear and straightforward, without rhetoric and conscious that the extreme situation requires a radical response, something that can convey the enormity of people's rage and dismay and disaffection.

'We – the fasting women – have therefore given substance where there was neither substantial nor symbolic opposition; there was neither the substance of state bodies, nor of flesh and blood bodies: the summer threatened to swallow us all up. . . . And we were instead quite visible. Visible against the symbolic invisibility of the mafia.'[39]

> We explained to a journalist from the *Boston Globe* that the fast is a form of struggle which has no place in the history of the women's movement in Italy but it means that we become present once again through our bodies. The fast is a sign of cleanness, of transparency for the sake of saving energy. It is a sign of immediate opposition to violence and to the enormous, gargantuan greed of the clans, to tyrannical, life-crushing behaviour. Nor is it just a metaphor for our hunger for justice and truth. Through this symbolic order which is apparent in the very heart of a city like Palermo, where the symbol still matters very much, we feel more confident about what we are doing and that they cannot corrupt us.[40]

The fast staged the spectacle of the women's absolute presence there as a group, each with her own body: a clear and powerful way of saying no, a way too of relating to the agony of the bodies torn apart by the bombs; the imperative of not deserting them and of being close to the relatives of these victims. A powerful feeling bound the fasting women together, a feeling communicated to all those who passed through Piazza Politeama that August. Simona wrote: 'Taking three days out of my life and placing them in this square; being part of this great collective lay penance of not eating, in memory of those who are no more and who can neither eat, nor walk, nor look at things; to transform my body which is mine and mine alone to dispose, into a tool of non-violent protest which is silent but louder than any shout.'[41]

Angela explained:

> I had no hesitation about it. I said to myself: I don't want anything to do with these people, I've finished with these Sicilians! And so I cut myself off from nourishment, which is the most important connection with others, because I don't want to have anything to do with mafia people. I felt that my body needed transparency, that I had to keep it away from all of that befouled situation . . . it is as if we had said that we didn't want to take on either the role of mothers or of women in a world that is not right. We no longer want to go along with it and so we remove ourselves from this shitty situation . . . for me it was an affirmation, not a negation.[42]

The message went straight to the hearts of those who had been directly stricken by the massacres; Piazza Politeama became a place where people could be comforted, people like the relatives of Emanuela Loi, who had come from Sardinia, and her friend Maria. ' "I am Maria, Manù's best friend. . . . I was expecting her, she had called me to say that she would finish her shift around seven. . . . You have no idea, I'm on my way back from there now. I keep finding pieces of Manuela's body. Thank you, your being here gives me a lot of strength!" We gather close around her and stroke her hair, her face and her hands.'[43] On the first anniversary of the massacre some of the fasting women went to visit Emanuela Loi's parents in Sardinia. The Tirrenia Line ferry they took from Palermo to Cagliari displayed a huge banner in memory of Emanuela.

Maria Dos Santos was there, the partner of Claudio Traino, his brother, Luciano, and Vito Schifani's mother, the parents of the police officer, Antonino Agostino, killed three years earlier, along with the parents of his young wife who had also been killed. Pina Maisano Grassi was there, Michela Buscemi was there and at the final demonstration on 23 May she read out her poems in Sicilian dialect.

One purpose of the fast was to give a collective sense to the private mourning of these people, as Piera recalled: 'It was a revolt against the fact that the grief of those who had loved these people who keep on dying in this city . . . should be a burden borne only by the relatives. I can't accept that people die for some collective idea of justice, rights and truth, and that this death then turns into something private, so private that it ceases to be a death with the right to justice.'[44]

Rita Borsellino, the sister of the murdered judge, emphasized the importance of the vigil in Piazza Politeama:

And I had turned my back on newspapers and TV because I didn't want to keep up with the news, yet instinctively I stopped in front of that poster and read it. It had a big effect on me. It touched a nerve in me and I decided that I too had to do something. . . . I was more or less stunned by my brother's death, I felt everything had disintegrated, as if there was nothing more that could be done, and yet at that moment I realized that something different had to start. What you were calling for, that peremptory demand for the resignations of those people, made me realize that this could actually be a point of departure, as if this was where something could be started with a new strength, and I felt that I had to do something too.[45]

Despite its obvious association with a pacifist tradition, the women's fast did not take on what one might call the 'classic' meaning or convey any threat akin to the extended hunger strike. Angela explained: 'Gandhi's hunger strike contained a moral blackmail: "My death will be your responsibility." But the fast never had this meaning for any of us; each of us fasted for three days and it never occurred to any of us to fast indefinitely. We were testifying to our wish to abstain from this society which produces such bestial slaughter. We are not going along with it, that's what our fast said.'[46]

However, it is interesting that men often reacted to the fast with feelings of being threatened by this deep-seated symbolic act of rejection. 'Some of the men viewed us with apprehension. One woman's fiancé, for instance, was terribly distressed and took it really badly. He didn't take his eyes off her. When she was a little bit unwell on the last day of her fast, he got really upset . . .'[47] The men who came regularly to the square usually showed respect and admiration, but they seemed disoriented by such an unprecedented political practice. With only a few exceptions, they did not take part in the fasts. 'When all is said and done their attitude was devoted and helpful, although to start with we had to reject some pushy attempts to impose political alignments on us,' recalled Bice.[48]

They were all appalled by Rita Atria's suicide. Later, it was they, 'the fasting women', who carried Rita's coffin into the little cemetery, along with Michela Buscemi and Letizia Battaglia from the Association of Sicilian Women against the Mafia and the women of Partanna. 'The fasting women walk through the silent desert of Partanna. What we did in Piazza Politeama is effective precisely inasmuch as people recognize it to be. It was an action radiating meaning. Here too behind the lowered blinds the quality of our action is measured.'[49]

With its caravan, tents and banners, beneath the emblem *I'm hungry for justice — fast against the mafia*, Piazza Politeama took on a significance beyond any demonstration or protest action. It was not just a square now, it was almost a country. People went in and out of the square almost as if it was a house. Simona said:

> And so in this undefined space, which is neither campsite nor public meeting, neither house nor street, the miracle of trust blossoms inside the caravan from one little bed to another amid a solitude that is only apparent. This sometimes happens on night train journeys, or in waiting rooms at hospitals; it happened during the war, among trainloads of evacuees and in shelters; it has happened countless times over centuries and millennia; an encounter between women, free of suspicions or ulterior motives; mutual trust, friendship against the ghastliness of the world and in the hope of changing it.[50]

A lot of people spent hours on end there, talking, painting their sheets, leaving one another messages. One woman left the following note: 'I'm giving you a citizen's advice. Arrest the wives of the fugitives. Remember that they have killed the wives of other men, Signora Falcone to start with. No more demonstrations but concrete action.' As an ironic comment on the awkwardness of contacts with the media, over the mid-August holiday the statues in the square were covered in newspapers; a way of stimulating discussion among the people of Palermo. Thousands of signatures were collected, with full names and addresses given. People were speaking out on a huge scale in a milieu accustomed to silence and *omertà*. 'If we can't trust people any more, if we can't talk any more because we don't know "who" we are talking to, then our banners and tables and tents and petition forms which are so important to everyone who has signed, are our contribution to making this city become real.'[51]

Journalists come and go, tourists, trade union and party representatives, ordinary people. It was a vast work in progress, as Luisa put it. People met who had never met before. 'I fasted for three days. I'd never have thought I'd be able to fast for three days, but I managed it because I really had so much anger I wanted to express, and my grief for what had happened, because I felt deeply wounded,' said one woman.[52] Daniela's memory is this: 'One night, a woman arrived all hot and sweating – she had run from the Capo, which is a market in the centre of old Palermo, with a carrier bag, probably with washing things in it, saying she wanted to spend the night with us and fast the next day.'[53]

None the less, this particular woman was an exception; the high-risk mafia neighbourhoods, the run-down districts of the city centre and the periphery were usually empty of any demonstrations against the mafia, even the acts of the 'new resistance'.

The movement of that Palermo summer spontaneously gave rise to a number of powerful symbols. The *Falcone Tree*, the tall ficus outside the judge's home in Via Notarbartolo, the *Olive of Peace*, which was planted in the bomb crater at Via D'Amelio, dedicated to Paolo Borsellino. On the first anniversary of the Capaci massacre, in May 1993, the 'fasting women' built a *Peace Tree*, with the leaves taped with ribbon for people to write messages on or just to sign. On 19 July, the anniversary of the Via D'Amelio massacre, they sent the tree, along with a letter, to the Chief Prosecutor Caselli. The women wrote: 'If you agree, we would like to entrust it to you, as a sign of our esteem and solidarity, and as a mark of the combined work of so many women who are committed to freeing themselves and freeing this city.'

This gesture encapsulates an enormous change between Palermo citizens, and one of the foremost representatives of the institutions. Caselli's reply is a further demonstration of it: 'I will carry with me the photograph that shows a little girl at the foot of the tree, a hope for our best future.'[54]

I have no concluding words. I am exhausted and emotionally fraught at the end of this involving journey through the good and evil in our present. I have spent sleepless nights, had nightmares, wept. To come close to so much suffering, even if 'only' through the written word, has enriched me and at the same time devoured my energies. I thank with all my heart all the women who are present in this book.

I want to end with some verses by Beatrice Monroy.[55]

Se solamente potessi separare
la mia vita da quella di quelli
che uccidono.
Se io potessi escluderli per
sempre dalla mia vita, dalla
mia memoria, dalla memoria
della gente che come me cerca
disperatamente solamente
un po' di libertà per vivere
e per respirare.
Un po' siamo colpevoli.
Le lacrime servono a poco.
La strada vera la conosciamo bene.
Ogni giorno un'attesa
ogni giorno aspettiamo
un dolore nuovo
e quand'esso arriva
non è novità terribile.
Ce l'aspettavamo . . .
La gente attorno a me muore
Pazza di morte.
Non c'è più tempo. Anch'io
sono invasa dalla pestilenza
Non c'è più scampo
Che scampo vuoi che ci sia
quando gli amici i parenti
i conoscenti muoiono uno ad
uno trascinati nel pestifero gorgo?
Salvaci, ma chi?
Salvateci, ma chi?
*Salviamoci.**

---

* (If I could only separate my life from the life of those who kill. If I could lock them out for ever from my life, from my memory, from the memory of people who search like me in desperation for some freedom to live and breathe. We are a little bit to blame. Tears are not much help. We know the true road well enough. Waiting every day, every day we wait for some new grief and when it comes it's no new shock. We expected it. . . . People around me die crazy from death. There's no more time. I too am plague-stricken. There's no escape. What escape can there be when friends family acquaintances die one by one dragged into the vortex of plague? Someone to save us, but who will it be? People to save us, but who will they be? Let us save ourselves.)

Notes

Introduction

1 Nando Dalla Chiesa, *Storie*, Einaudi, Turin 1990, p. ix.

2 Angela Lanza, 'Un sonno interrotto', in *Nosside*, no. 6, 1992, p. 35.

3 Leonardo Sciascia, *A futura memoria*, Bompiani, Milan 1989, p. 109.

4 *Mezzocielo*, July 1993.

5 Carol Gilligan, *In a Different Voice*, Harvard University Press, Cambridge, Mass., 1982, p. 129.

6 Giovanni Falcone and Marcelle Padovani, *Cose di Cosa Nostra*, Rizzoli, Milan 1991, p. 154.

7 Donald W. Winnicott, *The Family and Individual Development*, Tavistock, London 1965, p. 83.

8 Diego Gambetta, *La mafia siciliana*, Einaudi, Turin 1992, p. 170.

9 Parliamentary Anti-mafia Commission, 'Mafia e politica', *La Repubblica*, supplement, 10 April 1993, p. iii.

10 Fabrizio Calvi, *La vita quotidiana della mafia dal 1950 a oggi*, Rizzoli, Milan 1986, p. 75.

11 Filippo Di Forti, *Per una psicoanalisi della mafia*, Bertani, Verona 1982, p. 172.

1 A Men-only Society

1 Georg Simmel, 'Il segreto e la società segreta', in *Sociologia*, Edizione de Comunita, Milan 1989, p. 310.

2 Ibid., p. 323.

3 Elisabeth Badinter, *XY de l'identité masculine*, Editions Odile Jacob, Paris 1992, pp. 14, 15.

4 Giuseppe Casarrubea and Pia Blandano, *L'educazione mafiosa*, Sellerio, Palermo 1991, p. 103.

5 Badinter, p. 18.

6 Giovanni Falcone and Marcelle Padovani, *Cose di Cosa Nostra*, Rizzoli, Milan 1991, pp. 99–100.

7   Pino Arlacchi, *Gli uomini del disonore*, Mondadori, Milan 1992, pp. 5–7.

8   Pantaleone Sergi, *La 'santa' violenta*, Periferia, Cosenza 1991, p. 64.

9   Parliamentary Anti-mafia Commission, 'Mafia e potere', *L'Unità*, supplement, 15 April 1993.

10   In Arlacchi, p. 149.

11   Casarrubea and Blandano, p. 131.

12   Francis A. J. Ianni, *A Family Business: Kinship and Social Control in Organized Crime*, Russell Sage Foundation, New York 1972, p. 84.

13   Anonymous, *Uomo di rispetto*, Mondadori, Milan 1990, p. 97.

14   Diego Gambetta, *La mafia siciliana*, Einaudi, Turin 1992, pp. 210, 213, 215.

15   Falcone and Padovani, p. 97.

16   Ibid., p. 98.

17   Filippo Di Forti, *Per una psicoanalisi della mafia*, Bertani, Verona 1982, p. 18.

18   Badinter, p. 126.

19   Enzo Ciconte, *'Ndrangheta dall'Unità ad oggi*, Laterza, Bari 1992, p. 37.

20   Ibid., p. 31.

21   Calderone, in Arlacchi, p. 5.

22   Gambetta, p. 348.

23   Preface to Fabrizio Calvi, *La vita quotidiana della mafia dal 1950 a oggi*, Milan, Rizzoli 1986, p. 10.

24   Arlacchi, pp. 196–7.

25   Ibid., p. 248.

26   Anonymous, p. 24.

27   Jane Schneider and Peter Schneider, *Culture and Political Economy in Western Sicily*, Academic Press, New York 1976, pp. 105, 107.

28   Joseph Bonanno with Sergio Lalli, *A Man of Honour*, Unwin, London 1984, p. 167.

29   Calvi, p. 113.

30   Schneider and Schneider, p. 105.

31   Luigi M. Satriani Lombardo, 'Stratificazione sociale dinamica culturale e mafia nel Mezzogiorno contemporaneo', in Saverio di Bella (ed.), *Mafia e potere: società civile, organizzazione mafiosa ed esercizio dei poteri nel Mezzogiorno contemporaneo, atti convegno internazionale*, 2 vols, Rubbettino, Saveria Mannelli 1983, p. 209.

32   Falcone and Padovani, p. 28.

33   Ibid., p. 26.

34   Ianni, p. 10.

35   *Corriere della Sera*, 10 January 1993.

36   Anonymous, p. 212.

37   Antonio Zagari, *Ammazzare stanca*, Periferia, Cosenza 1992, p. 62.

38   Giorgio Bocca, *L'inferno*, Mondadori, Milan 1992, p. 31.

39 Marzano, in Luigi M. Lombardi Satriani, 'Faidè, perchè?', *Quaderni del Mezzogiorno e delle Isole*, X, no. 26, 1977, p. 55.

40 Falcone and Padovani, p. 27.

41 Zagari, p. 43.

42 Badinter, p. 79.

43 Ibid., p. 85.

44 Victor J. Seidler, *Rediscovering Masculinity – Reason, Language and Sexuality*, Routledge, London 1989, p. 157.

45 Jessica Benjamin, *The Bonds of Love*, Pantheon and Virago, New York and London 1988, 1990, pp. 75–6.

46 Ibid., p. 76.

47 Falcone and Padovani, p. 79.

48 *La Stampa*, 21 November 1992.

49 Seidler, pp. 7, 4.

50 Badinter, p. 75.

51 Ianni, p. 44.

52 Bonanno, pp. 171, 172.

53 Theodor W. Adorno, *Minima Moralia*, trans. E.F.N. Jephcott, Verso, London 1974, pp. 45–6.

54 Bonanno, p. 271.

55 Di Forti, pp. 45, 55, 115.

56 Anonymous, p. 233.

57 Bonanno, p. 95.

58 Leonardo Sciascia, *Il giorno della civetta*, Einaudi, Turin 1972 (translated as *The Day of the Owl*), p. 118.

59 Luigi M. Lombardi Satriani, 'Sulla cultura mafiosa e gli immediati dintorni', *Quaderni del Mezzogiorno e delle Isole*, XLIV, no. 42–3, 1977, p. 57.

60 Di Forti, p. 56.

61 Ibid., p. 45.

62 Ibid., p. 56.

2 *The Family*

1 Amelia Crisantino and Giovanni La Fiura, *La mafia come metodo e come sistema*, Pellegrini, Cosenza 1989, p. 121.

2 Diego Gambetta, *La mafia siciliana*, Einaudi, Turin 1992, p. 368.

3 Enzo Biagi, *Il boss è solo*, Mondadori, Milan 1990, p. 94.

4 From the FBI tape recording of an initiation ritual in Gambetta, p. 372.

5 Pino Arlacchi, *Gli uomini del disonore*, Mondadori, Milan 1992, p. 157.

6 Corrado Stajano, *Mafia – L'atto d'accuso dei giudici di Palermo*, Editori Riuniti, Rome 1992, p. 33.

7 Marcelle Padovani, *Les dernières années de la mafia*, Gallimard, Paris 1987, p. 66.

NOTES TO PAGES 29–37

8 Enzo Ciconte, *'Ndrangheta dall'Unità ad oggi*, Laterza, Bari 1992, p. 223.

9 Victor J. Seidler, *Rediscovering Masculinity – Reason, Language and Sexuality*, Routledge, London 1989, pp. 13, 18.

10 Giorgio Chinnici and Umberto Santini, *La violenza programmata*, Franco Angeli, Milan 1991, pp. 291–2.

11 Giovanni Falcone and Marcelle Padovani, *Cose di Cosa Nostra*, Rizzoli, Milan 1991, p. 31.

12 *La Repubblica*, 10–11 January 1993.

13 Salvatore Lupo, *Storia della mafia*, Donzelli, Rome 1993, p. 13.

14 Renate Siebert, *'È femmina, però è belle' – Tre generazioni di donne al Sud*, Rosenberg & Sellier, Turin 1991, Part 3.

15 Falcone and Padovani, p. 94.

16 Leonardo Sciascia, *Il giorno della civetta*, Einaudi, Turin 1972 (translated as *The Day of the Owl*), p. 110.

17 Pino Arlacchi, *Mafia Business* (trans. Martin Ryle), Verso, London 1987, p. 27.

18 Stajano, p. 43.

19 Luciano Violante, 'I corleonesi', *L'Unità*, supplement, 11 September 1993.

20 Parliamentary Anti-mafia Commission, 'Mafia e politica', *La Repubblica*, supplement, 10 April 1993, p. 7.

21 Georg Simmel, 'Il segreto e la società segreta', *Sociologia*, Edizione de Comunita, Milan 1989, p. 340.

22 Francis A. J. Ianni, *A Family Business: Kinship and Social Control in Organized Crime*, Russell Sage Foundation, New York 1972, p. 165.

23 Falcone and Padovani, p. 59.

24 Ibid., p. 58.

25 Stajano, p. 44.

26 Falcone and Padovani, p. 61.

27 Jane Schneider, 'Of vigilance and virgins', *Ethnology*, vol. 10, no. 1, 1971, p. 22.

28 John Davis, *People of the Mediterranean*, Routledge & Kegan Paul, London 1977, p. 98.

29 Ibid., p. 99.

30 Maria Pia Di Bella, 'L'onore in Sicilia e l'onore nella mafia. Convergenza e divergenza', in Saverio Di Bella (ed.), *Mafia e potere: società civile, organizzazione mafiosa ed esercizio dei poteri nel Mezzogiorno contemporaneo, atti convegno internazionale*, 2 vols, Rubbettino, Soveria Mannelli 1983, p. 235.

31 Ibid., p. 234.

32 Pezzino 1987, p. 243.

33 Schneider, p. 21.

34 Seidler, p. 102.

35   Franz Neumann, *The Democratic and the Authoritarian State*, The Free Press of Glencoe and Collier-Macmillan, London 1957, p. 274.

36   Schneider, p. 20.

37   Di Bella, p. 235.

38   Schneider, p. 22.

39   Luigi M. Lombardi Satriani and Mariano Meligrana, 'Il ruolo della donna mafia', *Quaderni del Mezzogiorno e delle Isole*, XIV, 1977, p. 325.

40   Ibid., p. 336.

41   Mariano Meligrana, 'Giuridicità popolare e potere mafioso. L'istituto della vendetta', in Saverio Di Bella, p. 346.

42   Luigi M. Lombardi Satriani and Mariano Meligrana, *Il ponte di San Giacome – L'ideologia della morte nella società contadina del Sud*, Rizzoli, Milan 1982, p. 346.

43   *Corriere della Sera*, 8 March 1993.

44   Meligrana, p. 245.

45   Anonymous, *Uomo di rispetto*, Mondadori, Milan 1990, p. 172.

46   Luigi M. Lombardi Satriani, 'Sulla culture mafiosa e gli immediati dintorni', *Quaderni del Mezzogiorno e delle Isole*, XIV, no. 42–3, 1977, p. 56.

47   Lombardi Satriani and Meligrana, 1982, p. 342.

48   Ibid.

49   Nick Gentile, *Vita di capomafia*, Editori Riuniti, Rome 1963, p. 91.

50   Joseph Bonanno with Sergio Lalli, *A Man of Honour*, Unwin, London 1984, p. 41.

51   Cf. Renate Siebert, *Le ali de un elefante – Sul rapporto adulti bambini in un paese della Calabria*, Franco Angeli, Milan 1984.

52   Pantaleone Sergi, *La 'santa' violenta*, Periferia, Cosenza 1991, pp. 123–4.

53   *La Repubblica*, 5 February 1993.

54   Arlacchi, 1992, p. 293.

55   Parliamentary Anti-mafia Commission, 'Mafia e potere', *L'Unità*, supplement, 15 April 1993.

56   Gay Talese, *Honour Thy Father*, Sphere, London 1972.

57   Giuseppe Casarrubea and Pia Blandano, *L'educazione mafiosa*, Sellerio, Palermo 1991, pp. 132, 138.

58   Calderone in Arlacchi, 1992, p. 7.

59   Bonanno, pp. 22, 35.

60   Gambetta, p. 51.

61   Arlacchi, 1987, p. 137.

62   Arlacchi, 1992, p. 126.

63   Arlacchi, 1987, p. 140.

64   Vera Pegna, *Tempo di lupi e di comunisti*, La Luna, Palermo 1992, pp. 52–3.

65   Umberto Santini (ed.), *L'antimafia difficile*, csd, Palermo 1989, p. 11.

66 Anna Puglisi and Umberto Santino, Preface to Felicia Bartolotta Impastato, *La mafia in case mia*, La Luna, Palermo 1987, p. 5.

67 Santino, p. 12.

68 Bartolotta Impastato, p. 8.

69 Bonanno, p. 187.

70 Talese, p. 11.

71 Bonanno pp. 289–90.

72 Sciascia, pp. 114–15.

73 Biagi, p. 77.

74 Arlacchi, 1992, p. 292.

3 Women

1 Diego Gambetta *La mafia siciliana*, Einaudi, Turin 1992, p. 165.

2 Pino Arlacchi, *Gli uomini del disonore*, Mondadori, Milan 1992, p. 56.

3 Nick Gentile, *Vita di capomafia*, Editori Riuniti, Rome 1963, p. 153.

4 Joseph Bonanno with Sergio Lalli, *A Man of Honour*, Unwin, London 1984, pp. 142, 311, 312.

5 Ibid., p. 389.

6 Ibid., p. 154.

7 Antonio Zagari, *Ammazzare stanca*, Periferia, Cosenza 1992, p. 119.

8 Ibid., p. 89.

9 Ibid., p. 11.

10 Ibid., p. 34.

11 Enzo Ciconte, *'Ndrangheta dall'Unità ad oggi*, Laterza, Bari 1992, p. 17.

12 Ibid., p. 87.

13 Arlacchi, p. 102.

14 Giovanni Falcone and Marcelle Padovani, *Cose di Cosa Nostra*, Rizzoli, Milan 1991, p. 76.

15 Cf. Klaus Thelweit, *Male Fantasies*, 2 vols, Polity Press, Cambridge 1987.

16 Filippo Di Forti, *Per una psicoanalisi della mafia*, Bertani, Verona 1982, p. 50.

17 Zagari, p. 49.

18 Leonardo Sciascia, *La Sicilia come metafora*, Mondadori, Milan 1979, p. 42.

19 Falcone and Padovani, p. 78.

20 Ibid., p. 76.

21 Gambetta, p. 165.

22 Zagari, p. 83.

23 Di Forti, p. 52.

24 Anonymous, *Uomo di rispetto*, Mondadori, Milan 1990, p. 49.

25 Luigi M. Lombardi Satriani, 'Sulla culture mafiosa e gli immediati

dintorni', *Quaderni del Mezzogiorno e delle Isole*, XIV, 1977, p 53.

26 Gianfranco Manfredi, *Il Messaggero*, 10 June 1993.

27 Giovanni Falcone, 'La mafia, tra criminalità e cultura', *Meridiana*, no. 5, 1989, p. 206.

28 Arlacchi, p. 165.

29 Gambetta, p. 168.

30 Arlacchi, pp. 167–8.

31 Anonymous, p. 128.

32 Ibid., p. 112.

33 Anton Blok, *The Mafia of the Sicilian Village, 1860–1960*, Basil Blackwell, Oxford 1974, p. 183.

34 Calderone, in Arlacchi, p. 166.

35 Elizabeth Badinter, *XY de l'identité masculine*, Editions Odile Jacob, Paris 1992, p. 177.

36 Ibid., p. 157.

37 Sciascia, p. 14.

38 Renate Siebert, 'Le sud des femmes: potentialités, intérêts, désirs', *Peuples Méditerranéens*, 'Femmes et Pouvoir', no. 48–9, 1989.

39 Sciascia, p. 74.

40 Falcone and Padovani, p. 76.

41 Jessica Benjamin, *The Bonds of Love*, Pantheon and Virago, New York and London, 1988, 1990, p. 78.

42 Renate Siebert, *'È femmina, però è belle' – Tre generazioni di donne al Sud*, Rosenberg & Sellier, Turin 1991, pp. 331–7.

43 Angela Lanza, 'Visibilità e invisibilità delle "donne del digiuno"', *Nosside*, no. 7–8, 1993, p. 106.

44 Zagari, p. 89.

45 Sciascia, p. 41.

46 Erich Fromm, *The Heart of Man*, Routledge & Kegan Paul, London 1965, pp. 98–9.

47 Di Forti, p. 117.

48 Ibid., pp. 180–1.

4 Death

1 Herbert Marcuse, *Eros and Civilisation*, Ark, London 1987, pp. 235–6.

2 Heinrich Popitz, *Fenomenologia del potere*, Il Mulino, Bologna 1990, p. 65.

3 Salvatore Lupo, *Storia della mafia*, Donzelli, Rome 1993, p. 232.

4 Librerie Associate, *Mafia – Anatomia di un regime*, Rome 1992, p. 94.

5 Enrico Deaglio, *Raccolto rosso*, Feltrinelli, Milan 1993, p. 67.

6 Pino Arlacchi, *Gli uomini del disonore*, Mondadori, Milan 1992, p. 200.

7 Franz Neumann, *The Democratic and the Authoritarian State*, The Free

Fress of Glencoe and Collier-Macmillan, London 1957, p. 270.

8   Saverio Abbruzzese, 'La paura', in Franco Occhiogrosso (ed.), *Ragazzi della mafia*, Franco Angeli, Milan 1993, p. 205.

9   Herbert Marcuse, 'The Ideology of Death', in Herman Feifel (ed.), *The Meaning of Death*, McGraw Hill, New York 1959, pp. 71, 74.

10   Popitz, p. 65.

11   Arlacchi, pp. 26, 58.

12   Filippo Di Forti, *Per una psicoanalisi della mafia*, Bertani, Verona 1982, p. 107.

13   Elias Canetti, *Potere e sopravvivenza*, Adelphi, Milan 1974, p. 13.

14   Enzo Biagi, *Il boss è solo*, Mondadori, Milan 1990, p. 182.

15   Canetti, pp. 14, 25.

16   Giorgio Chinnici and Umberto Santino, *La violenza programmata*, Franco Angeli, Milan 1991, p. 195.

17   Giorgio Bocca, *L'inferno*, Mondadori, Milan 1992, p. 182.

18   Giovanni Falcone and Marcelle Padovani, *Cose di Cosa Nostra*, Rizzoli, Milan 1991, p. 30.

19   Popitz, p. 71.

20   Parliamentary Anti-mafia Commission, 'Mafia e potere', *L'Unità*, supplement, 15 April 1993, p. 78.

21   Chinnici and Santino, p. 319.

22   Salvatore Lupo and Rosario Mangiameli, 'Mafia di ieri e mafia di oggi', *Meridiana*, no. 7–8, 1990, p. 34.

23   Fabrizio Calvi, *La vita quotidiana della mafia dal 1950 a oggi*, Rizzoli, Milan 1986, p. 276.

24   Popitz, p. 73.

25   Arlacchi, p. 220.

26   Anonimo del XX Secolo, *Una modesta proposta per pacificare la città di Palermo*, Qualecultura, Vibo Valentia 1984, pp. 52–3.

27   Giovanni Falcone, 'La mafia, tra criminalità e cultura', *Meridiana*, no. 5, 1989.

28   Pino Arlacchi, *Mafia Business*, trans. Martin Ryle, Verso, London 1987, pp. 152–3.

29   Antonio Zagari, *Ammazzare stanca*, Periferia, Cosenza 1992, p. 98.

30   Di Forti, p. 23.

31   Chinnici and Santino, p. 194.

32   Corrado Stajano, *Mafia – L'atto d'accusa dei giudici di Palermo*, Editori Riuniti, Rome 1992, pp. xiv–xv.

33   Petra Bonavita, *Donna Sicilia*, Centaurus, Pfaffenweiler 1993, p. 57.

34   Erich Fromm, *The Heart of Man*, Routledge & Kegan Paul, London 1965, p. 40.

35   Falcone and Padovani, p. 72.

36   Di Forti, p. 50.

37 Anonymous, *Uomo di rispetto*, Mondadori, Milan 1990, p. 117.
38 Arlacchi, 1992, p. 286.
39 Librerie Associate, p. 29.
40 Arlacchi, 1992, p. 308.
41 Canetti, 1974, p. 25.
42 Di Forti, p. 58.
43 Chinnici and Santino, p. 255.
44 Arlacchi, 1992, p. 307.
45 Nick Gentile, *Vita di capomafia*, Editori Riuniti, Rome 1963, p. 144.
46 Giovanna Fiume, 'Ci sono donne nella mafia?', *Meridiana*, no. 7–8, 1990, pp. 296–7.
47 Arlacchi, 1987, p. 158.
48 Bocca, p. 185.
49 Giuseppe Casarrubea and Pia Blandano, *L'educazione mafiosa*, Sellerio, Palermo 1991, p. 73.
50 Marcuse, 1987, p. 236.
51 Di Forti, p. 108.
52 Stajano, p. 71.
53 Zagari, p. 52.
54 Arlacchi, 1992, pp. 159–60.
55 Chinnici and Santino, pp. 325–6.
56 Ibid., p. 200.
57 Antonino Caponnetto, *I miei giorni a Palermo*, Garzanti, Milan 1992, p. 59.
58 Arlacchi, 1992, pp. 91–2.
59 Stajano, p. ix.
60 Canetti, pp. 22–3.
61 Caponnetto, pp. 61, 62.
62 Arlacchi, 1992, p. 149; my italics.
63 Amelia Crisantino and Giovanni La Fiura, *La mafia come metodo e come sistema*, Pellegrini, Cosenza 1989, p. 114.
64 Hannah Arendt, 'Eichmann in Jerusalem' (exchange of letters between Hannah Arendt and Gershom Scholem), *Encounter*, January 1964, p. 56.
65 Max Weber, 'Politics as a vocation', in H. H. Gerth and C. Wright Mills, *From Max Weber*, Kegan Paul, Trench, Trubner & Co., London 1947, p. 117.
66 Hannah Arendt, *Eichmann in Jerusalem*, Penguin, Harmondsworth 1963, 1977, p. 287.
67 Hannah Arendt, *The Life of the Mind*, Secker & Warburg, London 1978, p. 4.
68 Falcone and Padovani, pp. 70–1.
69 Ibid., pp. 111, 112.
70 Leonardo Sciascia, *Il giorno della civetta*, Einaudi, Turin 1972 (translated

as *The Day of the Owl*), p. 119.

71 Zagari, pp. 46, 60.

72 Arlacchi, 1992, pp. 27, 205.

73 Anonymous, p. 163.

74 Leonardo Sciascia, *A future memoria*, Bompiani, Milan 1989, pp. 50–1.

5 Eros against Thanatos

1 Vincenzo Consolo, *Le pietre di Pantalica*, Mondadori, Milan 1988, pp. 170, 172.

2 Pezzino in Librerie Associate, *Mafia – Anatomia di un regime*, Rome 1992, p. 35.

3 *Giornale di Sicilia*, 15 November 1984.

4 Felicia Bartolotta Impastato, *La mafia in casa mia*, La Luna, Palermo 1987, p. 64.

5 Pino Arlacchi, *Mafia Business*, trans. Martin Ryle, Verso, London 1987, p. 144.

6 Pino Arlacchi, *Gli uomini del disonore*, Mondadori, Milan 1992, pp. 308–9.

7 Giovanni Falcone and Marcelle Padovani, *Cose di Cosa Nostra*, Rizzoli, Milan 1991, p. 38.

8 Ibid., p. 83.

9 Vittorio Zucconi, *La Repubblica*, 10 March 1993.

10 Falcone and Padovani, p. 84.

11 Anonymous, *Uomo di rispetto*, Mondadori, Milan 1990, p. 185.

12 Herbert Marcuse, *Eros and Civilisation*, Ark, London 1987, p. 203.

13 Arlacchi, 1987, p. 129.

14 Giuseppe Casarrubea and Pia Blandano, *L'educazione mafiosa*, Sellerio, Palermo 1991, p. 60.

15 Antonino Caponnetto, *I miei giorni a Palermo*, Garzanti, Milan 1992, p. 57.

16 Giorgio Bocca, *L'inferno*, Mondadori, Milan 1992, pp. 173, 175.

17 Anonymous, pp. 157–8.

18 *Mezzocielo*, July 1993.

19 Marcuse, p. 149.

20 Giorgio Chinnici and Umberto Santino, *La violenza programmata*, Franco Angeli, Milan 1991, p. 125.

21 Arlacchi, 1992, p. 281.

22 Ibid., p. 289.

23 Falcone and Padovani, p. 83.

24 Ibid., p. 84.

25 RAI 1, 23 June 1993.

26 *La Stampa*, 27 November 1993.

27   *L'Unità*, 11 October 1993.

28   *La Repubblica*, 7 December 1993.

29   Arlacchi, 1992, p. 292.

30   Interview by Sandra Rizza, *Panorama*, 1 August 1993.

31   *Mezzocielo*, April 1993.

32   Roberto Alajmo, *Un lenzuolo contro la mafia*, Gelka, Palermo 1993, p. 88.

33   Sophocles, *Antigone*, translated by H. D. F. Kitto, OUP, Oxford 1962.

34   *La Repubblica*, 22–23 November 1992.

35   Sandra Rizza, *Una ragazza contro la mafia – Rita Atria*, La Luna, Palermo 1993, pp. 48, 127.

36   Saverio Abbruzzese, 'La paura', in Franco Occhiogrosso (ed.), *Ragazzi della mafia*, Franco Angeli, Milan 1993, p. 204.

37   Rizza, p. 49.

38   Ibid., p. 61.

39   *Giornale di Sicilia*, 26 July 1993.

40   Rizza, p. 63.

41   *Panorama*, 1 August 1993.

42   Rizza, pp. 64, 66.

43   Ibid., p. 69.

44   *Mezzocielo*, May 1993.

45   Rizza, p. 66.

46   *Mezzocielo*, July 1993.

47   Rizza, p. 96.

48   Silvia Vegetti Finzi, 'L'ospite perturbante', unpublished paper given to the seminar 'Der die das Fremde', Hanover, 1993.

49   Angela Lanza, *Donne contro la mafia. L'esperienza del digiuno a Palermo*, Data News, Rome 1994, p. 63.

50   Ibid., p. 68.

51   Gabriello Montemagno, *Il sogno spezzato di Rita Atria*, Edizioni della Battaglia, Palermo 1992, p. 33.

52   Rizza, pp. 129–30.

53   Alajmo, p. 88.

54   Rosaria Schifani and Felice Cavallaro, *Lettera ai mafiosi – vi perdono ma inginocchiatevi*, Pironti, Naples 1992, p. 182.

55   *L'Unità*, 27 July 1993.

56   Rizza, p. 137.

57   Silvia Ferraris, *Mezzocielo*, January 1993.

58   Interview with Rosetta Cerminara by Sandra Bonsanti, *La Repubblica*, 21 October 1992.

59   Interview by Ivo Carezzano, *Il Messaggero*, 21 October 1992.

60   Ibid.

61   Enclosure with the custody order for Molinaro and Rizzardi.

62   Rosa Masciopinto, *Donna d'onore*, Edizioni della Battaglia, Palermo 1994, p. 7.

63   *Il Messaggero*, 21 October 1992.

64   *Il Messaggero*, 14 July 1992.

65   *Il Messaggero*, 21 October 1992.

66   Anna Puglisi in *A Rosetta Cerminara*, 1992, p. 15.

67   Rosa Tavella, in ibid., 1992, p. 5.

68   *Il Messaggero*, 21 October 1992.

69   *A Rosetta Cerminara*, p. 30.

70   Donatella Mauro, in ibid., p. 30.

71   Gianfranco Manfredi, *Il Messaggero*, 14 July 1992.

72   *La Repubblica*, 21 October 1992.

73   Television interview transmitted during the ceremony for the Marisa Bellisario Foundation Prize, 8 March 1993, RAI 2.

74   *La Repubblica*, 18 November 1993.

75   Piero Bevilacqua, 'La mafia e la Spagna', *Meridiana*, no. 13, 1992, p. 119.

6 Emancipation?

1   *Narcomafie*, no. 3, April–May 1993.

2   Gabriella Gribaudi, 'Mafia, culture e gruppi sociali', *Meridiana*, no. 7–9, 1990, p. 349.

3   Francis A. J. Ianni, *A Family Business: Kinship and Social Control in Organized Crime*, Russell Sage Foundation, New York 1972, p. 11.

4   Piero Fantozzi, *Politica, clientela e regolazione sociale*, Rubbettino, Soveria Mannelli 1993, p. 129.

5   Giovanni Falcone and Marcelle Padovani, *Cose di Cosa Nostra*, Rizzoli, Milan 1991, pp. 81–2.

6   Fantozzi, p. 131.

7   Minervini, in Franco Occhiogrosso (ed.), *Ragazzi della mafia*, Franco Angeli, Milan 1993, pp. 269–70.

8   Giovanna Fiume, *La vecchia dell'aceto*, Gelka, Palermo 1990, p. 141.

9   Pantaleone Sergi, *La 'santa' violenta*, Periferia, Cosenza 1991, pp. 177–8.

10   Pino Arlacchi, *Gli uomini del disonore*, Mondadori, Milan 1992, pp. 168–9.

11   Fondazione Marisa Bellisario, *Donne e mafia: Dentro contro fuori*, Premio Marisa Bellisario, Palermo 1993, p. 43.

12   *Il Venerdì di Repubblica*, 1993.

13   Anna Rossi-Doria (ed.), *La libertà delle donne*, Rosenberg & Sellier, Turin 1990, pp. 289, 290.

14   Sara Ruddick, 'Maternal thinking', *Feminist Studies*, Summer 1980, pp. 347, 359.

15 *Il Diritto delle Donne*, no. 14, February 1992.

16 Cf. *La Repubblica*, 20 February 1986; Fabrizio Calvi, *La vita quotidiana della mafia dal 1950 a oggi*, Rizzoli, Milan 1986, p. 76.

17 *L'Unità*, May 1980.

18 Provisional custody order, pp. 202–24.

19 *Giornale di Sicilia*, 5 February 1984.

20 Corrado Stajano, *Mafia – L'atto d'accusa dei giudici di Palermo*, Editori Riuniti, Rome 1992, p. 89.

21 Ibid., p. 271.

22 Antonia Cascio and Anna Puglisi (eds), *Con e contro – Le donne nell'organizzazione mafiosa e nella lotta antimafia*, dossier 4, CSD, Palermo 1986, p. 13.

23 Anonimo del XX Secolo, *Una modesta proposta per pacificare la città di Palermo*, Qualecultura, Vibo Valentia 1984, pp. 56–7.

24 *Giornale di Sicilia*, 7 January 1984.

25 Cascio and Puglisi, p. 65.

26 Salvatore Lupo, *Storia della mafia*, Donzelli, Rome 1993, p. 193.

27 Giovanna Fiume, 'Ci sono donne nella mafia?', *Meridiana*, no. 7–8, 1990, p. 206.

28 Cf. Cascio and Puglisi, pp. 35–50.

29 *L'Ora*, 25 May 1993.

30 *Mezzocielo*, March 1993.

31 Cascio and Puglisi, p. 48.

32 Luigi M. Lombardi Satriani, Alfonso Madeo and Mariano Meligrana, 'Il ruolo della donna nella mafia', *Quaderni del Mezzogiorno e delle Isole*, XIV, no. 42–3, 1977, p. 109.

7 Subordination and Exploitation

1 Franco Cazzola, in Fondazione Marisa Bellisario, *Donne e mafia: Dentro contro fuori*, Premio Marisa Bellisario, Palermo 1993, p. 42.

2 Giovanna Fiume, 'Ci sono donne nella mafia?', *Meridiana*, no. 7–8, 1990, p. 294.

3 Salvatore Lupo, *Storia della mafia*, Donzelli, Rome 1993, p. 194.

4 Ibid., p. 194.

5 Marina Pino, *Le signore della droga*, La Luna, Palermo 1988, p. 34.

6 *Il Diritto delle Donne*, no. 14, February 1992.

7 Pino, pp. 5–6.

8 Ibid., p. 22.

9 Ibid., p. 15.

10 Ibid., p. 7.

11 Ibid., p. 101.

12 Ibid., p. 34.

13 Ibid., p. 25.

14 Ibid., p. 17.

15 Ibid., p. 14.

16 Ibid., p. 16.

17 Ibid., p. 6.

18 Ibid., p. 71.

19 Ibid., p. 73.

20 Ibid., p. 75.

21 Ibid., p. 76.

22 Giuseppe Martorani and Sergio Nigrelli, *Leonardo Messina, la carriera di un uomo d'onore*, Musumeci, Quart (Valle D'Aosta) 1993, p. 56.

23 Ibid.

24 *Giornale di Sicilia*, 5 November 1985.

25 *Giornale di Sicilia*, 6 October 1984, 16 November 1984.

26 *Giornale di Sicilia*, 20 February 1984.

27 Pino, p. 47.

28 Ibid., pp. 48–9.

29 Ibid., p. 59.

30 Ibid., p. 60.

31 *L'Ora*, 23 February 1982.

32 Pino, p. 62.

33 Ibid., p. 56.

34 Ibid., p. 58.

35 Ibid., p. 69.

36 Ibid., p. 70.

37 Anna Puglisi, 'Donne e mafia', unpublished, Centro Siciliano di Documentazione, Palermo 1991, p. 2.

38 Pino, p. 69.

39 *Giornale di Sicilia*, 19 January 1980.

40 *La Sicilia*, 8 April 1983.

41 Pantaleone Sergi, *La 'santa' violenta*, Periferia, Cosenza 1991, p. 135.

42 *Il Diritto delle Donne*, no. 14, February 1992.

43 Lupo, p. 136.

44 Pino Arlacchi, *Gli uomini del disonore*, Mondadori, Milan 1992, p. 170.

45 Ibid., p. 164.

46 *Il Diritto delle Donne*, no. 14, February 1992.

47 Giorgio Chinnici and Umberto Santino, *La violenza programmata*, Franco Angeli, Milan 1991, p. 235.

48 Danilo Dolci, *Spreco*, Einaudi, Turin 1960, pp. 271–2.

49 Chinnici and Santino, p. 343.

50 Ibid.

51 Luciano Violante, 'La politica', in Franco Occhiogrosso (ed.), *Ragazzi della mafia*, Franco Angeli, Milan 1993, p. 279.

52   Marcelle Padovani, *Les dernières années de la mafia*, Gallimard, Paris 1987, p. 11.

53   Chinnici and Santino, p. 356.

54   Michele Pantaleone, *Mafia e politica*, Einaudi, Turin 1966, p. 111.

55   Gabor Gellert, *Mafia*, Rubbettino, Soveria Mannelli 1987, p. 233.

56   Ibid., p. 234.

57   Felice Cavallaro (ed.), *Mafia – Album di Cosa Nostra*, Rizzoli, Milan 1992, p. 155.

58   Chinnici and Santino, p. 255.

59   Sergi, p. 135.

60   Pino Arlacchi, *Mafia Business*, trans. Martin Ryle, Verso, London 1987, p. 31.

61   Sergi, p. 137.

62   Ibid., p. 141.

63   Arlacchi, 1992, pp. 244–5.

64   Enrico Deaglio, *Raccolto rosso*, Feltrinelli, Milan 1993, p. 40.

8 Open Complicities

1   *L'Ora*, 15 February 1982.

2   *Giornale di Sicilia*, 16 February 1982.

3   Marina Pino, *Le signore della droga*, La Luna, Palermo 1988, pp. 77–90.

4   Ibid., pp. 79–80.

5   Ibid., p. 91.

6   Ibid., pp. 95, 96.

7   Ibid., p. 90.

8   Ibid., p. 91.

9   Ibid., p. 90.

10   *Mezzocielo*, April 1993.

11   Graziella Priulla, *Noi Donne*, March 1988, p. 55.

12   Enzo Biagi, *Il boss è solo*, Mondadori, Milan 1990, p. 111.

13   Hank Messick, *Syndicate Wife – The Story of Ann Drahmann Coppola*, Robert Hale, London 1969, pp. 84, 85.

14   Sandra Rizza, *Una ragazza contro la mafia – Rita Atria*, La Luna, Palermo 1993, p. 66.

15   Interview with Paola Zanuttini, *Venerdì di Repubblica*, 14 January 1994.

16   Pino Arlacchi, *Gli uomini del disonore*, Mondadori, Milan 1992, pp. 166, 167, 170.

17   Antoinette Giancana and Thomas C. Renner, *Mafia Princess*, George Allen & Unwin, London 1984, p. 30.

18   Corrado Stajano, *Mafia – L'atto d'accusa dei giudici di Palermo*, Editori Riuniti, Rome 1992, p. 246.

19   Giancana and Renner, pp. 46–7.

20   Gay Talese, *Honour Thy Father*, Sphere, London 1972, pp. 123, 124, 125.

21   Joseph Bonanno with Sergio Lalli, *A Man of Honour*, Unwin, London 1984, p. 312.

22   Interview with Silvana Mazzocchi.

23   Arlacchi, p. 250.

24   Ibid., p. 229.

25   Giovanni Falcone and Marcelle Padovani, *Cose di Cosa Nostra*, Rizzoli, Milan 1991, p. 85.

26   Giancana and Renner, p. 56.

27   Ibid., pp. 45–6.

28   Stajano, pp. 326, 178.

29   Giancana and Renner, pp. 45–6.

30   *Il Diritto delle Donne*, no. 14, February 1992.

31   *L'Unità*, May 1980.

32   Enzo Ciconte, *'Ndrangheta dall'Unità ad oggi*, Laterza, Bari 1992, p. 312.

33   Messick, p. 63.

34   Ibid., pp. 103–4.

35   Stajano, p. 82.

36   Enrico Deaglio, *Raccolto rosso*, Feltrinelli, Milan 1993, p. 198.

37   Ibid., p. 199.

38   Petra Bonavita, *Donna Sicilia*, Centaurus, Pfaffenweiler 1993, p. 110.

39   Deaglio, p. 200.

40   Stajano, p. 268.

41   Danilo Dolci, *Spreco*, Einaudi, Turin 1960, p. 133.

42   Interview with Paola Zanuttini, *Il Venerdì di Repubblica*, 1993.

43   Arlacchi, p. 168.

44   Ibid., pp. 240–1.

45   Nick Gentile, *Vita di capomafia*, Editori Riuniti, Rome 1963, p. 156.

46   Michele Pantaleone, *Mafia e droga*, Einaudi, Turin 1966, p. 101.

47   *La Sicilia*, 23 September 1983.

48   Antonino Caponnetto, *I miei giorni a Palermo*, Garzanti, Milan 1992, p. 136.

49   Falcone and Padovani, pp. 85–6.

50   Letter posted in the red box and circulated among Palermo women students during student meetings on the theme of sexual violence during winter 1988; *Mezzocielo*, March 1993.

51   Gentile, pp. 148–9.

52   Interview with Silvana Mazzocchi.

53   Giuseppe Fava, *I siciliani*, Cappelli, Bologna 1980, p. 102.

54   Gabor Gellert, *Mafia*, Rubbettino, Soveria Mannelli 1987, p. 245.

55   Biagi, pp. 237–8.

56   Attilio Bolzoni and Giuseppe D'Avanzo, *Il capo dei capi – Totò Riina*, Mondadori, Milan 1993, p. 66.

57 Falcone and Padovani, p. 84.
58 Giancana and Renner, p. 15.
59 Ibid., pp. 73, 79, 81.
60 Ibid., p. 39.
61 Francesco La Licata, *La Stampa*, 20 May 1993.
62 *L'Espresso*, 31 January 1993.
63 *Corriere della Sera*, 18 January 1993.
64 Pino Buongiorno, *Totò Riina*, Rizzoli, Milan 1993, p. 63.
65 Ibid., p. 62.
66 Ibid., p. 61.
67 Giuseppe Martorana and Sergio Nigrelli, *Totò Riina*, Musumeci, Quart (Valle D'Aosta) 1993, p. 60.
68 Bolzoni and D'Avanzo, p. 92.
69 Ibid., p. 107.
70 Martorana and Nigrelli, p. 61.
71 Buongiorno, p. 72.
72 Bolzoni and D'Avanzo, p. 112.
73 *Corriere della Sera*, 18 January 1993.
74 *L'Espresso*, 31 January 1993.
75 Martorana and Nigrelli, p. 66.
76 Buongiorno, pp. 79–80.
77 *La Repubblica*, 5 March 1993.
78 *L'Unità*, 19 January 1993.
79 Arlacchi, p. 167.
80 *Corriere della Sera*, 19 May 1993.
81 *Mezzocielo*, May 1993.
82 *La Stampa*, 16 May 1993.
83 Bertolt Brecht, *Poems 1913–1956*, trans. John Willett, Minerva, London 1994, p. 318.
84 *Mezzocielo*, May 1993.
85 Arlacchi, p. 167.
86 Ciconte, p. 82.
87 Sicilian Documentation Centre, 1979, p. 41.
88 *La Repubblica*, 1 April 1993.
89 Simona Dalla Chiesa, *La Repubblica*, 1 April 1993.
90 *Mezzocielo*, February 1993.
91 *Mezzocielo*, April 1993.
92 *Mezzocielo*, February 1993.
93 *Il Venerdì di Repubblica*, 5 March 1993.
94 *La Repubblica*, 2 March 1993.
95 *La Repubblica*, 22–23 August 1993.
96 *La Repubblica*, 12 January 1994.
97 Marisa Bellisario Foundation.

9 Emotions as a Resource

1 Carlo Levi, *Le parole sono pietre*, Einaudi, Turin 1979, p. 160.

2 Michele Pantaleone, *Mafia e politica*, Einaudi, Turin 1978, p. 155.

3 Levi, pp. 155.

4 Ibid., pp. 157–8.

5 Ibid., pp. 171–2.

6 Ibid., p. 172.

7 Ibid., pp. 166–7.

8 Ibid., p. 167.

9 Ibid., pp. 170, 173.

10 Ibid., p. 166.

11 *Giornale di Sicilia*, 6 November 1985.

12 *Corriere della Sera*, 7 November 1985.

13 Vera Pegna, *Tempo di lupi e di comunisti*, La Luna, Palermo 1992, p. 29.

14 Piera Fallucca, *Mezzocielo*, April 1993.

15 Roberto Alajmo, *Un lenzuolo contro la mafia*, Gelka, Palermo 1993, p. 22.

16 Rosario Schifani and Felice Cavallaro, *Lettera ai mafiosi – vi perdono ma inginocchiatevi*, Pironti, Naples 1992, p. 280.

17 Alajmo, p. 22.

18 Schifani and Cavallaro, p. 143.

19 Ibid., p. 268.

20 Ibid., p. 270.

21 Ibid., pp. 264–5.

22 Ibid., p. 16.

23 Ibid., p. 15, 20–1.

24 Gabriella Turnaturi and Carlo Donolo, 'Familismi morali', in Carlo Donolo and Franco Fichera, *Le vie dell'innovazione*, Feltrinelli, Milan 1988, p. 181.

25 Schifani and Cavallaro, p. 312.

26 Ibid., pp. 329–30.

27 Ibid., p. 354.

28 Ibid., p. 380.

29 Ibid., p. 364.

30 Ibid., p. 372.

31 Ibid., p. 377.

32 Ibid., p. 340.

33 Ibid., p. 441.

34 Ibid., pp. 395, 399.

35 Ibid., pp. 417–18.

36 Ibid., p. 429.

37 Ibid., p. 434.

38   Ibid., p. 454.

39   Ibid., p. 484.

40   Ibid., p. 458.

41   Gabriella Turnaturi, *Associate per amore*, Feltrinelli, Milan 1991, p. 95.

42   Schifani and Cavallaro, p. 443.

43   Turnaturi and Donolo, p. 165.

44   Gabriella Turnaturi, 'Fra interessi e dignita', *Democrazio e Diritto*, no. 2, 1992, p. 225.

45   Anna Puglisi and Umberto Santino, 'Intervista a Giovanna Terranova', unpublished, Sicilian Documentation Centre, Palermo 1985, p. 20.

46   Gabriella Turnaturi, 'Sentirsi sicuri', in Laura Balbo (ed.), *Friendly*, Anabasi, Milan 1993, p. 120.

47   Ibid., p. 123.

48   Ibid.

49   Schifani and Cavallaro, p. 398.

50   Turnaturi, 1993, p. 120.

51   *Narcomafie*, April 1993, p. 11.

52   Turnaturi and Donolo, p. 182.

53   Ibid., p. 174.

54   Alajmo, p. 25.

55   Giovanna Cirillo Rampolla, *Suicidio per mafia*, La Luna, Palermo 1986, p. 10.

10   Mothers, Sisters and Widows in Mourning: Women Alone

1   Giovanni Falcone and Marcelle Padovani, *Cose di Cosa Nostra*, Rizzoli, Milan 1991, p. 85.

2   Salvatore Lupo, *Storia della mafia*, Donzelli, Rome 1993, p. 226.

3   Antonia Cascio, in Umberto Santini (ed.), *L'antimafia difficile*, Sicilian Documentation Centre, Palermo 1989, p. 100.

4   Lupo, p. 226.

5   *Giornale di Sicilia*, 16 July 1981.

6   Pino Arlacchi, *Uomini del disonore*, Mondadori, Milan 1982, p. 226.

7   Anna Puglisi and Umberto Santini, 'Intervista a Giovanna Terranova', unpublished, Sicilian Documentation Centre, Palermo 1985, p. 8.

8   *L'Ora*, 14 February 1979.

9   Antonino Caponnetto, *I miei giorni a Palermo*, Garzanti, Milan 1992, p. 137.

10   *Giornale di Sicilia*, 16 July 1981.

11   *L'Isola*, no. 24.

12   *Giornale di Sicilia*, 16 July 1981.

13   Lupo, p. 226.

14   Gabor Gellert, *Mafia*, Rubbettino, Soveria Mannelli 1987, p. 232.

15 Caponnetto, pp. 137–8.

16 *Giornale di Calabria*, 9 May 1976.

17 *Giornale di Calabria*, 11 July 1976.

18 *Giornale di Calabria*, 14 July 1976.

19 Felicia Bartolotta Impastato, *La mafia in casa mia*, La Luna, Palermo 1987, p. 7.

20 Ibid., pp. 13–14.

21 Ibid., pp. 27, 29.

22 Vera Pegna, *Tempo di lupi e di comunisti*, La Luna, Palermo 1992, pp. 37–8.

23 Bartolotta Impastato, pp. 28, 30.

24 Ibid., p. 31.

25 PM, September 1984.

26 Bartolotta Impastato, p. 35.

27 Ibid., p. 40.

28 Ibid., p. 41.

29 Ibid., p. 43.

30 *Città d'Utopia*, no. 8, May–August 1993.

31 Bartolotta Impastato, p. 45.

32 *Donna Più*, September 1985.

33 PM, September 1984.

34 Interview with Claudio Fava, Canale 5, 1993.

35 *Donna Più*, September 1985.

36 Pegna, p. 43.

37 *Il Messaggero*, 8 June 1986.

38 *Donna Più*, September 1985.

39 Bartolotta Impastato, p. 54.

40 Ibid., p. 62.

41 Ibid., p. 60.

42 *Gente Mese*, February 1989, p. 104.

43 *Giornale di Sicilia*, 15 February 1986.

44 Anna Puglisi, *Sole contro la mafia*, La Luna, Palermo 1990, p. 43.

45 Ibid., pp. 48–9.

46 Ibid., pp. 45.

47 Ibid., pp. 39, 51.

48 Petra Bonavita, *Donna Sicilia*, Centaurus, Pfaffenweiler 1993, p. 31.

49 Puglisi, p. 81.

50 Ibid., pp. 84–5.

51 Ibid., Preface, p. 16.

52 Ibid., p. 87.

53 Ibid., p. 88.

54 Television interview, RAI, 1992.

55 Puglisi, p. 88.

56 *Gente Mese*, February 1989.
57 Fabrizio Calvi, *La vita quotidiana della mafia dal 1950 a oggi*, Rizzoli, Milan 1986, pp. 216–17.
58 *Gente Mese*, February 1989.
59 Umberto Santino, Preface to Puglisi, p. 15.
60 *Gente Mese*, February 1989.
61 *Giornale di Sicilia*, 12 February 1986.
62 *Gente Mese*, February 1989.
63 *Giornale di Sicilia*, 12 February 1986.
64 *Gente Mese*, February 1989.
65 Interview with Sandra Rizza, *L'Ora*, 14 November 1986.
66 Giovanna Fiume, 'Ci sono donne nella mafia?', *Meridiana*, no. 7–8, 1990, p. 295.
67 Puglisi, p. 93.
68 Fiume, p. 295.
69 Puglisi, p. 91.
70 Ibid., p. 95.
71 Fiume, pp. 297–8.
72 Ibid., p. 300.
73 Puglisi, p. 112.
74 Ibid., p. 116.
75 Ibid., p. 118.
76 Ibid., p. 115.
77 *L'Ora*, 11 November 1986.
78 Puglisi, p. 118.
79 Ibid., p. 119.
80 *Giornale di Sicilia*, 23 October 1986.
81 Birgit Kienzle and Maria Teresa Galluzzo, *Frauen gegen die Mafia*, Rowohlt, Hamburg 1990, p. 50.
82 Bonavita, p. 35.
83 Umberto Santino, Preface, in Puglisi, p. 18.
84 Sandra Rizza, *L'Ora*, 9 November 1988.
85 Kienzle and Galluzzo, p. 50.
86 Interview with Sandra Rizza, *L'Ora*, 14 November 1986.
87 Fiume, p. 296.
88 Ibid., p. 297.
89 Ibid., p. 302.
90 *Il Manifesto*, 16 February 1988.
91 *L'Ora*, 12 February 1988.
92 *Il Manifesto*, 5–6 April 1987.
93 Umberto Santino, *Il Manifesto*, 5–6 April 1987.
94 Puglisi, p. 18.
95 Ibid., p. 85.

96 Sicilian Documentation Centre, *Donne contro la mafia: dall'isolamento allo spettacolo. Ovvero: chi le ha aiutate e chi è stato a guardare*, dossier, CSD, Palermo 1989.

97 Gianfranco Manfredi, *Il Messaggero*, 9 April 1989.

98 Kienzle and Galluzzo, p. 109.

99 Ibid., pp. 106, 107.

100 Ibid., p. 108.

101 Ibid., p. 110.

102 Ibid.

103 *Il Messaggero*, 12 May 1987.

104 *Il Messaggero*, 10 May 1987.

105 *Il Messaggero*, 16 October 1988.

106 Giorgio Bocca, *L'inferno*, Mondadori, Milan 1992, p. 32.

107 *Il Messaggero*, 16 October 1988.

108 Ibid.

109 Ibid.

110 *Il Messaggero*, 19 July 1988.

111 *La Repubblica*, 23 May 1990.

112 Antonia Cascio and Anna Puglisi (eds), 'Intervista a Maria Benigno', unpublished, CSD, Palermo 1986, p. 8.

113 Kienzle and Galluzzo, p. 82.

114 Cascio and Puglisi, p. 7.

115 Ibid., p. 8.

116 Ibid., p. 9.

117 Ibid., p. 12.

118 Ibid., p. 13.

119 *Donna Più*, September 1985.

120 Cascio and Puglisi, p. 14.

121 *La Sicilia*, 23 October 1982.

122 Cascio and Puglisi, p. 13.

123 Kienzle and Galluzzo, p. 87.

124 *Donna Più*, September 1985.

125 Kienzle and Galluzzo, p. 85.

126 Cascio and Puglisi, pp. 16, 19, 21.

127 PM, September 1984.

11 The Women of 'Men against the Mafia'

1 *Giornale di Sicilia*, 10 October 1981.

2 Ibid.

3 Antonino Caponnetto, *I miei giorni a Palermo*, Garzanti, Milan 1992, p. 26.

4 *Mezzocielo*, July 1992.

5 Ibid.

6 *Il Diritto delle Donne*, no. 14, February 1992.

7 Francesco La Licata, *Storia di Giovanni Falcone*, Rizzoli, Milan 1993, p. 87.

8 Ibid., p. 81.

9 Ibid., p. 115.

10 Ibid., pp. 115–16.

11 Ibid., p. 140.

12 Ibid., p. 142, 143.

13 Roberto Alajmo, *Un lenzuolo contro la mafia*, Gelka, Palermo 1993, p. 116.

14 Anna Puglisi and Umberto Santino, 'Intervista a Giovanna Terranova', unpublished, CSD, Palermo 1985, pp. 14–15.

15 Ibid., p. 3.

16 Ibid., pp. 6, 7.

17 Ibid., p. 12.

18 Rosaria Schifani and Felice Cavallaro, *Lettera ai mafiosi – vi perdono ma inginocchiatevi*, Pironti, Naples 1992, p. 330.

19 Puglisi and Santino, pp. 14, 15.

20 *Giornale di Sicilia*, 4 October 1979.

21 Puglisi and Santino, pp. 15–16.

22 Ibid., p. 16.

23 Ibid., p. 17.

24 Ibid., pp. 17, 18–19.

25 *L'Ora*, 16 November 1982.

26 Puglisi and Santino, p. 20.

27 Ibid., p. 21.

28 Schifani and Cavallaro, p. 329.

29 Puglisi and Santino, p. 21.

30 Ibid., p. 22.

31 Birgit Kienzle and Maria Teresa Galluzzo, *Frauen gegen die Mafia*, Rowohlt, Hamburg 1990, p. 39.

32 *Donna Più*, September 1985.

33 Ibid.

34 Ibid.

35 *Corriere della Sera*, 19 November 1985.

36 *Donna Più*, September 1985.

37 *Corriere della Sera*, 19 November 1985.

38 Ibid.

39 Bianca Stancanelli, *L'Ora*, 19 June 1981.

40 *Giornale di Sicilia*, 6 August 1981; *L'Ora*, 19 June 1981.

41 *L'Ora*, 19 June 1981.

42 Ibid.

43 *Donna Più*, September 1985.

44 *L'Ora*, 19 June 1981.

45 *Donna Più*, September 1985.

46 *L'Ora*, 11 February 1981.

47 Schifani and Cavallaro, p. 300.

48 Ibid., p. 316.

49 Roselina Salemi, *Ragazzi di Palermo*, Rizzoli, Milan 1993, p. 151.

50 Ibid., p. 134.

51 Schifani and Cavallaro, pp. 299–300.

52 Ibid., p. 299.

53 Saverio Lodato, *Dieci anni di mafia*, Rizzoli, Milan 1992, p. 43.

54 Schifani and Cavallaro, p. 356.

55 *Mezzocielo*, July 1992.

56 *L'Ora*, 29 April 1983.

57 Ibid.

58 Schifani and Cavallaro, p. 355.

59 *L'Ora*, 29 April 1983.

60 Ibid.

61 Schifani and Cavallaro, pp. 349, 350.

62 Ibid., p. 348.

63 PM, September 1984.

64 *L'Ora*, 20 May 1982.

65 *L'Ora*, 29 April 1983.

66 Ibid.

67 Ibid.

68 *Corriere della Sera*, 7 November 1985.

69 *L'Unità*, 27 February 1981.

70 Ibid.

71 PM, September 1984.

72 *L'Ora*, 19 June 1981.

73 Schifani and Cavallaro, pp. 372, 373.

74 Canale 5, 12 May 1993.

75 Schifani and Cavallaro, p. 441.

76 Ibid., p. 442.

77 Ibid., p. 435.

78 Ibid., pp. 433, 434, 437.

79 Interview with Claudio Fava, Canale 5, 12 May 1993.

80 Schifani and Cavallaro, p. 400; Saverio Lodato, *Potenti*, Garzanti, Milan 1992, p. 41.

81 Luciano Violante, 'I corleonesi', *L'Unità*, supplement, 11 September 1993, p. 79.

82 Paolo Jedlowski, 'Nuovi ceti medi nel Mezzogiorno: fra clientelismo e professionalità', *Inchiesta*, XX, no. 88–9, p. 135.

83 Schifani and Cavallaro, p. 401.

84 *Giornale di Sicilia*, 29 August 1993.

85 Schifani and Cavallaro, p. 400.

86 Ibid., p. 397.

87 *La Repubblica*, 2 September 1993.

88 Schifani and Cavallaro, p. 390.

89 Ibid., p. 398.

90 Lodato, p. 42.

91 *Giornale di Sicilia*, 29 August 1993.

92 Lodato, p. 40.

93 Alajmo, pp. 10–11, 22.

94 Schifani and Cavallaro, p. 398.

95 Osservatorio Libero Grassi, *Mafia o sviluppo. Un dibattito con Libero Grassi*, Palermo 1992, p. 114.

96 Lodato, p. 53.

97 *Mezzocielo*, July 1993.

98 Schifani and Cavallaro, p. 378.

99 *Mezzocielo*, July 1993.

100 Schifani and Cavallaro, p. 383.

101 Ibid., pp. 380, 381, 382.

102 Giovanna Fiume, Introduction, Giovanna Cirillo Rampolla, *Suicidio per mafia*, La Luna, Palermo 1986, pp. 36, 37.

103 Schifani and Cavallaro, p. 383.

104 Ibid., p. 449.

105 Interview with Roselina Salemi, *Donna Più*, September 1985.

106 *L'Ora*, 24 July 1986.

107 *Donna Più*, September 1985.

108 Ibid.

109 Schifani and Cavallaro, p. 448.

110 *Donna Più*, September 1985.

111 Schifani and Cavallaro, pp. 451, 452.

112 Ibid., p. 446.

113 Interview with Claudio Fava, Canale 5, 30 June 1993.

114 Lodato, p. 46.

115 *Mezzocielo*, January 1993.

12 Women and Kidnappings

1 Frances Elliot, *The Diary of an Idle Woman in Sicily*, 2 vols, J. W. Arrowsmith, Bristol 1885, vol. 2, pp. 95, 96, 99.

2 Pino Buongiorno, *Totò Riina*, Rizzoli, Milan 1993, p. 89.

3 Pantaleone Sergi, *La 'santa' violenta*, Periferia, Cosenza 1991, p. 152.

4 Ibid., p. 154.

5 *La Repubblica*, 22–23 March 1987.

6 Sergi, Chapters 13, 14.

7 Cesari Casella, *743 Giorni Lontano da Casa*, Rizzoli, Milan 1990, pp. 9, 34.

8 Ibid., pp. 128–9.

9 *La Stampa*, 13 June 1989.

10 *Gazzetta del Sud*, 11 June 1989.

11 *La Stampa*, 13 June 1989.

12 *La Repubblica*, 15 June 1989.

13 *Corriere della Sera*, 17 June 1989.

14 *Corriere della Sera*, 14 June 1989.

15 *La Repubblica*, 16 June 1989.

16 *La Repubblica*, 18–19 June 1989.

17 *La Stampa*, 24 June 1989.

18 *Corriere della Sera*, 17 June 1989.

19 *La Stampa*, 16 June 1989.

20 Ibid.

21 *La Repubblica*, 17 June 1989.

22 *La Repubblica* and *Corriere della Sera*, 20 June 1989.

23 *Gazzetta del Sud*, 21 June 1989.

24 Gabriella Turnaturi, 'In nome degli affetti familiari', *Memoria*, no. 13, 1986, pp. 80, 81.

25 Ibid., p. 81.

26 Ibid., pp. 84, 85.

27 *Corriere della Sera*, 16 June 1989.

28 *La Stampa*, 17 June 1989.

29 *Gazzetta del Sud*, 16 June 1989.

30 *La Stampa*, 16 June 1989.

31 *Corriere della Sera*, 18 June 1989.

32 *Corriere della Sera*, 15 June 1989.

33 *La Stampa*, 18 June 1989.

34 *La Repubblica*, 20 June 1989.

13 'Between Killing and Dying There's a Third Way: Living'

1 Birgit Kienzle and Maria Teresa Galluzzo, *Frauen gegen die Mafia*, Rowohlt, Hamburg 1990, p. 133.

2 Anna Puglisi, *Sole contro la mafia*, La Luna, Palermo 1990, p. 16.

3 Umberto Santino (ed.), *L'antimafia difficile*, CSD, Palermo 1989, p. 156.

4 Renate Siebert, 'Intervista a Maria Di Carlo', unpublished, 1993.

5 *Il Diritto delle Donne*, February 1992, p. 11.

6 Siebert.

7   Ibid.

8   Anna Puglisi, *Il Diritto delle Donne*, February 1992, p. 11.

9   *Il Diritto delle Donne*, February 1992, p. 13.

10 Unpublished typescript.

11 Anna Puglisi and Umberto Santino, 'Intervista a Giovanna Terranova', unpublished, CSD, Palermo 1985, pp. 21–2.

12 Petra Bonavita, *Donna Sicilia*, Centaurus, Pfaffenweiler 1993, p. 47.

13 Enrico Deaglio, *Raccolto rosso*, Feltrinelli, Milan 1993, p. 66.

14 Antonia Cascia and Anna Puglisi (eds), *Con e contro − Le donne nell'organizzazione mafiosa e nella lotta antimafia*, dossier 4, CSD, Palermo 1986, p. 224.

15 *Giornale di Sicilia*, 6 December 1983.

16 Cascia and Puglisi, p. 273.

17 *Giornale di Sicilia*, 9 December 1984.

18 *Il Diritto delle Donne*, February 1992, p. 12.

19 *La Repubblica*, 13 March 1993.

20 *Mezzocielo*, October 1993, p. 3.

21 *Il Diritto delle Donne*, February 1992, p. 13.

22 Giovanna Fiume, in Roberto Alajmo, *Un lenzuolo contro la mafia*, Gelka, Palermo 1993, p. 5.

23 Alajmo, pp. 24–5.

24 Marta Cimino, *Mezzocielo*, July 1992.

25 Alajmo, p. 98.

26 Deaglio, p. 195.

27 Alajmo, p. 33.

28 Ibid., pp. 6–7.

29 Sara Ruddick, 'Maternal thinking', *Feminist Studies*, Summer 1980, p. 346.

30 Marinella Fiume, *Mezzocielo*, January 1993, p. 11.

31 Alajmo, p. 106.

32 Ibid., p. 66.

33 Guido, in ibid., p. 54.

34 Santino, 1989.

35 Alajmo, p. 51.

36 Angela Lanza, *Donne contro la mafia. L'esperienza delle donne del digiuno a Palermo*, Data News, Rome 1994, p. 11.

37 Ibid., p. 11.

38 *Smog*, May–June 1993.

39 Angela Lanza, 'Visibilità e invisibilità delle "donne del digiuno"', *Nosside*, no. 7–8, 1993, pp. 107–8.

40 Angela Lanza, 'Un sonno interotto', *Nosside*, no. 6, pp. 39–40.

41 Lanza, 1994, p. 12.

42 Ibid., p. 44.

43 Ibid., p. 16.

44   Stella Bertuglia, *Le digiune*, video, 1993.

45   Lanza, 1994, p. 65.

46   Ibid., p. 44.

47   Ibid., p. 45.

48   Ibid., p. 23.

49   Ibid., p. 28.

50   Ibid., p. 30.

51   Lanza, 1992, p. 35.

52   Bertuglia, 1993.

53   Ibid.

54   Lanza, 1994, p. 75.

55   Beatrice Monroy, *Palermo in tempo di peste*, Edizioni della Battaglia, Palermo 1979.

Bibliography

Autori vari (various authors), 1992, *A Rosetta Cerminara*, Lamezia Terme, privately published booklet.

Abbruzzese, Saverio, 1993, 'La paura', in Franco Occhiogrosso (ed.), op. cit.

Accati, Luisa, 1992, 'Il marito della santa. Ruolo paterno, ruolo materno e politica italiana', *Meridiana*, no. 13.

Adorno, Theodor W., 1974, *Minima Moralia*, trans. E. F. N. Jephcott, Verso, London.

Alajmo, Roberto, 1993, *Un lenzuolo contro la mafia*, Gelka, Palermo.

Amurri, Sandra (ed.), 1992, *L'Albero Falcone*, Fondazione Giovanni e Francesca Falcone, Palermo.

Anonimo (Anonymous), 1990, *Uomo di rispetto*, Mondadori, Milan.

Anonimo del XX secolo (U. Santino), 1984, *Una modesta proposta per pacificare la città di Palermo*, Qualecultura, Vibo Valentia.

Arendt, Hannah, 1963, 1977, *Eichmann in Jerusalem*, Penguin, Harmondsworth.

Arendt, Hannah, 1964, 'Eichmann in Jerusalem' (exchange of letters between Hannah Arendt and Gershom Scholem), *Encounter*, January 1964.

Arendt, Hannah, 1978, *The Life of the Mind*, Secker & Warburg, London.

Arlacchi, Pino, 1987, 'La condizione della donna in due tipi di società mediterranee tradizionali', *Quaderni del circolo semiologico siciliano*, no. 26–27, Palermo.

Arlacchi, Pino, 1987 [1983], *Mafia Business*, Verso, London, trans. by Martin Ryle.

Arlacchi, Pino, 1992, *Gli uomini del disonore*, Mondadori, Milan.

Badinter, Elisabeth, 1992, *XY de l'identité masculine*, Editions Odile Jacob, Paris.

Balbo, Laura (ed.), 1993, *Friendly*, Anabasi, Milan.

Barone, Lidia, 1990, 'L'ascesa della 'ndrangheta negli ultimi due decenni', *Meridiana*, no. 7–8.

Bartolotta Impastato, Felicia, 1987, *La mafia in casa mia*, La Luna, Palermo.

Benjamin, Jessica, 1988, 1990, *The Bonds of Love*, Pantheon, New York, Virago, London.

Bertuglia, Stella, 1993, *Le digiune*, VHS video, Zizzania, Palermo.

Bevilacqua, Piero, 1992, 'La mafia e la Spagna', *Meridiana*, no. 13.

Biagi, Enzo, 1990, *Il boss è solo*, Mondadori, Milan.

Blok, Anton, 1974, *The Mafia of the Sicilian Village, 1860–1960*, Basil Blackwell, Oxford.

Bocca, Giorgio, 1992, *L'inferno*, Mondadori, Milan.

Bolzoni, Attilio and D'Avanzo, Giuseppe, 1993, *Il capo dei capi – Totò Riina*, Mondadori, Milan.

Bonanno, Joseph with Sergio Lalli, 1984, *A Man of Honour*, Unwin, London.

Bonavita, Petra, 1993, *Donna Sicilia*, Centaurus, Pfaffenweiler.

Brecht, Bertolt, 1994, *Poems 1913–1956*, ed. J. Willett and Ralph Manheim, Minerva, London.

Buongiorno, Pino, 1993, *Totò Riina*, Rizzoli, Milan.

Calvi, Fabrizio, 1986, *La vita quotidiana della mafia dal 1950 a oggi*, Rizzoli, Milan.

Canetti, Elias, 1972, *Macht und Überleben*, Carl Hanser Verlag, Munich; 1974, *Potere e sopravvivenza*, Adelphi, Milan.

Caponnetto, Antonino, 1992, *I miei giorni a Palermo*, Garzanti, Milan.

Casarrubea, Giuseppe and Blandano, Pia, 1991, *L'educazione mafiosa*, Sellerio, Palermo.

Cascio, Antonia and Puglisi, Anna (eds), 1986, *Con e contro – Le donne nell'organizzazione mafiosa e nella lotta antimafia*, dossier 4, CSD, Palermo. (Many of the newspaper articles quoted in this work were taken from this dossier.)

Cascio, Antonia and Puglisi, Anna, 1986, 'Intervista a Maria Benigno', Centro Siciliano di Documentazione 'Giuseppe Impastato', unpublished typescript, Palermo.

Casella, Cesari, 1990, *743 Giorni Lontano da Casa*, Rizzoli, Milan.

Catanzaro, Raimondo, 1988, *Il delitto come impresa*, Liviana Editrice, Padua.

Cavallaro, Felice (ed.), 1992, *Mafia – Album di Cosa Nostra*, Rizzoli, Milan.

Centro Siciliano di Documentazione 'Giuseppe Impastato' (CSD, Sicilian Documentation Centre), 1989, *Donne contro la mafia: dall'isolamento allo spettacolo. Ovvero: chi le ha aiutate e chi è stato a guardare*, dossier, CSD, Palermo.

Chinnici, Giorgio and Santino, Umberto, 1991, *La violenza programmata*, Franco Angeli, Milan.

Chinnici, Giorgio, Santino Umberto, La Fiura, Giovanni and Adragna, Ugo, 1992, *Gabbie Vuote*, Franco Angeli, Milan.

Ciconte, Enzo, 1992, *'Ndrangheta dall'Unità ad oggi*, Laterza, Bari.

Cirillo Rampolla, Giovanna, 1986, *Suicidio per mafia*, La Luna, Palermo.

Comitato di Controinformazione Peppino Impastato *et al.*, 1979, *Accumulazione e culture mafiose*, Cento Fiori, Palermo.

Commissione Parlamentare Antimafia (Parliamentary Anti-mafia Commission), 1993, 'Mafia e politica', *La Repubblica*, supplement to 10 April edition.

Commissione Parlamentare Antimafia (Parliamentary Anti-mafia Commission), 1993, 'Mafia e potere', *L'Unità*, supplement to 15 April edition.

Consolo, Vincenzo, 1988, *Le pietre di Pantalica*, Mondadori, Milan.

Consolo, Vincenzo, 1993, *Requiem per le vittime della mafia*, Ila Palma, Palermo.

Crisantino, Amelia, 1990, *La città spugna*, Centro Siciliano di Documentazione 'Giuseppe Impastato', Palermo.

Crisantino, Amelia, 1991, *Cercando Palermo*, La Luna, Palermo.

Crisantino, Amelia and La Fiura, Giovanni, 1989, *La mafia come metodo e come sistema*, Pellegrini, Cosenza.

Crupi, Pasquino, 1992, L'anomalia selvaggia, Sellerio, Palermo.

Dalla Chiesa, Nando, 1990, *Storie*, Einaudi, Turin.

Dalla Chiesa, Simona *et al.*, 1987, *Cultura e politica contro la 'ndrangheta*, Pellegrini, Cosenza.

Davis, John, 1977, *People of the Mediterranean*, Routledge & Kegan Paul, London.

Deaglio, Enrico, 1993, *Raccolto rosso*, Feltrinelli, Milan.

De Stefani, Livia, 1991, *La Mafia alle mie spalle*, Mondadori, Milan.

Di Bella, Maria Pia, 1983, *L'onore in Sicilia e l'onore nella mafia. Convergenza e divergenze*, in Saverio Di Bella (ed.), op. cit.

Di Bella, Saverio (ed.), 1983, *Mafia e potere: società civile, organizzazione mafiosa ed esercizio dei poteri nel Mezzogiorno contemporaneo, atti convegno internazionale*, 2 vols, Rubbettino, Soveria Mannelli.

Di Forti, Filippo, 1982, *Per una psicoanalisi della mafia*, Bertani, Verona.

Di Maria, Franco *et al.*, 1989, *Il sentire mafioso*, Giuffrè, Milan.

Di Vita, Angela Maria (ed.), 1986, *Alle radici di un'immagine della mafia*, Franco Angeli, Milan.

Dolci, Danilo, 1960, *Spreco*, Einaudi, Turin.

Donolo, Carlo and Fichere, Carlo, 1988, *Le vie dell'innovazione*, Feltrinelli, Milan.

Duggan, Christopher, 1989, *Fascism and the Mafia*, Yale University Press, New Haven, Conn.

Elliot, Frances, 1885, *The Diary of an Idle Woman in Sicily*, 2 vols, J. W. Arrowsmith, Bristol.

Falcone, Giovanni, 1989, 'La mafia, tra criminalità e cultura', *Meridiana*, no. 5.

Falcone, Giovanni, 1992, 'Che cosa è la mafia', *Micromega*, no. 3.

Falcone Giovanni and Padovani, Marcelle, 1991, *Cose di Cosa Nostra*, Rizzoli, Milan.

Fantozzi, Piero, 1993, *Politica, clientela e regolazione sociale*, Rubbettino, Soveria Mannelli.

Fava, Claudio, 1991, *La mafia comanda a Catania 1960/91*, Laterza, Bari.

Fava, Giuseppe, 1980, *I siciliani*, Cappelli, Bologna.

Ferrarotti, Franco, 1978, *Rapporto sulla mafia: da costume locale a problema dello sviluppo nazionale*, Liguori, Naples.

Fiume, Giovanna, 1990, 'Ci sono donne nella mafia?', *Meridiana*, no. 7–8.

Fiume, Giovanna, 1990, *La vecchia dell'aceto*, Gelka, Palermo.

Fondazione, Marisa Bellisario, 1993, *Donne e mafia: Dentro contro fuori*, Premio Marisa Bellisario, Palermo.

Fromm, Erich, 1965, *The Heart of Man*, Routledge & Kegan Paul, London.

Gambetta, Diego, 1992, *La mafia siciliana*, Einaudi, Turin.

Gellert, Gabor, 1987, *Mafia*, Rubbettino, Soveria Mannelli.

Gentile, Nick, 1963, *Vita di capomafia*, Editori Riuniti, Rome.

Giancana, Antoinette and Renner, Thomas C., 1984, *Mafia Princess*, George Allen & Unwin, London.

Gilligan, Carol, 1982, *In a Different Voice*, Harvard University Press, Cambridge, Mass.

Gribaudi, Gabriella, 1990, 'Mafia, culture e gruppi sociali', *Meridiana*, no. 7–9.

Hess, Henner, 1970, *Mafia: Zentrale Herrschaft und Lokale Gegenmacht*, J. C. B. Muhr, Tübingen; 1973, *Mafia*, Laterza, Bari.

Ianni, Francis A. J., 1972, *A Family Business: Kinship and Social Control in Organized Crime*, Russell Sage Foundation, New York.

Jedlowski, Paolo, 1990, 'Nuovi ceti medi nel Mezzogiorno: fra clientelismo e professionalità', *Inchiesta*, XX, no. 88–89.

Kienzle, Birgit and Galluzzo, Maria Teresa, 1990, *Frauen gegen die Mafia*, Rowohlt, Hamburg.

La Licata, Francesco, 1993, *Storia di Giovanni Falcone*, Rizzoli, Milan.

Lanza, Angela, 1992, 'Un sonno interrotto', *Nosside*, no. 6.

Lanza, Angela, 1993, 'Visibilità e invisibilità delle "donne del digiuno"', *Nosside*, no. 7–8.

Lanza, Angela, 1994, *Donne contro la mafia. L'esperienza delle donne del digiuno a Palermo*, Data News, Rome.

Leccardi, Carmen, 1990, *Giovani in Calabria fra tradizione e modernità – Le culture del lavoro*, Marra, Cosenza.

Levi, Carlo, 1979, *Le parole sono pietre*, Einaudi, Turin.

Librerie Associate, 1992, *Mafia – Anatomia di un regime*, edition not for sale, Rome.

Lo Cascio, Gigliola (ed.), 1986, *L'immaginario mafioso*, Dedalo, Bari.

Lodato, Saverio, 1992, *Dieci anni di mafia*, Rizzoli, Milan.

Lodato, Saverio, 1992, *Potenti*, Garzanti, Milan.

Lombardi Satriani, Luigi M., 1973, 'Faide, perché?', *Quaderni del Mezzogiorno e delle Isole*, X, no. 29.

Lombardi Satriani, Luigi M., 1975, 'Culture subalterne e dominio di classe', *Classe*, no. 10.

Lombardi Satriani, Luigi M., 1977, 'Sulla culture mafiosa e gli immediati dintorni', *Quaderni del Mezzogiorno e delle Isole*, XIV, no. 42–43.

Lombardi Satriani, Luigi M., 1983, 'Stratificazione sociale dinamica culturale e mafia nel Mezzogiorno contemporaneo', in Saverio Di Bella (ed.), op. cit.

Lombardi Satriani, Luigi M. and Meligrana Mariano, 1982, *Il ponte di San Giacomo – L'ideologia della morte nella società contadina del Sud*, Rizzoli, Milan.

Lombardi Satriani, Luigi M., Madeo Alfonso and Meligrana Mariano, 1977, 'Il ruolo della donna nella mafia' (debate), *Quaderni del Mezzogiorno e delle Isole*, XIV, no. 42–43.

Lupo, Salvatore, 1993, *Storia della mafia*, Donzelli, Rome.

Lupo, Salvatore and Mangiameli, Rosario, 1990, 'Mafia di ieri mafia di oggi', *Meridiana*, no. 7–8.

Maletesta, Stefano, 1980, *L'armata Caltagirone*, Mondadori, Milan.

Marcuse, Herbert, 1959, 'The ideology of Death', in Herman Feifel (ed.), *The Meaning of Death*, McGraw Hill, New York.

Marcuse, Herbert, 1987, *Eros and Civilisation*, Ark, London.

Martelli, Franco, 1981, *La guerra mafiosa*, Editori Riuniti, Rome.

Martorana, Giuseppe and Nigrelli, Sergio, 1993, *Leonardo Messina, la carriera di un uomo d'onore*, Musumeci, Quart (Valle D'Aosta).

Martorana, Giuseppe and Nigrelli, Sergio, 1993, *Totò Riina*, Musumeci, Quart (Valle D'Aosta).

Masciopinto, Rosa, 1994, *Donna d'onore*, Edizioni della Battaglia, Palermo.

Meligrana, Mariano, 1977, 'Sull'origine e sulla funzione sociale della mafia', *Quaderni del Mezzogiorno e delle Isole*, XIV, no. 42–43.

Meligrana, Mariano, 1983, 'Giuridicità popolare e potere mafioso. L'istituto della vendetta', in Saverio Di Bella, op. cit.

Mercurio, Domenico, 1982, *Il padrino della 'Ndrangheta*, Eda, Turin.

Meridiana, 1990, 'Mafia', no. 7–8.

Messick, Hank, 1969, *Syndicate Wife – The Story of Ann Drahmann Coppola*, Robert Hale & Co., London.

Mignosi, Enzo, 1993, *Il Signore sia coi boss*, Edizioni Arbor, Palermo.

Minervini, Guglielmo, 1993, 'Un volontariato non violento contro il crimine organizzato', in Franco Occhiogrosso (ed.), op. cit.

Minna, Rosario, 1984, *Breve storia della mafia*, Editori Riuniti, Rome.

Minuti, Diego and Veltri Filippo, 1990, *Lettere a San Luca*, Abramo, Catanzaro.

Monroy, Beatrice, 1992, *Palermo in tempo di peste*, Edizioni della Battaglia, Palermo.

Montemagno, Gabriello, 1992, *Il sogno spezzato di Rita Atria*, Edizioni della Battaglia, Palermo.

Neumann, Franz, 1957, *The Democratic and the Authoritarian State*, The Free Press of Glencoe, Collier-Macmillan, London.

Occhiogrosso, Franco (ed.), 1993, *Ragazzi della mafia*, Franco Angeli, Milan.

Osservatorio Libero Grassi, 1992, *Mafia o sviluppo. Un dibattito con Libero Grassi*, Quaderni 1, Palermo.

Padovani, Marcelle, 1987, *Les dernières années de la mafia*, Gallimard, Paris.

Pantaleone, Michele, 1966, *Mafia e droga*, Einaudi, Turin.

Pantaleone, Michele, 1978, *Mafia e politica*, Einaudi, Turin.

Pegna, Vera, 1992, *Tempo di lupi e di comunisti*, La Luna, Palermo.

Pezzino, Paolo, 1989, 'Per una critica dell'onore mafioso', in Giovanna Fiume (ed.), *Onore e storia nelle società mediterranee*, La Luna, Palermo.

Pino, Marina, 1988, *Le signore della droga*, La Luna, Palermo.

Pizzorno, Alessandro, 1987, 'I mafiosi come classe media violenta', *Polis*, I, 1.

Popitz, Heinrich, 1986, *Phänomene der Macht*, J. C. B. Muhr, Tübingen; 1990, *Fenomenologia del potere*, Il Mulino, Bologna.

Puglisi, Anna, 1990, *Sole contro la mafia*, La Luna, Palermo.

Puglisi, Anna, 1991, *Donne e mafia*, Centro Siciliano di Documentazione 'Giuseppe Impastato', unpublished typescript, Palermo.

Puglisi, Anna and Santino, Umberto, 1985, 'Intervista a Giovanna Terranova', Centro Siciliano di Documentazione, unpublished typescript, Palermo.

Rizza, Sandra, 1993, *Una ragazza contro la mafia – Rita Atria*, La Luna, Palermo.

Rossi-Doria, Anna (ed.), 1990, *La libertà delle donne*, Rosenberg & Sellier, Turin.

Ruddick, Sara, 1980, 'Maternal thinking', *Feminist Studies*, Summer 1980, University of Maryland.

Salemi, Roselina, 1993, *Ragazzi di Palermo*, Rizzoli, Milan.

Santino, Umberto (ed.), 1989, *L'antimafia difficile*, Centro Siciliano Documentazione 'Giuseppe Impastato', Palermo.

Santino, Umberto, 1992, 'Il carretto e la piovra', *La balena bianca*, no. 4.

Santino, Umberto and La Fiura Giovanni, 1990, *L'impresa mafiosa*, Franco Angeli, Milan.

Santino, Umberto, Allegra, Gianni and Donarelli, Franco, 1988, *Mamilandia & d'intorni*, Edizioni Ellesse, Palermo.

Schifani, Rosaria and Cavallaro, Felice, 1992, *Lettera ai mafiosi – vi perdono ma inginocchiatevi*, Pironti, Naples.

Schneider, Jane, 1971, 'Of Vigilance and Virgins', *Ethnology*, vol. 10, no. 1.

Schneider, Jane and Schneider, Peter, 1976, *Culture and Political Economy in Western Sicily*, Academic Press, New York.

Sciascia, Leonardo, 1972, *Il Giorno della civetta*, Einaudi, Turin (translated by A. Colquhoun and A. Oliver as *The Day of the Owl*, 1987, Paladin, London).

Sciascia, Leonardo, 1979, *La Sicilia come metafora*, Mondadori, Milan.

Sciascia, Leonardo, 1989, *A future memoria*, Bompiani, Milan.

Seidler, Victor J., 1989, *Rediscovering Masculinity – Reason, Language and Sexuality*, Routledge, London.

Sergi, Pantaleone, 1991, *La 'santa' violenta*, Periferia, Cosenza.

Siebert, Renate, 1984, *Le ali di un elefante – Sul rapporto adulti bambini in un paese della Calabria*, Franco Angeli, Milan.

Siebert, Renate, 1989, 'Le sud des femmes: potentialités, intérêts, désirs', *Peuples Méditerranéens*, 'Femmes et Pouvoir', no. 48–49.

Siebert, Renate, 1991, *'È femmina, però è bella' – Tre generazioni di donne al Sud*, Rosenberg & Sellier, Turin.

Siebert, Renate, 1992, 'Don't forget – fragments of a negative tradition', in Luisa Passerini (ed.), *Memory and Totalitarianism*, International Yearbook of Oral History and Life Studies, vol. I, Oxford University Press, Oxford.

Siebert, Renate, 1993, 'Intervista a Maria Di Carlo', unpublished typescript.

Simmel, Georg, 1908, *Soziologie Untersuchungen über die Formen der Vergesellschaftung*, Duncker & Humblot, Berlin; 1989, 'Il segreto e la società segreta', *Sociologia*, Edizioni di comunità, Milan.

Stajano, Corrado, 1979, *Africo*, Einaudi, Turin.

Stajano, Corrado, 1991, *Un eroe borghese*, Einaudi, Turin.

Stajano, Corrado, 1992, *Mafia – L'atto d'accusa dei giudici di Palermo*, Editori Riuniti, Rome.

Talese, Gay, 1972, *Honour Thy Father*, Sphere, London.

Theweleit, Klaus, 1987, *Male Fantasies*, 2 vols, Polity Press, Cambridge.

Tranfaglia, Nicola, 1991, *La Mafia come metodo*, Laterza, Bari.

Turnaturi, Gabriella, 1986, 'In nome degli affetti familiari', *Memoria*, no. 13.

Turnaturi, Gabriella, 1991, *Associati per amore*, Feltrinelli, Milan.

Turnaturi, Gabriella, 1992, 'Fra interessi e dignità', *Democrazia e diritto*, no. 2.

Turnaturi, Gabriella, 1993, 'Sentirsi sicuri', in Laura Balbo (ed.), op. cit.

Turnaturi, Gabriella and Donolo, Carlo, 1988, 'Familismi morali', in Carlo Donolo and Franco Fichera, op. cit.

Uessler, Rolf, 1987, *Mafia*, Dietz, Berlin-Bonn.

Vegetti, Finzi Silvia, 1993, 'L'ospite perturbante', paper given to the seminar 'Der die das Fremde', Hanover, unpublished typescript.

Violante, Luciano, 1993, 'La politica', in Franco Occhiogrosso (ed.), op. cit.

Violante, Luciano, 1993, 'I corleonesi', *L'Unità*, supplement published 11 September.

Weber, Max, 1947 [48] 'Politics as a vocation', in *From Max Weber*, ed. H. H. Gerth and C. Wright Mills, Kegan Paul, Trench, Trubner & Co., London.

Winnicott, Donald W., 1965, *The Family and Individual Development*, Tavistock, London.

Zagari, Antonio, 1992, *Ammazzare stanca*, Periferia, Cosenza.